# Lecture Notes in Computer Scien

*Commenced Publication in 1973*
Founding and Former Series Editors:
Gerhard Goos, Juris Hartmanis, and Jan van Leeuwen

T0237766

## Editorial Board

David Hutchison
  *Lancaster University, UK*

Takeo Kanade
  *Carnegie Mellon University, Pittsburgh, PA, USA*

Josef Kittler
  *University of Surrey, Guildford, UK*

Jon M. Kleinberg
  *Cornell University, Ithaca, NY, USA*

Friedemann Mattern
  *ETH Zurich, Switzerland*

John C. Mitchell
  *Stanford University, CA, USA*

Moni Naor
  *Weizmann Institute of Science, Rehovot, Israel*

Oscar Nierstrasz
  *University of Bern, Switzerland*

C. Pandu Rangan
  *Indian Institute of Technology, Madras, India*

Bernhard Steffen
  *University of Dortmund, Germany*

Madhu Sudan
  *Massachusetts Institute of Technology, MA, USA*

Demetri Terzopoulos
  *University of California, Los Angeles, CA, USA*

Doug Tygar
  *University of California, Berkeley, CA, USA*

Moshe Y. Vardi
  *Rice University, Houston, TX, USA*

Gerhard Weikum
  *Max-Planck Institute of Computer Science, Saarbruecken, Germany*

Ernesto Damiani   Peng Liu (Eds.)

# Data and Applications Security XX

20th Annual IFIP WG 11.3 Working Conference on
Data and Applications Security
Sophia Antipolis, France, July 31–August 2, 2006
Proceedings

 Springer

Volume Editors

Ernesto Damiani
University of Milan
Department of Information Technology
Via Bramante 65, 26013 Crema, Italy
E-mail: damiani@dti.unimi.it

Peng Liu
Pennsylvania State University
College of Information Sciences and Technology
313G IST Building, University Park, PA 16802, USA
E-mail: pliu@ist.psu.edu

Library of Congress Control Number: 2006929592

CR Subject Classification (1998): E.3, D.4.6, C.2, F.2.1, J.1, K.6.5

LNCS Sublibrary: SL 3 – Information Systems and Application, incl. Internet/Web
and HCI

ISSN        0302-9743
ISBN-10     3-540-36796-9 Springer Berlin Heidelberg New York
ISBN-13     978-3-540-36796-3 Springer Berlin Heidelberg New York

Springer is a part of Springer Science+Business Media

springer.com

© IFIP International Federation for Information Processing, Hofstrasse 3, A-2361 Laxenburg, Austria 2006

Typesetting: Camera-ready by author, data conversion by Scientific Publishing Services, Chennai, India
Printed on acid-free paper      SPIN: 11805588      06/3142      5 4 3 2 1 0

# Preface

For 20 years, the IFIP WG 11.3 Working Conference on Data and Applications Security (DBSEC) has been a major forum for presenting original research results, practical experiences, and innovative ideas in data and applications security. Looking back, it is difficult not to appreciate the full extent of the change that has occurred in our field. Once considered afterthoughts in systems and application design, data protection, privacy and trust have become the key problems of our day. This central role of security in the information society has however brought increased responsibilities to the research community. Today practitioners and researchers alike need to find new ways to cope with the increasing scale and complexity of the security problems that must be solved on the global information infrastructure. Like the previous conference, the 20th DBSEC has proved to be up to this challenge.

DBSEC 2006 received 56 submissions, out of which the program committee selected 22 high-quality papers covering a number of diverse research topics such as access control, privacy, and identity management. We are glad to see that the final program contains a well-balanced mix of theoretical results and practical prototype systems, many of them converging and building off each other. Also, the DBSEC program includes a number of papers on new, emerging aspects of security research.

Putting together a top-level conference like DBSEC is always a team effort. We would like to thank a number of friends and colleagues for their valuable help and support, including our General Chair Andreas Schaad, our Publicity Chair Soon Ae Chun, IFIP WG 11.3 Chair Pierangela Samarati, all our program committee members, and, above all, the researchers who chose DBSEC as the forum to which to submit their work. In addition, we would like to thank SAP for sponsoring this conference.

August 2006                                    Ernesto Damiani, Peng Liu

# Organization

## General Chair

Andreas Schaad        SAP Labs, France

## Program Chairs

Ernesto Damiani        Università degli Studi di Milano, Italy
Peng Liu        Penn State University, USA

## Publicity Chair

Soon Ae Chun        City University of New York, USA

## IFIP WG 11.3 Chair

Pierangela Samarati        Università degli Studi di Milano, Italy

## Program Committee

| | |
|---|---|
| Gail-Joon Ahn | University of North Carolina at Charlotte, USA |
| Anne Anderson | Sun Microsystems, USA |
| Vijay Atluri | Rutgers University, USA |
| Sabrina De Capitani di Vimercati | Università degli Studi di Milano, Italy |
| Soon Ae Chun | City University of New York, USA |
| Chris Clifton | Purdue University, USA |
| Steve Demurjian | University of Connecticut, USA |
| Csilla Farkas | University of South Carolina, USA |
| Eduardo Fernandez-Medina | Univ. of Castilla-La Mancha, Spain |
| Simon Foley | University College Cork, Ireland |
| Qijun Gu | Texas State University, USA |
| Ehud Gudes | Ben-Gurion University, Israel |
| Sushil Jajodia | George Mason University, USA |
| Carl Landwehr | University of Maryland, USA |
| Tsau Young Lin | San Jose State University, USA |
| Patrick McDaniel | Pennsylvania State University, USA |
| Sharad Mehrotra | University of California Irvine, USA |
| Mukesh K. Mohania | IBM Research Labs, India |
| Ravi Mukkamala | Old Dominion University, USA |

| | |
|---|---|
| Peng Ning | North Carolina State University, USA |
| Sylvia Osborn | University of Western Ontario, Canada |
| Brajendra Panda | University of Arkansas, USA |
| Joon S. Park | Syracuse University, USA |
| Indrakshi Ray | Colorado State University, USA |
| Indrajit Ray | Colorado State University, USA |
| Pierangela Samarati | Università degli Studi di Milano, Italy |
| Andreas Schaad | SAP Labs, France |
| Sujeet Shenoi | University of Tulsa, USA |
| David Spooner | Rensselaer Polytechnic Institute, USA |
| Bhavani Thuraisingham | University of Texas Dallas, USA |
| T.C. Ting | University of Connecticut, USA |
| Duminda Wijesekera | George Mason University, USA |
| Meng Yu | Monmouth University, USA |
| Ting Yu | North Carolina State University, USA |

## Sponsoring Institutions

SAP Labs, Sophia Antipolis, France

# Table of Contents

# Creating Objects in the Flexible Authorization Framework*

Nicola Zannone[1,2], Sushil Jajodia[2], and Duminda Wijesekera[2]

[1] Dep. of Information and Communication Technology
University of Trento
`zannone@dit.unitn.it`
[2] Center for Secure Information Systems
George Mason University
{`jajodia, dwijesek`}`@gmu.edu`

**Abstract.** Access control is a crucial concern to build secure IT systems and, more specifically, to protect the confidentiality of information. However, access control is necessary, but not sufficient. Actually, IT systems can manipulate data to provide services to users. The results of a data processing may disclose information concerning the objects used in the data processing itself. Therefore, the control of information flow results fundamental to guarantee data protection. In the last years many information flow control models have been proposed. However, these frameworks mainly focus on the detection and prevention of improper information leaks and do not provide support for the dynamical creation of new objects.

In this paper we extend our previous work to automatically support the dynamical creation of objects by verifying the conditions under which objects can be created and automatically associating an access control policy to them. Moreover, our proposal includes mechanisms tailored to control the usage of information once it has been accessed.

## 1 Introduction

Access control is one of the main challenges in IT systems and has received significant attention in the last years. These efforts have matched with the development of many frameworks dealing with access control issues [1,2,3,4,5,6]. However, many of these proposals focus on the restriction on the release of information but not its propagation [7].

Actually, IT systems are developed not only to merely store data, but also to provide a number of functionalities designed to process data. Thereby, they may release information as part of their functionalities [8]. Yet, a malicious user can embed in some

---

* This material is based upon work supported by the National Science Foundation under grants IIS-0242237 and IIS-0430402. Any opinions, findings, and conclusions or recommendations expressed in this material are those of the author(s) and do not necessarily reflect the views of the National Science Foundation. This work was partly supported by the projects RBNE0195K5 FIRB-ASTRO, 016004 IST-FP6-FET-IP-SENSORIA, 27587 IST-FP6-IP-SERENITY, 2003-S116-00018 PAT-MOSTRO.

E. Damiani and P. Liu (Eds.): Data and Applications Security 2006, LNCS 4127, pp. 1–14, 2006.

application provided by the IT system, a Trojan horse that, once the application is executed, copies sensitive information in a file accessible by the malicious user [9]. In this setting, information flow control plays a key role in ensuring that derived objects do not disclose sensitive information to unauthorized users.

This issue has spurred the research and development of frameworks that improve authorization frameworks with some form of flow control. Sammarati et al. [10] proposed to detect unauthorized information flow by checking if the set of authorizations associated with a derived object are a subset of the intersection of the sets of authorizations associated with the objects used to derive it. Similar approaches [11,12] have associated with each object an access control list that is propagated together with the information in the object. However, in these approaches the creation of objects is implicit. Essentially, they attempt to identify leaking information, but do not deal with the creation of new objects.

Moreover, this approach is to rigid to implement real access control policies. Actually, it is not flexible enough to support information declassification [8]. For instance, the US Privacy Act allows an agency to disclose information to those officers and employees of the agency who need it to perform their duties without the consent of the data subject. Furthermore, the Act does not impose any constraint to data that do not disclose personal identifying information.

In this paper, we extend our previous work [13] in order to automatically enforce access control policies on objects dynamically created in Flexible Authorization Framework (FAF) [14]. This requires to deal with some issues:

– deciding if an object can be created;
– associating authorizations with the new object;
– verifying if the derived object does not disclose sensitive information to unauthorized users.

The first issue is addressed by introducing conditions under which a data processing can be performed and enforcing the system to verify them before creating new objects. To cope with the second issue, we allow system administrators to define the policies governing access to derived objects, based on the authorizations associated with the objects used to derive them.

However, this is not sufficient to fully guarantee data protection. Actually, if a user is authorized to execute an application in which a Trojan horse is embedded, such a malicious application is considered as legitimate by the authorization framework. To this end, we propose an approach based on [10,11,12] to block non safe information flow. However, it is up to system administrators to decide whether or not an information flow is safe. Thereby, we only provide support for detecting flows of information that may be harmful to data subjects.

Other issues come up when the proposed approach is integrated in FAF. Actually, its current architecture does not support the dynamical creation of objects. To this intent, we need to improve it together with its underlying logic-based framework.

The remainder of the paper is structured as follows. Next (§2) we provide a brief overview of FAF. Then, we illustrate our approach for dealing with the dynamical creation of objects (§3) and for automatically deriving their access control policy (§4).

Next, we propose a mechanism to control information flow and show how such a mechanism copes with the Trojan horse problem (§5). Finally, we discuss related work (§6) and conclude the paper (§7).

## 2 Flexible Authorization Framework

Flexible Authorization Framework (FAF) [14] is a logic-based framework developed to manage access to data by users. It consists of four stages that are applied in sequence. The first stage takes in input the extensional description of the system, as subject and object hierarchies and a set of authorizations, and propagates authorizations through the organizational structure of the system. However, in this stage it is possible to derive contradictory authorizations, that is, a subject could be authorized and denied to execute an action on an object at the same time. The second stage aims to resolve this problem by applying conflict resolution policies. Once authorizations are propagated and conflicts resolved, there is the possibility that some access is neither authorized nor denied. In the third stage, decision policies are used to ensure the completeness of authorizations. In the last stage, specific domain properties are verified using integrity constraints, and all authorizations that violate them are removed.

FAF provides a logic-based language, called authorization specification language (**ASL**), tailored for encoding security needs. Before defining the language, we introduce the logic programming terminology needed to understand the framework. Let $p$ be a predicate with arity $n$, and $t_1, \ldots, t_n$ be its appropriate terms. $p(t_1, \ldots, t_n)$ is called *atom*. Then, the term *literal* denotes an atom or its negation. **ASL** syntax includes the following predicates:

- A ternary predicate cando. Literal cando$(o, s, a)$ is used to represent authorizations directly defined by the system administrator where $o$ is an object, $s$ is a subject, and $a$ is a signed action terms. Depending on the sign, authorizations are permissions or prohibitions.
- A ternary predicate dercando that has the same arguments of predicate cando and is used to represent authorizations derived through propagation policies.
- A ternary predicate do that has the same arguments of predicate cando and represents effective permissions derived by applying conflicts resolution and decision policies.
- A 5-ary predicate done that is used to describe the actions executed by users. Intuitively, done$(o, s, r, a, t)$ holds if subject $s$ playing role $r$ has executed action $a$ on object $o$ at time $t$.
- A propositional symbol error. Its occurrence in the model corresponds to a violation of some integrity constraints.
- A set of hie-predicates. In particular, the ternary predicate in$(x, y, \mathsf{H})$ is used to denote that $x \leq y$ in hierarchy $\mathsf{H}$.
- A set of rel-predicates. They are specific domain predicates.

Based on the architecture previously presented, every authorization specification **AS** is a locally stratified program where stratification is implemented by assigning levels to predicates (Table 1 [14]). For any specification **AS**, **AS**$_i$ denotes the rules belonging to the $i$-th level.

**Table 1.** Strata in FAF specification

| Stratum | Predicate | Rules defining predicate |
|---|---|---|
| $AS_0$ | hie-predicates | base relations. |
| | rel-predicates | base relations. |
| | done | base relation. |
| $AS_1$ | cando | the body may contain done, hie- and rel-literals. |
| $AS_2$ | dercando | the body may contain cando, dercando, done, hie- and rel-literals. Occurrences of dercando literals must be positive. |
| $AS_3$ | do | the head must be of the form $do(\_, \_, +a)$ and the body may contain cando, dercando, done, hie- and rel-literals. |
| $AS_4$ | do | the head must be of the form $do(o, s, -a)$ and the body contains the literal $\neg do(o, s, +a)$. |
| $AS_5$ | error | the body may contain cando, dercando, do, done, hie- and rel-literals. |

For optimizing the access control process, Jajodia et al. [14] proposed a materialized view architecture, where instances of predicates corresponding to views are maintained. Because predicates belong to strata, the materialization structure results (locally) stratified. This guarantees that the specification has a unique stable model and well-founded semantics [15,16]. Following [14], we use the notation $\mathcal{M}(\mathbf{AS})$ to refer to the unique stable model of specification $\mathbf{AS}$.

## 3  Creating Objects

When a user requires to perform a data processing, the IT system should verify whether or not such a user has all necessary authorizations. In the remainder of this section, we address this issue.

Let O be the name space of all possible objects that may occur in the specification. We assume that they are organized into a hierarchical structure. This means that all possible objects are fully classified with respect to their type. Further, we assume that objects do not exist until they are created. This means that objects (together with their classification) may be not in the scope of the specification, although they are defined in O. Essentially, we assume that a possible object is considered only if some event demands its existence, that is, it is created.

Following [17], we introduce predicate exists, where exists($o$) holds if object $o$ exists, that is, it is already created. We define the *state of the system* as the set of existing objects and their relationships. To deal with the creation of objects, Liskov et al. [18] introduced two kinds of functions: *constructors* and *creators*. Constructors of a certain type return new objects of the corresponding type and creators initialize them. Essentially, constructors add object identifiers (i.e., names) to the state of the system and creators assign a value to such names. However, this approach distinguishes the identifier of an object from the values the object can assume. We merge this pair of functions into a single function, called *initiator*. Essentially, when an object is created, it exists together with its value. This allows us to be consistent with the semantics of FAF. Further, we assume that objects are never destroyed. From these assumptions, we can deduce that the set of objects belonging to a state of the system is a subset of the set of objects belonging to the next state.

IT systems process data as part of their functionalities by providing automatic procedures used to organize and manipulate data. As done in [13], we represent data processing through initiators and make explicit the objects used by data processing and the users who performs them. Thus, we introduce an initiator for each procedure supported by the IT system. For instance, we write

$$f(s, o_1, \ldots, o_m) = o$$

to indicate that object $o$ is the result of data processing $f$ when this is performed by subject $s$ and objects $o_1, \ldots, o_m$ are passed as input.[1] We assume that when an object is created (i.e., it enters in the scope of the specification), also its classification belongs to the specification. Notice that initiators do not belong to the specification language. We use them only to emphasize the objects used in the procedure and the subject that executes it.

Subjects may need to access exiting objects in order to create new objects. Moreover, only users that play a certain role or belong to a certain group may be entitled to perform a certain data processing. This means that an authorization framework should verify whether the subject has enough rights to access all objects needed to create the new one and whether he can execute the procedure.

Our idea is to enforce the system to verify the capabilities of the subject before an object is created. Based on this intuition, we redefine initiator $f$ as

$$f(s, o_1, \ldots, o_m) = \begin{cases} o & \text{if } \mathcal{C} \text{ is true} \\ \bot & \text{otherwise} \end{cases}$$

where $\mathcal{C}$ represents the condition that must be satisfied and $\bot$ means that object $o$ cannot be created since $s$ does not have sufficient rights to execute the procedure.

Initiators are implemented in our framework through rules, called *creating rules*. These rules enforce the system to verify the conditions under which a user can create the object.

**Definition 1.** *Let $f$ be an initiator, $s$ be the subject executing $f$, $o_1, \ldots, o_m$ be the objects required by $f$, and $o = f(s, o_1, \ldots, o_m)$ be the derived object. A creating rule has the form*

$$\text{exists}(o) \leftarrow L_1 \& \ldots \& L_n \& \text{exists}(o_1) \& \ldots \& \text{exists}(o_m).$$

*where $L_1, \ldots, L_n$ are* cando, dercando, do, done, hie-, *or* rel-*literals.* cando, dercando, do *literals may refer only to* $o_1, \ldots, o_m$.

Essentially, the conjunction of literals $L_1, \ldots, L_n$ represents the condition that a subject must satisfy in order to create object $o$. Last part of the body of the rule ensures that all objects necessary to create the new object already exist.

---

[1] Notice that initiators are not total functions since if one combines personal data of different users for creating an account, such account is not a valid object.

*Example 1.* A bank needs customer personal information, namely name, shipping address, and phone number, for creating an account. The bank IT system provides the procedure *openA* for creating new accounts. Suppose a customer discloses his name $(n)$, shipping address $(sa)$, and phone number $(p)$ to the bank. A bank employee $s$ will be able to create *account* $(= openA(s, n, sa, p))$ only if it is authorized to read customer data and he works in the Customer Services Division (CSD). In symbol,

$$\text{exists}(account) \leftarrow \text{do}(n, s, +\text{read}) \ \& \ \text{do}(sa, s, +\text{read}) \ \& \ \text{do}(p, s, +\text{read}) \ \&$$
$$\text{in}(s, CSD\text{-}employee, \text{ASH}) \ \& \ \text{exists}(n) \ \& \ \text{exists}(sa) \ \& \ \text{exists}(p).$$

The outcome of a data processing may then be used to derive further objects. We represent the process to create an object as a tree, called *creation tree*, where the root is the "final" object and the leaves are *primitive objects* (i.e., objects that are directly stored in the system by users). In order to rebuild the creation tree, the system should keep trace of the process used to create the object. To this end, we introduce the binary predicate derivedFrom where derivedFrom$(o_1, o_2)$ is used to indicate that object $o_2$ is used to derive object $o_1$. As for classification literals, derivedFrom literals referring an object are added to the model only when the object is created.

*Example 2.* Back to Example 1, the bank IT system stores the following set of literals:

$$\{\text{derivedFrom}(account, n), \text{derivedFrom}(account, sa), \text{derivedFrom}(account, p)\}$$

## 4    Associating Authorizations with New Objects

Once an object has been created, authorizations should be associated with it. Since the object is not independent from the objects used to derive it, the policy associated with it should take into account the authorizations associated with them. Some proposals [11,12] associate with each object an access control list (ACL) that is propagated together with the information in the object. Essentially, the ACL associated with the new object is given by the intersection of all ACLs associated with the objects used to create it. However, when a system administrator specifies an access control policy for derived objects, he should consider that not all data processing disclose individually identifiable information [8]. For example, the sum of all account balances at a bank branch does not disclose data that allows to recover information associating a user with his own account balance.

We propose a flexible framework in order to allow system administrators to determine how authorizations are propagated to new objects. The idea is that authorizations associated with the objects used to derive the new one can be used to determine the authorizations associated with it. However, this approach cannot be directly implemented in FAF since the specification results no more stratified [13]. Next, we propose how FAF can be modified in order to support access control on derived objects maintaining the locally stratified structure.

### 4.1    Redefining Rules

To maintain the locally stratified structure, we need to redefine *creating rules, authorization rules* [14], *derivation rules* [14], and *positive decision rules* [14] by enforcing some syntactic constraints to predicates occurring in the body of rules. Before doing this, we have also to redefine the predicates defined in FAF. Essentially, we introduce a new parameter representing the depth of the creation tree of the object into predicates exists, cando, dercando and do. Further, we enforce rules to be applied only to existing objects.

**Definition 2.** *Let $f$ be an initiator, $s$ be the subject executing $f$, $o_1, \ldots, o_m$ be the objects required by data processing $f$, and $o = f(s, o_1, \ldots, o_m)$ be the derived object. A* creating rule *is a rule of the form*

$$\text{exists}(i, o) \leftarrow L_1 \& \ldots \& L_n \& \text{exists}(j_1, o_1) \& \ldots \& \text{exists}(j_m, o_m).$$

*where $o$ is an object, $i$ represents the current iteration, and $L_1, \ldots, L_n$ are* cando, dercando, do, done, hie-, *or* rel-*literals.* cando, dercando, do *literals refer only to $o_1, \ldots, o_m$ and $0 \leq j_1, \ldots, j_m < i$.*

Once an object has been introduced in the scope of the specification, its access control policy is inferred by the system through authorization rules.

**Definition 3.** *An* authorization rule *is a rule of the form*

$$\text{cando}(i, o, s, a) \leftarrow L_1 \& \ldots \& L_n \& \text{exists}(i, o).$$

*where $o$, $s$ and $a$ are respectively an object, a subject and a signed action, $i$ represents the current iteration, and $L_1, \ldots, L_n$ are* cando, dercando, do, done, derivedFrom, hie-, *or* rel-literals. *Every* cando, dercando *and* do *literal must be inferred at an iteration $j$ such that $0 \leq j < i$.*

*Example 3.* A customer may prefer to not receive advertising on new services offered by the bank. Therefore, he specifies that his information (i.e., name ($n$), shipping address ($sa$), and phone number ($p$)) cannot be accessed by the Marketing Division (MD).

$$\text{cando}(0, n, x_s, -\text{read}) \leftarrow \text{in}(x_s, MD\text{-}employee, \text{ASH}) \& \text{exists}(i, n).$$
$$\text{cando}(0, sa, x_s, -\text{read}) \leftarrow \text{in}(x_s, MD\text{-}employee, \text{ASH}) \& \text{exists}(i, sa).$$
$$\text{cando}(0, p, x_s, -\text{read}) \leftarrow \text{in}(x_s, MD\text{-}employee, \text{ASH}) \& \text{exists}(i, p).$$

It is possible that no authorization is explicitly defined for the user with respect to a request access. Thereby, the framework allows system administrators to specify policies to propagate authorizations through the organizational structure of the system.

**Definition 4.** *A* derivation rule *is a rule of the form*

$$\text{dercando}(i, o, s, a) \leftarrow L_1 \& \ldots \& L_n \& \text{exists}(i, o).$$

*where $o$, $s$ and $a$ are respectively an object, a subject and a signed action, $i$ represents the current iteration, and $L_1, \ldots, L_n$ are* cando, dercando, do, done, derivedFrom, hie-, *or* rel-literals. *Every* cando, over *and positive* dercando *literal must be inferred at an iteration $j$ such that $0 \leq j \leq i$, and every* do *and negative* dercando *literal at an iteration $k$ such that $0 \leq k < i$.*

*Example 4.* Employees of the Customer Services Division are authorized to manage bank accounts. However, the actions that they can perform depend on the actions that they are authorized to perform on the customer information used to create such an account.

$$\text{dercando}(i, x_{o_1}, x_s, x_a) \leftarrow \text{in}(x_{o_1}, Account, \text{AOH}) \ \& \ \text{derivedFrom}(x_{o_1}, x_{o_2}) \ \& \\ \text{do}(j, x_{o_2}, x_s, x_a) \ \& \ \text{in}(x_s, CSD\text{-}employee, \text{ASH}) \ \& \\ \text{exists}(i, x_{o_1}) \ \& \ j < i.$$

Using derivation rules, a system administrator can specify very flexible policies for propagating authorizations. However, such a propagation may lead conflicting authorizations. Decision rules are introduced to cope with this issue.

**Definition 5.** *A* positive decision rule *is a rule of the form*

$$\text{do}(i, o, s, +a) \leftarrow L_1 \ \& \ \ldots \ \& \ L_n \ \& \ \text{exists}(i, o).$$

*where $o$, $s$ and $a$ are respectively an object, a subject and an action, $i$ represents the current iteration, and $L_1, \ldots, L_n$ are* cando, dercando, do, done, derivedFrom, *hie-, or rel-literals. Every* cando *and* dercando *literal must be inferred at an iteration $j$ such that $0 \leq j \leq i$, and every* do *literal at an iteration $k$ such that $0 \leq k < i$.*

*Example 5.* Information on accounts is also required by employees of other divisions of the bank in order to perform their duties. Thus, bank employees are entitled to access an account only if they are not explicitly denied to access the account and the information of its owner.

$$\text{do}(i, x_{o_1}, x_s, +\text{read}) \leftarrow \neg \ \text{dercando}(i, x_{o_1}, x_s, -\text{read}) \ \& \ \text{in}(x_{o_1}, Account, \text{AOH}) \ \& \\ \text{derivedFrom}(x_{o_1}, x_{o_2}) \ \& \ \neg \ \text{do}(j, x_{o_2}, x_s, -\text{read}) \ \& \\ \text{in}(x_s, employee, \text{ASH}) \ \& \ \text{exists}(i, x_{o_1}) \ \& \ j < i.$$

### 4.2  Materialized Views

The architecture proposed in [14] works properly when authorizations refer to primitive objects, but it is not able to completely enforce access control policies when objects are dynamically created. The main problem is when objects are "introduced" in the state of the system. If derived objects are introduced before applying propagation policies, they could not be created since required authorizations might be not yet computed. Otherwise, if they are introduced after applying propagation policies, authorizations on derived objects are not propagated.

Authorizations on new objects could depend on the authorizations associated with those objects used to create them. To maintain the flexibility provided by FAF, we permit any authorization predicate to occur in the body of rules. However, this affects the process for enforcing access control policies. In particular, the locally stratified structure of specifications is not preserved. Next, we present the process to enforce access control policies when objects are dynamically created.

The idea is to iterate the access control process proposed in [14] for $n+1$ times where $n$ is the greatest depth of creation trees. At each step $i$, we compute the stable model of

$\mathbf{AS}^i \cup \mathcal{M}(\mathbf{AS}^{i-1})$, where $\mathbf{AS}^i$ is the set of authorization specifications applied at the $i$-th iteration and $\mathcal{M}(\mathbf{AS}^{i-1})$ is the unique stable model of specification $\mathbf{AS}^{i-1}$. Next, we describe the process for computing this materialization.

The first step corresponds to the "standard" FAF process where only primitive objects are considered. Essentially, creating rules add to the state of the system objects that occur as leaves in some creation tree. Then, authorizations on these objects are propagated, possible conflicts are resolved, and decision policies are applied. If authorizations comply with integrity constraints, the output of the first iteration, $\mathcal{M}(\mathbf{AS}^0)$, is used as input for the second iteration where objects derived by one derivation step are considered. Repeatedly, the process proceeds until all derived objects are considered where the $i$-th iteration takes in input the output of the previous iteration, $\mathcal{M}(\mathbf{AS}^{i-1})$, and creating rules add to the state of the system objects whose creation tree has depth equal to $i$.

We now analyze the computation of the unique stable model of an authorization specification $\mathbf{AS}$ during one step of the previous process. This process is, in turn, an iterative process that, at each step $i$, computes the model of $\mathbf{AS}^i_j \cup \mathcal{M}(\mathbf{AS}^i_{j-1})$, where $\mathcal{M}(\mathbf{AS}^i_{j-1})$ is the unique stable model of stratum $\mathbf{AS}^i_{j-1}$. Next, we describe the different steps of this materialization computation process at the $i$-th iteration.

**Step (0):** $\mathbf{AS}^i_0$ represents the lowest stratum. This stratum contains facts derived at the $i-1$-th iteration, $\mathcal{M}(\mathbf{AS}^{i-1})$, and creation rules used to derive objects that are the root of a creation tree having depth equal to $i$. Creating rules are recursive, but, in agreement with Definition 2, exists literals occurring in the body of such rules must be derived in one of previous iterations so that they belong to $\mathcal{M}(\mathbf{AS}^{i-1})$. Moreover, Definition 2 allows only cando, dercando and do derived in previous iterations to occur in the body of creating rules. This guarantees that such literals belong to $\mathcal{M}(\mathbf{AS}^{i-1})$.

**Step (1):** $\mathbf{AS}^i_1$ contains facts derived at the previous stratum, $\mathcal{M}(\mathbf{AS}^i_0)$, and authorization rules. Differently from [14], here authorization rules are recursive. However, according to Definition 3, cando literals occurring in the body of such rules must be derived in previous iterations so that they belong to $\mathcal{M}(\mathbf{AS}^{i-1})$. This holds also for dercando and do literals. Moreover, Definition 3 allows only exists literals derived in the previous step to occur in the body of authorizations rules. Therefore, we can conclude that if a cando literal is added to the model, every literal that can occur in the body of the authorization rule belongs to $\mathcal{M}(\mathbf{AS}^i_0)$.

**Step (2):** $\mathbf{AS}^i_2$ contains facts derived at the previous stratum, $\mathcal{M}(\mathbf{AS}^i_1)$, and derivation rules. As in [14], derivation rules permit a "real" (positive) recursion. In particular, positive dercando literals having iteration parameter equal to $i$ can occur in the body of the rule. It is possible to prove, along the same lines as done in [14], the correctness of the materialized view. Essentially, the body of derivation rules is split into two parts: positive dercando literals having iteration parameter equal to $i$ and the rest. By Definition 4, we can easily verify that the literals belonging to the last set either are in $\mathcal{M}(\mathbf{AS}^{i-1})$ or are derived in one of previous steps. Thereby, they belong to $\mathcal{M}(\mathbf{AS}^i_1)$. On the other side, we refer to [14] for the fixpoint evaluation procedure that proves the correctness of $\mathcal{M}(\mathbf{AS}^i_2)$.

**Step (3):** $\mathbf{AS}_3^i$ contains facts derived at the previous stratum, $\mathcal{M}(\mathbf{AS}_2^i)$, and positive decision rules. By Definition 5, we can easily verify that literals occurring in the body either are in $\mathcal{M}(\mathbf{AS}^{i-1})$ or are derived in one of previous steps. Thus, do literals are added to the specification only if every literal that can occur in the body of positive decision rules belongs to $\mathcal{M}(\mathbf{AS}_2^i)$.

**Step (4)** *and* **Step (5)** are analogous to the ones presented in [14].

The above process ensures that the stable model computed during one iteration is a superset of the stable model computed in previous iterations. Further, it guarantees that every literal derived during an iteration refers to objects created in that iteration.

**Theorem 1.** *Let* $\mathbf{AS}^{i-1}$ *and* $\mathbf{AS}^i$ *be authorization specifications at* $i - 1$-*th and* $i$-*th iterations, respectively. The following statements hold.*

*1.* $\mathcal{M}(\mathbf{AS}^{i-1}) \subseteq \mathcal{M}(\mathbf{AS}^i)$
*2. Every literal in* $\mathcal{M}(\mathbf{AS}^i) \backslash \mathcal{M}(\mathbf{AS}^{i-1})$ *refers to objects created at the* $i$-*th iteration.*

In [14], authors have proved the locally stratified structure by assigning a level to each type of predicates. In our setting, this is not sufficient since the level of the head predicate could be strictly lower than that of predicates occurring in its body. However, the locally stratified structure is maintained by distinguishing the iteration in which facts are deduced and limiting the application of rules to existing objects. Essentially, strata are ordered with respect to a lexicographic order: the first component is the iteration, and the second corresponds to the level as defined in [14].

**Theorem 2.** *Every authorization specification is a locally stratified logic program.*

This result ensures that the specification has a unique stable model [16]. Baral et al. [15] proved that well-founded semantics coincide with stable model for locally stratified logic programs. This guarantees that the stable model of authorization specifications can be computed in quadratic time on data complexity [19].

## 5   Information Flow Control

Data subjects want that their information is not misused once it has been accessed. However, FAF does not provide any form of control on the usage of information. This lack makes this authorization framework vulnerable to Trojan horses embedded in applications. If a user executing a tampered application has the required authorizations, the Trojan horse will copy sensible information into a file accessible by a malicious and unauthorized user. Therefore, it is necessary to characterize the flow of information within the system.

FAF supports an integrity constraints phase in order to verify the consistency of the system with respect to specific domain properties. Our idea is to use integrity constraints also to verify the presence of leaks in the information flow. Similarly to [10,11,12,20], we propose to verify that the set of authorizations associated with a derived object is a subset of the intersection of the authorizations associated with the objects used to create it. Essentially, we want to ensure that a derived object does not disclose more information that the objects used to derive it does.

To this end, we define the 4-ary predicate warning. The intuition is that literal warning$(o_1, o_2, s, a)$ holds if subject $s$ can perform action $a$ on object $o_1$, but he cannot perform $a$ on object $o_2$ where $o_2$ is used to derive $o_1$. Notice that warnings are different from errors: they are failure of integrity constraints, like errors, but the system administrator may be perfectly happy with a system that does not satisfy them since information should be disclosed for complying with availability requirements. Thus, if the system reports a warning, the system administrator has to establish whether a leak complies with system requirements or corresponds to a system vulnerability.

**Definition 6.** *An* information flow constraint *is a rule of the form*

$$\text{warning}(o_1, o_2, s, a) \leftarrow \text{do}(i, o_1, s, a)\&\ \text{derivedFrom}(o_1, o_2)\&\ \neg\text{do}(j, o_2, s, a).$$

*where s and a are respectively a subject and an action, i and j are iterations such that $0 \leq j < i$, and object $o_2$ is used to derive object $o_1$.*

Essentially, the presence of warning literals in the model corresponds to the presence of covert channels [21] in the system. Therefore, we can detect possible illegal information flow by checking the occurrence of warning in the model.

**Theorem 3.** *If* warning *does not occur in the model, all information flows are safe.*

We remark that it is up to the system administration decides if an "unauthorized" flow is permitted or not. Every time a warning literal occurs in the model, he has to decide if it corresponds to an unauthorized leakage and, in this case, fix it.

*Example 6.* Suppose a malicious user, Mallory, has tampered the procedure *openA* provided by the bank IT system for creating new accounts. In this setting, the modified procedure copies customer information in a file (*foo*) accessible by the malicious user himself along with its legal functionalities. Such information will then sell to bank competitors by Mallory.

Accordingly, the malicious user defines the following rules

$$\begin{aligned}
\text{exists}(i, foo) \leftarrow\ &\text{do}(j, n, s, +\text{read})\ \&\ \text{do}(j, sa, s, +\text{read})\ \&\\
&\text{do}(j, p, s, +\text{read})\ \&\ \text{in}(s, CSD\text{-}employee, \text{ASH})\ \&\\
&\text{exists}(j, n)\ \&\ \text{exists}(j, sa)\ \&\ \text{exists}(j, p).\\
\text{cando}(i, foo, Mallory, +\text{read}) \leftarrow\ &\text{exists}(i, foo).\\
\text{dercando}(i, foo, Mallory, +\text{read}) \leftarrow\ &\text{cando}(i, foo, Mallory, +\text{read})\ \&\ \text{exists}(i, foo).\\
\text{do}(i, foo, Mallory, +\text{read}) \leftarrow\ &\text{dercando}(i, foo, Mallory, +\text{read})\ \&\ \text{exists}(i, foo).
\end{aligned}$$

The first rule sets the permissions necessary to create file *foo*. The other rules are needed by Mallory to access such a file.

Once an employee of Customer Services Division has run the procedure *openA*, the bank account is created together with file *foo*. The authorization framework then infers that Mallory is entitled to read *foo*. However, the bank IT system keeps trace that *foo* is derived by customer information by storing the following literals:

$$\{\text{derivedFrom}(foo, n), \text{derivedFrom}(foo, sa), \text{derivedFrom}(foo, p)\}$$

Applying the information flow constraint to this scenario, the system spots a harmful situation for the data subject since his information can be accessed by unauthorized users.

Notice that we have proposed to verify only step-by-step flow, that is, we compare authorizations associated with an object only with those associated with the objects directly used to derive it. We adopt this solution since we claim that, if a system administrator has already allowed an "unauthorized" flow, an additional warning on the same flow is unnecessary. However, we can easily verify information flow with respect to primitive information by making relation derivedFrom transitive.

## 6   Related Work

Proposals for enforcing access control policies can be classified under three main classes: discretionary access control (DAC) [4,5], mandatory access control (MAC) [1,2,3], and role based access control (RBAC) [6]. DAC allows users to specify which subjects can access their objects by directly defining an access control policy for each of their own objects. In MAC approaches, users cannot fully control the access to their objects, but it is the system that entirely determine the access that is to be granted. RBAC improves DAC and MAC proposals by integrating access control policies into the organizational structure of the system.

DAC models restrict access to objects on the basis of the identity of the invoking user and authorizations defining the actions he can execute on such objects. However, DAC models do not provide any form of support to control the usage of information once it is has been accessed [9]. Thereby, they are vulnerable to Trojan horse attacks [22]. This awareness has been matched by a number of research proposals on incorporating information flow control into access control models. Some proposals [11,12] associate with each object an ACL and propagate it together with the information in the object. In particular, the access control list associated with a new object is given by the intersection of all ACLs associated with the objects used to create it. Similarly, in [20,10] an information flow is defined to be safe if the ACL associated with the new object is a subset of the intersection of the sets of authorizations associated with the objects used to derive it. However, contrarily to our work, these proposals do not deal with the dynamic creation of objects.

Among MAC models, the model proposed by Bell and LaPadula [1] is a milestone for later work. Essentially, the model categorizes the security levels of objects and subjects, and enforces information flow to comply with "no read up" and "no write down" rules. Then, this model was generalized into the lattice model [2,3]. The above rules are very robust but have some disadvantages. The main drawback is covert channels [21]. A covert channel represents an implicit information flow that cannot be controlled by the security policy. Several proposals have been presented to cope with this problem [23,24,25]. However, their focus is on the detection of improper information leaks rather than on the the dynamic creation of objects.

Osborn [26] proposed to verify information flow in the RBAC model through a MAC approach. Essentially, they propose to map a role graph [27] (i.e., a graphical notation for representing RBAC hierarchies) into an information flow graphs which shows the information flow among roles. However, in this work information flow refers to the propagation of primitive information with respect to hierarchies of roles, rather than to derived information.

Yusuda et al. [28] propose a purpose-oriented access control model. Essentially, purpose-oriented access rules identify which operations associated with an object can invoke operations associated with other objects modifying the objects themselves. These operations are classified with respect to the type of information flow. Based on this classification, they build an invocation graph that, together with a MAC model, is used to detect information leakages. Izaki et al. [29] integrate the RBAC model into the purpose-oriented model. Essentially, the purpose-oriented model is enhanced by introducing the concept of role. The idea underlying this approach is to classify object methods and derive a flow graph from method invocations. From such a graph, non-secure information flows can be identified.

# 7  Conclusion

The main contribution of this paper is a procedure for dynamically creating objects and automatically deriving access control policies to be associated with them. First, we have introduced creating rules in order to verify the conditions under which objects can be created and add "legal" objects to the state of the system. Then, we have defined a flexible framework for associating with a new object an access control policy based on the authorizations associated with the objects used to create it. However, the architecture of FAF does not support the dynamical creation of objects. Thus, we have improved it together with its underlying logic-based framework in order to preserve the locally stratified structure. This ensures the validity of advantage gained by FAF over its predecessors in specifying and enforcing access control policies. Finally, we have provided a mechanism in order to detect information leakages in the specification.

# References

1. Bell, D.E., LaPadula, L.J.: Secure Computer System: Unified Exposition and MULTICS Interpretation. Technical Report MTR-2997 Rev. 1, The MITRE Corporation, Bedford, MA (1976)
2. Brewer, D.F.C., Nash, M.J.: The chinese wall security policy. In: Proc. of Symp. on Sec. and Privacy, IEEE Press (1989) 206–214
3. Denning, D.E., Denning, P.J.: Certification of programs for secure information flow. CACM **20**(7) (1977) 504–513
4. Downs, D., Rub, J., Kung, K., Jordan, C.: Issues in Discretionary Access Control. In: Proc. of Symp. on Sec. and Privacy, IEEE Press (1985) 208–218
5. Griffiths, P.P., Wade, B.W.: An authorization mechanism for a relational database system. TODS **1**(3) (1976) 242–255
6. Sandhu, R.S., Coyne, E.J., Feinstein, H.L., Youman, C.E.: Role-based access control models. IEEE Comp. **29**(2) (1996) 38–47
7. Sabelfeld, A., Myers, A.C.: Language-Based Information-Flow Security. IEEE J. on Selected Areas in Comm. **21**(1) (2003) 5–19
8. Chong, S., Myers, A.C.: Security Policies for Downgrading. In: Proc. of CCS'04, ACM Press (2004) 198–209
9. Bertino, E., Samarati, P., Jajodia, S.: High assurance discretionary access control for object bases. In: Proc. of CCS'93, ACM Press (1993) 140–150

10. Samarati, P., Bertino, E., Ciampichetti, A., Jajodia, S.: Information flow control in object-oriented systems. TKDE **9**(4) (1997) 524–538

11. McCollum, C.D., Messing, J.R., Notargiacomo, L.: Beyond the pale of MAC and DAC-defining new forms of access control. In: Proc. of Symp. on Sec. and Privacy, IEEE Press (1990) 190–200

12. Stoughton, A.: Access flow: A protection model which integrates access control and information flow. In: Proc. of Symp. on Sec. and Privacy, IEEE Press (1981) 9–18

13. Zannone, N., Jajodia, S., Massacci, F., Wijesekera, D.: Maintaining Privacy on Derived Objects. In: Proc. of WPES'05, ACM Press (2005) 10–19

14. Jajodia, S., Samarati, P., Sapino, M.L., Subrahmanian, V.S.: Flexible support for multiple access control policies. TODS **26**(2) (2001) 214–260

15. Baral, C.R., Subrahmanian, V.S.: Stable and extension class theory for logic programs and default logics. J. of Autom. Reas. **8**(3) (1992) 345–366

16. Gelfond, M., Lifschitz, V.: The stable model semantics for logic programming. In: Proc. of ICLP'88, MIT Press (1988) 1070–1080

17. Scott, D.S.: Identity and existence in intuitionistic logic. In: Application of Sheaves. Volume 753 of Lecture Notes in Mathematics. Springer Verlag (1979) 660–696

18. Liskov, B.H., Wing, J.M.: A Behavioral Notion of Subtyping. TOPLAS **16**(6) (1994) 1811–1841

19. van Gelder, A.: The alternating fixpoint of logic programs with negation. In: Proc. of PODS'89, ACM Press (1989) 1–10

20. Ferrari, E., Samarati, P., Bertino, E., Jajodia, S.: Providing flexibility in information flow control for object oriented systems. In: Proc. of Symp. on Sec. and Privacy, IEEE Press (1997) 130–140

21. Focardi, R., Gorrieri, R.: The Compositional Security Checker: A Tool for the Verification of Information Flow Security Properties. TSE **23**(9) (1997) 550–571

22. Samarati, P., di Vimercati, S.D.C.: Access Control: Policies, Models, and Mechanisms. In: FOSAD 2001/2002. Volume 2946 of LNCS. Springer (2001) 137–196

23. He, J., Gligor, V.D.: Information-Flow Analysis for Covert-Channel Identification in Multilevel Secure Operating Systems. In: Proc. of the 3rd IEEE Comp. Sec. Found. Workshop, IEEE Press (1990) 139–149

24. National Computer Security Center: A Guide to Understanding Covert Channel Analysis of Trusted Systems. Technical Report NCSC-TG-030, Library No. S-240,572, National Security Agency (1993)

25. Pernul, G.: Database Security. Advances in Computers **38** (1994) 1–72

26. Osborn, S.L.: Information flow analysis of an RBAC system. In: Proc. of SACMAT'02, ACM Press (2002) 163–168

27. Nyanchama, M., Osborn, S.: The role graph model and conflict of interest. TISSEC **2**(1) (1999) 3–33

28. Yasuda, M., Tachikawa, T., Takizawa, M.: Information Flow in a Purpose-Oriented Access Control Model. In: Proc. of ICPADS'97, IEEE Press (1997) 244–249

29. Izaki, K., Tanaka, K., Takizawa, M.: Information flow control in role-based model for distributed objects. In: Proc. of ICPADS'01, IEEE Press (2001) 363–370

# Detection and Resolution of Anomalies in Firewall Policy Rules

Muhammad Abedin, Syeda Nessa, Latifur Khan,
and Bhavani Thuraisingham

Department Of Computer Science
The University of Texas at Dallas
{maa056000, skn051000, lkhan, bxt043000}@utdallas.edu

**Abstract.** A firewall is a system acting as an interface of a network to one or more external networks. It implements the security policy of the network by deciding which packets to let through based on rules defined by the network administrator. Any error in defining the rules may compromise the system security by letting unwanted traffic pass or blocking desired traffic. Manual definition of rules often results in a set that contains conflicting, redundant or overshadowed rules, resulting in anomalies in the policy. Manually detecting and resolving these anomalies is a critical but tedious and error prone task. Existing research on this problem have been focused on the analysis and detection of the anomalies in firewall policy. Previous works define the possible relations between rules and also define anomalies in terms of the relations and present algorithms to detect the anomalies by analyzing the rules. In this paper, we discuss some necessary modifications to the existing definitions of the relations. We present a new algorithm that will simultaneously detect and resolve any anomaly present in the policy rules by necessary reorder and split operations to generate a new anomaly free rule set. We also present proof of correctness of the algorithm. Then we present an algorithm to merge rules where possible in order to reduce the number of rules and hence increase efficiency of the firewall.

**Keywords:** Packet Filters, Network Security, Firewalls, Anomalies, Security Policy.

## 1 Introduction

A firewall is a system that acts as an interface of a network to one or more external networks and regulates the network traffic passing through it. The firewall decides which packets to allow to go through or to drop based on a set of "rules" defined by the administrator. These rules have to be defined and maintained with utmost care, as any slight mistake in defining the rules may allow unwanted traffic to be able to enter or leave the network, or deny passage to quite legitimate traffic. Unfortunately, the process of manual definition of the rules and trying to detect mistakes in the rule set by inspection is very prone to errors and consumes a lot of time. Thus, research in the direction of detecting

E. Damiani and P. Liu (Eds.): Data and Applications Security 2006, LNCS 4127, pp. 15–29, 2006.

anomalies in firewall rules have gained momentum of recent. Our work focuses on automating the process of detecting and resolving the anomalies in the rule set.

Firewall rules are usually in the form of a criteria and an action to take if any packet matches the criteria. Actions are usually *accept* and *reject*. A packet arriving at a firewall is tested with each rule sequentially. Whenever it matches with the criteria of a rule, the action specified in the rule is executed, and the rest of the rules are skipped. For this reason, firewall rules are order sensitive. When a packet matches with more than one rules, the first such rule is executed. Thus, if the set of packets matched by two rules are not disjoint, they will create anomalies. For instance, the set of packets matching a rule may be a superset of those matched by a subsequent rule. In this case, all the packets that the second rule could have matched will be matched and handled by the first one and the second rule will never be executed. More complicated anomalies may arise when the sets of packets matched by two rules are overlapped.

If no rule matches the packet, then the default action of the firewall is taken. Usually such packets are dropped silently so that nothing unwanted can enter or exit the network. In this paper, we assume that the default action of the firewall system is to *reject* and develop our algorithms accordingly.

Of recent, research work on detecting and resolving anomalies in firewall policy rules have gained momentum. Mayer et al. present tools for analyzing firewalls in [13]. In [8], Eronen et al. propose the approach of representing the rules as a knowledge base, and present a tool based on *Constraint Logic Programming* to allow the user to write higher level operations and queries. Works focusing on automating the process of detecting anomalies in policy include [12] where Hazelhurst describes an algorithm to represent the rules as a *Binary Decision Diagram* and presents a set of algorithms to analyze the rules. Eppstein et al. give an efficient algorithm for determining whether a rule set contains conflicts in [7]. Al-Shaer et al. define the possible relations between firewall rules in [1, 2, 4], and then define anomalies that can occur in a rule set in terms of these definitions. They also give an algorithm to detect these anomalies, and present policy advisor tools using these definitions and algorithm. They extend their work to distributed firewall systems in [3, 5]. A work that focuses on detecting and resolving anomalies in firewall policy rules is [11], where they propose a scheme for resolving conflicts by adding resolve filters. However, this algorithm requires the support of prioritized rules, which is not always available in firewalls. Also their treatment of the criterion values only as prefixes makes their work specific. In [9], Fu et al. define high level security requirements, and develop mechanisms to detect and resolve conflicts among IPSec policies. Golnabi et al. describe a Data Mining approach to the anomaly resolution in [10].

Majority of current research focus on the analysis and detection of anomalies in rules. Those that do address the resolution of anomalies require special features or provisions from the firewall, or focus on specific areas. In this paper, we base our work on the research of Al-Shaer et. al. in [1, 2, 3] whose analysis is applicable to all rule based firewalls in general. However, their work is limited to the detection of anomalies. We also show that one of their definitions is redundant, and the set of definitions do not cover all possibilities. In our work, we remove the redundant definition, and modify one definition to cover all the possible relations between rules. We also describe the anomalies in terms of the modified definitions. Then we present a set of algorithms to simultaneously detect and resolve these anomalies to produce an anomaly-free rule set. We also present an algorithm to merge rules whenever possible. Reports are also produced by the algorithms describing the anomalies that were found, how they were resolved and which rules were merged.

The organization of the paper is as follows. In Sect. 2, we discuss the basic concepts of firewall systems, representation of rules in firewalls, possible relations between rules, and possible anomalies between rules in a firewall policy definition. In Sect. 3, we first present our algorithm for detecting and resolving anomalies and its proof of correctness. Then we provide an illustrative example showing how the algorithm works. After that we present our algorithm to merge rules and provide an example of its application. Finally, in Sect. 4, we present the conclusions drawn from our work and propose some directions for future work.

## 2    Firewall Concepts

In this section, we first discuss the basic concepts of firewall systems and their policy definition. We present our modified definitions of the relationships between the rules in a firewall policy, and then present the anomalies as described in [1].

### 2.1    Representation of Rules

A rule is defined as a set of criteria and an action to perform when a packet matches the criteria. The criteria of a rule consist of the elements direction, protocol, source IP, source port, destination IP and destination port. Therefore a complete rule may be defined by the ordered tuple ⟨direction, protocol, source IP, source port, destination IP, destination port, action⟩. Each attribute can be defined as a range of values, which can be represented and analyzed as sets.

### 2.2    Relation Between Two Rules

The relation between two rules essentially mean the relation between the set of packets they match. Thus the action field does not come into play when considering the relation between two rules. As the values of the other attributes of firewall rules can be represented as sets, we can consider a rule to be a set of sets, and we can compare two rules using the set relations described in Fig. 1. Two rules can be exactly equal if every criteria in the rules match exactly, one rule can be the subset of the other if each criterion of one rule is a subset of or equal to the other rule's criteria, or they can be overlapped if the rules are not disjoint and at least one of the criteria are overlapped. In the last case, a rule would match a portion of the packets matched by the other but not every

18      M. Abedin et al.

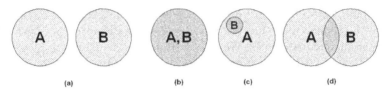

**Fig. 1.** (a) Sets $A$ and $B$ are disjoint, $A \cap B = \phi$; (b) Sets $A$ and $B$ are equal, $A = B$; (c) Set $B$ is a subset of set $A$, $B \subset A$; (d) Sets $A$ and $B$ are overlapped, $A \cap B \neq \phi$, but $A \not\subset B$ and $B \not\subset A$

packet, and the other rule would also match a portion of the packets matched by the first rule, but not all.

Al-Shaer et al. discuss these possible relations in [1] and they define the relations *completely disjoint*, *exactly matched*, *inclusively matched*, *partially disjoint* and *correlated*. We propose some modifications to the relations defined in [1]. First we note that it is not needed to distinguish between *completely disjoint* and *partially disjoint* rules as two rules will match entirely different set of packets if they differ in even only in one field. Further, we observe that the formal definition of *correlated* rules does not include the possibility of overlapped field in which the fields are neither disjoint nor subset of one or the other. We propose the following modified set of relations between the rules.

**Disjoint.** Two rules $r$ and $s$ are *disjoint*, denoted as $r\Re_D s$, if they have at least one criterion for which they have completely disjoint values. Formally,
$r\Re_D s$ if $\exists a \in attr[r.a \cap s.a = \phi]$

**Exactly Matching.** Two rules $r$ and $s$ are *exactly matched*, denoted by $r\Re_{EM} s$, if each criterion of the rules match exactly. Formally,
$r\Re_{EM} s$ if $\forall a \in attr[r.a = s.a]$

**Inclusively Matching.** A rule $r$ is a *subset*, or *inclusively matched* of another rule $s$, denoted by $r\Re_{IM} s$, if there exists at least one criterion for which $r$'s value is a subset of $s$'s value and for the rest of the attributes $r$'s value is equal to $s$'s value. Formally,
$r\Re_{IM} s$ if $\exists_{a \subset attr} [a \neq \phi \land \forall_{x \in a} [r.x \subset s.x] \land \forall_{y \in a^c} [r.y = s.y]]$

**Correlated.** Two rules $r$ and $s$ are *correlated*, denoted by $r\Re_C s$, if $r$ and $s$ are not disjoint, but neither is the subset of the other. Formally,
$r\Re_C s$ if $(r \not\Re_D s) \land (r \not\Re_{IM} s) \land (s \not\Re_{IM} r)$

### 2.3 Possible Anomalies Between Two Rules

In [1], Al-Shaer et al. give formal definitions of the possible anomalies between rules in terms of the relations defined in [1]. Of these anomalies, we consider *generalization* not to be an anomaly, as it is used in practice to specially handle a specific group of addresses within a larger group, and as such we omit it from our consideration. Here, we define the anomalies in terms of the relations in Sect. 2.2.

**Shadowing Anomaly.** A rule $r$ is shadowed by another rule $s$ if $s$ precedes $r$ in the policy, and $s$ can match all the packets matched by $r$. The effect is that $r$ is never activated. Formally, rule $r$ is shadowed by $s$ if $s$ precedes $r$, $r\Re_{EM}s$, and $r.action \neq s.action$, or $s$ precedes $r$, $r\Re_{IM}s$, and $r.action \neq s.action$.

**Correlation Anomaly.** Two rules $r$ and $s$ are correlated if they have different filtering actions and the $r$ matches some packets that match $s$ and the $s$ matches some packets that $r$ matches. Formally rules $r$ and $s$ have a correlation anomaly if $r\Re_{C}s, r.action \neq s.action$

**Redundancy Anomaly.** A redundant rule $r$ performs the same action on the same packets as another rule $s$ such that if $r$ is removed the security policy will not be affected. Formally rule $r$ is redundant of rule $s$ if $s$ precedes $r$, $r\Re_{EM}s$, and $r.action = s.action$, or $s$ precedes $r$, $r\Re_{IM}s$, and $r.action = s.action$; whereas rule $s$ is redundant to rule $r$ if $s$ precedes $r$, $s\Re_{IM}r$, $r.action = s.action$ and $\not\exists t$ where $s$ precedes $t$ and $t$ precedes $r$, $s\{\Re_{IM}, \Re_{C}\}t$, $r.action \neq t.action$

# 3   Anomaly Resolution Algorithms

This section describes the algorithms to detect and resolve the anomalies present in a set of firewall rules as defined in the previous section. The algorithm is in two parts. The first part analyzes the rules and generates a set of disjoint firewall rules that do not contain any anomaly. The second part analyzes the set of rules and tries to merge the rules in order to reduce the number of rules thus generated without introducing any new anomaly.

## 3.1   Algorithms for Finding and Resolving Anomalies

In this section, we present our algorithm to detect and resolve anomalies. In this algorithm, we resolve the anomalies as follows: in case of *shadowing anomaly*, when rules are *exactly matched*, we keep the one with the reject action. When the rules are *inclusively matched*, we reorder the rules to bring the subset rule before the superset rule. In case of *correlation anomaly*, we break down the rules into disjoint parts and insert them into the list. Of the part that is common to the correlated rules, we keep the one with the reject action. In case of *redundancy anomaly*, we remove the redundant rule.

In our algorithm, we maintain two global lists of firewall rules, *old_rules_list* and *new_rules_list*. The *old_rules_list* will contain the rules as they are in the original firewall configuration, and the *new_rules_list* will contain the output of the algorithm, a set of firewall rules without any anomaly. The approach taken here is incremental, we take each rule in the *old_rules_list* and insert it into *new_rules_list* in such a way that *new_rules_list* remains free from anomalies.

Algorithm RESOLVE-ANOMALIES controls the whole process. After initializing the global lists in lines 1 and 2, it takes each rule from the *old_rules_list* and invokes algorithm INSERT on it in lines 3 to 4. Then, it scans the *new_rules_list* to resolve any redundancy anomalies that might remain in the list in lines 5 to 10 by looking for and removing any rule that is a subset of a subsequent rule with same action.

**Algorithm.** RESOLVE-ANOMALIES: Resolve anomalies in firewall rules file

1. *old_rules_list* ← read rules from config file
2. *new_rules_list* ← empty list
3. **for all** $r \in old\_rules\_list$ **do**
4.      INSERT($r$, *new_rules_list*)
5. **for all** $r \in new\_rules\_list$ **do**
6.      **for all** $s \in new\_rules\_list$ after $r$ **do**
7.          **if** $r \subset s$ **then**
8.              **if** $r.action = s.action$ **then**
9.                  Remove $r$ from *new_rules_list*
10.             **break**

Algorithm INSERT inserts a rule into the *new_rules_list* in such a way that the list remains anomaly free. If the list is empty, the rule is unconditionally inserted in line 2. Otherwise, INSERT tests the rule with all the rules in *new_rules_list* using the RESOLVE algorithm in the **for** loop in line 5. If the rule conflicts with any rule in the list, RESOLVE will handle it and return *true*, breaking the loop. So, at line 10, if *insert_flag* is *true*, it means that RESOLVE has already handled the rule. Otherwise, the rule is disjoint or superset with all the rules in *new_rules_list* and it is inserted at the end of the list in line 11.

**Algorithm.** INSERT($r$,*new_rules_list*): Insert the rule $r$ into *new_rules_list*

1. **if** *new_rules_list* is empty **then**
2.      insert $r$ into *new_rules_list*
3. **else**
4.      *inserted* ← *false*
5.      FOR ALL $s \in new\_rules\_list$ **do**
6.          **if** $r$ and $s$ are not disjoint **then**
7.              *inserted* ← RESOLVE($r$, $s$)
8.              **if** *inserted* = *true* **then**
9.                  **break**
10.     **if** *inserted* = *false* **then**
11.         Insert $r$ into *new_rules_list*

The algorithm RESOLVE is used to detect and resolve anomalies between two non-disjoint rules. This algorithm is used by the INSERT algorithm. The first rule passed to RESOLVE, $r$, is the rule being inserted, and the second parameter, $s$ is a rule already in the *new_rules_list*. In comparing them, following are the possibilities:

1. *r and s are equal.* If they are equal, and their actions are same, then any one can be discarded. If the actions are different, then the one with the *reject* action is retained. This case is handled in lines 1 to 6.

2. *r is a subset of s.* In this case, we simply insert $r$ before $s$ regardless of the action. This case is handled in lines 7 to 9.
3. *r is a superset of s.* In this case, $r$ may match with rules further down the list, so it is allowed to be checked further. No operation is performed in this case. This case is handled in lines 10 to 11.
4. *r and s are correlated.* In this case, we need to break up the correlated rules into disjoint rules. This case is handled in lines 12 to 19. First the set of attributes in which the two rules differ is determined in line 13, and then SPLIT is invoked for each of the differing attributes in the **for** loop in line 14. After SPLIT returns, $r$ and $s$ contain the common part of the rules, which is then inserted.

**Algorithm.** RESOLVE($r$, $s$): Resolve anomalies between two rules $r$ and $s$

1. **if** $r = s$ **then**
2.     **if** $r.action \neq s.action$ **then**
3.         set $s.action$ to REJECT and report anomaly
4.     **else**
5.         report removal of $r$
6.     **return** *true*
7. **if** $r \subset s$ **then**
8.     insert $r$ before $s$ into *new_rules_list* and report reordering
9.     **return** *true*
10. **if** $s \subset r$ **then**
11.     **return** *false*
12. Remove $s$ from *new_rules_list*
13. Find set of attributes $a = \{x | r.x \neq s.x\}$
14. **for all** $a_i \in a$ **do**
15.     SPLIT($r$, $s$, $a_i$)
16. **if** $r.action \neq s.action$ **then**
17.     $s.action \leftarrow$ REJECT
18. INSERT($s$, *new_rules_list*)
19. **return** *true*

Algorithm SPLIT, is used to split two non-disjoint rules. It is passed the two rules and the attribute on which the rules differ. It first extracts the parts of the rules that are disjoint to the two rules and invokes the INSERT algorithm on them. Then it computes the common part of the two rules. Let $r$ and $s$ be two rules and let $a$ be the attribute for which SPLIT is invoked. As can be readily seen from the examples in Fig. 2(a) and 2(b), the common part will always start with $\max(r.a.start, s.a.start)$ and end with $\min(r.a.end, s.a.end)$. The disjoint part before the common part begins with $\min(r.a.start, s.a.start)$ and ends with $\max(r.a.start, s.a.start) - 1$, and the disjoint part after the common part starts with $\min(r.a.end, s.a.end) + 1$ and ends with $\max(r.a.end, s.a.end)$. As these two parts are disjoint with $r$ and $s$, but we do not know their relation with the other rules in *new_rules_list*, they are inserted into the *new_rules_list* by invoking

INSERT procedure. The common part of the two rules is computed in lines 13 and 14. The disjoint part before the common part is computed and inserted in lines 5 to 8. The disjoint part after the common part is computed and inserted in lines 9 to 12.

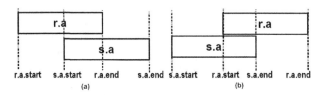

**Fig. 2.** (a) $r.a.start < s.a.start$ & $r.a.end < s.a.end$, so the ranges can be broken into $[r.a.start, s.a.start - 1]$, $[s.a.start, r.a.end]$ and $[r.a.end + 1, s.a.end]$. (b) $r.a.start > s.a.start$ & $r.a.end > s.a.end$, so the ranges can be broken into $[s.a.start, r.a.start - 1]$, $[r.a.start, s.a.end]$ and $[s.a.end + 1, r.a.end]$.

**Algorithm.** SPLIT($r$,$s$,$a$): Split overlapping rules $r$ and $s$ based on attribute $a$

1. $left \leftarrow \min(r.a.start, s.a.start)$
2. $right \leftarrow \max(r.a.end, s.a.end)$
3. $common\_start \leftarrow \max(r.a.start, s.a.start)$
4. $common\_end \leftarrow \min(r.a.end, s.a.end)$
5. **if** $r.a.start > s.a.start$ **then**
6.     INSERT($\langle(left, common\_start - 1)$, rest of $s$'s attributes$\rangle$, $new\_rules\_list$)
7. **else if** $r.a.start < s.a.start$ **then**
8.     INSERT($\langle(left, common\_start - 1)$, rest of $r$'s attributes$\rangle$, $new\_rules\_list$)
9. **if** $r.a.end > s.a.end$ **then**
10.     INSERT($\langle(common\_end + 1, right)$, rest of $r$'s attributes$\rangle$, $new\_rules\_list$)
11. **else if** $r.a.end < s.a.end$ **then**
12.     INSERT($\langle(common\_end + 1, right)$, rest of $s$'s attributes$\rangle$, $new\_rules\_list$)
13. $r \leftarrow \langle(common\_start, common\_end)$, rest of $r$'s attributes$\rangle$
14. $s \leftarrow \langle(common\_start, common\_end)$, rest of $s$'s attributes$\rangle$

After completion of the RESOLVE-ANOMALIES algorithm, $new\_rules\_list$ will contain the list of firewall rules that are free from all the anomalies in consideration.

### 3.2  Proof of Correctness

To prove the correctness of our algorithm, we first present and prove the following theorem.

**Theorem 1.** *A set of rules $R[1\dots n]$ is free from* shadowing, correlation *and* redundancy *anomalies if for $1 \leq i < j \leq n$, exactly one of the following three conditions hold:*

1. $R[i] \Re_D R[j]$
2. $R[i] \Re_{IM} R[j]$ and $R[i].action \neq R[j].action$
3. $R[i] \Re_{IM} R[j]$ and $R[i].action = R[j].action$ only if there exists some $k$ such that $i < k < j$ and $R[i] \Re_{IM} R[k]$ and $R[i].action \neq R[k].action$

*Proof. Shadowing anomaly* cannot exist in the list as for $R[i]$ cannot be a subset of $R[j]$ if $i > j$. *Correlation anomaly* cannot exist in the list as the only relations allowed in the list are $\Re_D$ and $\Re_{IM}$. The absence of *redundancy anomaly* is ensured by conditions 2 and 3.                                          □

We show by using loop invariants [6] that after the completion of Algorithm RESOLVE-ANOMALIES, *new_rules_list* will maintain these properties and so it will be anomaly free. The loop invariant is:

> At the start of each iteration of the **for** loop in line 3 of Algorithm RESOLVE-ANOMALIES, for $1 \leq i < j \leq m$, exactly one of the following holds:
> 1. *new_rules_list*$[i] \Re_D$*new_rules_list*$[j]$
> 2. *new_rules_list*$[i] \Re_{IM}$*new_rules_list*$[j]$
> where $m$ is the size of *new_rules_list*.

**Initialization.** Before the first iteration, the *new_rules_list* is initialized to *empty* and the invariant holds trivially.

**Maintenance.** Let $r$ be the rule being inserted in an iteration. When INSERT is invoked on $r$, the following cases are possible:

1. *new_rules_list* is empty. Then $r$ is inserted into *new_rules_list*, and the iteration is complete, with the invariant holding trivially.
2. $r$ is disjoint with every rule in *new_rules_list*. In this case, $r$ is inserted at the end of the list. The iteration is complete, and the loop invariant holds.
3. $r$ is not disjoint with rule $s \in$ *new_rules_list*. Then the procedure RESOLVE is invoked with $r$ and $s$, which checks the following possibilities:
   (a) $r \Re_{EM} s$. In this case, if their actions are same, $r$ is redundant and need not be inserted. If their actions are different, then $r$ and $s$ are conflicting rules, and we simply change the action of $s$ to *reject*, without inserting $r$. In both cases, the iteration completes without inserting anything, so the loop invariant holds.
   (b) $r \Re_{IM} s$. In this case, $r$ is inserted before $s$ in *new_rules_list* . The iteration is complete, and the loop invariant holds.
   (c) $s \Re_{IM} r$. In this case, RESOLVE returns *false* so that the loop in line 5 in INSERT can continue until either the end of *new_rules_list* has been reached, or for some subsequent rule $t$ has been found that is not disjoint with $r$ and call to RESOLVE$(r, t)$ has returned *true*. In the first case, all the rules after $s$ in *new_rules_list* are disjoint with $r$, so $r$ can be appended to *new_rules_list* without violating the loop invariant. In the second case, the call to RESOLVE$(r, t)$ has handled $r$ without violating the loop invariant, so in both cases the invariant holds.

(d) $r\Re_C s$. In this case, first $s$ is removed from *new_rules_list* as $r$ and $s$ are going to be broken into disjoint rules. Then, algorithm SPLIT is invoked for each attribute for which $r$ and $s$ differ. SPLIT breaks up the attribute's value into the part common to the rules and the parts unique to the rules. The unique parts are by definition disjoint, so they are inserted into the list by calling INSERT. After breaking up all the non-matching attributes, $r$ and $s$ are exactly matched. If they are of different action, then *s.action* is set to *reject*, otherwise $s$ already contains the common action. Then $s$ is inserted into *new_rules_list* by INSERT procedure. This completes the iteration, and ensures that the loop invariant holds.

**Termination.** The loop terminates when all the rules in *old_rules_list* has been inserted into *new_rules_list*, and as the loop invariant holds for each iteration, we have that conditions of the loop invariant hold for the entire *new_rules_list*.

Thus, at the end of the **for** loop in line 3 of Algorithm RESOLVE-ANOMALIES, each element of the *new_rules_list* is either disjoint with or subset of the subsequent elements. The **for** loop at line 5 scans and removes any redundancy anomalies present in the *new_rules_list*. If any rule $r$ in *new_rules_list* is subset of any subsequent rule $s$ in *new_rules_list* with the same action, $r$ is removed as it is redundant. So at the end of this loop, *new_rules_list* will maintain the three properties stated in Theorem 1, and so *new_rules_list* will be free from *shadowing*, *correlation* and *redundancy* anomalies.

### 3.3   Cost Analysis

The cost of running the algorithm depends on the nature of the rules in the input. If a rule is disjoint or superset with the other rules of the *new_rules_list* then the rule is inserted into the list without further invoking procedure INSERT. In this case the **for** loop in line 5 of Algorithm INSERT has to traverse the whole *new_rules_list*. If a rule is subset of any rule in the *new_rules_list*, then the rule is inserted just before the superset rule and the loop terminates immediately. So in the worst case the whole *new_rules_list* may have to be traversed. A rule is discarded if it is equal to any rule in the *new_rules_list*, and in the worst case the whole *new_rules_list* may have to be traversed. If a rule is correlated with a rule in the *new_rules_list* then they will be divided into a set of mutually disjoint rules. In the worst case the number of rules thus generated will be up to twice the number of attributes plus one, and these rules will be inserted into the *new_rules_list* by invoking INSERT recursively. RESOLVE-ANOMALIES invokes INSERT once for each rule in *new_rules_list* in the **for** loop in line 3, and removes the redundancy anomalies in the **for** loop in line 5. The running time of RESOLVE-ANOMALIES is dominated by the number of times INSERT is invoked, which depends on the number of correlated rules. In the worst case, if all rules are correlated, the running time may deteriorate to exponential order.

## 3.4   Illustrative Example

Let us consider the following set of firewall rules for analysis with the algorithm.

1. ⟨IN, TCP, 129.110.96.117, ANY, ANY, 80, REJECT⟩
2. ⟨IN, TCP, 129.110.96.*, ANY, ANY, 80, ACCEPT⟩
3. ⟨IN, TCP, ANY, ANY, 129.110.96.80, 80, ACCEPT⟩
4. ⟨IN, TCP, 129.110.96.*, ANY, 129.110.96.80, 80, REJECT⟩
5. ⟨OUT, TCP, 129.110.96.80, 22, ANY, ANY, REJECT⟩
6. ⟨IN, TCP, 129.110.96.117, ANY, 129.110.96.80, 22, REJECT⟩
7. ⟨IN, UDP, 129.110.96.117, ANY, 129.110.96.*, 22, REJECT⟩
8. ⟨IN, UDP, 129.110.96.117, ANY, 129.110.96.80, 22, REJECT⟩
9. ⟨IN, UDP, 129.110.96.117, ANY, 129.110.96.117, 22, ACCEPT⟩
10. ⟨IN, UDP, 129.110.96.117, ANY, 129.110.96.117, 22, REJECT⟩
11. ⟨OUT, UDP, ANY, ANY, ANY, ANY, REJECT⟩

**Step-1.** As the *new_rules_list* is empty, rule-1 is inserted as it is.

**Step-2.** When rule-2 is inserted, *new_rules_list* contains only one rule, the one that was inserted in the previous step. We have, $r = $ ⟨IN, TCP, 129.110.96.*, ANY, ANY, 80, ACCEPT⟩ and $s = $ ⟨IN, TCP, 129.110.96.117, ANY, ANY, 80, REJECT⟩. Here, $s \subset r$, so $r$ is inserted into *new_rules_list* after $s$.

**Step-3.** In this step, $r = $ ⟨IN, TCP, ANY, ANY, 129.110.96.80, 80, ACCEPT⟩. In the first iteration, $s = $ ⟨IN,TCP,129.110.96.117,ANY,ANY,80,REJECT⟩. Clearly these two rules are correlated, with $s.srcip \subset r.srcip$ and $r.destip \subset s.destip$. Therefore these rules must be broken down. After splitting the rules into disjoint parts, we have the following rules in *new_rules_list*:

1. ⟨IN, TCP, 129.110.96.1-116, ANY, 129.110.96.80, 80, ACCEPT⟩
2. ⟨IN, TCP, 129.110.96.118-254, ANY, 129.110.96.80, 80, ACCEPT⟩
3. ⟨IN, TCP, 129.110.96.117, ANY, 129.110.96.1-79, 80, REJECT⟩
4. ⟨IN, TCP, 129.110.96.117, ANY, 129.110.96.81-254, 80, REJECT⟩
5. ⟨IN, TCP, 129.110.96.117, ANY, 129.110.96.80, 80, REJECT⟩
6. ⟨IN, TCP, 129.110.96.*, ANY, ANY, 80, ACCEPT⟩

After completion of the first **for** loop in line 3 in the algorithm RESOLVE-ANOMALIES, the *new_rules_list* will hold the following rules:

1. ⟨IN, TCP, 129.110.96.1-116, ANY, 129.110.96.80, 80, ACCEPT⟩
2. ⟨IN, TCP, 129.110.96.118-254, ANY, 129.110.96.80, 80, ACCEPT⟩
3. ⟨IN, TCP, 129.110.96.117, ANY, 129.110.96.1-79, 80, REJECT⟩
4. ⟨IN, TCP, 129.110.96.117, ANY, 129.110.96.81-254, 80, REJECT⟩
5. ⟨IN, TCP, 129.110.96.117, ANY, 129.110.96.80, 80, REJECT⟩
6. ⟨IN, TCP, 129.110.96.*, ANY, 129.110.96.80, 80, REJECT⟩
7. ⟨IN, TCP, 129.110.96.*, ANY, ANY, 80, ACCEPT⟩
8. ⟨OUT, TCP, 129.110.96.80, 22, ANY, ANY, REJECT⟩
9. ⟨IN, TCP, 129.110.96.117, ANY, 129.110.96.80, 22, REJECT⟩
10. ⟨IN, UDP, 129.110.96.117, ANY, 129.110.96.80, 22, REJECT⟩
11. ⟨IN, UDP, 129.110.96.117, ANY, 129.110.96.117, 22, REJECT⟩

12. ⟨IN, UDP, 129.110.96.117, ANY, 129.110.96.*, 22, REJECT⟩
13. ⟨OUT, UDP, ANY, ANY, ANY, ANY, REJECT⟩

The next step is to scan this list to find and resolve the redundancy anomalies. In this list, rule-1 is a subset of rule-6, but as the rules have different action, rule-1 is retained. Similarly, rule-2, which is also a subset of rule-6 with differing action, is also retained. Rules 3 and 4 are subsets of rule-7, but are retained as they have different action than rule-7. Rule-5 is a subset of rule-6, and as they have the same action, rule-5 is removed. After removing these rules, the list is free from all the anomalies.

### 3.5  Algorithms for Merging Rules

After the completion of the anomaly resolution algorithm, there are no correlated rules in the list. In this list, we can merge rules having attributes with consecutive ranges with the same action. To accomplish this, we construct a tree using Algorithm TREEINSERT. Each node of the tree represents an attribute. The edges leading out of the nodes represent values of the attribute. Each edge in the tree represents a particular range of value for the attribute of the source node, and it points to a node for the next attribute in the rule represented by the path. For example, the root node of the tree represents the attribute *Direction*, and there can be two edges out of the root representing *IN* and *OUT*. We consider a firewall rule to be represented by the ordered tuple as mentioned in Sect. 2.1. So, the edge representing the value *IN* coming out of the root node would point to a node for *Protocol*. The leaf nodes always represent the attribute *Action*. A complete path from the root to a leaf corresponds to one firewall rule in the policy. For example, the leftmost path in the tree in Fig. 3(a) represents the firewall rule ⟨IN, TCP, 202.80.169.29-63, 483, 129.110.96.64-127, 100-110, ACCEPT⟩.

Algorithm TREEINSERT, takes as input a rule and a node of the tree. It checks if the value of the rule for the attribute represented by the node matches any of the values of the edges out of the node. If it matches any edge of the node, then it recursively invokes TREEINSERT on the node pointed by the edge with the rule. Otherwise it creates a new edge and adds it to the list of edges of the node.

**Algorithm.** TREEINSERT($n$, $r$): Inserts rule $r$ into the node $n$ of the rule tree

1. **for all** *edge* $e_i \in n.edges$ **do**
2.    **if** $r.(n.attribute) = e_i.range$ **then**
3.       TREEINSERT($e_i.vertex$, $r$)
4.       **return**
5. $v \leftarrow$ new Vertex(next attribute after $n.attribute$, NULL)
6. Insert new edge ⟨$r.(n.attribute), r.(n.attribute),$ v ⟩ in $n.edges$
7. TREEINSERT($v$, $r$)

We use Algorithm MERGE on the tree to merge those edges of the tree that has consecutive values of attributes, and has exactly matching subtrees. It first calls itself recursively on each of its children in line 2 to ensure that their sub-trees are already merged. Then, it takes each edge and matches its range with all the other edges to see if they can be merged. Whether two edges can be merged depends on two criteria. First, their ranges must be contiguous i.e. the range of one starts immediately after the end of the other. Second, the subtrees of the nodes pointed to by the edges must match exactly. This criterion ensures that all the attributes after this attribute are same for all the rules below this node. If these two criteria are met, they are merged into one edge in place of the original two edges. After merging the possible rules, the number of rules defined in the firewall policy is reduced and it helps to increase the efficiency of firewall policy management. The example given in Fig. 3 illustrate how the merge procedure works.

**Algorithm.** MERGE($n$): Merges edges of node $n$ representing a continuous range

1. **for all** *edge $e \in n.edges$* **do**
2.     MERGE(*e.node*)
3. **for all** *edge $e \in n.edges$* **do**
4.     **for all** *edge $e' \neq e \in n.edges$* **do**
5.         **if** $e$'s and $e'$'s ranges are *contiguous* and Subtree($e$)=Subtree($e'$) **then**
6.             Merge *e.range* and *e'.range* into *e.range*
7.             Remove $e'$ from *n.edges*

## 3.6   Illustrative Example of the Merge Algorithm

To illustrate the merging algorithm, we start with the following set of non-anomalous rules. We deliberately chose a set of rules with the same action since rules with different action will never be merged.

1. ⟨IN, TCP, 202.80.169.29-63, 483, 129.110.96.64-127, 100-110, ACCEPT⟩
2. ⟨IN, TCP, 202.80.169.29-63, 483, 129.110.96.64-127, 111-127, ACCEPT⟩
3. ⟨IN, TCP, 202.80.169.29-63, 483, 129.110.96.128-164, 100-127, ACCEPT⟩
4. ⟨IN, TCP, 202.80.169.29-63, 484, 129.110.96.64-99, 100-127, ACCEPT⟩
5. ⟨IN, TCP, 202.80.169.29-63, 484, 129.110.96.100-164, 100-127, ACCEPT⟩
6. ⟨IN, TCP, 202.80.169.64-110, 483-484, 129.110.96.64-164, 100-127, ACCEPT⟩

From this rules list we generate the tree as in Fig 3(a) by the TREEINSERT algorithm. On this tree, the Merge procedure is run. The Merge algorithm traverses the tree in post order. Thus, the first node to be processed is node 14. As it has only one child, it returns without any operation. The next node in order is 15, which also has only one child. The next node to be processed is node 9. The attribute represented by node 9 is destination port. The ranges of its two children, 100-110 and 111-127 are consecutive, and also their subtrees are the same. Thus, these two edges are merged to obtain one edge with the range 100-127.

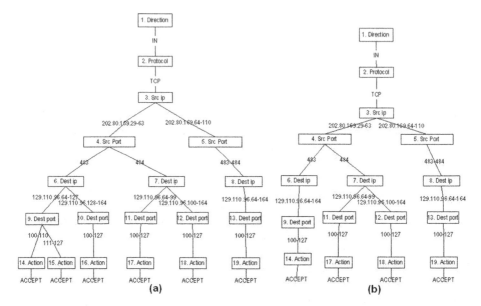

**Fig. 3.** (a) Tree generated from the example rules list by the TreeInsert algorithm. (b) Intermediate state of the tree: node 7's children are going to be merged next.

Of the nodes that are going to be processed now, nodes 16 and 10 are each of one child only, so they do not require any further processing. However, node 6, representing destination IP address, has two children, and their IP address ranges, 129.110.96.64-127 and 129.110.96.128-164, are consecutive. Also, the subtrees from the nodes 9 and 10 are also the same. Hence, they are merged to become one edge with range value of 129.110.96.128-164.

So far, we have eliminated three nodes, 15, 16 and 10. Of the next nodes to be processed, nodes 17, 11, 18 and 12 has only one child, and hence incur no processing. At node 7, as shown in Fig 3(b), the represented attribute is destination IP address, and the ranges of its children are 129.110.96.64-99 and 129.110.96.100-164. The ranges being consecutive, they are merged into one edge of range 129.110.96.64-164, eliminating node 12 and 18.

After the MERGE algorithm is complete on the entire tree, we are left with the single rule ⟨IN, TCP, 202.80.169.29-110, 483-484, 129.110.96.64-164, 100-127, ACCEPT⟩ .

## 4   Conclusion and Future Works

Resolution of anomalies from firewall policy rules is vital to the network's security as anomalies can introduce unwarranted and hard to find security holes. Our work presents an automated process for detecting and resolving such anomalies. The anomaly resolution algorithm and the merging algorithm should produce a compact yet anomaly free rule set that would be easier to understand and maintain. This algorithms can also be integrated into policy advisor and editing tools. The paper also establishes the complete definition and analysis of the relations between rules.

In future, this analysis can be extended to distributed firewalls. Also, we propose to use data mining techniques to analyze the log files of the firewall and discover other kinds of anomalies. These techniques should be applied only after the rules have been made free from anomaly by applying the algorithms in this paper. That way it would be ensured that not only syntactic but also semantic mistakes in the rules will be captured. Research in this direction has already started.

# References

[1] E. Al-Shaer and H. Hamed. Design and implementation of firewall policy advisor tools. Technical Report CTI-techrep0801, School of Computer Science Telecommunications and Information Systems, DePaul University, August 2002.

[2] E. Al-Shaer and H. Hamed. Firewall policy advisor for anomaly detection and rule editing. In *IEEE/IFIP Integrated Management Conference (IM'2003)*, March 2003.

[3] E. Al-Shaer and H. Hamed. Discovery of policy anomalies in distributed firewalls. In *Proc. 23rd Conf. IEEE Communications Soc. (INFOCOM 2004), Vol. 23, No. 1*, pages 2605–2616, March 2004.

[4] E. Al-Shaer and H. Hamed. Taxonomy of conflicts in network security policies. *IEEE Communications Magazine*, 44(3), March 2006.

[5] E. Al-Shaer, H. Hamed, R. Boutaba, and M. Hasan. Conflict classification and analysis of distributed firewall policies. *IEEE Journal on Selected Areas in Communications (JSAC)*, 23(10), October 2005.

[6] T. H. Cormen, C. E. Leiserson, R. L. Rivest, and C. Stein. *Introduction to Algorithms*. MIT Press, Cambridge, MA, U.S.A, 2nd edition, 2001.

[7] D. Eppstein and S. Muthukrishnan. Internet packet filter management and rectangle geometry. In *Proceedings of the 12th Annual ACM–SIAM Symposium on Discrete Algorithms (SODA 2001)*, pages 827–835, January 2001.

[8] P. Eronen and J. Zitting. An expert system for analyzing firewall rules. In *Proceedings of the 6th Nordic Workshop on Secure IT Systems (NordSec 2001)*, pages 100–107, November 2001.

[9] Z. Fu, S. F. Wu, H. Huang, K. Loh, F. Gong, I. Baldine, and C. Xu. IPSec/VPN security policy: Correctness, conflict detection, and resolution. In *Proceedings of Policy2001 Workshop*, January 2001.

[10] K. Golnabi, R. K. Min, L. Khan, and E. Al-Shaer. Analysis of firewall policy rules using data mining techniques. In *IEEE/IFIP Network Operations and Management Symposium (NOMS 2006)*, April 2006.

[11] A. Hari, S. Suri, and G. M. Parulkar. Detecting and resolving packet filter conflicts. In *INFOCOM (3)*, pages 1203–1212, March 2000.

[12] S. Hazelhurst. Algorithms for analysing firewall and router access lists. Technical Report TR-WitsCS-1999-5, Department of Computer Science, University of the Witwatersrand, South Africa, July 1999.

[13] A. Mayer, A. Wool, and E. Ziskind. Fang: A firewall analysis engine. In *Proceedings, IEEE Symposium on Security and Privacy*, pages 177–187. IEEE CS Press, May 2000.

# On Finding an Inference-Proof Complete Database for Controlled Query Evaluation

Joachim Biskup and Lena Wiese

Universität Dortmund, 44221 Dortmund, Germany
{biskup, wiese}@ls6.cs.uni-dortmund.de
http://ls6-www.cs.uni-dortmund.de/issi/

**Abstract.** Controlled Query Evaluation (CQE) offers a logical framework to prevent a user of a database from inadvertently gaining knowledge he is not allowed to know. By modeling the user's a priori knowledge in an appropriate way, a CQE system can control not only plain access to database entries but also inferences made by the user. A dynamic CQE system that enforces inference control at runtime has already been investigated. In this article, we pursue a static approach that constructs an inference-proof database in a preprocessing step. The inference-proof database can respond to any query without enabling the user to infer confidential information. We illustrate the semantics of the system by a comprehensive example and state the essential requirements for an inference-proof and highly available database. We present an algorithm that accomplishes the preprocessing by combining SAT solving and "Branch and Bound".

**Keywords:** Controlled Query Evaluation, inference control, lying, confidentiality of data, complete database systems, propositional logic, SAT solving, Branch and Bound.

## 1 Introduction and Related Work

Controlled query evaluation (cf. [1,2,3]) aims at preserving the confidentiality of some secret information in a sequence of queries to a database. Not only plain access to certain database entries is denied but also information that can be gained by logical reasoning is taken into consideration. This is what is usually called *inference control*. There are a lot of different approaches addressing inference control for example for statistical databases [9], distributed databases [5], relational databases with fuzzy values [15] and for XML documents [19]. In [11] the authors give a comprehensive overview of existing inference control techniques and state some of the fundamental problems in this area. Wang et al. [18] name two typical protection mechanisms (in their case for online analytical processing (OLAP) systems): *restriction* (deleting some values in the query result) and *perturbation* (changing some values in the query result). In general, any method for avoiding inferences has an effect on the accuracy of the returned answers. Hence, there is a trade-off between *confidentiality* of secret information and *availability* of information; in order to protect the secret information, some

E. Damiani and P. Liu (Eds.): Data and Applications Security 2006, LNCS 4127, pp. 30–43, 2006.

(even non-secret) information may be modified. *Reliability* may also be reduced by protection mechanisms; the user may be unsure of whether he got a correct or a modified answer.

The above mentioned approaches are typically based on specialized data structures (relational data model, XML documents); Controlled Query Evaluation (CQE) however offers a flexible framework to execute inference control based on an arbitrary logic. In this paper, we construct an inference-proof database in the CQE framework considering the original database, a user's a priori knowledge and a set of secrets. In Section 2 we introduce the CQE framework and state the prerequisites assumed in this paper. In Section 3 we formalize the notion of an inference-proof and highly available database. Section 4 shows a transformation of our problem to SAT solving and presents an algorithm that computes an inference-proof database. A comprehensive example illustrates our approach in Subsections 2.1 and 4.3.

## 2 Controlled Query Evaluation

Basically, a system model for Controlled Query Evaluation consists of:

1. a database that contains some freely accessible information and some secret information
2. a single user (or a group of collaborating users, respectively) having a certain amount of information as a priori knowledge of the database and the world in general; the case that several different users independently query the database is not considered as the database cannot distinguish whether a group of users collaborates or not

The user sends queries to the database and the database sends corresponding answers to the user. To prevent the user from inferring confidential information from the answers and his assumed a priori knowledge, appropriate restriction or perturbation is done by the CQE system on the database side. In CQE on the one hand *refusal* is used as a means of restriction: to a critical query the database refuses to answer (i.e., just returns mum). On the other hand, *lying* is employed as a means of perturbation: the database returns a false value or declares the query answer as undefined although a value exists in the database. In this way, the CQE approach automates the enforcement of confidentiality: wanting to restrict access to some secret information, a database administrator just specifies which information has to be kept secret; then, the CQE system computes the inference-proof answers. No human being ever has to consider inferences potentially made by the user, because the CQE system computes these inferences and employs the above mentioned protection mechanisms such that only "safe" answers are returned to the user. However, the database should be as cooperative as possible: only a minimum of answers should be distorted to ensure the confidentiality of the secret information. CQE can be varied based on several different parameters:

- complete information systems are considered with a model-theoretic approach (see [2]) while incomplete information systems are treated with a proof-theoretic approach (see [4])

- the secret information can be represented by two distinct types of "confidentiality policies": either secrecies (no truth value may be known by the user – be it *true* or *false*) or potential secrets (the user may know that a secret is *false* or possibly undefined, but the user may not know that a secret is *true*)
- the user may or may not know what kind of information is to be kept secret; therefore the "user awareness" can be divided into the known policy and the unknown policy case
- as the protection mechanism (also called "enforcement method") either lying or refusal or a combination of both can be employed (see [3])

In this paper we focus on a *complete* information system in *propositional logic* with a security policy of *potential secrets* and a *known* policy. Additionally, we only use *lying* as a protection mechanism. Thus, in this paper a CQE system is based on the following:

- a finite alphabet $\mathcal{P}$ of propositional variables; formulas can be built from the variables with the connectives $\neg$, $\vee$ and $\wedge$;[1] formulas contain "positive literals" (variables) and "negative literals" (negations of variables)
- a database $db \subset \mathcal{P}$ that represents an interpretation $I$ of the propositional variables: for each $A \in \mathcal{P}$, if $A \in db$, then $I$ assigns $A$ the value *true* (written as $I(A) = 1$), else $I$ assigns $A$ the value *false* (written as $I(A) = 0$); this means that we have a complete database: to each query the database returns either *true* or *false*
- the user's queries to the database as formulas $\Phi$ over $\mathcal{P}$
- a security policy *pot_sec* as a set of formulas over $\mathcal{P}$ of "potential secrets"; these potential secrets represent the secret information; the semantics is that for each formula $\Psi \in pot\_sec$, if $\Psi$ evaluates to *true* according to $db$ then the user may not know this, but the user may believe that the formula evaluates to *false* (that is, the negation of $\Psi$ evaluates to *true* according to $db$).
- the user's a priori knowledge as a set of formulas over $\mathcal{P}$ called *prior*; *prior* may contain general knowledge (like implications over $\mathcal{P}$) or knowledge of $db$ (like semantic constraints)

There are some prerequisites our system has to fulfill. In this paper, we presume that:

(a) [**consistent knowledge**] *prior* is consistent and the user cannot be made believe inconsistent information at any time
(b) [**monotone knowledge**] the user cannot be "brainwashed" and forced to forget some part of his knowledge
(c) [**single source of information**] the database $db$ is the user's only source of information (besides *prior*)
(d) [**unknown secrets**] for all $\Psi \in pot\_sec$: $prior \not\models \Psi$
(e) [**implicit closure under disjunction**] the user may not know (a priori) that the disjunction of the potential secrets is true:

$$prior \not\models pot\_sec\_disj \quad (\text{where } pot\_sec\_disj := \bigvee_{\Psi \in\ pot\_sec} \Psi) \qquad (1)$$

---

[1] Two consecutive negations cancel each other out: $\neg\neg A \equiv A$.

We require (d) because if the user already knows a potential secret, we obviously cannot protect the secret anymore. Moreover, in the case of lying as the only protection mechanism, we even have to be more strict: requirement (e) is necessary, because otherwise the system could run into a situation where even a lie reveals a secret. To illustrate this, assume $pot\_sec = \{\alpha, \beta\}$ (for formulas $\alpha$ and $\beta$ that are both *true* according to *db*) and $prior = \{\alpha \vee \beta\}$; to the query $\Phi = \alpha$ the CQE system would return the lie $\neg\alpha$, but this would enable the user to conclude that $\beta$ were true (and he is not allowed to know this); thus, we require *prior* to fulfill Equation (1). This line of reasoning also demands that the CQE system lie to every query entailing the disjunction of some potential secrets. See [1,3] for more information.

## 2.1 An Example System

The following example shall clarify the system design. Let us imagine that we have a database with Alice's medical records. The curious user Mallory wants to find out whether she is incapable of working or has financial problems. We use the alphabet

$$\mathcal{P} = \{\texttt{cancer}, \texttt{brokenArm}, \texttt{brokenLeg}, \texttt{highCosts}, \texttt{lowWorkCpcty}\}.$$

Poor Alice is badly ill and her medical records (as a set of literals) look like this:

$$record = \{\texttt{cancer}, \texttt{brokenArm}, \texttt{brokenLeg}\}.$$

It is generally known that cancer leads to high medical costs and low work capacity and that a broken arm leads to low work capacity and a broken leg to high medical costs. Expressing these implications as formulas, we have the general knowledge

$$genknowl = \{ \quad \neg\texttt{cancer} \vee \texttt{highCosts}, \neg\texttt{cancer} \vee \texttt{lowWorkCpcty},$$
$$\neg\texttt{brokenArm} \vee \texttt{lowWorkCpcty}, \neg\texttt{brokenLeg} \vee \texttt{highCosts}\}.$$

The database *db* contains the medical record *record* and is compliant with the general knowledge *genknowl*; thus, in this example we have

$$db = \mathcal{P}.$$

Mallory just knows what is also generally known:

$$prior = genknowl.$$

Now we can specify the potential secrets. As a first example we have just one formula consisting of one literal:

$$pot\_sec_1 = \{\texttt{lowWorkCpcty}\}.$$

To the query $\Phi = \texttt{cancer}$ the database should now return the lie *false* (as otherwise Mallory would conclude from his a priori knowledge that Alice has low work capacity). The same applies to the queries `brokenArm` and `lowWorkCpcty`. However, to the queries `brokenLeg` and `highCosts` the database should return the correct answer *true*.

A conjunction of two literals means that Mallory may know one of the literals but may not know both at the same time. As an example, consider the secret

$$pot\_sec_2 = \{\texttt{highCosts} \land \texttt{lowWorkCpcty}\}.$$

To one of the queries $\Phi_1 = \texttt{brokenArm}$ and $\Phi_2 = \texttt{brokenLeg}$ the database can return the correct answer *true*; however, to the other query the database has to return the lie *false* (otherwise both high medical costs and low work capacity can be concluded).

The meaning of a disjunction of two literals implies that Mallory may know neither of the literals. Consider

$$pot\_sec_3 = \{\texttt{highCosts} \lor \texttt{lowWorkCpcty}\}.$$

To every possible atomic query $\Phi \in \mathcal{P}$ the database has to return the lie *false* (as otherwise either high medical costs or low work capacity or both can be concluded).

The intended semantics of *pot_sec* can inductively be extended to non-singleton sets of arbitrary formulas.

As can be seen from the above examples, confidentiality of secret information is considered more important than a correct and reliable answer. Secret information has to be kept secret even at the risk of returning inaccurate information.

## 3    Constructing an Inference-Proof Database

Given a database $db$, a security policy *pot_sec* in the form of potential secrets, and the user's a priori knowledge *prior* as described in the previous section, we now want to construct a database $db'$ that is inference-proof with respect to every possible sequence of queries the user may come up with. We demand the following for $db'$ to be fulfilled:

i. [**inference-proof**] $db'$ does not satisfy any of the potential secrets: $db' \not\models \Psi$ for every $\Psi \in pot\_sec$
ii. [**complete**] $db'$ is complete (as is $db$)
iii. [**highly available**] $db'$ contains as few lies as possible; we want to remove, add or change only a minimum of entries (with respect to the original database $db$): $db'$ shall contain a lie only if otherwise a potential secret would be endangered
iv. [**consistent**] $db'$ is consistent in itself and also consistent with *prior* as the user's a priori knowledge is fixed and we cannot make the user believe inconsistent information

As for the inference-proofness and completeness features (i. and ii.), we want $db'$ to represent an interpretation $I'$ that assigns a value to every propositional variable in $\mathcal{P}$. Hence the database $db'$ must return an answer (*true* or *false*) to every query – also to a query containing a potential secret. As we consider here the *known policy* case, the user knows that he gets the answer *false* when querying a potential secret (because he is not allowed to know that a potential secret is true). So concluding from completeness and the user's awareness of the security policy, as one property of the database $db'$ we have:

$$db' \models \neg\Psi \text{ for every } \Psi \in pot\_sec \tag{2}$$

We define the set of formulas $Neg(pot\_sec) := \{\neg\Psi | \Psi \in pot\_sec\}$ and try to find an interpretation $I'$ that satisfies all formulas in $Neg(pot\_sec)$ in order for $db'$ to fulfill (2).

Now, let us turn to the availability feature (iii.).[2] To have a measure for the availability of $db'$ we define a distance between an interpretation $I$ and an interpretation $J$ with respect to a set of propositional variables $\mathcal{V}$ as follows: $dist_{\mathcal{V}}(I, J) := ||\{A | A \in \mathcal{V}, I(A) \neq J(A)\}||$. That is, we count all variables in $\mathcal{V}$ having in one interpretation a value distinct from the value in the other interpretation. As we want to maximize availability, we have to minimize the distance of the new interpretation $I'$ with respect to the original interpretation $I$ and all variables in $\mathcal{P}$: $dist_{\mathcal{P}}(I, I') \longrightarrow min$.

The consistency feature (iv.) means that we want to find an interpretation $I'$ such that all formulas in *prior* are satisfied.

All in all we conclude that $I'$ has to be an interpretation (for the variables in $\mathcal{P}$) that has minimal distance to the original interpretation $I$ and satisfies the set of formulas $prior \cup Neg(pot\_sec)$.

Under the requirements (a)–(e) given in Section 2, such a satisfying interpretation always exists. To prove this, first of all note that requirement (e) implies that $pot\_sec\_disj$ is not a tautology. Combining requirements (a) and (e), we conclude that *prior* is consistent with the set $Neg(pot\_sec)$. Thus, there exists at least one interpretation $I'$ satisfying $prior \cup Neg(pot\_sec)$.

## 4   A "Branch and Bound"-SAT-Solver

In order to find interpretation $I'$, we combine SAT-solving (for the completeness and satisfiability requirements) with "Branch and Bound" (for the minimization requirement). The database $db'$ representing $I'$ will be inference-proof by construction, as we describe in the following.

SAT-solvers try to find a satisfying interpretation for a set of clauses (i.e. disjunctions of literals). The basis for nearly all non-probabilistic SAT-solvers is the so-called DLL-algorithm (see [7,6]). It implements:

1. "elimination of one-literal clauses" (also called "boolean constraint propagation", BCP): a unit clause (i.e., a clause consisting of just one literal) must be evaluated to *true*

---

[2] Availability in this context is defined as "containing as much correct information as possible"; in contrast, reliability is defined as "the user knows that the answer he got from $db'$ is correct".

2. "affirmative-negative rule": if in all clauses only the positive literal or only the negative literal of a variable occurs (a so-called "pure literal"), then the literal can be evaluated to *true*
3. splitting on variables: take one yet uninterpreted variable, set it to *false* (to get one subproblem) and to *true* (to get a second subproblem), and try to find a solution for at least one of the subproblems

Whenever a value is assigned to a variable, the set of clauses can be simplified by subsumption (if a clause contains a literal that is evaluated to *true*, remove the whole clause) or resolution (if a clause contains a literal that is evaluated to *false*, remove this literal from the clause but keep the remaining clause).

"Branch and Bound" (B&B, for short) is a method for finding solutions to an optimization problem. It offers the features "branching" (dividing the problem into adequate subproblems), "bounding" (efficiently computing local lower and upper bounds for subproblems), and "pruning" (discarding a subproblem due to a bad bound value). For a minimization problem a global upper bound is maintained stating the currently best value. A B&B-algorithm may have a superpolynomial running time; however, execution may be stopped with the assurance that the optimal solution's value is in between the global upper bound and the minimum of the local lower bounds.

## 4.1   The Algorithm

First of all, we consider the case where $prior \cup Neg(pot\_sec)$ is a set of formulas in conjunctive normal form (CNF); the general case will be treated in Section 4.2. We define the set of clauses $C_{decision}$ as

$$C_{decision} := \bigcup_{\Psi \in prior \cup Neg(pot\_sec)} \texttt{clauses}(\Psi)$$

where $\texttt{clauses}(\Psi)$ is a set of clauses representing $\Psi \in prior \cup Neg(pot\_sec)$. $C_{decision}$ is the input to our SAT-solving algorithm. Let $\mathcal{P}_{decision} \subset \mathcal{P}$ be the set of all variables occurring in $C_{decision}$; these are the "decision variables". Our SAT-solver finds an interpretation $I'_{decision}$ for all decision variables; all other variables get assigned the same truth value as before: $I'(A) := I(A)$ if $A \in \mathcal{P} \setminus \mathcal{P}_{decision}$. Thus, we have $dist_{\mathcal{P} \setminus \mathcal{P}_{decision}}(I, I') = 0$. We find an interpretation $I'_{decision}$ for $\mathcal{P}_{decision}$ satisfying $C_{decision}$ with minimal distance to $I$ by employing a branch and bound algorithm. Listings 1, 2, 3 and 4 show the four functions "initialization", "best-first-search splitting", "boolean constraint propagation", and "simplification of clauses" of our algorithm. In the following we describe each function in detail.

B&B on the set $\mathcal{P}_{decision}$ yields a binary tree; its maximal depth is the cardinality of $\mathcal{P}_{decision}$: $depth_{max} = ||\mathcal{P}_{decision}||$. The binary structure of the tree is created as follows. In every node $v$ a "splitting variable" $A \in \mathcal{P}_{decision}$ is selected; we refer to this variable by $splitvar(v)$. Then, a left and a right child node $v_{left}$ and $v_{right}$ are constructed; in one of the child nodes $A$ is set to *true* and in the other child node $A$ is set to *false*. This is the splitting step of the DLL-algorithm

1. **Initialization** for the root node $r$
   1.1. $I_r(A) := undefined$ for all $A \in \mathcal{P}_{decision}$
   1.2. $lb_r := 0$; $ub_r := depth_{max}$; $ub_{global} := ub_r$
   1.3. $C_r := C_{decision}$
   1.4. BCP($I_r$,$C_r$,$lb_r$,$ub_r$)

**Listing 1.** Initialization for root node $r$

as well as the branching step of B&B. We conduct a "best-first search" with our
B&B algorithm: in the left child node we assign $splitvar(v)$ the same truth value
as in $I$ (this choice yields better local bounds and we process the left child node
first; see Listing 2, line 2.3.), and in the right child node we assign $splitvar(v)$
the opposite truth value $\overline{I(splitvar(v))}$ (which yields worse local bounds; see
line 2.6.). A splitting step is pictured in Figure 1.

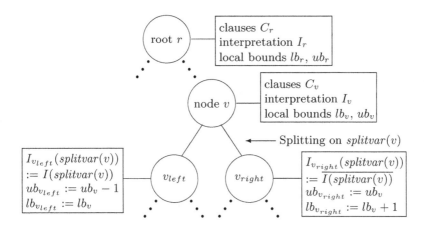

**Fig. 1.** A splitting step

Each node $v$ has its own set of clauses $C_v$. The child nodes get each a simplified
set of clauses constructed from $C_v$ by subsumption and resolution (see lines 2.5.1.
and 2.8.1. and Listing 4). Initially, for the root node $r$ the set of clauses is
$C_r = C_{decision}$ (see Listing 1, line 1.3.).

Before splitting takes place in node $v$, we carry out BCP: unit clauses are
repeatedly eliminated from $C_v$ until there are none left (see Listing 3, line 3.2.).
Variables in unit clauses are assigned a value without splitting on these variables;
thus, BCP reduces the number of branches in the tree.

Each node $v$ represents an interpretation $I_v$ containing all variable assignments
occurring on the path from the root node $r$ to the node $v$. Initially, for the root
node $r$ all values are undefined (see Listing 1, line 1.1.).

In each node $v$ also the local lower bound $lb_v$ and the local upper bound $ub_v$
are defined. The global upper bound is called $ub_{global}$. We compute the bounds
using the availability distance defined above; this is the bounding step of B&B.

2. $\text{SPLIT}(I_v, C_v, lb_v, ub_v)$: **Best-First-Search-Splitting** on $A \in \mathcal{P}_{decision}$
   2.1. generate two child nodes $v_{left}$ and $v_{right}$
   2.2. copy $I_v$ into $I_{v_{left}}$ and $I_{v_{right}}$
   2.3. $I_{v_{left}}(A) := I(A)$; $ub_{v_{left}} := ub_v - 1$; $lb_{v_{left}} := lb_v$
   2.4. `if` $(lb_{v_{left}} > ub_{global})$ { `GOTO` line 2.6. }
   2.5. `else`
      2.5.1. $C_{v_{left}} := \text{SIMP}(I_{v_{left}}, C_v, ub_v)$
      2.5.2. $\text{BCP}(I_{v_{left}}, C_{v_{left}}, lb_{v_{left}}, ub_{v_{left}})$
   2.6. $I_{v_{right}}(A) := \overline{I(A)}$; $ub_{v_{right}} := ub_v$; $lb_{v_{right}} := lb_v + 1$
   2.7. `if` $(lb_{v_{right}} > ub_{global})$ { `RETURN` }
   2.8. `else`
      2.8.1. $C_{v_{right}} := \text{SIMP}(I_{v_{right}}, C_v, ub_v)$
      2.8.2. $\text{BCP}(I_{v_{right}}, C_{v_{right}}, lb_{v_{right}}, ub_{v_{right}})$

**Listing 2.** Best-First-Search Splitting

3. $\text{BCP}(I_v, C_v, lb_v, ub_v)$: **Boolean Constraint Propagation** in node $v$
   3.1. $C_v^{unit} :=$ set of unit clauses of $C_v$
   3.2. `while` $(C_v^{unit} \neq \emptyset)$
      3.2.1. `foreach` clause $[l] \in C_v^{unit}$ (with $l = A$ or $l = \neg A$ for an $A \in \mathcal{P}_{decision}$)
         3.2.1.1. remove $[l]$ from $C_v^{unit}$; set $I_v(A)$ such that $I_v \models l$
         3.2.1.2. `if` $(I_v(A) == I(A))$ $\{ub_v - -\}$
         3.2.1.3. `else` $\{lb_v + +\}$
      3.2.2. `if` $(lb_v > ub_{global})$ { `RETURN` }
      3.2.3. `else`
         3.2.3.1. $C_v :- \text{SIMP}(I_v, C_v, ub_v)$; $C_v^{unit} :=$ set of unit clauses of $C_v$
   3.3. `if` $(v == r$ and $ub_{global} > ub_r)$ $\{ub_{global} := ub_r\}$
   3.4. `if` $(C_v \neq \emptyset)$ $\{\text{SPLIT}(I_v, C_v, lb_v, ub_v)\}$

**Listing 3.** Boolean Constraint Propagation

The lower bound $lb_v$ is the number of variables that are assigned in $I_v$ a value distinct from the value in the original interpretation $I$; the upper bound $ub_v$ is $lb_v$ plus the number of variables that are still undefined in $I_v$; if the final interpretation $I'_{decision}$ can be found in this branch, it has at least distance $lb_v$ and at most distance $ub_v$ from $I$: $lb_v \leq dist_{\mathcal{P}_{decision}}(I, I'_{decision}) \leq ub_v$. Initially, the bounds are $lb_r = 0$ and $ub_r = depth_{max}$; $ub_{global}$ is initialized to $depth_{max}$, too (see line 1.2.).

During BCP the bounds are accordingly adjusted (see lines 3.2.1.2. and 3.2.1.3.). After BCP in the root node $r$, the global upper bound can already be decremented (see line 3.3.); every satisfying assignment $I'_{decision}$ has to satisfy the unit clauses in the root node. Subsequently, $ub_{global}$ may only be adjusted when a complete and satisfying interpretation $I_v$ is found and $ub_v < ub_{global}$ (see line 4.3.).

During splitting in an arbitrary node $v$, in the left child node only the upper bound has to be decremented, while in the right child node only the lower bound has to be incremented (see lines 2.3. and 2.6.).

4. SIMP($I_v$,$C_v$,$ub_v$): **Simplification** of a set of clauses $C_v$ given interpretation $I_v$
   4.1. initialize set of clauses $C_{return} := \emptyset$
   4.2. **foreach** clause $c$ in $C_v$
      4.2.1. **foreach** literal $l$ in $c$:
         4.2.1.1. **if** ($I_v \models l$) {**Subsumption:** CONTINUE (ignore $c$)}
         4.2.1.2. **else if** ($I_v \not\models l$) {**Resolution:** remove $l$ from $c$}
      4.2.2. **if** ($c$ empty clause) { RETURN ($I_v$ not satisfying)}
      4.2.3. **else** {add $c$ to $C_{return}$}
   4.3. **if** ($C_{return} == \emptyset$ and $ub_{global} > ub_v$) {$ub_{global} := ub_v$}
   4.4. **return** $C_{return}$

**Listing 4.** Simplification of clauses

For the pruning of B&B to take place, there are two possible conditions:

1. **[bad lower bound]** the local lower bound of node $v$ is worse than the current global upper bound: $lb_v > ub_{global}$; we have already found a better solution and we are not able to expand $I_v$ to an interpretation for all decision variables with minimal distance
2. **[unsatisfiability]** while constructing $I_v$ we encountered an inconsistency: we are not able to expand $I_v$ to an interpretation for all decision variables that satisfies $C_{decision}$

The lower bound condition is checked in lines 2.4., 2.7. and 3.2.2. after new lower bounds have been calculated. The unsatisfiability condition is checked in line 4.2.2. during simplification: if an empty clause is generated, the current interpretation is not satisfying.

In the subsumption step it may happen that variables "disappear" from the clauses: there are no clauses left that contain the variables. Thus, it may be the case that in the final interpretation $I'_{decision}$ there are still some undefined variables (they are often referred to as "don't care variables"). However, these variables had no influence on the satisfiability of the clauses; these variables are removed from $P_{decision}$ and thus are assigned the same truth value as in the original interpretation.

Having found $I'_{decision}$ satisfying $C_{decision}$ and having minimal distance to $I$, we can construct our inference-proof database $db'$ as follows:

$$\text{for all } A \in \mathcal{P}_{decision} : \quad A \in db' \text{ iff } I'_{decision}(A) = 1$$
$$\text{for all } A \in \mathcal{P} \setminus \mathcal{P}_{decision} : A \in db' \text{ iff } A \in db \text{ (that is } I(A) = 1)$$

If $||\mathcal{P}_{decision}|| \ll ||\mathcal{P}||$, it may be more efficient to just maintain a small separate database $db_{decision}$, in this special case including possibly negated entries:

$$\text{for all } A \in \mathcal{P}_{decision} \begin{cases} A \in db_{decision} & \text{iff } I'_{decision}(A) = 1 \\ \neg A \in db_{decision} & \text{iff } I'_{decision}(A) = 0 \end{cases}$$

$db_{decision}$ returns the truth values for all variables from $\mathcal{P}_{decision}$. The original database $db$ returns the truth values of variables from $\mathcal{P} \setminus \mathcal{P}_{decision}$.

## 4.2   Some Remarks on Further Techniques

There exist several adaptations of the basic DLL-algorithm to non-CNF for-mulas. For example, Ganai et al. [13] introduce hybrid SAT for boolean circuits where only newly added ("learned") clauses are in CNF. Propagation in circuits is supported by a lookup table and "watched literals" (see also [21]). Giunchiglia et al. [14] apply renaming of subformulas by adding new variables (thus construct-ing an equisatisfiable formula in CNF for a non-CNF input formula) but propose to split only on the original ("independent") variables. Thiffault et al. [17] repre-sent the non-CNF input formula as a directed acyclic graph and base propagation on "watch children" and "don't care watch parents". With such techniques our B&B-algorithm can be extended to accept non-CNF formulas. Moreover, a vast number of optimization techniques and splitting heuristics have been proposed for the basic DLL-algorithm; for example, subsumption removal [20], reduction of the number of clauses [10] or elimination of variables [16]. Such techniques can be employed to speed up the search process.

Our availability distance may not be the only optimization criterion; the bounding can easily be extended by other measures to guide the search and determine the quality of a solution. Equally, a preference relation on proposi-tions can be employed so that lying for a lower-ranked proposition is preferred to lying for a higher-ranked proposition.

Lastly, let us note that in our algorithm pure literals cannot be removed, that is, the DLL-"affirmative-negative rule" cannot be applied: setting pure literals to *true* may lead to an interpretation that does not have minimal distance. Anyway, detection of pure literals is expensive (see for example [21]) and often omitted in SAT-solver implementations.

## 4.3   An Example Run

Let us come back to our example. We consider *db*, *prior* and $pot\_sec_1$. The set $prior \cup Neg(pot\_sec_1)$ is a set of CNF-formulas and we have as a set of clauses (clauses are written with square brackets):

$$C_{decision} = \{[\neg\texttt{brokenArm}, \texttt{lowWorkCpcty}], [\neg\texttt{brokenLeg}, \texttt{highCosts}],$$
$$[\neg\texttt{cancer}, \texttt{highCosts}], [\neg\texttt{cancer}, \texttt{lowWorkCpcty}], [\neg\texttt{lowWorkCpcty}]\}.$$

Figure 2 shows the tree created by our algorithm. We need just one splitting step; all other assignments are determined by BCP.

In root $r$ we have two BCP steps: the first one on $\{[\neg\texttt{lowWorkCpcty}]\}$ and the second one on $\{[\neg\texttt{cancer}], [\neg\texttt{brokenArm}]\}$. This yields the interpretation $I_r(\texttt{cancer}) = I_r(\texttt{brokenArm}) = I_r(\texttt{lowWorkCpcty}) = 0$ and from this we com-pute the bounds $lb_r = 3$ and $ub_{global} = ub_r = 5$.

Next we split on $splitvar(r) = \texttt{brokenLeg}$: we construct the child nodes $r_{left}$ and $r_{right}$ and begin with $I_{r_{left}}(\texttt{brokenLeg}) = 1$ (best-first search). We have $lb_{r_{left}} = 3$ and $ub_{r_{left}} = 4$ and simplification produces the new unit clause $[\texttt{highCosts}]$. BCP on this clause results in $lb_{r_{left}} = 3$ and $ub_{r_{left}} = 3$; we

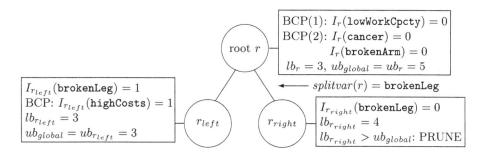

**Fig. 2.** An example run

have found a complete and satisfying interpretation in this branch and we set $ub_{global} = ub_{r_{left}} = 3$.

We now treat $r_{right}$ and set $I_{r_{right}}(\texttt{brokenLeg}) = 0$, $lb_{r_{right}} = 4$ and $ub_{r_{right}} = 5$. We find that $lb_{r_{right}} > ub_{global}$ and this branch is pruned.

Thus, the optimal solution is $I'(\texttt{brokenLeg}) = I'(\texttt{highCosts}) = 1$ on the one hand and $I'(\texttt{cancer}) = I'(\texttt{brokenArm}) = I'(\texttt{lowWorkCpcty}) = 0$ on the other hand; the transformed database is $db' = \{\texttt{brokenLeg}, \texttt{highCosts}\}$ with distance 3 to the original database.

## 5   Conclusion and Future Work

We presented an algorithm to preprocess an inference-proof database based on a user's a priori knowledge and a specification of secret information. While the worst-case runtime is exponential, there is a good chance to find an acceptable (or even optimal) solution in a smaller amount of time. Even if we stop the algorithm prematurely and accept a suboptimal solution, it is a solution that is definitely inference-proof; it might only be suboptimal with respect to availability: there may be more lies in the database than necessary.

Future work shall investigate how this approach can be adapted to other CQE parameters, namely, the unknown policy case, refusal as a restriction method and incomplete databases. Furthermore, this method shall be expanded to other logics (for example first-order logic). In a wider setting, we want to connect CQE to other established research areas, for example linear or constraint programming [12] and theory merging [8]. Moreover, a comparison of the CQE system to existing approaches for general purpose databases (see e.g. [11]) has already been initiated.

One of the fundamental problems inherent to every inference control system still remains: It is difficult – if not impossible – to appropriately model the user's knowledge in the system. Apart from that, there are other interesting questions regarding the user's knowledge in the approach presented here. For example, if there is one transformed database $db'_1$ for a fixed $prior_1$, is it possible to reuse (parts of) $db'_1$ to construct a $db'_2$ for a different $prior_2$? Similarly, if we allow the user's knowledge to change at runtime due to input from external sources, is it possible to adjust $db'$ to the new situation? These topics will be covered in the near future.

## Acknowledgements

This work was funded by the German Research Council (DFG) under a grant for the Research Training Group (Graduiertenkolleg) "Mathematical and Engineering Methods for Secure Data Transfer and Information Mediation" organized at Ruhr-Universität Bochum, Universität Dortmund, Universität Essen and Fernuniversität Hagen.

## References

1. Joachim Biskup and Piero A. Bonatti. Lying versus refusal for known potential secrets. *Data & Knowledge Engineering*, 38(2):199–222, 2001.
2. Joachim Biskup and Piero A. Bonatti. Controlled query evaluation for enforcing confidentiality in complete information systems. *International Journal of Information Security*, 3(1):14–27, 2004.
3. Joachim Biskup and Piero A. Bonatti. Controlled query evaluation for known policies by combining lying and refusal. *Annals of Mathematics and Artificial Intelligence*, 40(1-2):37–62, 2004.
4. Joachim Biskup and Torben Weibert. Refusal in incomplete databases. In Csilla Farkas and Pierangela Samarati, editors, *18th Annual IFIP WG 11.3 Conference on Data and Applications Security, Proceedings*, pages 143–157. Kluwer, 2004.
5. LiWu Chang and Ira S. Moskowitz. A study of inference problems in distributed databases. In Ehud Gudes and Sujeet Shenoi, editors, *16th Annual IFIP WG 11.3 Conference on Data and Applications Security, Proceedings*, pages 191–204. Kluwer, 2002.
6. Martin Davis, George Logemann, and Donald W. Loveland. A machine program for theorem-proving. *Communications of the ACM*, 5(7):394–397, 1962.
7. Martin Davis and Hilary Putnam. A computing procedure for quantification theory. *Journal of the ACM*, 7(3):201–215, 1960.
8. James P. Delgrande and Torsten Schaub. Two approaches to merging knowledge bases. In José Júlio Alferes and João Alexandre Leite, editors, *9th European Conference on Logics in Artificial Intelligence, Proceedings*, volume 3229 of *Lecture Notes in Computer Science*, pages 426–438. Springer, 2004.
9. Josep Domingo-Ferrer, editor. *Inference Control in Statistical Databases, From Theory to Practice*, volume 2316 of *Lecture Notes in Computer Science*. Springer, 2002.
10. Niklas Eén and Armin Biere. Effective preprocessing in SAT through variable and clause elimination. In Fahiem Bacchus and Toby Walsh, editors, *8th International Conference on Theory and Applications of Satisfiability Testing, Proceedings*, volume 3569 of *Lecture Notes in Computer Science*, pages 61–75. Springer, 2005.
11. Csilla Farkas and Sushil Jajodia. The inference problem: A survey. *SIGKDD Explorations*, 4(2):6–11, 2002.
12. Thom Frühwirth and Slim Abdennadher. *Essentials of Constraint Programming*. Springer, 2003.

13. Malay K. Ganai, Pranav Ashar, Aarti Gupta, Lintao Zhang, and Sharad Malik. Combining strengths of circuit-based and CNF-based algorithms for a high-performance SAT solver. In *39th Design Automation Conference, Proceedings*, pages 747–750. ACM, 2002.

14. Enrico Giunchiglia and Roberto Sebastiani. Applying the Davis-Putnam procedure to non-clausal formulas. In Evelina Lamma and Paola Mello, editors, *6th Congress of the Italian Association for Artificial Intelligence, Proceedings*, volume 1792 of *Lecture Notes in Computer Science*, pages 84–94. Springer, 2000.

15. John Hale and Sujeet Shenoi. Analyzing fd inference in relational databases. *Data & Knowledge Engineering*, 18(2):167–183, 1996.

16. Sathiamoorthy Subbarayan and Dhiraj K. Pradhan. Niver: Non increasing variable elimination resolution for preprocessing SAT instances. In *7th International Conference on Theory and Applications of Satisfiability Testing, Online Proceedings*, 2004.

17. Christian Thiffault, Fahiem Bacchus, and Toby Walsh. Solving non-clausal formulas with DPLL search. In *7th International Conference on Theory and Applications of Satisfiability Testing, Online Proceedings*, 2004.

18. Lingyu Wang, Yingjiu Li, Duminda Wijesekera, and Sushil Jajodia. Precisely answering multi-dimensional range queries without privacy breaches. In Einar Snekkenes and Dieter Gollmann, editors, *8th European Symposium on Research in Computer Security, Proceedings*, volume 2808 of *Lecture Notes in Computer Science*, pages 100–115. Springer, 2003.

19. Xiaochun Yang and Chen Li. Secure XML publishing without information leakage in the presence of data inference. In Mario A. Nascimento, M. Tamer Özsu, Donald Kossmann, Renée J. Miller, José A. Blakeley, and K. Bernhard Schiefer, editors, *30th International Conference on Very Large Data Bases, Proceedings*, pages 96–107. Morgan Kaufmann, 2004.

20. Lintao Zhang. On subsumption removal and on-the-fly CNF simplification. In Fahiem Bacchus and Toby Walsh, editors, *8th International Conference on Theory and Applications of Satisfiability Testing, Proceedings*, volume 3569 of *Lecture Notes in Computer Science*, pages 482–489. Springer, 2005.

21. Lintao Zhang and Sharad Malik. The quest for efficient boolean satisfiability solvers. In Andrei Voronkov, editor, *18th International Conference on Automated Deduction, Proceedings*, volume 2392 of *Lecture Notes in Computer Science*, pages 295–313. Springer, 2002.

# Consolidating the Access Control of Composite Applications and Workflows

Martin Wimmer[1], Alfons Kemper[1], Maarten Rits[2], and Volkmar Lotz[2]

[1] Technische Universität München, 85748 Garching b. München, Germany
[2] SAP Research, Font de l'Orme, 06250 Mougins, France
{wimmerma, kemper}@in.tum.de, {maarten.rits, volkmar.lotz}@sap.com

**Abstract.** The need for enterprise application integration projects leads to complex composite applications. For the sake of security and efficiency, consolidated access control policies for composite applications should be provided. Such a policy is based on the policies of the corresponding autonomous sub-applications and has the following properties: On the one hand, it needs to be as restrictive as possible to block requests which do not comply with the integrated sub-applications' policies. Thereby, unsuccessful executions of requests are prevented at an early stage. On the other hand, the composite policy must grant all necessary privileges in order to make the intended functionality available to legitimate users.

In this paper, we present our formal model and respective algorithmic solutions for consolidating the access control of composite applications. The generated policies conform to the presented requirements of the least privileges paradigm and, thus, allow to revise and optimize the access control of composite applications. We demonstrate this by means of Web service workflows that constitute the state of the art for the realization of business processes.

## 1 Introduction

Composite applications are applications that rely on sub-applications (also called sub-activities) to integrate their functionality. There are numerous examples for such applications including quite simple Web applications as well as large scale enterprise resource planning systems (ERP) that rely on database backends. Also, business processes that are realized as Web service workflows constitute complex composite applications. In general, sub-applications are self-contained software components, like Web services that autonomously enforce their own security policy. When integrating autonomous sub-activities into workflows, security dependencies must be considered. As an example consider the e-health workflow illustrated in Figure 1 that will be executed when a patient is transferred to the cardiology department of a hospital. Depending on the diagnostic findings, either an in-patient treatment is applied or an electrocardiogram (ECG) is made in order to acquire further insight. Each of the individual sub-activities that are depicted in the figure are autonomously enforcing their security policies. In case, these policies are not consolidated, reliable workflow execution might be hindered. Administrative employees, for instance, are allowed to query the medical records of patients, but are not permitted to perform any medical treatment.

E. Damiani and P. Liu (Eds.): Data and Applications Security 2006, LNCS 4127, pp. 44–59, 2006.
© IFIP International Federation for Information Processing 2006

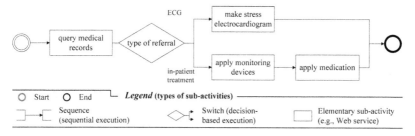

**Fig. 1.** Example of an e-health workflow

Thus, requests might be authorized by some sub-activities but rejected by others, which results in performance drawbacks due to unsuccessful workflow executions and can require transaction rollbacks or costly compensating actions.

In order to perform an early-filtering of the requests to avoid unsuccessful executions, a consolidated view onto the access control of workflows or general composite applications is needed. Thereby, we can identify two different perspectives onto the security configuration of a composite application. From the security officer's point of view, access control should be defined as tight as possible to avoid security vulnerabilities. Too restrictive policies on the other hand can hinder legitimate users to execute the application which contradicts the process-centered viewpoint of the application developer. Therefore, a consolidated policy is required that is tailored to the functionality of the composite application. The consolidation process derives the following information: (1) what are the least required privileges for the execution of the composite application and (2) who is granted these privileges. The first aspect allows to meet the security officer's requirements by defining access rules and role profiles that are restricted to the functionality of the composite application. The second supports the application developer in detecting unintended configurations. For instance, if only highly privileged users (e.g., administrators) are authorized to perform the workflow, this might be an indication for the design of the application itself having to be revised.

In [1] we presented a security engineering approach for optimizing the access control of Web service compositions by determining the maximum set of authorized subjects. As we will show in this paper, in order to treat generic composite applications, privilege relaxation tests are required in addition. Our contributions are a formal model and corresponding algorithmic solutions for the consolidation of the access control of generic composite applications. The consolidation is performed from the *single-user / single-role*-perspective, meaning that a user can execute the application by the activation of one task specific role. This complies with most business processes, which are typically representing job specific functions and are thus designed for specific groups of employees.

The remainder of this contribution is structured as follows: Section 2 introduces the syntax and semantics of our policy algebra, which constitutes the basis of the policy consolidation approach presented in Section 3. In Section 4 elementary algorithms of the policy consolidation process are described. Section 5 gives an overview over related work and Section 6 concludes the paper.

# 2   Policy Model

First, we introduce the policy algebra which constitutes the basis for the formal specification of the proposed policy consolidation technique. Policies are described in an attribute based way and are not restricted to identity based description. For instance, subjects can be specified through characterizing properties like role-membership, age, profession skills and so on. The policy model allows to express discretionary access control (DAC) rules and supports role based access control (RBAC) models which are suitable security concepts for almost all commercial applications. The formal syntax and semantics of our policy model are based on those introduced by Bonatti et al. [2]. We adapted and extended this model where necessary, e.g., by introducing additional operators.

## 2.1   Notation

*Predicates.* A predicate defines an attribute comparison of the form ($attribute\text{-}identifier \circ constant$). Depending on the attribute's domain, the comparison operator $\circ$ is in $\{<, \leq, =, \geq, >\}$ for totally ordered sets and in $\{\sqsubset, \sqsubseteq, =, \sqsupseteq, \sqsupset\}$ for partially ordered finite sets.

*Subjects, objects, actions, and conditions.* Let *Attr* be the set of distinguished attribute identifiers. *Attr* is subdivided into disjoint sets of subject, object, action, and environment attribute identifiers (denoted as *S-Attr*, *O-Attr*, *A-Attr*, and *E-Attr* respectively). A set of subjects $S$ is represented by a disjunction of predicate conjunctions over *S-Attr*. That is, $S = ((s_{1,1} \wedge \ldots \wedge s_{1,l}) \vee \ldots \vee (s_{k,1} \wedge \ldots \wedge s_{k,l}))$, with each $s_{i,d}$ being a predicate conjunction that applies to one attribute. The cardinality of *S-Attr* is denoted by $l$. The elements of *S-Attr* are also called dimensions of a subject specification. Representations of objects $O$ and actions $A$ are defined in a similar way. $S$, $O$, and $A$ are inequality-free. A condition $c$ is a boolean formula defined over attributes of *E-Attr* that can include user defined functions with Boolean codomain (e.g., *isWeekday(date)*).

*Rules and policies.* A rule $R$ is a quadruple $(S, O, A, c)$, consisting of specifications of subjects $S$, objects $O$, and actions $A$. A rule assigns a set of permissions specified by $(O, A)$ to a set of subjects. The scope of the assignment is restricted through $c$. Individual rules $R_1, \ldots, R_n$ can be aggregated in a policy $P = \{R_1, \ldots, R_n\}$.

*Evaluation context.* An evaluation context $e \in \mathcal{E}$ is a partial mapping of the attributes defined in *Attr*. If $D_1, \ldots, D_m$ are the domains of the attributes in *Attr*, then $\mathcal{E}$ is defined as $D_1^{\perp} \times \ldots \times D_m^{\perp}$, with $D_j^{\perp} = D_j \cup \{\perp\}$ and $\perp$ representing an unspecified attribute value.

## 2.2   Semantics

*Evaluation of rules.* An evaluation context $e$ is evaluated against the individual components of rules. A subject specification $S$ applies to $e$, iff $S$ maps to *true* w.r.t. the attribute values of $e$. That is, $[\![S]\!]_e := S(e) = (true|false)$. The semantics of $O$, $A$ and $c$ are defined analogously. The applicability of a rule $R$ w.r.t. $e$ is defined as $[\![R]\!]_e := [\![S]\!]_e \wedge [\![O]\!]_e \wedge [\![A]\!]_e \wedge [\![c]\!]_e$.

*Evaluation of policies.* The semantics of a policy $P$ depend on the employed *policy evaluation algorithm* (abbrev. *pe-alg*). We define the evaluation algorithms *pe-all* and *pe-any*, with $[\![P]\!]_e^{pe\text{-}all} := \bigwedge_{R \in P} [\![R]\!]_e$ and $[\![P]\!]_e^{pe\text{-}any} := \bigvee_{R \in P} [\![R]\!]_e$. *pe-all* can be applied to realize a static policy enforcement, in cases when access control can be performed once for a composite application and all its sub-activities before the execution. *pe-any* is useful for gradually performing access control, when runtime information needs to be considered. In order to characterize unrestricted specifications (i.e., tautologies) we use the symbol $\Upsilon$, with $\forall e \in \mathcal{E} : [\![\Upsilon]\!]_e^{pe\text{-}alg} = true$.

## Policy Combining Operators

*Conjunction.* Let $S$ and $S'$ be two subject specifications. The conjunction of $S$ and $S'$ is denoted as $S \wedge S'$ with $[\![S \wedge S']\!]_e = [\![S]\!]_e \wedge [\![S']\!]_e$. The conjunction operator is analogously defined on objects, actions, conditions, and rules.

*Subtraction.* The subtraction of two subject specifications $S$ and $S'$ is defined as $S - S'$ with $[\![S - S']\!]_e = [\![S]\!]_e \wedge \neg([\![S']\!]_e)$. Analogously, subtraction is also defined on objects, actions, conditions and rules.

*Projection.* Let $R = (S, O, A, c)$ be a rule. The projection on the subjects part of $R$ is defined as $\Pi_{\mathcal{S}}(R) = S$. Analogously, $\Pi_{\mathcal{O}}(R) = O$, $\Pi_{\mathcal{A}}(R) = A$, $\Pi_{\mathcal{C}}(R) = c$, and $\Pi_{\mathcal{O},\mathcal{A}}(R) = (O, A)$.

Let $P = \{R_1, \ldots, R_n\}$ be a policy. $\Pi_{\mathcal{S}}(P)$ is defined as $\Pi_{\mathcal{S}}(P) = \{\Pi_{\mathcal{S}}(R_1), \ldots, \Pi_{\mathcal{S}}(R_n)\}$. Other projection operators on policies are defined in a similar way. We use the abbreviation $\mathcal{S}(P) = \bigwedge_{1 \leq i \leq n} \Pi_{\mathcal{S}}(R_i)$ to denote those subjects that are granted all privileges defined in $P$.

**Privilege, Rule, and Policy Relaxation.** A privilege $(O', A')$ relaxes a privilege $(O, A)$, denoted as $(O, A) \sqsubseteq (O', A')$, iff it applies to more (or the same) actions on more (or the same) objects. That is, $([\![(O, A)]\!]_e = true)$ implies $([\![(O', A')]\!]_e = true)$ for any evaluation context $e$. Analogously, a rule $R'$ relaxes a rule $R$, $R \sqsubseteq R'$, iff it grants more or the same privileges to more or the same users under the same or less restrictive conditions. That is, $\forall e \in \mathcal{E}$ with $([\![R]\!]_e = true) \Rightarrow ([\![R']\!]_e = true)$. In the same way, $P \sqsubseteq^{pe\text{-}alg} P'$, iff $\forall e \in \mathcal{E} : ([\![P]\!]_e^{pe\text{-}alg} = true) \Rightarrow ([\![P']\!]_e^{pe\text{-}alg} = true)$.

**Reduced Policies.** In order to efficiently consolidate the policy of composite applications we are focussing on reduced policies as motivated in Section 3.1: Let the applied policy evaluation algorithm be *pe-all*. $P$ is called *reduced*, iff

(1) $\forall R, R' \in P, R \neq R' : \nexists e \in \mathcal{E} : ([\![\Pi_{\mathcal{O},\mathcal{A}}(R) \wedge \Pi_{\mathcal{O},\mathcal{A}}(R')]\!]_e = true)$    and

(2) $\forall R \in P : \mathcal{S}(P) = \Pi_{\mathcal{S}}(R)$

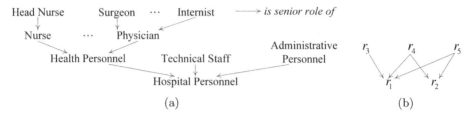

**Fig. 2.** Example for limited (a) and general (b) role hierarchies

A policy fulfilling (2) but not (1) can be reduced as follows: Let $R_a, R_b \in P$, $R_a \neq R_b : \exists e \in \mathcal{E} : ([\![\Pi_{\mathcal{O},\mathcal{A}}(R_a) \wedge \Pi_{\mathcal{O},\mathcal{A}}(R_b)]\!]_e = true)$. Substitute the two rules $R_a, R_b$ through the three combined rules $R_{a-b}, R_{a \wedge b}, R_{b-a}$ with $R_{a-b} = (\mathcal{S}(P), \Pi_{\mathcal{O},\mathcal{A}}(R_a) - \Pi_{\mathcal{O},\mathcal{A}}(R_b), \Pi_{\mathcal{C}}(R_a))$, $R_{a \wedge b} = (R_a \wedge R_b)$, and $R_{b-a} = (\mathcal{S}(P), \Pi_{\mathcal{O},\mathcal{A}}(R_b) - \Pi_{\mathcal{O},\mathcal{A}}(R_a), \Pi_{\mathcal{C}}(R_b))$.

### 2.3   Role Based Access Control

Policy administration can easily become unmanageable if privileges are independently assigned to each user. Scalability is provided through role based access control (RBAC, see [3] and [4]). Using RBAC, privileges required for performing a certain task are grouped by roles. Users acquire these privileges via the indirection of being granted those roles. Roles can be organized in a hierarchy that defines a partial order. Senior roles, which are at higher levels in the hierarchy, inherit all privileges that are granted to their junior roles. To give an example, the role *Internist* in Figure 2(a) is senior to *Physician*, denoted as *Internist* $\sqsupseteq$ *Physician*. Accordingly, *Physician* is called junior role of *Internist*.

A role $r'$ is an *immediate descendant* of a role $r$ if $r' \sqsubseteq r$ and there is no $r''$ with $r \neq r''$ and $r'' \neq r'$ such that $r' \sqsubseteq r'' \sqsubseteq r$. A role hierarchy is called *limited* if each role has at most one immediate descendant. This is the case for the example hierarchy illustrated in Figure 2(a). In contrast to this, *general role hierarchies* like the one shown in Figure 2(b) support the concept of multiple (access right) inheritance.

## 3   Policy Consolidation

### 3.1   Problem Specification

Let $\text{APP}_1, \ldots, \text{APP}_N$ be $N \geq 1$ (autonomous) sub-activities of the composite application $\text{APP}_0$ and $P_i$ be the policy that applies to $\text{APP}_i$ (for $1 \leq i \leq N$). We equate the permission to execute the $i^{\text{th}}$ sub-activity with the set of privileges that apply to the accesses performed by $\text{APP}_i$ (which itself can be a composite application, too). These are defined by $\Pi_{\mathcal{O},\mathcal{A}}(P_i)$. In order to enforce all of these access rights, we use *pe-all* as evaluation algorithm. We assume $P_i$ to be a reduced policy. Thus, as defined in Section 2.2, $P_i$ has the following two characteristics: First, the privileges defined in $P_i$ are disjoint. This property can be assured through the preprocessing described in Section 2.2. Second, its rules apply to the same set of subjects. In some cases it might be required, that the privileges $\Pi_{\mathcal{O},\mathcal{A}}(P_i)$ are granted to different groups of users under distinguished conditions. In order to efficiently process the set of constraints, the policy is decomposed into policies conforming to Section 2.2 that are evaluated individually.

Let $P_0$ be the reduced policy for $\text{APP}_0$. In many cases, there might be no predefined policy for $\text{APP}_0$, i.e., $P_0$ is equivalent to $\Upsilon$. Nevertheless, policy prototypes can be pre-defined specifying intended configurations. The objective of the policy consolidation process is to evaluate $P_0$ against the policies of the underlying applications. Its result is an optimized policy $P^{\text{opt}}$ that fulfills the following two criteria:

*LP. Least privilege criterion*: Each privilege defined in $P^{\text{opt}}$ must also be defined in at least one policy $P_i$ with $1 \leq i \leq N$. The privileges defined in $P^{\text{opt}}$ must be sufficient to perform $\text{APP}_0$ and its respective sub-activities.

*MS. Maximum set of subjects criterion*: Each subject that is authorized based on the original policy configurations $(P_i)_{0 \leq i \leq N}$ must also be authorized by $P^{\text{opt}}$. Each subject that is defined in $P^{\text{opt}}$ must also be defined in at least one policy $P_i$ with $1 \leq i \leq N$ and in $P_0$.

## 3.2   Workflow Dependencies

Sub-activities of a composite application can for example be executed in sequence or in parallel. Also, iterations (i.e., loops) are possible. From an access control point of view it is of importance that **all** sub-activities will be performed. We represent this fact through the SEQUENCE pattern. Furthermore, conditional and event based executions can be defined. From the access control perspective this denotes that only **one** sub-activity will be invoked, which we represent through the so-called SWITCH template. SEQUENCE and SWITCH templates can be nested to model complex workflows. Apart from these kinds of control flow dependencies further interdependencies influencing access control can exist:

a) *Data-flow dependencies* are given, if an output parameter $x$ of a sub-activity $\text{APP}_i$ is input to $\text{APP}_j$ and the value of $x$ determines the result of the evaluation of the policy $P_j$.
b) *External dependencies* are dependencies by parameters external to the system, like time. For example, $P_i$ and $P_j$ might define time constraints that restrict the execution of $\text{APP}_i$ and $\text{APP}_j$ to disjoint time frames. That is, the conjunction of conditions defined in $P_i$ and $P_j$ respectively constitute a contradiction. Nevertheless, the control-flow can be consistent due to the execution order (e.g., think of delays during long-running transactions).

We first describe the consolidation of access control policies for the two patterns SEQUENCE and SWITCH before we return to discuss the influence of interdependencies a) and b).

### 3.3   Analysis of Sequence Patterns

For a SEQUENCE pattern to be consistent from the access control perspective, the following two conditions must be met: First, the access rights defined in $P_0$ must include those privileges defined in the policies $(P_i)_{1 \leq i \leq N}$. Second, there must be at least one subject that is granted these privileges. Otherwise, the access specifications are conflicting, preventing the execution of $\text{APP}_0$. Formally:

$$\forall 1 \leq i \leq N : \forall R \in P_i : \exists R' \in P_0 : \Pi_{\mathcal{O},\mathcal{A}}(R) \sqsubseteq \Pi_{\mathcal{O},\mathcal{A}}(R') \tag{1}$$

$$\exists e \in \mathcal{E} : [\![S_{\text{all}}]\!]_e = true \ \ \text{for} \ \ S_{\text{all}} = \bigwedge_{0 \leq i \leq N} \mathcal{S}(P_i) \tag{2}$$

The consolidated policy $P_{(\text{all})}^{\text{opt}}$ is defined as:

$$\begin{aligned}
P_{(\text{all})}^{\text{opt}} = \{(S_{\text{all}}, \Pi_{\mathcal{O},\mathcal{A}}(R), (\Pi_{\mathcal{C}}(R) \wedge \Pi_{\mathcal{C}}(R'))) \mid \forall i \in \{1, \dots, N\} : \\
R \in P_i, R' \in P_0 : \Pi_{\mathcal{O},\mathcal{A}}(R) \sqsubseteq \Pi_{\mathcal{O},\mathcal{A}}(R')\}
\end{aligned} \tag{3}$$

The applied evaluation algorithm is *pe-all*. If the policies $(P_i)_{1 \leq i \leq N}$ fulfill LP, then LP can also be inferred for $P_{(\text{all})}^{\text{opt}}$, as the privileges in $P_{(\text{all})}^{\text{opt}}$ are restricted to those defined in $(P_i)_{1 \leq i \leq N}$ and its rules are constrained through conjunctions of the respective conditions defined in these policies and $P_0$. Sub-activities can perform similar accesses on the same objects, like scans of the same tables of a database. Thus, $P_{(\text{all})}^{\text{opt}}$ – which aggregates the privileges defined in $(P_i)_{1 \leq i \leq N}$ – might contain redundancies that can be eliminated according to Section 2.2.

### 3.4   Analysis of Switch Patterns

The access control configurations for SWITCH patterns can be defined from two different perspectives. The *full-authorization* approach enforces each subject defined in the consolidated policy to be authorized for any of the $(\text{APP}_i)_{1 \leq i \leq N}$, irrespective which sub-activity will actually be executed. As a consequence, the consolidated policy corresponds to $P_{(\text{all})}^{\text{opt}}$ defined in the previous paragraph.

On the opposite side, *partial-authorization* distinguishes the different execution paths. Subjects might be authorized to execute $\text{APP}_0$ in case a particular $\text{APP}_i$ is invoked next, but will be blocked in any other case. Thus, in order to efficiently evaluate a SWITCH pattern the distinguished execution branches have to be analyzed separately. Consequently, up to $N$ security configurations have to be considered. In order to specify the optimized policy for the $i^{\text{th}}$ branch, the policies $P_0$ and $P_i$ are consolidated and the following must be true:

$$\forall R \in P_i : \exists R' \in P_0 : \Pi_{\mathcal{O},\mathcal{A}}(R) \sqsubseteq \Pi_{\mathcal{O},\mathcal{A}}(R') \tag{4}$$

$$\exists e \in \mathcal{E} : [\![S^{(i)}]\!]_e = true \ \ \text{for} \ \ S^{(i)} = \mathcal{S}(P_0) \wedge \mathcal{S}(P_i) \tag{5}$$

The consolidated policy for the $i^{\text{th}}$ branch (using *pe-all*) is defined as:

$$\begin{aligned}
P_{(i)}^{\text{opt}} = \{(S^{(i)}, \Pi_{\mathcal{O},\mathcal{A}}(R), (\Pi_{\mathcal{C}}(R) \wedge \Pi_{\mathcal{C}}(R'))) \mid R \in P_i, R' \in P_0 : \\
\Pi_{\mathcal{O},\mathcal{A}}(R) \sqsubseteq \Pi_{\mathcal{O},\mathcal{A}}(R')\}
\end{aligned} \tag{6}$$

## 3.5   The Benefits of Policy Consolidation

The policy consolidation technique performs a static analysis of the policy of a composite application $\text{APP}_0$ by comparing it with the security configuration of its underlying sub-activities $\text{APP}_1, \ldots, \text{APP}_N$. Its result is an optimized policy $P^{\text{opt}}$ for $\text{APP}_0$ and all sub-activities ($P^{\text{opt}} = P^{\text{opt}}_{(\text{all})}$) or specific branches $\text{APP}_0 \rightarrow \text{APP}_i$ ($P^{\text{opt}} = P^{\text{opt}}_{(i)}$), respectively. In case no external or dataflow dependencies exist, the access control costs can be reduced significantly. As each execution which is granted based on $P^{\text{opt}}$ will also be granted by the sub-activities, it is sufficient to enforce access control solely at $\text{APP}_0$, thus, saving redundant enforcements through the sub-activities. In case interdependencies 3.2.a) or 3.2.b) have to be considered at runtime, no single point of access control can be established. Nevertheless, the static analysis allows to receive a consolidated view onto the set of authorized users (MS) and the least required privileges (LP) enabling the following optimizations:

*Evaluation of MS.* $\mathcal{S}(P^{\text{opt}})$ specifies those subjects that are authorized to execute the workflow (branch) or general composite application, respectively. It allows application developers to check more easily whether the policy complies with the intended security specifications, e.g., detecting over-privileged users or conflicts. Furthermore, in case role based access control is employed, *least required roles* can be inferred. In this regard, a least required role is a role that grants process execution without demanding for further intermediary role activations. This "one role will do"-approach is especially relevant for business processes that are typically defined for specific job functions. Least required roles are identified through the predicate reduction introduced in Alg. 1 and are unique for limited role hierarchies but not necessarily for general role hierarchies. For example, the infima of the role hierarchy shown in Figure 2(b) are $r_1$ and $r_2$. The respective least required roles are least common senior roles, i.e., $r_4$ and $r_5$ in the example.

*Evaluation of LP.* $\Pi_{\mathcal{O}, \mathcal{A}}(P^{\text{opt}})$ represents the aggregated set of privileges tailored to the access requirements of the composite application. In the meaning of a reverse security engineering, this information allows to generate *task specific roles* which are appropriate for the application. They are called *task specific* as they group exactly those rights that are required for the composite application's functionality (while *least required* roles can be more generic).

## 3.6   Case Study: Web Service Workflows

Sub-activities of the intra-organizational workflow illustrated in Figure 1 on the one hand represent practical activities that require human interaction like a medication. On the other hand, they stand for information processing tasks, like an update of the stock of pharmaceuticals in the database. In the following we concentrate on the technical aspects of the workflow and assume the sub-activities to be realized as Web services with the following access rules:

– Health personnel with permanent employment and administrative personnel are allowed to access the medical records of patients. The subject specification $S_{\mathrm{MR}}$ applying to the sub-activity *query medical records* is defined as

$$S_{\mathrm{MR}} = ((\mathit{role} \sqsupseteq \text{Health Pers.} \land \mathit{employment} = \text{permanent})$$
$$\lor (\mathit{role} \sqsupseteq \text{Admin. Pers.}))$$

– Nurses of the cardiology and internists are allowed to update medical records, e.g., by inserting ECG results. Users allowed to execute *make stress electrocardiogram* are in
$$S_{\mathrm{ECG}} = ((\mathit{role} \sqsupseteq \text{Nurse} \land \mathit{field\text{-}of\text{-}activity} = \text{cardiology}) \lor (\mathit{role} \sqsupseteq \text{Internist}))$$
– Internists are allowed to perform the sub-activity *apply monitoring devices*:
$$S_{\mathrm{App}} = (\mathit{role} \sqsupseteq \text{Internist}).$$
– The sub-activity *apply medication* can be performed by nurses and physicians:
$$S_{\mathrm{Med}} = ((\mathit{role} \sqsupseteq \text{Nurse}) \lor (\mathit{role} \sqsupseteq \text{Physician})).$$

As motivated in Section 3.2, the workflow can be modeled as a composition of SEQUENCE and SWITCH patterns. This allows the authorization dependencies of the workflow to be represented as a tree as shown in Figure 3. Through a bottom-up analysis, the consolidated access control configuration for the workflow can be inferred. Typically, no access control policies are defined for the control structures – i.e, $\mathcal{P}_0 \equiv \varUpsilon$ for SEQUENCE and SWITCH nodes. Hence, the privileges defined for the individual Web services, are iteratively aggregated without demanding for relaxation tests. We thus focus on determining the set of authorized users which proceeds as follows: First, $S_{\mathrm{App}}$ and $S_{\mathrm{Med}}$ are intersected as both sub-activities are linked in sequence. It holds $S_{\mathrm{App}} \land S_{\mathrm{Med}} = (\mathit{role} \sqsupseteq \text{Internist})$. Next, the SWITCH node is evaluated. The subjects that are granted full-authorization are defined by $S = (\mathit{role} \sqsupseteq \text{Internist})$. In contrast to this, nurses are only granted partial authorization for the *ECG*-branch: $S' = (\mathit{role} \sqsupseteq \text{Nurse} \land \mathit{field\text{-}of\text{-}activity} = \text{cardiology})$. Finally, $S$ and $S'$ have to be intersected with $S_{\mathrm{MR}}$. We receive:

$$S_{\mathrm{all}} = (S_{\mathrm{MR}} \land S) = (\mathit{role} \sqsupseteq \text{Internist} \land \mathit{employment} = \text{permanent})$$
$$S^{(ECG)} = (S_{\mathrm{MR}} \land S') = (\mathit{role} \sqsupseteq \text{Nurse} \land \mathit{field\text{-}of\text{-}activity} = \text{cardiology}$$
$$\land \mathit{employment} = \text{permanent})$$

Thus, the workflow is executable for nurses and internists, whereby nurses are only granted partial authorization. This allows the following optimization of access control at the workflow layer: Internists that fulfill the specification of $S_{\mathrm{all}}$ need only be authorized at the workflow layer. For nurses, access control has to be performed twice: On top of the workflow layer and when entering the SWITCH part. All other subjects, like those granted the *Administrative Personnel* role, can be blocked right from the beginning, as they will never succeed in reaching an end state of the workflow. The optimization capabilities can be realized to the maximum extent possible, if the access control of the sub-activities can be controlled by the composite application, for instance by building up a security context between the workflow execution system and the autonomous services,

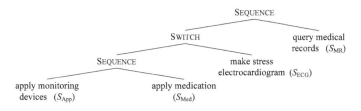

**Fig. 3.** Tree representation of the e-health business process

e.g., employing WS-SecureConversation [5]. In any case, policy enforcement at the workflow layer helps to reduce unnecessary service executions, transaction rollbacks and compensating actions.

## 4    Algorithmic Solutions

For an implementation of the described policy consolidation technique, algorithmic solutions for the evaluation of predicate conjunctions and subtractions, and the validation of privilege relaxation are required.

### 4.1    Implementing the Conjunction Operator

Equations (2) and (5) introduce $S_{all}$ and $S^{(i)}$ as conjunctions of subject specifications. The conjunction operator is semantically equivalent to the set theoretical intersection operator. That is, $S_{all}$ and $S^{(i)}$ can be interpreted as the intersection of subject sets. Let $S$ and $S'$ be two subject specifications. According to the policy model, $S$ and $S'$ are represented via disjunctions of predicate conjunctions over attributes in $S\text{-}Attr$:

$$S = s_1 \lor \ldots \lor s_k = (s_{1,1} \land \ldots \land s_{1,l}) \lor \ldots \lor (s_{k,1} \land \ldots \land s_{k,l}) \quad \text{and}$$
$$S' = s'_1 \lor \ldots \lor s'_{k'} = (s'_{1,1} \land \ldots \land s'_{1,l}) \lor \ldots \lor (s'_{k',1} \land \ldots \land s'_{k',l})$$

The attributes in $S\text{-}Attr$ are also called the dimensions of subject specifications. We assume all dimensions in $S$ and $S'$ to be specified. If a conjunction $s_i$ is not constrained in dimension $d$, then the respective predicate $s_{i,d}$ represents the whole domain of $d$. According to Section 2.2 the intersection of $S$ and $S'$ is: $S \land S' = \bigvee_{1 \leq i \leq k, 1 \leq j \leq k'} (\bigwedge_{1 \leq d \leq l} (s_{i,d} \land s'_{j,d}))$. Nevertheless, conjunctions $(s_{i,d} \land s'_{j,d})$ can be contradictory, i.e., unsatisfiable by any evaluation context. Such terms constitute unnecessary parts of a policy and shall be omitted to keep policy specifications clear. Alg. 1 illustrates an approach for computing a condensed representation of $S \land S'$. We illustrate the algorithm by means of an example. Consider the following two subject descriptions (based on the example role hierarchy shown in Figure 2(a)):

$$S = (s_1) = (role \sqsupseteq \text{Nurse} \land yop \geq 1) \quad \text{and}$$
$$S' = (s'_1 \lor s'_2) = (role \sqsupseteq \text{Admin. Pers.} \land yop \geq 0) \lor$$
$$(role \sqsupseteq \text{Health Pers.} \land yop \geq 2 \land yop \leq 4)$$

**Algorithm 1.** *intersect*$(S, S')$, with $S \equiv s_1 \vee \ldots \vee s_k$, and $S' \equiv s'_1 \vee \ldots \vee s'_{k'}$

```
1: Ψ = false
2: for all conjunctions sᵢ of S do
3:     for all conjunctions s'ⱼ of S' do
4:         for all dimensions d = 1 . . . l do
5:             ψ_d = reduce(s_{i,d} ∧ s'_{j,d})
6:         end for
7:         Ψ = Ψ ∨ (ψ₁ ∧ . . . ∧ ψ_l)
8:     end for
9: end for
10: return Ψ
```

$$\Psi \equiv S \wedge S' = \bigvee_{1 \leq i \leq k, 1 \leq j \leq k'} \left( \bigwedge_{1 \leq d \leq l} \left( s_{i,d} \wedge s'_{j,d} \right) \right)$$

$S$ represents all subjects that are granted the *Nurse* role and that have at least one year of practice (abbrev. *yop*). $S'$ represents administrative employees and all subjects that are granted senior roles of the *Health Personnel* role with at least two and at most four years of practice. Thus, the dimensions are *role* and *yop*. While the domain of *role* is a finite lattice (defined by the role hierarchy shown in Figure 2(a)), the domain of *yop* is $[0, +\infty[$.

The terms $s_1$ and $s'_1$ are disjoint, because they do not overlap in the *role*-dimension, i.e., $(s_{1,\mathrm{role}} \wedge s'_{1,\mathrm{role}})$ is a contradiction and needs not be considered in line 1. In contrast to this, $s_1$ and $s'_2$ overlap in each dimension. The conjunction $(yop \geq 1) \wedge (yop \geq 2 \wedge yop \leq 4)$ is reduced to $(yop \geq 2 \wedge yop \leq 4)$. The predicates $s_{1,\mathrm{role}}$ and $s'_{2,\mathrm{role}}$ define the two finite sets $\Phi_1 = \{Nurse, Head\ Nurse\}$ and $\Phi'_2 = \{Nurse, Head\ Nurse, Physician, Internist, Surgeon\}$. Thus, $(s_{1,\mathrm{role}} \wedge s'_{2,\mathrm{role}})$ is equivalent to $\Phi_1 \cap \Phi'_2 = \{Nurse, Head\ Nurse\}$. The intersection can be represented through the predicate $(role \sqsupseteq Nurse)$, as *Nurse* is the infimum of $\Phi_1 \cap \Phi'_2$ according to the example role hierachy. Thus, $S_1 \wedge S_2 = (role \sqsupseteq Nurse \wedge yop \geq 2 \wedge yop \leq 4)$. That is, the intersection consists of those subjects that are granted the *Nurse* role and that have at least two and at most four years of practice.

## 4.2   Checking Privilege Relaxation

Let $(O, A)$ and $(O', A')$ be two privileges. As objects and actions are defined on disjoint sets of attribute identifiers (*O-Attr* and *A-Attr*, see Section 2.1) and according to the definition of privilege relaxation (Section 2.2), $(O', A')$ relaxes $(O, A)$, if the following holds: $\forall e \in \mathcal{E} : (\llbracket O \rrbracket_e = true \wedge \llbracket A \rrbracket_e = true) \Rightarrow (\llbracket O' \rrbracket_e = true \wedge \llbracket A' \rrbracket_e = true)$. Therefore, the privilege relaxation problem can be reduced to the implication problem: Let $T = (t_1 \vee \ldots \vee t_k)$ and $T' = (t'_1 \vee \ldots \vee t'_{k'})$ be disjunctions of predicate conjunctions. $T$ implies $T'$, denoted as $T \Rightarrow T'$, if and only if every evaluation context which is satisfying $T$ is also satisfying $T'$ [6]. Informally, $T \Rightarrow T'$ means that $T'$ is more generic than $T$. To evaluate whether $T \Rightarrow T'$ holds, each predicate conjunction $t_i$ of $T$ is evaluated against the predicate conjunctions $t'_j$ of $T'$. The following three cases can arrive:

1. $t_i$ implies $t'_j$, i.e., $t_i \Rightarrow t'_j$. Then a match for $t_i$ has been found.
2. $t_i$ and $t'_j$ are incomparable, i.e., $(t_i \wedge \neg t'_j) = t_i$. Then $t_i$ has to be compared with the remaining predicate conjunctions of $T'$ to find possible matches.

**Algorithm 2.** $implies(T, T')$, with $T = t_1 \vee \ldots \vee t_k$ and $T' = t'_1 \vee \ldots \vee t'_{k'}$

```
 1: if k' = 0 then
 2:     return T      // i.e., T' = false
 3: end if
 4: Δ = false
 5: for all conjunctive terms t_i of T = (t_1 ∨ ... ∨ t_k) do
 6:     δ = subtract(t_i, t'_1)
 7:     if δ ≠ false then
 8:         Δ = Δ ∨ implies(δ, t'_2 ∨ ... ∨ t'_{k'})
 9:     end if
10: end for                         (T ⇒ T') ⇔ (Δ = false)
11: return Δ
```

3. $t_i$ and $t'_j$ overlap partially. Then, the remainder $(t_i \wedge \neg t'_j)$ is separately compared with the predicate conjunctions of $T'$.

Alg. 2 shows a pseudo-code implementation of *implies* for evaluating predicate implications. $T$ implies $T'$, if all predicate conjunctions $t_i$ of $T$ are subsumed by $T'$. In this case the remainder $\Delta$ is equal to *false*. In line 2 the sub-procedure *subtract* is invoked which calculates the remainder of $t_i$ w.r.t. $t'_1$, i.e., $\delta = (t_i \wedge \neg t'_1)$, given in disjunctive normal form (DNF). The individual predicate conjunctions of $\delta$ are separately compared to the remaining conjunctions of $T'$ through a recursive invocation of *implies* in line 2 of Alg. 2.

A pseudo-code implementation of *subtract* is depicted in Alg. 3. Computing the predicate subtraction is done in a way similar to Alg. 1 by iteratively comparing the conjunctive terms $t_i$ and $t'_j$ in each dimension $d$ (line 3–3). If $t_i$ and $t'_j$ do not overlap in any dimension $d$, $t_i$ and $t'_j$ represent disjoint data sets and the remainder is $t_i$. Otherwise, the overall overlap of $t_i$ and $t'_j$ is iteratively computed and stored in the variable *work*. The non-matching parts are described by $\delta$.

As an example assume a relational database with the table *Employees* with the attributes *Name*, *Gender*, *Salary*, and *Job* (abbrev. *na*, *ge*, *sa*, and *jo*). Parameter values of *jo* are health, administrative, and technical personnel (for short *HP*,

**Algorithm 3.** $subtract(t_i, t'_j)$, with $t_i = t_{i,1} \wedge \ldots \wedge t_{i,l}$ and $t'_j = t_{j,1} \wedge \ldots \wedge t_{j,l}$

```
 1: δ = false, work = t_i     // work = w_1 ∧ ... ∧ w_l
 2: for d = 1 ... l do
 3:     w'_d = (t_{i,d} ∧ t'_{j,d})   // the overlap of t_{i,d} and t'_{j,d}
 4:     work = (w'_1 ∧ ... ∧ w'_{d-1} ∧ w'_d ∧ w_{d+1} ... ∧ w_l)
 5:     if w'_d ≡ false then
 6:         return t_i    // t_i and t'_j represent disjoint data sets
 7:     else if w'_d ≠ t_{i,d} then
 8:         ω = t_{i,d} ∧ ¬t'_{j,d}   // the remainder of t_{i,d} minus t'_{j,d}
 9:         δ = δ ∨ (w'_1 ∧ ... ∧ w'_{d-1} ∧ ω ∧ w_{d+1} ... ∧ w_l)
10:     end if
11: end for
12: return DNF of δ    // ω in line 3 is a predicate disjunction
```

*AP*, and *TP*). Two privileges are defined on this relation. The first privilege states that the complete table can be accessed via *select*. The second restricts the *select*-access to the data of female health care employees that earn more than $50'\,\$$ and less than $100'\,\$$. We use the symbol $\bot$ to represent unrestricted attribute values. The object specifications of both privileges are represented by the following two predicate conjunctions:

$$t = (na = \bot \wedge ge = \bot \wedge sa = \bot \wedge jo = \bot)$$
$$t' = (na = \bot \wedge ge = female \wedge\ sa > 50' \wedge\ sa < 100' \wedge\ jo = HP)$$

It can easily be verified that $t$ relaxes $t'$. Let's assume that on the other way round it shall be examined whether $t'$ relaxes $t$, which is obviously not the case. The following table shows the evaluation steps of *subtract*, in case the attributes are processed in the order *Name*, *Gender*, *Salary*, and *Job*.

| | Variable *work* | Remainders | |
|---|---|---|---|
| 1. | $(na = \bot \wedge ge = \bot \wedge sa = \bot \wedge jo = \bot)$ | —— | |
| 2. | $(na = \bot \wedge ge = female \wedge\ sa = \bot \wedge jo = \bot)$ | $\delta_1 = (na = \bot \wedge ge = male \wedge\ sa = \bot \wedge jo = \bot)$ | |
| 3. | $(na = \bot \wedge ge = female \wedge$ $sa > 50' \wedge\ sa < 100' \wedge\ jo = \bot)$ | $\delta_2 = (na = \bot \wedge ge = female \wedge\ sa \le 50' \wedge\ jo = \bot)$ $\delta_3 = (na = \bot \wedge ge = female \wedge\ sa \ge 100' \wedge\ jo = \bot)$ | |
| 4. | $(na = \bot \wedge ge = female \wedge$ $sa > 50' \wedge\ sa < 100' \wedge\ jo = HP)$ | $\delta_4 = (na = \bot \wedge ge = female \wedge\ sa > 50' \wedge$ $sa < 100' \wedge jo \in \{TP, AP\})$ | |

When comparing the terms in the *Salary*-dimension $t$ divides *work* into three components, the overlapping part and two remainder predicates $\delta_2$ and $\delta_3$. This is the maximum number of remainder predicates that can be generated in one step if the attribute's domain is a totally ordered uncountable set (the domain of *Salary* is $[0, +\infty[$). Things are different if the attribute's domain is a partially ordered finite set, as is the case for the dimension *Job*. Instead of enumerating all attribute values (*AP* and *TP*) in distinct predicates, the internal representation is an aggregate of the form $(jo \in \{AP, TP\})$ as illustrated in the table.

As a consequence, a comparison of two predicate conjunctions results in up to $2l$ remainder predicate conjunctions in the worst case. As each of these are individually compared with $T'$ (line 2 of Alg. 2) this leads to an exponential worst case complexity of *implies* w.r.t. the input parameter $k'$. Thus, the described privilege implication problem is closely related to other well known computationally hard issues like query subsumption or the satisfiability problem [6]. Nevertheless, the worst case is supposed to arrive rarely. This is due to the fact that, for the worst case to occur, privileges have to be described through distinguished, partially overlapping predicate conjunctions – which would be the case if policies are written in a complex (unstructured and almost unmanageable) way. Instead, average complexity is assumed to be close to the best case complexity, which is in polynomial time.

### 4.3   Implementing the Subtraction Operator

The semantics of the subtraction of two terms $T$ and $T'$ are defined as $[\![T - T']\!]_e = [\![T]\!]_e \wedge \neg([\![T']\!]_e)$. Thus, the subtraction operator can be realized through the already presented algorithm *implies* (Alg. 2), as the remainder $\Delta$ of $implies(T, T')$ is equivalent to $T - T'$.

## 5   Related Literature

In Section 2 we defined the policy model that constitutes the basis for the specification of our proposed policy consolidation technique. Syntax and semantics of this policy model are closely related to those proposed by Bonatti et al. [2] and Wijesekera and Jajodia [7]. We extended them through additional operators and relaxation rules for defining policy consolidation. The access control policy of a composite application is composed of rules that codify the individual access rights that relate to the underlying sub-activities. The enforcement of such a policy depends on the applied evaluation algorithm. If negative or mixed authorization should be employed, which could be expressed in our model as well by means of the subtraction operator, conflict resolution techniques like those proposed by Jajodia et al. [8] have to be employed. In this work we focussed on positive authorization which is suitable for almost all enterprise applications.

Our work is also related to research on models for the specification and analysis of workflow processes. Adam et al. [9] use Petri-nets to model and evaluate control flow dependencies. Bettini et al. [10] identify temporal constraints that might cause inconsistencies which restrict the executability of workflows. Temporal constraints must also be considered when interpreting the result of the static policy analysis (see 3.2.b)). Nevertheless, even if dynamic dependencies have to be evaluated at runtime, policy consolidation still offers optimization potential. The composed policy allows to perform access control at the workflow layer, filtering unsuccessful execution attempts as early as possible. The enforcement of access rules at the workflow layer is also proposed by Gudes et al. [11]. Access control models and architectures for workflow systems are for example proposed by [12,13] and [14]. Atluri et al. [13] present an approach for analyzing dependencies between sub-activities that operate on the same data but are assigned to different security levels. A framework supporting static and dynamic separation of duties is provided by Bertino et al. [14]. In contrast to this, we concentrate on *single-user / single-role* execution schemes which we assume to be prevalent for most enterprise applications. Identifying the set of authorized users of composite applications was also addressed in previous work [15]. There, a practical approach was shown, how task-specific user profiles and roles can be determined by analyzing the source code. In this paper we presented a generic, implementation independent policy consolidation framework which also supports the reverse engineering of appropriate user / role profiles by determining the least required privileges. Compliance with LP can be inferred if the policies of the underlying sub-activities have been preprocessed and minimized. How this can be achieved for Web services that rely on database interaction has been shown in foregoing work [16].

## 6   Conclusions and Ongoing Work

As motivated in the beginning of this paper, introducing access control on the layer of composite applications that depend on autonomous sub-applications can be employed to filter unsuccessful execution attempts as early as possible, thus, avoiding unnecessary work. Additionally, a consolidated view onto the access control of a composite application allows to revise the security configuration by restricting it to the applications' functionality. Further optimization potential is given, in case the access control of the underlying sub-activities can be regulated through the composite application.

Based on the formal specification of policy consolidation, a prototype has been implemented to show its feasibility regarding the consolidation of the access control of Web service workflows. We employ XACML as policy language which due to the attribute based description of access rules is well suited to map our policy model. Workflows are specified using BPEL4WS. Currently, we are working on the integration of the consolidation functionality in a business process modeling tool [17] and the extension of the prototype to support all kinds of policy consolidations as described in Section 3 of this paper.

# References

1. M. Wimmer, M.-C. Albutiu, and A. Kemper, "Optimized Workflow Authorization in Service Oriented Architectures," in *Proceedings of the International Conference on Emerging Trends in Information and Communication Security (ETRICS)*, vol. 3995 of *LNCS*, (Freiburg, Germany), pp. 30–44, June 2006.
2. P. Bonatti, S. De Capitani di Vimercati, and P. Samarati, "An Algebra for Composing Access Control Policies," *ACM Transactions on Information and System Security (TISSEC)*, vol. 5, no. 1, pp. 1–35, 2002.
3. R. S. Sandhu, E. J. Coyne, H. L. Feinstein, and C. E. Youman, "Role-Based Access Control Models," *IEEE Computer*, vol. 29, no. 2, pp. 38–47, 1996.
4. ANSI INCITS 359-2004, *Role Based Access Control*. American National Standards Institute, Inc. (ANSI), New York, NY, USA, Feb. 2004.
5. A. Nadalin *et al.*, "Web Services Secure Conversation Language (WS-SecureConversation)." http://www-128.ibm.com/developerworks/library/specification/ws-secon/, Feb. 2005.
6. S. Guo, W. Sun, and M. A. Weiss, "Solving Satisfiability and Implication Problems in Database Systems," *ACM Trans. Database Syst.*, vol. 21, no. 2, pp. 270–293, 1996.
7. D. Wijesekera and S. Jajodia, "A Propositional Policy Algebra for Access Control," *ACM Transactions on Information and System Security (TISSEC)*, vol. 6, no. 2, pp. 286–325, 2003.
8. S. Jajodia, P. Samarati, M. L. Sapino, and V. S. Subrahmanian, "Flexible Support for Multiple Access Control Policies," *ACM Transactions on Information and System Security (TISSEC)*, vol. 26, no. 2, pp. 214–260, 2001.
9. N. R. Adam, V. Atluri, and W.-K. Huang, "Modeling and Analysis of Workflows Using Petri Nets," *Journal of Intell. Inf. Syst.*, vol. 10, no. 2, pp. 131–158, 1998.
10. C. Bettini, X. S. Wang, and S. Jajodia, "Temporal Reasoning in Workflow Systems," *Distrib. Parallel Databases*, vol. 11, no. 3, pp. 269–306, 2002.
11. E. Gudes, M. S. Olivier, and R. P. van de Riet, "Modelling, Specifying and Implementing Workflow Security in Cyberspace," *Journal of Computer Security*, vol. 7, no. 4, pp. 287–315, 1999.
12. W.-K. Huang and V. Atluri, "SecureFlow: a Secure Web-enabled Workflow Management System," in *RBAC '99: Proceedings of the 4th ACM Workshop on Role-based Access Control*, (New York, NY, USA), pp. 83–94, ACM Press, 1999.

13. V. Atluri, W.-K. Huang, and E. Bertino, "A Semantic-Based Execution Model for Multilevel Secure Workflows," *Journal of Computer Security*, vol. 8, no. 1, 2000.
14. E. Bertino, E. Ferrari, and V. Atluri, "The Specification and Enforcement of Authorization Constraints in Workflow Management Systems," *ACM Trans. Inf. Syst. Secur.*, vol. 2, pp. 65–104, Feb. 1999.
15. M. Rits, B. D. Boe, and A. Schaad, "Xact: a Bridge between Resource Management and Access Control in Multi-layered Applications," in *SESS '05: Proceedings of the 2005 Workshop on Software Engineering for Secure Systems*, (New York, NY, USA), pp. 1–7, ACM Press, 2005.
16. M. Wimmer, D. Eberhardt, P. Ehrnlechner, and A. Kemper, "Reliable and Adaptable Security Engineering for Database-Web Services," in *Proceedings of the Fourth International Conference on Web Engineering*, vol. 3140 of *LNCS*, (Munich, Germany), pp. 502–515, July 2004.
17. "Advanced Technologies for interoperability of Heterogeneous Enterprise Networks and their Applications (ATHENA), European project." Project homepage: http://www.athena-ip.org.

# Authenticating Multi-dimensional Query Results in Data Publishing

Weiwei Cheng[1], HweeHwa Pang[2], and Kian-Lee Tan[1]

[1] Department of Computer Science, National University of Singapore
[2] School of Information Systems, Singapore Management University

**Abstract.** In data publishing, the owner delegates the role of satisfying user queries to a third-party publisher. As the publisher may be untrusted or susceptible to attacks, it could produce incorrect query results. This paper introduces a mechanism for users to verify that their query answers on a *multi-dimensional dataset* are correct, in the sense of being complete (i.e., no qualifying data points are omitted) and authentic (i.e., all the result values originated from the owner). Our approach is to add authentication information into a spatial data structure, by constructing certified chains on the points within each partition, as well as on all the partitions in the data space. Given a query, we generate proof that every data point within those intervals of the certified chains that overlap the query window either is returned as a result value, or fails to meet some query condition. We study two instantiations of the approach: Verifiable KD-tree (VKDtree) that is based on space partitioning, and Verifiable R-tree (VRtree) that is based on data partitioning. The schemes are evaluated on window queries, and results show that VRtree is highly precise, meaning that few data points outside of a query result are disclosed in the course of proving its correctness.

## 1 Introduction

In data publishing, a data owner delegates the role of satisfying user queries to a third-party publisher [6,10]. This model is applicable to a wide range of computing platforms, including database caching [8], content delivery network [23], edge computing [9], P2P databases [7], etc.

The data publishing model offers a number of advantages over conventional client-server architecture where the owner also undertakes the processing of user queries. By pushing application logic and data processing from the owner's data center out to multiple publisher servers situated near user clusters, network latency can be reduced. Adding publisher servers is also likely to be a cheaper way to achieve scalability than fortifying the owner's data center and provisioning more network bandwidth for every user. Finally, the data publishing model removes the single point of failure in the owner's data center, hence reducing the database's susceptibility to denial of service attacks and improving service availability.

However, since the publishers are outside of the administrative domain of the data owner, and in fact may reside on poorly secured platforms, the query results

E. Damiani and P. Liu (Eds.): Data and Applications Security 2006, LNCS 4127, pp. 60–73, 2006.
© IFIP International Federation for Information Processing 2006

that they generate cannot be accepted at face value, especially where they are used as basis for critical decisions. Instead, there must be provisions for the user to check the "correctness" of a query answer.

**Schema:**
[ id, x-coord, y-coord, user-name, account#, ... ]

**Data:**

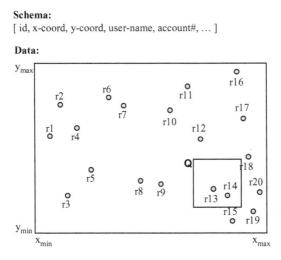

**Fig. 1.** Running Example

Consider a dataset containing 20 data points in two-dimensional space as shown in Figure 1. The figure also includes a window query **Q**, for which $\{r13, r14\}$ is the correct result. A rogue publisher may return a wrong result $\{r13, r14, r100\}$, which includes a spurious point $r100$, or $\{r13^*, r14\}$ in which some attribute values of $r13$ have been tampered with. To detect such incorrect values, the user should be able to verify the *authenticity* of query result. A different threat is that the publisher may omit some result points, for example by returning only $\{r13\}$ for query **Q**. This threat relates to the *completeness* of query result.

Most of the existing works provide for checking the authenticity [11,16] and completeness [6,15] of query results on *one-dimensional* datasets. The exception is Devanbu's scheme [6] which handles multiple key attributes by essentially concatenating them in some preferred order $key_1|key_2|..|key_d$. However, the scheme is expected to be very inefficient for symmetric queries, such as window and nearest neighbor queries, that are typical in multi-dimensional context.

In this paper, we propose a mechanism for users to verify that their query results on a *multi-dimensional dataset* are authentic and complete. Our approach is to build authentication information into a spatial data structure, by constructing certified chains on the points within each partition, as well as on all the partitions in the data space. We introduce two schemes based on this approach. The first, the Verifiable KD-tree (VKDtree), is based on the space partitioning k-d tree. The second, the Verifiable R-tree (VRtree), employs data partitioning and is based on the R-tree. The schemes are evaluated on window queries, and results show that VRtree is highly precise, meaning that few data points outside of a query result are disclosed in the course of proving its correctness. Moreover, both schemes are computationally secure, and incur low processing and update overheads. To the best of our knowledge, the authentication mechanism introduced in this paper is the first that enables a user to verify the *completeness* of a *multi-dimensional* query result generated by an untrusted server.

The remainder of this paper is organized as follows. Section 2 provides the background on data publishing model and the associated threats, and describes some cryptographic primitives. Our authentication schemes are introduced in Sections 3 and 4, while Section 5 presents results from a performance study. Finally, Section 6 concludes the paper.

## 2    Background

In this section, we first present the target system deployment model and the associated security threats. Next, we define some cryptographic primitives that are used in our solution.

### 2.1    System and Threat Models

Figure 2 depicts the data publishing model, which supports three distinct roles:

- The data owner maintains a master database, and distributes it with one or more associated signatures that prove the authenticity of the database. Any data that has a matching signature is accepted by the user to be trustworthy.
- The publisher hosts the database, and executes queries on behalf of the owner. There could be several publisher servers that are situated at the edge of the network, near the user applications. The publisher is not required to be trusted, so the query results that it generates must be accompanied by some "correctness proof", derived from the database and signatures issued by the owner.
- The user issues queries to the publisher explicitly, or else gets redirected to the publisher, e.g. by the owner or a directory service. To verify the signatures in the query results, the user obtains the public key of the owner through an authenticated channel, such as a public key certificate issued by a certificate authority.

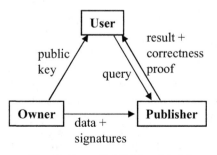

**Fig. 2.** Data Publishing Model

Our primary concern addressed in this paper is the threat that a dishonest publisher may return incorrect query results to the users, whether intentionally or under the influence of an adversary. An adversary who is cognizant of the data organization in the publisher server may make logical alterations to the data, thus inducing incorrect query results. Even if the data organization is hidden, for example through data encryption or steganographic schemes (e.g., [17]), the adversary may still sabotage the database by overwriting physical pages within the storage volume. In addition, a compromised publisher server could be made to return incomplete query results by withholding data intentionally. Therefore mechanisms for users to verify the completeness as well as authenticity of their query results are essential for the data publishing model. While there are several other security considerations in the data publishing model (such as privacy, user authentication and access control), these have been studied extensively (e.g. [1], [17], [12], [22]), and are orthogonal to our work here.

## 2.2   Cryptographic Primitives

Our proposed solution and many of the related work are based on the following cryptographic primitives:

**One-way hash function:** A one-way hash function, denoted as $h(.)$, is a hash function that works in one direction: it is easy to compute a fixed-length digest $h(m)$ from a variable-length pre-image $m$; however, it is hard to find a pre-image that hashes to a given hash value. Examples include MD5 [18] and SHA [3]. We will use the terms hash, hash value and digest interchangeably.

**Digital signature:** A digital signature algorithm is a cryptographic tool for authenticating the integrity and origin of a signed message. In the algorithm, the signer uses a private key to generate digital signatures on messages, while a corresponding public key is used by anyone to verify the signatures. RSA [19] and DSA [2] are two commonly-used signature algorithms.

**Signature aggregation:** As introduced in [5], this is a multi-signer scheme that aggregates signatures generated by distinct signers on different messages into one signature. Signing a message $m$ involves computing the message hash $h(m)$ and then the signature on the hash value. To aggregate $t$ signatures, one simply multiplies the individual signatures, so the aggregated signature has the same size as each individual signature. Verification of an aggregated signature involves computing the product of all message hashes and then matching with the aggregated signature.

**Signature chain:** In [15], a signature chain scheme is proposed that enables clients to verify the completeness of answers of range queries. A very nice property of the scheme is that only result values are returned, thus ensuring that there is no violation of access control. The scheme is based on two concepts: (a) The signature of a record is derived from its own digest as well as its left and right neighbors'. In this way, an attempt to drop any value from the answer of a range query will be detected since it would no longer be possible to derive the correct signature for the record that depends on the dropped value. (b) For the boundaries of the answer, a collaborative scheme that involves both the publisher and the client is proposed – the publisher performs partial computation based on but not revealing the two records bounding the answer and the query range, while the client completes the computation based on the two end points of the query range.

## 3   Signature Chain in Multi-dimensional Space

The goal of our work is to devise a solution for checking the correctness of query answers on multi-dimensional datasets. The design objectives include:

- Completeness: The user can verify that all the data points that satisfy a window query are included in the answer.
- Authenticity: The user can check that all the values in a query answer originated from the data owner. They have not been tampered with, nor have spurious data points been introduced.
- Precision: Proving the correctness of a query answer entails minimal disclosure of data points that lie beyond the query window. We define precision as the ratio of the number of data points within the query window, to the number of data points returned to the user.
- Security: It is computationally infeasible for the publisher to cheat by generating a valid proof for an incorrect query answer.
- Efficiency: The procedure for the publisher to generate the proof for a query answer has polynomial complexity. Likewise the procedure for the user to check the proof has polynomial complexity.

Without loss of generality, we assume that the data in the multi-dimensional space are split into partitions – this can be done using a spatial data structure. To ensure that the answer for a window query is complete, two issues must be addressed. First, we need to prove that the answer covers all the partitions that overlap the query window. We refer to these partitions as candidate partitions. Second, we need to prove that all qualifying values within each candidate partition are returned. The first issue is dependent on the partitioning strategy adopted, and is deferred to Section 4. In the rest of this section, we shall focus on the second issue.

Assuming we have proven that the query answer covers all the candidate partitions, we now need to ensure that all the qualifying values in those partitions have not been dropped. Consider a candidate partition $P$ for the window query $Q = [(q_{l1}, q_{l2}, \ldots, q_{ld}), (q_{u1}, q_{u2}, \ldots, q_{ud})]$. There are three possible cases: (a) $Q$ contains $P$. Since the window query bounds the partition, we need to ensure that *all* the points in $P$ are returned. (b) $P$ contains $Q$. The query window is within the space covered by the partition. A naive solution is to return all the points in $P$. A better solution, which we advocate, is to return only those points that are necessary for users to check for completeness. In both cases, our concern is to ensure the secrecy of points that are outside $Q$. (c) $P$ overlaps $Q$. This case can be handled by splitting $P$ into two parts: the part of $P$ that contains $Q$, and the part of $P$ that does not overlap $Q$. The former is handled in case (b), while nothing needs to be done for the latter. Thus, we shall focus on cases (a) and (b), and not discuss case (c) any further.

Our solution extends the signature chain concept in [15] to multi-dimensional space. This is done by ordering the points within the partition, and then constructing the signature chain. In this paper, we adopt a simple scheme of ordering the points based on increasing $(x_1, x_2, \ldots, x_d)$ value. In 2-d space, $(x_1, y_1)$ is ordered before $(x_2, y_2)$ if $x_1 < x_2$, or $x_1 = x_2$ and $y_1 < y_2$. Based on this ordering, we need to return all the points whose first dimension is within the range $[q_{l1}, q_{u1}]$, as well as the bounding points. Of course, some of these points may fall beyond the query window along the second dimension. *For such points that should not be part of the answer, we return only their digests rather than the actual values*, in order to protect their secrecy and achieve high precision.

We choose this simple ordering scheme over more sophisticated space filling curves [20] because: (a) A partition (corresponding to a 4K or 8K block/page) typically consists of a small number of points (100-200). Moreover, the actual number of points within a partition would be smaller than the maximum capacity (since the page is typically not full). As such, it may not be worthwhile to employ a complicated scheme. (b) None of the existing space filling curves perform well in all cases. Thus, they really offer no significant advantage over the simple scheme (especially given the small number of points).

For the example in figure 1, assuming that the entire space corresponds to one partition, the points would be ordered from $r_1$ to $r_{20}$. For case (a) where the query bounds the partition, $r_1$ to $r_{20}$ would be returned; for case (b) where the query (i.e., the box that bounds $r_{13}$ and $r_{14}$) is within the partition, we return the values of $r_{13}$ and $r_{14}$ and the digest of the various dimensions for $r_{11}$, $r_{12}$, $r_{15}$, $r_{16}$ and $r_{17}$. We now present the details of our solution that extends the signature chain scheme to multi-dimensional setting.

**Construction:** Let $L = (L_1, L_2, \ldots, L_d)$ and $U = (U_1, U_2, \ldots, U_d)$ be two points that bound the entire data space, where $L_r \leq U_r$ for all $r$. $L$ and $U$ are known to all users. Consider a partition $P$ bounded by two points $p_0 = (x_{01}, x_{02}, \ldots, x_{0d})$ and $p_{k+1} = (x_{(k+1),1}, x_{(k+1),2}, \ldots, x_{(k+1),d})$ where $x_{0r} \leq x_{(k+1),r}$ for all $r$. Suppose $P$ contains $k$ data points $p_1 = (x_{11}, x_{12}, \ldots, x_{1d}), \ldots p_k = (x_{k1}, x_{k2}, \ldots, x_{kd})$. Without loss of generality, we assume that $p_i$ is ordered before $p_j$ for $1 \leq i < j \leq k$. Clearly, $p_0$ is ordered before $p_1$ and $p_{k+1}$ is ordered after $p_k$.

Our multi-dimensional signature chain constructs for each point within $P$ an associated signature (based on [15]):

$$sig(p_i) = s(h(g(p_{i-1})|g(p_i)|g(p_{i+1}))) \tag{1}$$

where $s$ is a signature function using the owner's private key, $h$ is a one-way hash function, and $|$ denotes concatenation. $g(p_i)$ is a function to produce a digest for point $p_i$:

$$g(p_i) = \sum_{r=1}^{d} h^{U_r - x_{ir} - 1}(x_{ir}) | h^{x_{ir} - L_r - 1}(x_{ir}) \tag{2}$$

where $h^j(x_{ir}) = h^{j-1}(h(x_{ir}))$ and $h^0(x_{ir})$ applies a one-way hash function on $x$.[1]

Moreover, for the two delimiters,

$$sig(p_0) = s(h(h(L_1| \ldots |L_d)|g(p_0)|g(p_1))) \tag{3}$$

$$sig(p_{k+1}) = s(h(g(p_k)|g(p_{k+1})|h(U_1| \ldots |U_d))) \tag{4}$$

In addition, each partition $P$ has an associated signature:

$$sig(P) = s(h(g(p_0)|g(p_{k+1})|h(k))) \tag{5}$$

**Query Processing:** Assuming that a partition $P$ is returned. We have to prove that all the data points within $P$ that fall within the query window $Q$ are returned.

**Case (a): $Q$ contains $P$.** The verification process for this case is straightforward. The publisher server returns $p_0$ to $p_{k+1}$, and $k$, together with the respective signatures $sig(p_0)$ to $sig(p_{k+1})$ and $sig(P)$. (To reduce traffic overhead, we could send just one combined signature instead of the individual signatures, using the signature aggregation technique in [5].) The user first verifies that

$$s^{-1}(sig(P)) = h(g(p_0)|g(p_{k+1})|h(k))$$

Then, for each $p_i$, $1 \le i \le k$, the user verifies that $p_i$ is indeed in $P$ (by checking that $P$ bounds $p_i$). Finally, for each $p_i$, $1 \le i \le k$, the user computes its digest and checks whether

$$s^{-1}(sig(p_i)) = h(g(p_{i-1})|g(p_i)|g(p_{i+1}))$$

If all the above checks are successful, the answer contains all the data points in $P$.

**Case (b): $P$ contains $Q$.** Let $p_i = (x_{i1}, x_{i2}, \ldots, x_{id})$. The data points in $P$ can be separated into: (a) $p_\alpha, p_{\alpha+1}, \ldots, p_{\beta-1}, p_\beta$ such that $x_{i1} \in [q_{l1}, q_{u1}]$ for $\alpha \le i \le \beta$. These points can be further categorized into answer points ($\mathcal{A}$) and false positives ($\mathcal{F}$). For each answer point $p_i \in \mathcal{A}$, $\forall r$ $x_{ir} \in [q_{lr}, q_{ur}]$, whereas for each false positive $p_i \in \mathcal{F}$, $\exists r$ $x_{ir} \notin [q_{lr}, q_{ur}]$. (b) $p_1, \ldots, p_{\alpha-1}, p_{\beta+1}, \ldots, p_k$, which are clearly not answer points.

---

[1] To achieve tighter security, $h^0(x_{ir})$ can be redefined as $h^0(x_{ir}|rand(p_i))$ where $rand(p_i)$ is a random number associated with $p_i$; in which case we will need to supply the corresponding $rand(p_i)$ with each returned record. For ease of presentation, we shall adopt the simpler definition of $h^0(x_{ir})$.

(i) For each point $p_i \in \mathcal{A}$, the server returns $p_i$ and $sig(p_i)$.
(ii) For each point $p_i \in \mathcal{F} \cup \{p_{\alpha-1}, p_{\beta+1}\}$, the server returns several pieces of information: (i) if $x_{ir} \in [q_{lr}, q_{ur}]$, $h^{U_r - x_{ir} - 1}(x_{ir}) | h^{x_{ir} - L_r - 1}(x_{ir})$ is returned; (ii) if $x_{ir} < q_{lr}$, $h^{q_{ur} - x_{ir} - 1}(x_{ir})$ and $h^{x_{ir} - L_r - 1}(x_{ir})$ are returned; (iii) if $x_{ir} > q_{ur}$, $h^{U_r - x_{ir} - 1}(x_{ir})$ and $h^{x_{ir} - q_{lr} - 1}(x_{ir})$ are returned.
(iii) The server also returns $p_0$, $p_{k+1}$, $k$, $sig(p_0)$, $sig(p_{k+1})$ and $sig(P)$.

With information from step (ii), the user can compute $g(p_i)$ without knowing the actual value of $p_i$:

- If $x_{ir} < q_{lr}$, the user applies $h$ on $(h^{q_{ur} - x_{ir} - 1}(x_{ir}))$ $(U_r - q_{ur})$ times to get $(h^{U_r - x_{ir} - 1}(x_{ir}))$.
- If $x_{ir} > q_{ur}$, the user applies $h$ on $(h^{x_{ir} - q_{lr} - 1}(x_{ir}))$ $(q_{lr} - L_r)$ times to get $(h^{x_{ir} - L_r - 1}(x_{ir}))$.
- The user computes $g(p_i)$ using Equation (2).

The above procedure is secure against cheating by the publisher provided $h^i(p)$ for $i < 0$ is either undefined or computationally infeasible to derive. We use an iterative hash function for $h^i(p)$, because there is no known algebraic function that satisfies the requirement. To ensure that $h^{-1}(p) \neq p$, a hash function is chosen that outputs a different digest length from the length of $p$.

Similar to case (a), the user verifies the completeness of the query answer as follows:

- Verify that the bounding box is correct using information from step (iii), and determine whether $s^{-1}(sig(P)) = h(g(p_0) | g(p_{k+1}) | h(k))$.
- Verify that each point $p$ in $\mathcal{A}$ is in $P$ by checking that $p$ is bounded by $P$.
- Verify that each point $p_i \in \mathcal{A}$ is authentic using information in step (ii) and the derived information to check $s^{-1}(sig(p_i)) = h(g(p_{i-1}) | g(p_i) | g(p_{i+1}))$.

Again, any attempt by the publisher server to cheat would lead to an unsuccessful match in at least one of the above cases.

Finally, we emphasize that extra data points that are returned for proving completeness are in the form of digests. Thus only the existence of the data points are revealed, but not their actual content. [2]

## 4  Verifying the Data Partitions

Having shown how to prove that all qualifying data points in a candidate partition (that overlaps the query window) are returned correctly, we now look at the first issue of verifying that the query answer covers all the candidate partitions.

A naive solution is to treat the entire data space as a single large partition, so that the mechanism described in Section 3 alone suffices. However, we expect this solution to have poor precision.

---

[2] If a non-answer $p_i \in \mathcal{F}$ has the same coordinate as an answer point $p_j \in \mathcal{A}$ along some dimension, both points will have the same digest for that dimension and $p_i$'s coordinate will be revealed. This can be overcome by simply adopting $h^0(x_{ir} | rand(p_i))$ as explained in footnote 1.

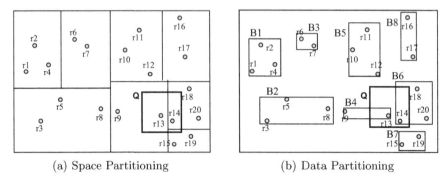

(a) Space Partitioning        (b) Data Partitioning

**Fig. 3.** Partitioning Strategies

To achieve high precision, we adopt partition-based strategies so that only those partitions that contain some qualifying data points need to be considered for a query. In this way, any potential information leakage is limited to only those partitions that contribute to the query answer, rather than across the entire data space. We present our solution based on two partitioning techniques (see Figure 3): space partitioning and data partitioning.

### 4.1    Space Partitioning

With space partitioning schemes, the partitions are disjoint but their union covers the entire data space. As such, all we need to do is to verify that the bounding boxes of the returned partitions are correct, and that the union of these partitions covers the query scope. The former has already been addressed in Section 3, while the latter is just a simple check on the partition boundaries.

To illustrate, Figure 3(a) shows the data space being partitioned through a k-d tree [4]. In the figure, the window of the query **Q** overlaps three partitions, so only data from these three partitions are returned in the answer.

Besides the k-d tree, other spatial indexing techniques like the grid file [13] and quadtree [21] can also be employed to help the publisher to locate the candidate partitions quickly. Our authentication mechanism entails no changes to the spatial data structures. (As we shall see shortly, this is not the case for data partitioning schemes.)

### 4.2    Data Partitioning

With data partitioning approach (e.g., R-tree), the union of all the partitions may not cover the entire data space. Thus, space that contains no data points may not be covered by any partition, as illustrated in Figure 3(b). The existence of empty space poses a challenge to verifying the completeness of query answers: How does the user know that portions of a query window that are not covered by any returned partitions indeed are empty spaces, without physically examining all the partitions? Referring to Figure 3(b), how can the user be sure that Q only intersects boxes B4 and B6 and not the other partitions?

Our solution is to extend the signature chain concept to the partitions. Specifically, we order the partitions by their starting boundaries along a selected dimension (as is done for point data), then chain the partitions so that the signature of a partition is dependent on the neighboring partitions to its left and right.

Let the bounding box of the $i$th partition be demarcated by $[l, u]$ where $l = (l_{i1}, l_{i2}, \ldots, l_{id})$, and $u = (u_{i1}, u_{i2}, \ldots, u_{id})$. Each partition $P_i$ has an associated signature (based on signature chaining):

$$sig(P_i) = s(h(g(P_{i-1})|g(P_i)|g(P_{i+1}))) \qquad (6)$$

where $P_{i-1}$ and $P_{i+1}$ are the left and right sibling partitions of $P_i$, and $g(P_i)$ is defined as follows:

$$g(P_i) = h(h(l_{i1}|\ldots|l_{id})|h(u_{i1}|\ldots|u_{id})|h(k_i)) \qquad (7)$$

where $k_i$ is the number of points within $P_i$.

In addition, we define two fictitious partitions as delimiters. This is similar to what we did in building the signature chain for data points in Section 3, so we shall not elaborate further.

During query processing, all the partition information along with their signatures are returned as part of the query answer. The user can be certain that no partition is omitted, otherwise some signatures will not match. For those partitions that overlap the query window, the user then proceeds to check their data points using the mechanism in Section 3. The remaining partitions that do not intersect the query window are dropped from further consideration.

To minimize the extra partitions that are disclosed to the user, and to reduce performance overheads, we apply a hierarchical data partitioning indexing structure like the R-tree on the data. The partitions within each internal node of the R-tree are chained as described above. Given a window query, the publisher server iteratively expands the child nodes corresponding to those candidate partitions in the current node, starting from the root down to the leaf nodes. All the partition information and signatures along the path of traversal are added to the query answer for user verification.

# 5   A Performance Study

In this section, we report results of an experimental study conducted to evaluate the effectiveness of our authentication mechanisms, which we have implemented in Java. We study three schemes: Verifiable KDtree (VKDtree) scheme that is based on space partitioning using the k-d tree; Verifiable Rtree (VRtree) scheme that is based on data partitioning using the R-tree; and Z-ordering scheme which employs Z-ordering [14] on the entire data space (as a single partition). The performance metric is the precision of query answers. Again, a low precision reveals the existence of extra data points and incurs traffic overhead, but not the actual content of those data points.

Unless stated otherwise, the following default parameter settings are used: the number of dimensions is 4, the data distribution is Gaussian, the number of data points is $1,000,000$. The domain of each dimension is $[1, 10M]$. The node capacity is 50 (i.e., each node holds up to 50 data points). Queries are generated by picking a point randomly from the dataset, then marking out the query window with the chosen point as center. The length of the query window along each dimension is $l \times domain\_size$; by default, $l$ is set to 0.1. For each experiment, we run 500 queries, and take the average precision.

## 5.1  Effect of Number of Dimensions

We first vary the number of dimensions from 2 to 5. The results are summarized in Figure 4(a). As expected, as the number of dimensions increases, all the schemes lose precision, because more non-answer points must be provided to verify the completeness of the query answers.

We also observe that the VKDtree scheme performs well for two-dimensional space, but its precision drops dramatically at higher dimensions. This is because more partitions are returned as a result of their overlapping the query window. The result for Z-ordering is, surprisingly, similar to the VKDtree scheme. In fact, it even performs better than VKDtree in some cases. Investigation shows that this is because the coverage of the partitions returned under VKDtree may be larger than the region covered by the Z-ordering scheme. Finally, the VRtree scheme achieves precisions of at least 60%, is least affected by dimensionality, and appears to perform the best overall. This is because the data partitioning scheme is able to effectively limit the number of candidate partitions returned in the query answers.

## 5.2  Effect of Different Data Distributions

In the second experiment, we study the effect of different data distributions. Figure 4(b) shows the precisions of the various schemes under three different distributions: Exponential, Uniform and Gaussian. The precisions of all the schemes are better with the exponential dataset, because the data generated under the exponential distribution are clustered toward one corner (the origin) of the data space, whereas they are more spread out under the other two distributions.

The relative performance of the three schemes remain largely the same as before: with VRtree performing the best, while VKDtree and Z-ordering exhibit similar performance. We also note that VRtree is much more effective than VKDtree and Z-ordering under uniform data distribution.

## 5.3  Effect of Dataset Sizes

With a fixed data space, the size of the dataset will have an effect on the performance of the schemes. In particular, for large datasets, the data space becomes more densely populated. For a fixed-size query, this means that the precision will, with high probability, be higher (compared to one with small dataset size). This intuition is confirmed in our study, as shown in Figure 4(c) which presents the results for dataset sizes of 1,000,000, 100,000, and 10,000. The relative performance of the various schemes remain largely the same as in the earlier experiments, though VRtree is less affected by the size of the datasets compared to VKDtree and Z-ordering.

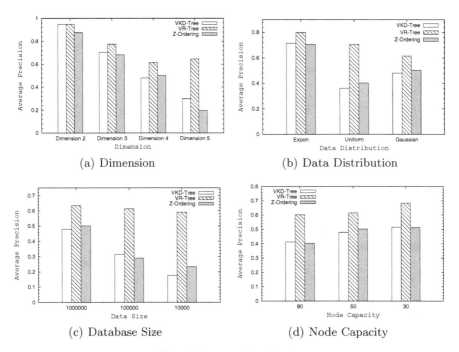

**Fig. 4.** Comparative Study

### 5.4 Effect of Node Capacity

In this study, we examine the effect of node capacity, which determines the maximum number of points allowed per partition. Obviously, a larger node capacity means that it is more likely that more non-answer points are returned (compared to a smaller node capacity), thus yielding lower precisions. Figure 4(d) shows the results for node capacities of 30, 50 and 80. From the figure, we notice that the precision of all the schemes improve as the node capacity reduces from 80 to 50 and then to 30.

### 5.5 Client Computation Cost

In this section, we evaluate the overhead of computation cost at the client side in authenticating the query results. For both VKDtree and VRtree, the client computation cost includes result entry verification cost ($C_{RV}$), boundary verification cost($C_{BV}$) and signature verification cost ($C_{SV}$). Figure 5 shows the authentication overhead of VKD-tree and VR-tree conducted in our experiment, where the overhead is measured as

$$client\ computation\ cost\ -\ processing\ cost$$
$$processing\ cost$$

where the processing cost refers to the cost for verifying only answer tuples. It turns out that there is no significant differences between the two schemes -

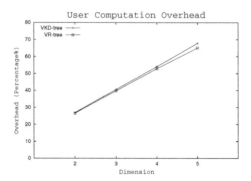

**Fig. 5.** Client Computation Cost

while VRtree incurs lower cost to verify the answers (lower false drops), it incurs additional cost to verify the chaining of partitions; whereas VKDtree does not need to deal with partition chaining but it returns more false drops and hence incur larger cost to verify the answers.

## 6    Conclusion

In this paper, we introduce a mechanism for users to verify that their query answers on a *multi-dimensional dataset* are correct. The mechanism follows a partition-based strategy, and comprises two steps: (a) verify that all partitions relevant to the query are returned, and (b) verify that all qualifying data points within each relevant partition are returned. The *signature chain* technique from [15] is used to chain up points and partitions so that any malicious omissions can be detected by the user. We study two schemes: Verifiable KD-tree (VKDtree) that is based on space partitioning, and Verifiable R-tree (VRtree) that is based on data partitioning. The schemes are evaluated on window queries, and results show that the VRtree is highly precise, meaning that few data points outside of a query answer are disclosed in the course of proving its correctness.

## Acknowledgements

This project is partially supported by a research grant (R-252-000-228-112) from the National University of Singapore, and a research grant from the Singapore Management University.

## References

1. Encrypting File System (EFS) for Windows 2000.   http://www.microsoft.com windows2000/techinfo/howitworks/security/encrypt.asp.
2. Proposed Federal Information Processing Standard for Digital Signature Standard (DSS). *Federal Register*, 56(169):42980–42982, 1991.
3. *Secure Hashing Algorithm.* National Institute of Science and Technology. FIPS 180-2, 2001.

4. J. Bentley. Multidimensional Binary Search Trees Used For Associative Searching. *Communications of the ACM*, 18(9):509–517, September 1975.
5. D. Boneh, C. Gentry, B. Lynn, and H. Shacham. Aggregate and Verifiably Encrypted Signatures from Bilinear Maps. In *Proceedings of Advances in Cryptology – EUROCRYPT'03, E. Biham, Ed., LNCS, Springer-Verlag*, 2003.
6. P. Devanbu, M. Gertz, C. Martel, and S. Stubblebine. Authentic Data Publication over the Internet. In *14th IFIP 11.3 Working Conference in Database Security*, pages 102–112, 2000.
7. R. Huebsch, J. Hellerstein, N. Lanham, B. Loo, S. Shenker, and I. Stoica. Querying the Internet with PIER. In *Proceedings of the 29th International Conference on Very Large Databases*, pages 321–332, 2003.
8. Q. Luo, S. Krishnamurthy, C. Mohan, H. Pirahesh, H. Woo, B. Lindsay, and J. Naughton. Middle-Tier Database Caching for E-Business. In *Proceedings of the 2002 ACM SIGMOD International Conference on Management of Data*, pages 600–611, 2002.
9. D. Margulius. Apps on the Edge. *InfoWorld*, 24(21), May 2002. http://www. infoworld.com/article/02/05/23/ 020527feedgetci_1.html.
10. G. Miklau and D. Suciu. Controlling Access to Published Data Using Cryptography. In *Proceedings of the 29th International Conference on Very Large Data Bases*, pages 898–909, 2003.
11. E. Mykletun, M. Narasimha, and G. Tsudik. Authentication and Integrity in Outsourced Databases. In *Proceedings of the Network and Distributed System Security Symposium*, February 2004.
12. B. Neuman and T. Tso. Kerberos: An Authentication Service for Computer Networks. *IEEE Communications Magazine*, 32(9):33–38, 1994.
13. J. Nievergelt, H. Hinterberger, and K. Sevcik. The Grid File: An Adaptable, Symmetric Multikey File Structure. *ACM Transactions on Database Systems*, 9(1):38–71, March 1984.
14. J. A. Orenstein and T. H. Merrett. A class of data structures for associative searching. In *Proceedings of the 3rd ACM SIGACT-SIGMOD Symposium on Principles of Database Systems (PODS)*, pages 181–190, 1984.
15. H. Pang, A. Jain, K. Ramamritham, and K. Tan. Verifying Completeness of Relational Query Results in Data Publishing. In *Proceedings of the 2005 ACM SIGMOD International Conference on Management of Data*, 2005.
16. H. Pang and K. Tan. Authenticating Query Results in Edge Computing. In *IEEE International Conference on Data Engineering*, pages 560–571, March 2004.
17. H. Pang, K. Tan, and X. Zhou. StegFS: A Steganographic File System. In *Proceedings of the 19th International Conference on Data Engineering*, pages 657–668, Bangalore, India, March 2003.
18. R. Rivest. *RFC 1321: The MD5 Message-Digest Algorithm*. Internet Activities Board, 1992.
19. R. Rivest, A. Shamir, and L. Adleman. A Method for Obtaining Digital Signatures and Public-Key Cryptosystems. *Communications of the ACM*, 21(2):120–126, 1978.
20. H. Sagan. *Space-Filling Curves*. Springer-Verlag, New York, 1994.
21. H. Samet. The Quadtree and Related Hierarchical Data Structures. *ACM Computing Surveys*, 16(2):187–260, June 1984.
22. R. Sandhu and P. Samarati. Access Control: Principles and Practice. *IEEE Communications Magazine*, 32(9):40–48, 1994.
23. S. Saroiu, K. Gummadi, R. Dunn, S. Gribble, and H. Levy. An Analysis of Internet Content Delivery Systems. In *Proceedings of the 5th Symposium on Operating Systems Design and Implementation*, pages 315–327, 2002.

# Xml Streams Watermarking*

Julien Lafaye and David Gross-Amblard

Laboratoire CEDRIC (EA 1395) – CC 432
Conservatoire national des arts et métiers
292 rue Saint Martin
75141 PARIS Cedex 3, France
{julien.lafaye, david.gross-amblard}@cnam.fr

**Abstract.** Xml streams are valuable, continuous, high-throughput sources of information whose owners must be protected against illegal redistributions. Watermarking is a known technique for hiding copyrights marks within documents, thus preventing redistributions. Here, we introduce a watermarking algorithm for Xml streams so that (i) the watermark embedding and detection processes are done online and use only a constant memory, (ii) the stream distortion is controlled, (iii) the type of the stream is preserved and finally (iv) the detection procedure does not require the original stream. We also evaluate, analytically and experimentally, the robustness of the algorithm against watermark removal attempts.

## 1 Introduction

*Streams.* Data streams are *high throughput* sequences of *tokens*, potentially *infinite*. They are used in a growing number of applications (see e.g. [3]) and their specificities make them a challenging application [12]. Since Xml has become the standard for specifying exchange formats between applications, the focus in this paper is on Xml streams. Xml streams can be purchased online and processed by distant peers. Data *producers*, e.g. news providers distributing news item in RSS (an Xml dialect) format, generate the tokens of the stream which is later on processed by *consumers*. We focus on automatic consumers, i.e. consumers defined by means of a program (or a Web Service). Hence, consumers, as any program, do not accept arbitrary streams, but place restrictions on their *input types*. Streams with invalid types can not be sold to consumers. For Xml based systems, types are usually specified through a Document Type Definition (DTD) or an Xml Schema. High throughput requirement puts severe constraints on consumers: they must be able to process each token of the stream quickly and cannot buffer an arbitrary number of tokens (bounded memory). For any arbitrary DTD, typechecking Xml streams can not be done while respecting these constraints. Hence, we focus on *acyclic* DTDs , where no element is a sub-element of itself (for example, Rss is an acyclic DTD). Under this hypothesis, typechecking can be done using deterministic finite automata (DFA) and types can be specified using regular expressions [15].

---

* Work supported by the ACI Sécurité & Informatique TADORNE grant (2004-2007).

E. Damiani and P. Liu (Eds.): Data and Applications Security 2006, LNCS 4127, pp. 74–88, 2006.

*Example 1.* The XML news feed of Fig. 1 may be regarded as a stream on an alphabet of *closing and ending tags* (< news >, < /date >..), *letters* (S,o,d,e,1,...) and predefined *sequences of letters* (Cinema, Politics, ...). It can be typechecked using      the      regular      language      `<news><priority>[123]</priority>` `<title>(.*)</title>..<date>`$D$`</date>...</news>`,      where      the      expression `D=(19|20)[0-9][0-9]-(0[1-9]|1[0-2])-(3[0-1]|0[1-9]|[1-2][0-9])` captures valid dates (for simplicity we do not try to check dates like 2005-02-31). Observe that the DTD standard does not allow the definition of a precise date format, since the contents of elements are mostly of type PCDATA (i.e. almost any sequence of letters). A more sophisticated model like XML Schema allows for such precise definitions. Our model applies to both formalisms.

```
...</news><news>
  <priority>1</priority>
  <title>Soderbergh won the Golden Palm</title>
  <url>http://www.imdb.com/title/tt0098724/</url>
  <date>1989-05-23</date>
  <text>Soderbergh's movie, Sex, lies and videotapes, won the ...</text>
  <category>Cinema</category>
</news><news>...
```

**Fig. 1.** An XML stream snapshot

*Watermarking.* High-quality streams carry a great intellectual and/or industrial value. Malicious users may be tempted to make quick profit by stealing and redistributing streams illegally. Therefore, data producers are interested in having a way to prove their ownership over these illicit copies. *Watermarking* is known to bring a solution to that issue by hiding copyright marks within documents, in an imperceptible and robust manner. It consists of a *voluntary alteration* of the content of the document. This alteration is parameterized by a key, kept secret by the owner. Accordingly, the secret key is needed to detect the mark and thus, to prove ownership. The robustness of the method relies on the key in the sense that removing the mark without its knowledge is very difficult. A first challenge of streams watermarking is to control and minimize the alteration of the stream, i.e. to *preserve* its *quality*. We measure the alteration by means of a relative edit-distance and propose a watermarking algorithm that introduces a bounded distortion according to this measure. A second challenge is to *preserve the type of the stream* so that it remains usable by its intended consumers. Existing XML watermarking schemes embed watermarks by modifications of the content of text nodes. We believe that other embedding areas may be used, e.g. within the tree-like structure itself. Obviously, altering the structure can not be done naïvely. For instance, in some pure text watermarking schemes, bits are embedded by switching words of the document with their synonyms. This can not be directly applied to our context: if the name of an opening tag is switched, the corresponding closing tag has to be switched to ensure well-formedness. Even if tag names are switched consistently, the resulting document may become invalid with respect to its original type. In that case, watermarked documents are *unusable* by their target consumers. Remark also that a good watermarking method must be *robust*, i.e. still detects marks within streams altered (random noise, statistical analysis, ..) by an attacker (up to a reasonable limit).

*Our Contribution.* In this paper, we introduce the $\ell$-détour algorithm, a robust watermarking scheme for XML streams, which respects the quality of the stream as well as its type, specified by means of an acyclic DTD. The idea of $\ell$-détour is the following. We identify two relevant parts of the stream, based on its semantics. The first *unalterable* part can not be altered by any attack without destroying the semantics of the stream. The second *alterable* part is still useful for the application, but can be altered within reasonable limits. For the automaton of Figure 1, the *unalterable* part will be e.g. the path name in the url element (but not the host name, since it can easily be replaced by an IP number). The alterable part will be e.g. the two digits of the day in the date element. Alterable parts can capture purely textual information as well as structuring one. A finite portion of the *unalterable* part, combined with a secret key known only by the data owner, is used to form a *synchronization key*. A noninvertible (cryptographic) pseudo-random number generator, seeded with this synchronization key, determines how the *alterable* part of the stream is modified to embed the watermark. This process, repeated along the stream, introduces *local dependencies* between parts of the data stream. These dependencies, invisible to anybody who does not possess the key used for watermarking, are checked at detection time by the owner. Only the private key and the suspect stream are needed. It can be viewed as an extension of Agrawal and Kiernan's method [2] which considered relational databases watermarking (primary keys played the role of our synchronization keys). In order to respect the type constraint, we simulate the DFA that typechecks the stream. Each time the insertion of a dependency is required, we change a sequence of tokens of the stream so the walk on the automaton follows a *detour*, leading to the *same* state. If the altered sequence lead to state $q$, the chosen detour still leads to $q$. The length $\ell$ of the detours and the frequency of the alteration control the quality of the stream. The DFA is also used to define the alterable and unalterable parts of the stream.

*Organization.* In Section 2, we present our main contribution: the $\ell$-détour algorithm, which allows for watermarking XML streams so that (i) the watermark embedding and detection processes are done online and use only a constant memory, (ii) the stream distortion is controlled, (iii) the type of the stream is preserved and finally (iv) the detection procedure does not require the original stream. In Section 3, we discuss on the robustness of $\ell$-détour against attempts to remove the watermark and show that attackers have to alter more the streams than the watermarking process did to remove the mark. Comparison with related work is presented in Section 4. Section 5 concludes.

# 2    The ℓ-détour Algorithm

## 2.1    Preliminaries

In this paper, we use $\omega$-rational languages on words, i.e. a simple, yet expressive, extension of regular languages suited to infinite words.

- **Streams:** *Let $\Sigma$ be a finite alphabet. Letters from $\Sigma$ are called tokens. A $\Sigma$-stream $\sigma$ is an infinite sequence of tokens from $\Sigma$.*
- **Stream Automaton:** *A stream automaton is a deterministic finite state automaton such that all states are accepting, except one which has no outcoming edge to an accepting state. This state is called the blocking state.*
- **Stream Acceptance:** *Let $G$ be a stream automaton. A stream $\sigma$ is accepted by $G$ if the walk on $G$ due to $\sigma$ never enters the blocking state.*
- **Stream Types:** *A set of streams $\mathcal{L}$ is a stream type if there exists a stream automaton $G$ such that $\mathcal{L}$ is the set of all streams accepted by $G$.*

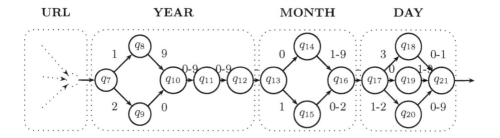

**Fig. 2.** A partial specification of the stream type for news items (`date` element)

*Example 2.* Figure 2 shows a partial specification of a stream automaton for the input type of a news items consumer. It checks that the syntax of the date is correct. The part checking that the stream is well-formed and conforms to the complete DTD is not depicted here. All unspecified transitions lead to the blocking state.

As a means to measure the distortion introduced by watermarking algorithms, we introduce the *relative edit-distance*. It is based on the edit-distance for strings [10]. In our context, the edit-distance $d_e(x, y)$ between words $x$ and $y$ is defined as the minimum number of operations (substitution/deletion/insertion of a token) that are needed to transform $x$ into $y$. For instance, if $y$ has been obtained by substituting one symbol of $x$, $d_e(x, y) = 1$. The *relative edit-distance* between $x$ and $y$ is defined as the average number of operations per symbol that are needed to transform $x$ into $y$. We measure the *relative edit-distance* from finite prefixes of streams:

**Definition 1 (Distance).** *Given* $\sigma^N$ *(resp.* $\sigma'^M$*) a finite initial segment of a stream of length* $N$ *(resp.* $M$*), the relative edit distance* $d(\sigma^N, \sigma'^M)$ *is defined by:*

$$d(\sigma^N, \sigma'^M) = \frac{d_e(\sigma^N, \sigma'^M)}{\sqrt{N}\sqrt{M}}.$$

*Example 3.* $d(babba, dabba) = 1/5$. Letter $b$ has been substituted for $d$ (edit-distance 1), and both words have length 5.

## 2.2   Informal Introduction to $\ell$-détour

Suppose that we want to watermark a data stream $\sigma$ flowing from a producer $\mathcal{P}$ to a consumer $\mathcal{C}$ whose input type is specified by a stream automaton $G$. Since $\mathcal{P}$ produces a usable stream for $\mathcal{C}$, its outputs correspond to non blocking walks on $G$. Assume that there exist in $G$ two different edges (paths of length 1), labelled by different tokens, and having same start and same end (for example, paths from $q_{17}$ to $q_{20}$ in Fig. 2). These edges can be loops on a single node. The idea of our algorithm is to change the value of some tokens of the stream so that the walk on $G$ follows one of these edges rather than the other (for instance, $q_{17} \xrightarrow{1} q_{20}$ instead of $q_{17} \xrightarrow{2} q_{20}$). These tokens are chosen as a function of (1) the secret key $K_p$ of the owner and (2) a finite portion, carefully chosen, of the path previously covered. The original walk on the automaton is diverted, and becomes specific to the data owner. This process is repeated along the stream. Notice that following an edge once does not imply that it will always be chosen because the path previously covered varies. Then, a watermarked stream is composed of alternated sequences of *unaltered* segments (*synchronization* segments) and *altered* segments of length 1. The value of an altered segment cryptographically depends on the value of its preceding synchronization segment. This method ensures that the type of the stream is respected. Furthermore, the modified stream is close to the original: each choice between two different paths adds at most 1 to the *edit-distance* between the original and the watermarked stream (and less to the relative edit-distance).

## 2.3   Finding Detours

The previous paragraph gave the idea of the 1-détour algorithm because paths of length 1 were altered in order to embed the watermark. The extension of this algorithm to path of length exactly $\ell$ is given the name of $\ell$-détour. In $\ell$-détour, not all paths of length $\ell$ may be changed but only those called *detours*:

**Definition 2 (Detours).** *Let* $G$ *be a stream automaton. The path* $p = q_i \rightarrow \ldots \rightarrow q_j$ *is a detour of length* $\ell$ *in* $G$ *if its length is* $\ell$ *and if there is no path* $p'$ *in* $G$*, distinct from* $p$*, of length at most* $\ell$*, having the same end points* $q_i$ *and* $q_j$*, and an internal node in common.*

*Example 4.* In any stream automaton, all edges are detours of length 1 since they do not contain any internal node. Remark also that as soon as $\ell > 1$, cycles are not allowed in detours of length $\ell$. On the automaton of Fig. 2, there are detours of length 2: $q_7 \xrightarrow{1} q_8 \xrightarrow{9} q_{10}$ and $q_7 \xrightarrow{2} q_9 \xrightarrow{0} q_{10}$. Conversely, paths from $q_{13}$ to $q_{16}$ going through $q_{14}$ are not detours because $q_{14}$ is an internal node common to 9 paths of length 2 between $q_{13}$ and $q_{16}$. There are 9 paths from $q_{14}$ to $q_{16}$ labeled by 1 to 9.

The proof of proposition 1 provides a constructive way to compute detours. Due to space reasons, it is not detailed. Remark that space complexity of the method is $O(n^2|\Sigma|\ell)$ whereas it is usually $O(n^2|\Sigma|^\ell)$ to compute paths (and not detours) of length $\ell$.

**Proposition 1.** *Let $\Sigma$ be the alphabet, $n$ the number of states of the automaton and $\ell \in \mathbb{N}$, $\ell > 0$. Detours of length $\ell$ can be computed in space complexity $O(n^2|\Sigma|\ell)$ and time complexity $O(n^3\ell)$.*

*Proof.* (sketch) Since detours are paths, i.e. finite sequences of labelled edges, a first naïve strategy is to compute the set of paths of length $\ell$ and remove paths which are not detours. If $S^k(i,j)$ is the set of paths of length $k$ between states $i$ and $j$, the formula $S^{k+1}(i,j) = \bigcup_{q \in states(G)} S^k(i,q) \times S^1(q,j)$ permits to define an iterative algorithm to compute $S^k(i,j)$ for any $k > 0$ (if $R, S$ are two sets, $R \times S$ is defined as the set containing the concatenation of every item of $R$ with every item of $S$). Unfortunately, this leads to an exponential blowup because the number of paths of length $\ell$ is $n|\Sigma|^\ell$ in the worst case. This blowup can be avoided by getting rid of paths which will not become detours, at each iteration. Indeed, if $p, p'$ are two detours having the same end points and $e$ is an edge in $G$, $p.e$ and $p'.e$ are not detours because they share an internal node: $end(p) = end(p')$. This fact remains true for any two paths which have $p$ and $p'$ as prefixes. Similarly, if $p$ is a detour of length $k$ between $i$ and $q$ and $e, e'$ are two edges between $q$ and $j$, $p.e$ and $p.e'$ are not detours. Hence, we can reduce the number of paths which are detours in the sets computed by the naïve algorithm by modifying the definition of the $\times$ operator: if $R$ and $S$ are not singletons, $R \times S = \emptyset$. This can be checked in constant time. Another condition is necessary to strictly compute sets of detours: if $p_1$ (resp. $p_2$) is the only detour of length $k > 1$ between states $i$ and $q_1$ (resp. $q_2$) and $e_1$ (resp. $e_2$) is the only edge between states $q_1$ (resp. $q_2$) and $j$, $p_1.e_1$ and $p_2.e_2$ are detours of length $k + 1$, unless $p_1$ and $p_2$ share their first edges. To check this when computing $R \times S$, buffering only the first edge of each path in $R$ is needed. There are at most $|\Sigma|$ such edges.

This leads to a time complexity $O(n^3\ell)$ and a space complexity $O(n^2|\Sigma|\ell)$. At each of the $\ell$ iterations, there are $n^2$ sets of detours to compute, each step requiring at most $n$ operations. Space complexity is $O(n^2|\Sigma|\ell)$ because the number of detours is at most $|\Sigma|$ between any two states (two detours can not begin with the same edge). There are $n^2$ pairs of states and the maximum length of a detour is $\ell$.

Interesting detours are likely to be found in real applications. For example, there are 9 detours of length 2 in the Rss specification, 39 detours of length 1 in a valid email addresses recognizer, and 48 detours of length 1 in a checker of valid IP numbers. In the sequel, only detours of length exactly $\ell$ are used. A straightforward extension not shown here allows for using all detours of length at most $\ell$.

## 2.4    Watermark Embedding

The $\ell$-détour algorithm can be divided into three successive steps. Steps (1) and (2) are performed once for all, while step (3) is used online and requires constant memory.

(1) *Choice* of the automaton and *Precomputation* of the detours given a target detour length $\ell$.
(2) *Annotation of the automaton.* The set of detours is split up into the set of *alterable* ones and the set of *unalterable* ones. Among the set of remaining edges (i.e. edges not part of a detour or part of an unalterable detour), a subset of *synchronization* edges is selected.
(3) *On-the-fly watermarking.* The stream is continuously rewritten by substituting some sequences of $\ell$ tokens.

***STEP 1:*** *Precomputation.* For a given input type, a canonical choice for the stream automaton is the minimal deterministic recognizer of the DTD, but any equivalent deterministic recognizer may be used. A strategy is to start with the minimal one and to compute the detours using Prop. 1. If their number is too small or if they do not fit the owner's needs, the automaton can be unfolded into an equivalent one by splitting nodes and duplicating edges, and detours recomputed.

***STEP 2:*** *Annotation of the automaton.* Not all detours are suitable for watermarking. For instance, on Fig. 2, there are two detours of length 2 between states $q_7$ and $q_{10}$: $q_7 \xrightarrow{1} q_8 \xrightarrow{9} q_{10}$ and $q_7 \xrightarrow{2} q_9 \xrightarrow{0} q_{10}$. Using these detours for watermark embedding would imply changing the millennium of a news item, resulting in an important loss of semantics. A solution is to divide the previously computed set of detours into two subsets: the subset of *alterable* detours and the subset of *unalterable* ones. This partition is done by the owner based on semantical criteria. All the remaining edges can not be used as *synchronization edges*. Indeed, some of them may be changed by an attacker without too much altering the semantics of the data which would result in the impossibility to resynchronize during the detection process and makes the watermark ineffective. For instance, we should not use the title as synchronization key because it can be altered, e.g. by adding spaces or changing the case of some characters, without changing its semantics. Conversely, the path in the url is not likely to be changed in an uninvertible manner (e.g. replacing letter 'a' by code %61). The corresponding edges in the automaton can be chosen as *synchronization* ones.

*Example 5.* A natural choice for watermarking news items is to modify the least significant part of the date. This can be achieved by using only detours from states $q_{17}$ to $q_{20}$, detours from states $q_{18}$ to $q_{21}$ and detours from states $q_{19}$ to $q_{21}$ as *alterable* ones.

**STEP 3:** *On-the-fly Watermarking.* In this last step, the core of $\ell$-détour, some portions of the stream are changed to insert the watermark. It is called `streamWatermark` and sketched on Fig. 3. Its execution is basically a walk on the automaton used to typecheck the stream. At each move, the last covered edges are changed if they match an alterable detour of length $\ell$. Inputs of `streamWatermark` are a stream $\sigma$, the private key $K_p$ of its owner and an extra parameter $\gamma$ used to change the alteration rate (on average, one alterable detour out of $\gamma$ is altered).

The `streamWatermark` procedure uses two variables: $p$ and $K_s$. The path $p$ is a finite queue having size at most $\ell$ containing the last covered edges, used as a finite FIFO: before adding a new edge at the end of a full $p$, its first edge is discarded. When $p$ is full, it contains a candidate detour, likely to be changed if it matches an *alterable* detour. The second variable $K_s$ stands for the synchronization key. It is used as a bounded-size queue of tokens. It will contain any symbol that corresponds to a synchronization edge.

The `streamWatermark` algorithm starts in **A** and regularly loops back to this cell. In **A**, we read a token from the input stream which generates a move on the automaton. The covered edge is added to $p$. Then, we move to cell **B**. If length($p$)$< \ell$, we move back to **A**. When length($p$)$= \ell$, we move to **C**. In cell **C**, we test whether $p$ is going to be changed i.e. whether $p$ is an alterable detour (from states $i$ to $j$) and whether there is at least one another other detour from $i$ to $j$. When these two conditions are met, we move to the watermark cell **E**. In **E**, the path $p$ is converted into an integer: its rank in an arbitrary ordering of all detours from $i$ to $j$. This integer, together with the synchronization key $K_s$, the private key of the owner $K_p$ and $\gamma$, is passed to the procedure `intWatermark` (Alg. 1). Its output is the number of a new detour whose labelling symbols will be added to the output stream. This procedure, derived from [2], uses a pseudo-random generator $\mathcal{R}$ seeded with $K_s.K_p$ to choose (1) whether the passed integer is going to be altered or not (2) which bit of the passed integer is going to be modified and (3) what will the new value of this bit. The synchronization key $K_s$ is reseted to the empty queue. Remark that this modification only depends on the private key of the owner and tokens of the stream which are not altered. If the conditions to move to cell **E** are not met, we move to cell **D**. Path $p$ not being an alterable detour does not mean that its suffix of length $\ell - 1$ is not the prefix of another detour. So, in **D**, the first edge of $p$ is discarded and, if it is a synchronization edge, its labelling token $c$ added to $K_s$. Simultaneously, $c$ is added to the output stream. The process loops back to the initial cell **A**.

Hence, the $\ell$-détour algorithm outputs 0,1 or $\ell$ tokens every time it reads a token from the input stream. If $N$ tokens have been read from the input stream, at least $N - \ell$ and at most $N$ tokens have been outputted which makes the process a real-time one. The output of `streamWatermark` is a stream of the form

$c_1 e_1 c_2 e_2...$ where each $c_i$ comes from the input stream and $e_i$ is the result of a pseudo-random choice seeded with the synchronization part of $c_i$ concatenated with the private key of the owner. Each segment $e_i$ has length $\ell$.

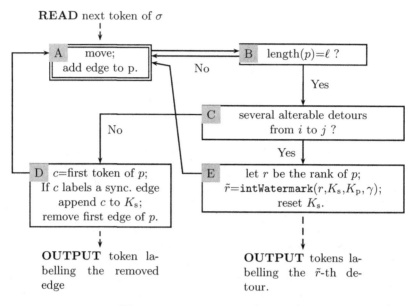

**Fig. 3.** streamWatermark$(\sigma, K_p, \gamma)$

*Example 6.* Suppose that we are in the middle of the watermarking process of the XML segment of Fig. 1. Detours of length $\ell = 1$ have been chosen and the partition of detours has been done in Example 5. Suppose also that the algorithm has just reached cell **A**, that the current position on the automaton is state $q_{13}$ (last read token is -), that $K_s = K_s^0 =$<url>http://www.imdb...</url> and $p = q_{12} \overset{-}{\to} q_{13}$. The path $q_{12} \overset{-}{\to} q_{13}$ has length 1 but is not a detour, so we move to cell **D** through cell **C**. In cell **D**, the first token of $p$, - is removed, appended to $K_s$ and added to the output stream. Then, $p = []$ and we move to cell **A**. The token 0 is read from the input stream and the edge $q_{13} \overset{0}{\to} q_{14}$ appended to $p$. Still, $p$ is not an *alterable* detour and the same sequence of steps through cells **B,C,D** is performed. Then, the algorithm moves through edges $q_{14} \overset{5}{\to} q_{16}$, $q_{16} \overset{-}{\to} q_{17}$ and $q_{17} \overset{2}{\to} q_{20}$; the tokens 5,-,2 are processed the same way the token 0 was. The token 3 coding for the lowest significant digit of the day in the month is read in cell **A**. The path $p = q_{20} \overset{3}{\to} q_{21}$ is a detour of length 1 from states $q_{20}$ to $q_{21}$. Since there are 10 detours between these states, we move to watermarking cell **E**. The intWatermark procedure is called with $K_s = K_s^0$.05-2 and $r = 4$ ($p$ is the fourth detour from $q_{20}$ to $q_{21}$). A one-way cryptographic choice of a new detour is done by Alg. 1, depending only on $K_s$ and $K_p$. For instance, if intWatermark outputs 7, the seventh detour is chosen and the token 6 added to

**Algorithm 1.** intWatermark($i, K_s, K_p, \gamma$)

   **Output**: $1 \leq j \leq n$

1  $\mathcal{R}.seed(K_s.K_p)$;                    /* seed the random generator */

   // (1) decide whether $i$ is going to be changed

2  **if** $\mathcal{R}.nextInt()$ % $\gamma = 0$ **then**

3     |   $p = \mathcal{R}.nextInt()$ % $\lceil \log_2(n) \rceil$; /* (2) choose which bit of $i$ to change */

4     |   $b = \mathcal{R}.nextInt()$ % 2;                    /* (3) new value of bit $p$ of $i$ */

5     |   $j := i$ where bit $p$ is forced to $b$;

6     |   **return** $j$;

the output stream. The watermarked date is 1989-05-26. Then, $K_s$ and $p$ are reseted and we loop back to **A**.

### 2.5 Quality Preservation: Setting Alteration Frequency $\gamma$

The following theorem quantifies to what extent the quality of a watermarked stream is preserved. Let $G$ be a stream automaton. Let $S$ (resp. $E$) be the set of starting (resp. ending) nodes of the *alterable* detours. We define the *inter-detours* distance $c$ as the length of the shortest path between a node in $E \cup q_0$ and a node in $S$. For the automaton of Fig. 2, $\{q_{17}, q_{18}, q_{19}\} \subseteq S$ and $\{q_{20}, q_{21}\} \subseteq E$ so $c$ is at most the minimum of the distances between $q_0$ and $q_{17}$ and between $q_{21}$ and $q_{17}$ (the actual *inter-detours* distance can not be given because of the partial specification).

**Theorem 1.** *Let $\sigma^N$ a finite prefix of a stream and $\tilde{\sigma}^N$ its watermarked version using $\ell$-détour. Then, at most $d(\sigma^N, \tilde{\sigma}^N) \leq (1 + \frac{c}{\ell})^{-1}$ and on average $d(\sigma^N, \tilde{\sigma}^N) \leq \frac{1}{\gamma}(1 + \frac{c}{\ell})^{-1}$.*

*Proof.* A finite segment $\sigma^N$ of a stream $\sigma$ can be written as $\sigma^N = c_1 e_1 .. c_n e_n r$ where $c_1, .., c_n$ are token sequences used as synchronization keys, $e_1, .., e_n$ are token sequences labelling detours and $r$ is the remaining. $\ell$-détour introduces a distortion of at most $n\ell$. Since the length of each $c_i$ is at least $c$, the relative distortion $\varepsilon = \frac{n\ell}{\sum_{1,n} |c_i| + n\ell + |r|}$ is such that $\varepsilon \leq (1 + c/l)^{-1}$. On average, $\frac{1}{\gamma}$ pairs $c_i e_i$ are altered.

Hence, for a maximum error rate $e = 0.1\%$, a detour length $\ell = 2$ and an inter-detour distance $c = 10$, the value of $\gamma$ is chosen so that $\frac{1}{\gamma}(1 + \frac{c}{\ell})^{-1} \leq e$ i.e. $\gamma \approx 6000$. So, on average, one over 6000 tokens labelling *alterable* detours should be altered to comply with this error rate.

### 2.6 Watermark Detection

Since the alterations performed by the watermarking process depend only on the value of the private key $K_p$ of the owner, exhibiting a key and making the dependencies appear is a strong proof of ownership. The detection process locates the synchronization keys and checks whether the detours taken by the suspect stream match what would be their watermarked value. It is very close from the watermarking algorithm except that the content f the stream is not changed. We use two counters, $tc$ and $mc$, $tc$ standing for *total count* and $mc$ for *match count*. We increment $tc$ every time we meet a detour that would be watermarked (this corresponds to line 2 of Alg. 1). We increment $mc$ every time a detour matches what would be its watermarked value. Therefore, $tc \geq mc$. When $tc = mc$, we can conclude of the presence of a watermark. When $tc > 0, mc = 0$, we are probably in front of an attacker who successfully inverted every bit of the mark. This inversion is considered as suspicious as the full presence of the mark (think of it as a negative image of a black and white picture). For a non-watermarked stream, we can assume that there is no correlation between the distribution of the data and the pseudo-random watermark embedding process (assumption verified in our experiments). In this case, the probability that each bit of a detour matches what would be its watermarked value is $1/2$. Then, we can await for $tc$ to be twice the value of $mc$ when there is no mark. To sum up, the watermark is found when $|mc/tc - 1/2| > \alpha$, where $\alpha$ is a predefined threshold. The choice of $\alpha$ is very important: if $\alpha$ is too large, the detection raises false alarms; if $\alpha$ is too small, slightly altered marks become undetectable, raising false negatives. The choice of $\alpha$ is discussed in the next section. Remark also that only the suspect stream and the private key of the owner are needed to check for a watermark.

## 3   Robustness: Analysis and Experiments

A watermarking algorithm is said to be *robust* when an attacker, unaware of the secret key used for watermark embedding, has to alter more the data than the watermarking process did, in order to remove the mark. In that case, the attacked stream suffers a huge loss of semantics, which is very likely to destroy their quality.

### 3.1   Synchronization Attacks

A watermarked stream can be attacked by modifying synchronization parts. Indeed, $\ell$-détour requires these parts to remain identical for detection. Such attacks are limited by the *constant requirement to keep streams valid with respect to the input type of their consumers*. A non-valid stream cannot be resold by a malicious user. As explained in **STEP 2** of $\ell$-détour, synchronization parts are chosen to be semantically relevant which means that they cannot be changed without widely affecting its semantics. Therefore, a type breaking attack requires to alter data semantics more than the watermarking process did.

### 3.2   Detours Attacks

Since the attacker is unaware of which detours were actually altered, two strategies are available to him. First, he can try to remove the mark by randomly modifying the altered detours. We model this attack as a *random attack*.

*Random Attack.* For $0 < p < 1$, a random attack of parameter $p$ is an attack inverting each bit of the watermark with a probability at most $p$. The false negative occurrence probability $p_{fn}(p)$ is the probability that an attacker performing a random attack of parameter $p$ cheats the detector. Theorem 2 (see [7] for a complete proof) shows how to choose $\alpha$ (detection threshold) and $tc$ (number of altered detours to poll) to get this probability maximally bounded by an owner-defined probability $\delta$ (e.g. $\delta = 10^{-6}$). These parameters also allows for a false positive occurrence probability $p_{fp}$ bounded by $\delta$.

**Theorem 2.** *Let* $0 < \delta, p < 1$, $tc \in \mathbb{N}$, $p \neq 1/2$, $tc_0 = \frac{-\log(\delta/2)}{2(1-2p)^2}$, $\alpha_1(tc) = \frac{-\log(\delta/2)}{2tc}$ *and* $\alpha_2(tc) = \frac{1}{2} - p - \sqrt{\frac{-\log(\delta/2)}{2tc}}$. *Then,*

$$(tc \geq tc_0 \text{ and } \alpha_1(tc) \leq \alpha \leq \alpha_2(tc)) \Rightarrow (p_{fp} \leq \delta \text{ and } p_{fn}(p) \leq \delta).$$

*Proof.* (sketch) The fact that a detour matches its watermarked value is seen as the outcome of a Bernoulli's law of parameter $1/2$. Suppose that we are able to retrieve $n$ possibly watermarked positions in the stream. The probability that a false positive occurs is exactly the probability that the number of positive outcomes in $n$ outcomes of Bernoulli's experiments deviates from the standard value $n/2$ by a distance $\alpha.n$. The higher $n$ is, the smaller this probability. It can be bounded using a Hoeffding inequality [8] to obtain a maximal bound for the occurrence of a false positive. Similarly, one can bound the probability that a false negative occurs. By combining these two results, we find the minimum number of potentially watermarked detours one must consider to test the presence of a watermark and simultaneously stay under the target probability $\delta$.

*Listen & Learn Attack.* When a synchronization key is met twice, the two corresponding watermarked bits will have the same position and the same value. If $c.e_1$ and $c.e_2$ are two sequences *synchronization key.detour*, the watermarked bit is among the set of bits which have the same value in the binary representations of the rank of $e_1$ and the rank of $e_2$. An attacker may try to learn such dependencies in order to perform a *Listen & learn* attack. This attack consists of the following two steps. First, *learning* associations between synchronization keys values and watermarked bits. Second, *attacking* the watermark using this knowledge. Notice that this can not be done in constant memory and requires an external and efficient storage. This does not comply with computational constraints on streams, that also apply to the attacker.

### 3.3 Experiments

*Test Sample.* We used Rss news feeds provided by CNN [1] from September 8th 2005 to September 14th 2005 for a total of 1694 news items (or 523041 tokens). *Alterable* detours were chosen to be the edges associated to the highest significant digit of the minutes field and the lowest significant digit of the seconds field. Hence, dates of news item are changed by at most 50 minutes and 9 seconds. Synchronization keys include the content of the `link` element and edges not part of an alterable detour in the `pubDate` element.

*Detour-witching Attack.* A *detour-switching* attack consists of randomly switching *all* alterable detours. It is parameterized by the alteration frequency $q$: with probability $1/q$ each detour is replaced by another one, having same start and same end, randomly chosen. We performed experiments for various values of $q$ and $\gamma$. A summary of the results is displayed in Table 1(a). For each combination of $q$ and $\gamma$, the set of news items was watermarked and attacked 100 times. We count the number of positive detections **PD** of the watermark and the relative extra alteration **QL** introduced by the attack, compared to the watermarking process. If the watermarking process alters **WL** tokens of the stream, then the attack has an overall distortion of **WL+QL**. For instance, when $q = 1$ and $\gamma = 3$, the attack successfully erases the watermark (**PD**= 0%) but at the price of a significant quality loss **QL**= 0.39% compared to the alterations introduced by the watermarking process **WL**= 0.22%. On the contrary, for $q = 1$ and $\gamma = 1$, the attack is a success (**PD**= 0%, **QL**= 0%). This shows that choosing $\gamma = 1$ is a bad idea for the data owner, as it means watermarking *every* possible position, hence giving a severe hint to the attacker. As soon as $\gamma > 1$, the mark is not removed if the attack does not alter more the stream than the watermarking process did.

**Table 1.** Attack Experiments: **WL** (quality loss due to watermarking), **QL** (*extra* quality loss due to attacks), **PD** (ratio of positive detections)

| $q$ \ $\gamma$ | 1 (high rate) | 2 | 3 (low rate) |
|---|---|---|---|
| 1 | **WL**:0.65% **QL**:0% **PD**:0% | **WL**:0.32% **QL**:0.38% **PD**:0% | **WL**:0.22% **QL**:0.39% **PD**:0% |
| 2 | **WL**:0.65% **QL**:0% **PD**:100% | **WL**:0.32% **QL**:0.19% **PD**:100% | **WL**:0.22% **QL**:0.19% **PD**:100% |
| 3 | **WL**:0.65% **QL**:0% **PD**:100% | **WL**:0.32% **QL**:0.13% **PD**:100% | **WL**:0.22% **QL**:0.13% **PD**:100% |

| strategy \ *ltime* | 100 | 500 | 1500 |
|---|---|---|---|
| surge | **QL**:0.27% **PD**:100% | **QL**:0.39% **PD**:100% | **QL**:0.24% **PD**:100% |
| destructive | **QL**:0.57% **PD**:52% | **QL**:0.49% **PD**:100% | **QL**:0.27% **PD**:100% |

(a) Random Attack
Failure probability $\delta = 0.01$

(b) Listen & Learn Attack
$\delta = 0.01$, $\gamma = 3$ and **WL**= 0.22%

*Listen & Learn Attack.* We performed experiments of this attack using two strategies. In the *destructive* strategy we change every *alterable* detour unless we know it is a watermarked one. In the *surge* strategy, a detour is altered only if we are sure it is a watermarked one. We performed experiments for different learning times, *ltime* ranging from 100 detours to 1500. The detection process begins after the end of the learning period to maximize the effect of the learning attack. For each strategy and learning time combination, 100 experiments were performed. Results are presented in Table 1(b). In only one case, the watermark is removed. This is not surprising because when *ltime* = 100, the destructive strategy is a random attack with $p = 1$. Indeed, not enough knowledge has been acquired. Even for longer learning times, the attack does not affect the detection.

# 4   Related Work

Our work is an extension of [2] which considered relational database watermarking. In [2] and its further extension [11], the watermarked information is located in the least significant bits of numerical values whereas ours is located at any position, provided this position can be localized by an automaton. Type-preservation is implicit since the structure of the databases (relation name, attribute names, key constraints) is not altered. In the XML context, structure is far more flexible and can be used to embed watermarking bits. This motivates structural modifications in the purpose of watermarking, but while keeping the data usable, i.e. respecting its original type. Such structural modifications are not discussed in [2]. It is noteworthy that our automata-based model can mimic their algorithm for numerical values with a fixed size (which is a usual hypothesis in practice).

In [16], a watermarking scheme for sensor streams is proposed. Streams are defined as continuous sequences of numerical values. Watermarking is based on a continuity hypothesis and is performed by altering salient points of the stream. This method does not consider typing problems. Keys and alterations are to be found in numerical values, whereas this can change in our approach according to the form of the stream.

Other works [6,4,13,17,9,14] address watermarking XML information in various contexts. In all these works XML documents are viewed as a whole, and not as streaming information. In [4,17,9,13], watermark embedding values are located through the use of specific XPATH queries. It is not discussed whether these techniques can be applied in a streaming context but it must be observed that XPATH can not be efficiently evaluated over streaming data [5]. Only one work [9] considers structural modification as bandwidth for watermarking which are often viewed as attacks [17,14] watermarkers must deal with. A theoretical work [6] explores the watermarking of XML databases while preserving constraints which are specified trough parametric queries. Type and stream constraints does not fit this framework.

# 5   Conclusion and Future Work

In this work, we have presented the $\ell$-détour algorithm which permits the embedding and the detection of copyright marks into XML streams. Thus, it enables detections of illegal redistributions of such objects. Future work is to study whether it is possible to detect watermarks after one or several transformations by consumers. Obviously, this is impossible in the most general setting but preliminary results [7] show that this question can be answered for a restricted class of transformations, expressing deterministically invertible stream rewritings.

# References

1. CNN RSS http://www.cnn.com/services/rss/.
2. R. Agrawal, P. J. Haas, and J. Kiernan. Watermarking Relational Data: Framework, Algorithms and Analysis. *VLDB J.*, 12(2):157–169, 2003.

3. A. Arasu, B. Babcock, S. Babu, M. Datar, K. Ito, R. Motwani, I. Nishizawa, U. Srivastava, D. Thomas, R. Varma, and J. Widom. STREAM: The Stanford Stream Data Manager. *IEEE Data Eng. Bull.*, 26(1):19–26, 2003.

4. D. G.-A. Camelia Constantin and M. Guerrouani. Watermill: an optimized finger-printing tool for highly constrained data. In *ACM Workshop on Multimedia and Security (MMSec)*, pages 143–155, August 1-2 2005.

5. G. Gottlob, C. Koch, and R. Pichler. Efficient algorithms for processing xpath queries. *ACM Trans. Database Syst.*, 30(2):444–491, 2005.

6. D. Gross-Amblard. Query-preserving watermarking of relational databases and XML documents. In *Symposium on Principles of Database Systems*, pages 191–201. ACM, 2003.

7. D. Gross-Amblard and J. Lafaye. Xml streams watermarking. Technical report, CEDRIC, 2005. CEDRIC TR-976.

8. W. Hoeffding. Probability Inequalities for Sums of Bounded Random Variables. *Journal of the American Statistical Association*, 58(301):13–30, March 1963.

9. S. Inoue, K. Makino, I. Murase, O. Takizawa, T. Matsumoto, and H. Nakagawa. Proposal on information hiding method using xml. In *The 1st Workshop on NLP and XML*, 2001.

10. V. Levenshtein. Binary Codes Capable of Correcting Deletions, Insertions and Reversals. *Soviet Physics Doklady*, 10(7):707–710, 1966.

11. Y. Li, V. Swarup, and S. Jajodia. Fingerprinting relational databases: Schemes and specialties. *IEEE Trans. Dependable Sec. Comput.*, 2(1):34–45, 2005.

12. B. Ludäscher, P. Mukhopadhyay, and Y. Papakonstantinou. A Transducer-Based XML Query Processor. In *VLDB*, pages 227–238, 2002.

13. W. Ng and H. L. Lau. Effective approaches for watermarking xml data. In *DAS-FAA*, pages 68–80, 2005.

14. M. A. Radu Sion and S. Prabhakar. Resilient information hiding for abstract semi-structures. In S. Verlag, editor, *Proceedings of the Workshop on Digital Water-marking IWDW*, volume 2939, pages 141–153, 2003.

15. L. Segoufin and V. Vianu. Validating Streaming XML Documents. In *Symposium on Principles of Database Systems*, pages 53–64, 2002.

16. R. Sion, M. Atallah, and S. Prabhakar. Resilient Rights Protection for Sensor Streams. In *Proc. of the 30th International Conference on Very Large Data Bases*, Toronto, 2004.

17. X. Zhou, H. Pang, K.-L. Tan, and D. Mangla. Wmxml: A system for watermarking xml data. In *VLDB*, pages 1318–1321, 2005.

# Aggregation Queries in the Database-As-a-Service Model*

Einar Mykletun and Gene Tsudik

Computer Science Department
School of Information and Computer Science
University of California, Irvine
{mykletun, gts}@ics.uci.edu

**Abstract.** In the Database-As-a-Service (DAS) model, clients store their database contents at servers belonging to potentially untrusted service providers. To maintain data confidentiality, clients need to outsource their data to servers in encrypted form. At the same time, clients must still be able to execute queries over encrypted data. One prominent and fairly effective technique for executing SQL-style range queries over encrypted data involves partitioning (or bucketization) of encrypted attributes.

However, executing aggregation-type queries over encrypted data is a notoriously difficult problem. One well-known cryptographic tool often utilized to support encrypted aggregation is homomorphic encryption; it enables arithmetic operations over encrypted data. One technique based on a specific homomorphic encryption function was recently proposed in the context of the DAS model. Unfortunately, as shown in this paper, this technique is insecure against ciphertext-only attacks. We propose a simple alternative for handling encrypted aggregation queries and describe its implementation. We also consider a different flavor of the DAS model which involves mixed databases, where some attributes are encrypted and some are left in the clear. We show how range queries can be executed in this model.

## 1 Introduction

The Database-As-a-Service (DAS) model was introduced by Haĉigümus, et al. in [1] and, since then, has received a lot of attention from the research community. DAS involves clients outsourcing their private databases to database service providers (servers) who offer storage facilities and necessary expertise. Clients, in general, do not trust service providers with the contents of their databases and, therefore, store the databases in encrypted format. The central challenge is how to enable an untrusted service provider to run SQL-style queries over encrypted data.

In [1], Haĉigümus, et al. suggested a method for supporting range queries in the DAS model. Since encryption by itself does not facilitate range queries, [2] involves bucketizing (partitioning) attributes upon which range queries will

---

* This work was supported by in part by NSF Awards 0331707 (ITR-DAS) and 0220069 (ITR-RESCUE).

E. Damiani and P. Liu (Eds.): Data and Applications Security 2006, LNCS 4127, pp. 89–103, 2006.

be based. This involves dividing the range of values in the specific domains of the attribute into *buckets* and providing explicit labels for each partition. These bucket labels are then stored along with the encrypted tuples at the server. Based on the same bucketization strategy, the follow-on work in [3] addresses aggregation queries in DAS by proposing the use of a particular homomorphic encryption function. In general, homomorphic encryption is a technique that allows entities who only possess encrypted values (but no decryption keys) to perform certain arithmetic operations directly over these values. For example, given two values $E(A)$ and $E(B)$ encrypted under some homomorphic encryption function $E()$, one can efficiently compute $E(A + B)$. It is easy to see that such functions can easily support $SUM$ operations over a desired range of values.

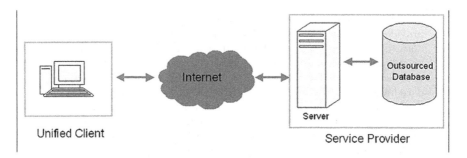

**Fig. 1.** Database-As-a-Service Overview

In this paper we show that the homomorphic encryption scheme in [3] is insecure by demonstrating its suspectability to a ciphertext-only attack. This makes it possible for the server (or any other party with access to the encrypted data) to obtain the corresponding cleartext. We propose a very simple alternative for handling aggregation queries at the server, which does not involve homomorphic encryption functions. We further describe the protocols for formulating and executing queries as well as updating encrypted tuples. We then focus on a variant of DAS which has not been explored thus far: the so-called mixed DAS model, where some attributes are sensitive (and thus stored encrypted) while others are not (and are thus left in the clear).

*Organization:* This paper is organized as follows: Section 2 describes the salient features of the DAS model and the bucketization technique. Section 3 introduces homomorphic encryption functions and describes our attack on the scheme in [3]. Section 4 describes our simple solution for supporting aggregation-style queries in the DAS model. and Section 5 addresses query processing in the mixed-DAS model. Section 6 overviews related work and Section 7 concludes the paper.

## 2   The DAS Model

The Database-As-a-Service (DAS) model is a specific instance of the well-known Application-As-a-Service model. DAS was first introduced by Haĉigümus, et al.

[1] in 2002. It involves clients storing (outsourcing) their data at servers administered by potentially untrusted service providers. Although servers are relied upon for the management/administration and availability of clients' data, they are generally not trusted with the actual data contents. In this setting, the main security goal is to limit the amount of information about the data that the server can derive, while still allowing the latter to execute queries over encrypted databases. (A related issue is how to maintain authenticity and integrity of clients' outsourced data; this has been addressed by the related work in [4,5,6].)

Before outsourcing, a DAS client is assumed to encrypt its data under a set of secret keys. These keys are, of course, never revealed to the servers. The client also creates, for each queri-able attribute, a bucketization index and accompanying metadata to help in formulating queries. For every encrypted tuple, each attribute index is reflected in a separate label (bucket id) which is given to the server. Table 1 shows an example of partitioning for a *salary* attribute. Clients maintain the metadata describing the partitions.

**Table 1.** Bucketization

| employee.salary | |
|---|---|
| **Partition** | **ID** |
| [0,25K] | 41 |
| (25K, 50K] | 64 |
| (50K, 75K] | 9 |
| (75K, 100K] | 22 |

Although the term "DAS client" generally refers to an organizational entity, the actual client who queries the outsourced data may be a weak device, such as a cell-phone or a PDA. Thus, it is important to minimize both bandwidth and computation overhead for such clients.

## 2.1 Bucketization

There are two basic strategies for selecting bucket boundaries: equi-width and equi-depth. With the former, each bucket has the same range. Table 1 is an example of equi-width bucketization where each partition covers 25K. However, if the attribute is distributed non-uniformly, this bucketization technique essentially reveals (to the server) the accurate bucket-width histogram of the encrypted attribute. In contrast, equi-depth bucketization attempts to avoid this problem by having each bucket contain the same number of items, thereby hiding the actual distribution of values. The downside of this approach is that, in the presence of frequent database updates, the equi-depth partition needs to be adjusted periodically. This requires additional (and non-trivial) interaction between the server and the client (database owner).

Although useful and practical, bucketization has an unavoidable side-effect of privacy loss since labels (bucket id-s) disclose some information about the cleartext. Unless there are as many buckets as there are distinct values in the domain of an attribute, some statistical information about the underlying data is disclosed through bucket id-s. Some recent results [7,8] analyze and estimate the loss of privacy due to bucketization. These results show that, although some degree of privacy is invariably lost (since statistical information is revealed), only very limited information can be deduced from encrypted tuples and associated labels [8].

| eid | age | salary |
|-----|-----|--------|
| 12  | 40  | 58K    |
| 18  | 32  | 65K    |
| 51  | 25  | 40K    |
| 68  | 27  | 76K    |

| $etuple(encrypted)$ | $eid^{id}$ | $age^{id}$ | $salary^{id}$ | $age^h$ | $salary^h$ |
|---------------------|-----------|-----------|---------------|---------|-----------|
| %j#9*&JbB@...       | 72        | 51        | 9             | 52      | 73        |
| P 5g4*H$j0aO...     | 72        | 3         | 9             | 29      | 65        |
| X!f(63¡glö3...      | 26        | 33        | 64            | 90      | 43        |
| ,f3+Wb5P@r-Cs...    | 85        | 33        | 22            | 81      | 38        |

(a)                                    (b)

**Fig. 2.** Relation *employee* in (a) plaintext form and (b) encrypted and bucketized form

Figure 2 (a) shows a subset of a table *employee* with the attributes: *employee id, age,* and *salary*. The encrypted version of the table, stored at the server, is shown in Figure 2 (b). It contains the fields: *etuple*, bucket identifiers each of the original attributes, and additional ciphertext values denoted by *fieldname$^h$* that will be utilized when the server computes aggregation queries (see Section 3). If the server aggregates data during range queries, it will be unable to include values from encrypted tuples. It should therefore be possible for the service provider to execute certain commands upon the sets selected during range queries, and the next section describes the use of homomorphic encryption which allows arithmetic operations directly over ciphertexts.

## 2.2   Query Processing

A client's SQL query is transformed, based upon metadata, into server-side and client-side queries ($Q^s$ and $Q^c$). The first is executed by the server over encrypted data. The results are returned to the client where they are decrypted and serve as input to the second query. When $Q^c$ is run at the client, it produces the correct results. As described below, the results from executing $Q^s$ form a superset of those produced by $Q^c$. In other words, after the decryption of the tuples returned by $Q^s$, $Q^c$ filters out extraneous tuples.

The use of bucketization limits the granularity of range limits in server-side queries. This is because the server cannot differentiate between tuples within the same bucket (i.e., tuples with identical labels). Therefore, server-side queries are further decomposed into *certain* and *maybe* queries, denoted by $Q^s_c$ and $Q^s_m$, respectively. The former will select tuples that certainly fall within the range specified in the query and its results can be aggregated at the server. $Q^s_m$ selects *etuples* corresponding to records that may qualify the conditions of the range query, but which cannot be determined without decryption and further selection by the client. This query's result set consists of the *etuples* from the border buckets in the range query. Upon receiving the two result sets the client runs query $Q^c$ to produce the final results.

Figure 3 illustrates the procedure whereby a client query $Q$ is decomposed into $Q^c, Q_c^s, Q_m^s$. Using Table data as an example, if a query specified the range of salaries between \$30-75K, then $Q_c^s$ would identify bucket 9 and $Q_m^s$ bucket 64. This query-splitting necessitates post-processing by the client – running $Q^c$ against the results returned by the server after running $Q^s$. We refer to [2] for details about the query-splitting.

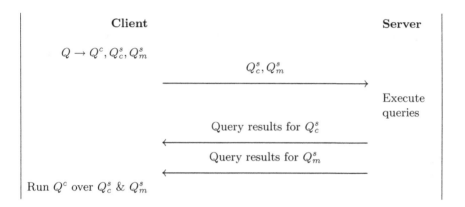

**Fig. 3.** Transformation of Client Query

# 3   Querying over Encrypted Data

The bucketization technique described above enables a server to run range queries over encrypted tuples. However, we have yet to describe any useful functions that can be computed in conjunction with such range queries. This section focuses on aggregation queries over encrypted data. More specifically, we are interested in mechanisms for computing the most rudimentary (and popular) aggregation function: SUM over a set of tuples selected as a result of a range query.

## 3.1   Homomorphic Encryption

A homomorphic encryption function allows manipulation of two (or more) ciphertexts to produce a new ciphertext corresponding to some arithmetic function of the two respective plaintexts, without having any information about the plaintext or the encryption/decryption keys. For example, if $E()$ is multiplicatively homomorphic, given two ciphertext $E(A)$ and $E(B)$, it is easy to compute $E(A * B)$. Whereas, if $E()$ is additively homomorphic, then computing $E(A + B)$ is also easy. One well-known example of a multiplicatively homomorphic encryption function is textbook RSA.[1] An example of an additively homomorphic encryption function is Paillier [10].

In more detail (as described in [3]) a homomorphic encryption function can be defined as follows:

> Assume $\mathcal{A}$ is the domain of unencrypted values, $\mathcal{E}_k$ an encryption function using key $k$, and $\mathcal{D}_k$ the corresponding decryption function, i.e., $\forall a \in \mathcal{A}, \mathcal{D}_k(\mathcal{E}_k(a)) = a$. Let $\alpha$ and $\beta$ be two (related) functions. The function $\alpha$ is defined on the domain $\mathcal{A}$ and the function $\beta$ is defined on the domain of encrypted values of $\mathcal{A}$. Then $(\mathcal{E}_k, \mathcal{D}_k, \alpha, \beta)$ is defined as a homomorphic encryption function if $\mathcal{D}_k(\beta(\mathcal{E}_k(a_1), \mathcal{E}_k(a_2), ..., \mathcal{E}_k(a_m))) = \alpha(a_1, a_2, ..., a_m)$. Informally, $(\mathcal{E}_k, \mathcal{D}_k, \alpha, \beta)$ is homomorphic over domain $\mathcal{A}$ if the result of the application of function $\alpha$ on values may be obtained by decrypting the result of $\beta$ applied to the encrypted form of the same values.

Homomorphic encryption functions were originally proposed as a method for performing arithmetic computations over private databanks [11]. Since then, they have become part of various secure computation schemes and more recently, homomorphic properties have been utilized by numerous digital signature schemes [12,4]. As mentioned above, some encryption functions are either additively or multiplicatively homomorphic. An open problem in the research community is whether there are any cryptographically secure encryption functions that are both additively and multiplicatively homomorphic. (It is widely believed that none exist.)

## 3.2  Homomorphic Function in [3]

The homomorphic encryption function proposed in [3] is based upon the so-called Privacy Homomorphism (PH) scheme [11]. PH is a symmetric encryption function with claimed security based on the difficulty of factoring large composite integers (similar to RSA). PH encryption works as follows:

- **Key Setup:**
  $k = (p, q)$, where $p$ and $q$ are large secret primes. Their product: $n = pq$ is made public.
- **Encryption:** Given plaintext (an integer) $a$,
  $\mathcal{E}_k(a) = C = (c_1, c_2) = (a \pmod{p} + R(a) \times p, a \pmod{q} + R(a) \times q)$, where $a \in \mathcal{Z}_n$ and $R(x)$ is a pseudorandom number generator (PRNG) seeded by $x$.
- **Decryption:** Given ciphertext $(c_1, c_2)$,
  $\mathcal{D}_k(c_1, c_2) = (c_1 \mod p)qq^{-1} + (c_2 \mod q)pp^{-1} \pmod{n}$

This encryption function exhibits both additive and multiplicative properties (component-wise). The addition of "noise" – through the use of $R(x)$ – is done

---

[1] In practice, RSA encryption is not homomorphic since plaintext is usually padded and encryption is made to be *plaintext-aware*, according to the OAEP specifications [9].

in multiples of $p$ and $q$, respectively, which is meant to make encryption non-deterministic and make it more difficult for an attacker to guess the secret key $k$. However, as we show below, this actually makes it easier to attack this encryption scheme through their extensions to the original homomorphic scheme.

There are several types of textbook-style attacks against encryption functions [13]. At the very least, an encryption function is required to withstand the most rudimentary attack type – *ciphertext-only attack*. Such an attack occurs when the adversary is able to discover the plaintext (or worse, the encryption key) while only having access to ciphertexts (encrypted values). We now show that the above PH-based encryption is subject to a trivial ciphertext-only attack, which results not only in the leakage of plaintext, but also in recovery of the secret keys. The attack is based on the use of a well-known Greatest Common Divisor (GCD) algorithm.

To make the attack work we make one simple assumption: that there are repeated (duplicate) plaintext values. This assumption is clearly realistic since it holds for most typical integer attributes, e.g., salary, age, date-of-birth, height, weight, etc. Of course, PH encryption ensures that identical plaintext values are encrypted into different ciphertexts, owing to the addition of *noise*.

We denote a repeated plaintext value by $M$ and two corresponding encryptions of that value as $C' = (c'_1, c'_2)$ and $C'' = (c_1'', c_2'')$. Let $R'$ and $R''$ represent the respective random noise values for the first half of each ciphertext. Recall that: $c'_1 = M \pmod{p} + R' \times p$ and $c_1'' = M \pmod{p} + R'' \times p$. Then, we have: $c'_1 - c_1'' = R' \times p - R'' \times p = (R' - R'') \times p$.

Since $R'$ and $R''$ are relatively small[2] factoring $(c'_1 - c_1'')$ is trivial. Hence, obtaining $p$ (and, likewise, $q$) is relatively easy. Moreover, we observe that, even if factoring $(c'_1 - c_1'')$ were to be hard (which it is not), it is equally trivial to compute the greatest common divisor of $(c'_1 - c_1'')$ and $n$. Note that $p = GCD(n, c'_1 - c_1'') = GCD(pq, (R' - R'')p)$.

This attack can be performed by the server by simply iterating through pairs of ciphertexts corresponding to a single database attribute, until a pair of duplicate-plaintext ciphertexts are found. In general, given $t$ ciphertexts (for a given attribute), the server would have to perform at most $O(t^2)$ GCD computations before computing $p$ and $q$. Once $p$ and $q$ are obtained, decrypting all ciphertexts is an easy task.

There are other weaknesses associated with the homomorphic scheme proposed in [3]. An extension is for accommodating encryption of negative numbers stipulates how values should be transformed prior to encryption. However, when such ciphertexts are multiplied, decryption simply fails! A separate issue arises due to the use of noise introduced through the use of $R(x)$. This function produces a pseudo-random number used as a multiplicative coefficient of $p$ and $q$, both of which are already large integers. Therefore, the resulting ciphertexts increase in size, taking significant storage at the server.

---

[2] If $R_i$ values were large, then the resulting ciphertexts would become even larger than their current size, especially since encryption does not include the noise component in its modular reductions.

### 3.3   Other Homomorphic Encryption Functions

Since the encryption function proposed in [3] is insecure, it is worthwhile to investigate whether there are other homomorphic encryption functions that can replace it. Recent cryptographic literature contains several encryption schemes that exhibit the additively homomorphic property. (Note that we are not as interested in multiplicatively homomorphic property because multiplication is not as frequent as addition in aggregation queries). Candidates include cryptosystems proposed by Paillier [10], Benaloh [14], the elliptic-curve variant of ElGamal [15] and Okamoto/Uchiyama [16]. One common feature of these schemes is that, unlike PH encryption, they are all provably secure public-key cryptosystems based upon solid number-theoretic assumptions. An unfortunate consequence is that ciphertexts tend to get rather large, and the operation of combining ciphertexts can be computationally intensive. This is problematic when dealing with computationally weak clients, such as cellphones or PDAs.

One very different alternative is a symmetric encryption function recently proposed by Castelluccia, et al. [17] in the context of secure aggregation in sensor networks. This function requires no number-theoretic assumptions, is very efficient and incurs only a minor ciphertext expansion [17]. It is based on a variant of a well-known counter (CTR) mode [13] of encryption and can be used in conjunction with any block cipher, such as Triple-DES or AES [18,19]. (The only notable difference is that it uses an arithmetic addition operation, instead of exclusive-OR to perform the actual encryption. The keystream is generated according to the normal counter mode.)

All of the above homomorphic encryption functions are secure, when used correctly. However, we show – in Section 4 – that there are simpler mechanisms for achieving aggregation over encrypted data.

## 4   Proposed Approach

With the exception of total summation queries, most aggregation queries are typically predicated upon a range selection over one or more attributes. However, if all tuple attributes are encrypted, aggregation is impossible without some form of bucketization or partitioning. Assuming a bucketization scheme (as described in Section 2.1), we now describe a trivial alternative for supporting aggregation-style queries. This technique does not require any homomorphic encryption and demands negligible extra storage as well as negligible amount of computation.

Our approach involves the data owner pre-computing aggregate values, such as SUM and COUNT, for each bucket, and storing them in encrypted form at the server. This allows the server, in response to a bucket-level aggregation query, to directly reply with such encrypted aggregate values, instead of computing them on-the-fly at query processing time. The encrypted bucket-level aggregate values can be stored separately. Table 2 shows sample table with SUM and COUNT values per *salary* attribute bucket, based on the data in Table 1.

The number of rows in this table is the same as the number of buckets for the bucketized attribute. During execution of a range query, the server simply

**Table 2.** Aggregate values stored per bucket

| employee.salary.aggregates | | |
|---|---|---|
| **Bucket ID** | **SUM** | **COUNT** |
| 41 | Enc(930) | Enc(15) |
| 64 | Enc(1020) | Enc(13) |
| 9 | Enc(774) | Enc(9) |
| 22 | Enc(568) | Enc(6) |

looks up the appropriate values from the aggregate table and returns them to the client. This frees the server from expensive computation with homomorphic encryption functions and also obviates any security risks.

We recognize two drawbacks in the proposed technique: (1) extra storage for encrypted aggregates, and (2) additional computation following database update operations. The first is not an actual concern since extra space is truly negligible in comparison to that stemming from ciphertext expansion in either PH-based or public key homomorphic encryption functions. The second does present a slight complication which we address below. The main benefit is that the server is relieved from adding ciphertexts during query execution, removing this computational overhead.

### 4.1  Aggregation Query Processing

We now describe the processing of aggregation-style range queries using the proposed technique. As before, each query is partitioned into client- and server-side sub-queries $Q^c$ and $Q^s$, respectively. $Q^c$ is basically the original query and $Q^s$ is its bucket-level "translation" and split into $Q^s_c$ and $Q^s_m$ (*certain* and *maybe* queries). However, unlike bucket-level range queries, aggregation queries result in the server returning one or more bucket-level encrypted aggregate values as the query response to $Q^s_c$. $Q^s_m$ executes as in [1] (described in Section 2.2) and returns the *etuples* belonging to bordering buckets which may be part of the final query response. For example, consider the following query:

*SELECT SUM, COUNT from employee WHERE*
*(employee.salary ≥ 30K) and (employee.salary ≤ 75K)*

The corresponding server-side query $Q^s$ would be: *SELECT SUM, COUNT from employee.salary.agg WHERE (id=64) or (id=9)*

The corresponding query reply would consist of:

1. Enc(1020) and Enc(13) for bucket id 64
   – as well as:
2. *etuples* for all tuples with bucket id 9

As a final step, the client needs (1) decrypt, filter and aggregate the *etuples*, (2) to decrypt and sum up the respective bucket aggregates, and (3) combine results from the two steps to compute correct aggregates.

## 4.2 Handling Updates

Whenever a data owner updates its outsourced database to modify, delete or insert tuples involving bucketized attributes, the aggregate values need to be updated as well. An update query may therefore require two communication rounds with the server: the stored aggregate values need to be returned by the server in the first round, and then updated and returned by the data owner in the second round. In between the two rounds, the owner modifies the aggregate values accordingly (i.e., computes new SUM and/or new COUNT). This procedure is shown in figure 4, where a client inserts a new tuple and updates the *salary* aggregate table simultaneously.

We use the term *data owner* as opposed to *client* to capture the fact that there may be many clients who are authorized to query the outsourced data (and who have appropriate decryption keys). Whereas, the there might be only one *owner*, i.e., the entity authorized to modify the database. Thus, while an owner is always a client, the opposite is not always true.

We also note that the two-round interaction shown in figure 4 is not necessary if there is only one owner (but many clients). Recall that, for each database, its owner as well all other clients are required to store certain metadata (bucketization scheme) for each bucketized attribute. The size of the bucketization metadata is proportional to the number of buckets. Consequently, it is reasonable to require the (single) owner to store up-to-date bucket-level aggregate values for each bucketized attribute. (In other words, the additional storage is insignificant as it at most doubles the amount of metadata.) Consequently, the first round of communication (as part of update) is unnecessary.

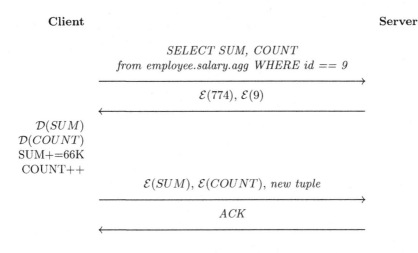

**Fig. 4.** Owner/Client inserts new tuple

# 5   Mixed Databases

Up until this point we have discussed a DAS model in which all the client's data is encrypted. We now look at execution of aggregation queries in a novel DAS flavor, where some attributes are encrypted and some are left in the clear. We label this as a *mixed database*. Such databases provide de facto access control since individuals not in possession of decryption keys cannot access sensitive data. Differentiating between confidential and non-confidential attributes also reduces the computational load related to encryption at both the server and client.

An interesting aggregation query in a mixed database specifies a range over a plaintext value while aggregating an encrypted attribute. Table 3 illustrates a mixed database where the *emp id* and age attributes are kept in the clear while *salary* is encrypted. A potential query asks for the total salary of all employees within a certain age group. Such queries cannot be executed with the proposed solution in Section 4, because the attribute over which the range is defined is not bucketized (since it is not encrypted). Instead, this plaintext attribute either has an index built over it or not. In the former case the index is utilized to select the matching tuples, while in the latter, a complete table scan is necessary during query execution. It still remains necessary for the server to aggregate over encrypted data, and we therefore return our focus to homomorphic encryptions functions. Next we compare and analyze the homomorphic functions introduced in Section 3.3 to determine the most appropriate candidate function for the mixed DAS model.

## 5.1   Additive Homomorphic Encryption Scheme Candidates

We are interested in comparing provably secure additive homomorphic encryption schemes. Criteria used to evaluate schemes included the size of their ciphertexts, the cost of adding ciphertexts, and that of decryption. Cost of encryption is of less importance since it is a one-time offline computation performed by the data owner, and has no effect on query response time.

The four homomorphic encryption schemes that we consider are Paillier [10], Benaloh [14], Okamoto-Uchiyama (OU) [16] and the elliptic-curve variant of ElGamal (EC-EG) [15]. [20] describes each of these schemes in greater detail. The privacy homomorphism in [3] does not qualify as a viable candidate because of its weak security, which is pointed out in Section 3.2. Castelluccia et al.'s secret key homomorphic scheme [17] requires that additional data be returned to the client for decryption. This data consists of unique identifiers for each aggregated ciphertext and is proportionate in length to the number of aggregated values. Such bandwidth overhead diminishes the value of data aggregation, and we therefore omit this scheme from our pool of candidates[3].

---

[3] It is possible to remove the additional bandwidth overhead by storing additional encrypted data at the server, but a description of this technique is outside the scope of this paper.

**Table 3.** Mixed Database

| faculty.salary | | |
|---|---|---|
| emp id | age | salary$^h$ |
| 31 | 52 | 87 |
| 32 | 45 | 12 |
| 33 | 38 | 41 |

## 5.2   Analysis and Comparison of Cryptoschemes

When comparing cryptosystems built upon different mathematical structures (EC-EG operates over elliptic curves while the OU and Benaloh work over multiplicative fields), it is important to devise a common computational unit of measurement for purposes of fair comparison. We choose that unit to be *1024-bit modular multiplications* and follow the same methodology for comparison as in [21]. The fundamental operation in EC-EG is elliptic curve point addition. [20] describes how to derive the equivalent number of modular multiplications to that of an elliptic curve point addition. The number of 1024-bit modular multiplications will define the computational cost of summing ciphertexts at the server and decryption of aggregate values at the client.

**Table 4.** Performance Comparison of Additive Homomorphic Cryptosystems

| Scheme | Addition | Decryption | Bandwidth |
|---|---|---|---|
| Paillier | 4 | 1536 | 2048 |
| EC-EG | 1 | 16384 | 328 |
| OU | 1 | 512 | 1024 |
| Benaloh | 1 | 131072 | 1024 |

Table 4 shows the comparison of the three homomorphic cryptosystems. The size of ciphertexts reflects both the overhead of storage at the server and transmission of aggregate values. It is measured in bits. The cost of homomorphic addition (summing two ciphertexts) and decryption is measured by the number of 1024-bit modular multiplications required by the operations.

The parameters for each of the four cryptosystems have been selected such as to obtain an equal 1024-bit level of security. For *Paillier, Benaloh* and *OU*, primes $p$ and $q$ are selected such that $|n| = 1024$, while $EC - EG$ uses one of the standard (IEEE) ECC curves over $F_{163}$ defined in [22]. Random nonces are assumed to be 80-bits[4].

The decryption cost for Benaloh and EC-EG depend on the size of the aggregated values to be decrypted. These values in turn are a result of the size of the attribute aggregated and the number of values aggregated. Both cryptosystems employ a baby-giant step algorithm during decryption. These algorithms work

---

[4] Random nonces are used in cryptosystems to make them non-deterministic, in that encryption of identical plaintexts will yield different ciphertexts.

by searching for the plaintext in its possible value range, while using tables of pre-computed values (at regular intervals) to speed up the search. The size of these tables directly affect the efficiency of the search in that the larger the tables the faster the search. When deriving the results in Table 4, we assumed aggregation of 10,000 20-bit bit values (e.g. up to million dollar salaries). Let $max$ denote the number of bits required to represent the largest possible aggregate value. In our case, $max = 34$. As is common with baby-giant step algorithms, $\sqrt{max}$ pre-computed values are stored in a table, and $\frac{\sqrt{max}}{2}$ computations are required for the search (on average). This means that $2^{17}$ computations will be required during Benaloh and EC-EG decryption, along with pre-computed tables of 2.6MB and 16.7MB, respectively.

## 5.3 Recommendations

OU and Paillier clearly stand out amongst the four candidate schemes, mainly due to their lower decryption costs. This is of importance since decryption will be performed by clients, which may be computationally limited devices (e.g. cell phone). Between the two, OU is the preferred choice in each of the measured performance categories. This is a result of Paillier's cryptosystem requirement of a larger group structure (2048 versus 1024 bits), resulting in greater storage and bandwidth overhead, as well as more expensive computations. The large cost difference in summation of ciphertexts (4 to 1 ratio) also plays a significant role, since this operation will be executed very frequently by the server. We therefore declare OU to be the algorithm of choice for aggregation queries in mixed-databases.

EC-EG and Benaloh are poor candidate choices because of their extremely high decryption costs and the large storage requirements (at clients) associated with their baby-giant step algorithms. This poor performance reflects the database environment in which they are evaluated, where tables may contain several thousand tuples, creating a large value space to search through (during decryption). The two algorithms are seemingly good choices in alternative settings that only require a few number of small values to be aggregated (e.g. certain sensor networks) [20].

# 6   Related Work

The Database-As-a-Service (DAS) model was introduced by Haĉigümus, et al. in [1] and, since then, has received a lot of attention from the research community. The specific technique of bucketizing data to support range queries over encrypted tuples was described in [2]. Bucketization involves dividing the range of values in the specific domains of the attribute into *buckets* and providing explicit labels for each partition. Recent work [7,8] analyze and estimate the loss of privacy due to bucketization. Since statistical information is revealed, some degree of privacy is invariably lost, but these results show that only very limited information can be deduced from the encrypted tuples and their corresponding bucket identifiers [8].

[11] is the first work describing homomorphic encryption functions (referred to as a Privacy Homomorphisms (PHs) by the respective authors). Such functions were originally proposed as a method for performing arithmetic computations over private databanks. [3] suggests a specific homomorphic encryption function to use within a DAS model that utilizes bucketization. The additional functionality provided by this function expands upon the range of queries that can be executed by the DAS server, specifically supporting a set of aggregation operations (SUM, COUNT and AVG).

An alternative DAS flavor involves the use of a Secure Coprocessor (SC) to aid with processing of server-side queries. A SC is a computer that can be trusted with executing its computations correctly and unmolested, even when attackers gain physical access to the device. It also provides tamper resistance, allowing for secure storage of sensitive data such as cryptographic keys. [23] describes a high-level framework for incorporating a SC in a DAS setting, including the query splitting between the client, server and SC, and suggest [24] as a SC candidate.

# 7   Conclusion

In conclusion, we proposed an alternative technique to homomorphic encryption functions to support aggregation queries over encrypted tuples in the Database-as-a-Server Model. The previously suggested solution in [3] was shown to be insecure. Our technique if simple and reduces the computational overhead associated with aggregation queries on both the server and client. Next we explored mixed databases, where certain attributes are encrypted while others are left in the clear. Additively homomorphic encryption functions are needed to support basic aggregation queries for such databases. We analyzed and compared a set of homomorphic encryption candidates and selected our preferred algorithm.

# References

1. H. Hacigumus, B. Iyer, and S. Mehrotra, "Providing database as a service," in *International Conference on Data Engineering*, March 2002.
2. H. Hacigumus, B. Iyer, C. Li, and S. Mehrotra, "Executing sql over encrypted data in the database-service-provider model," in *ACM SIGMOD Conference on Management of Data*, pp. 216–227, ACM Press, June 2002.
3. H. Hacigumus, B. Iyer, and S. Mehrotra, "Efficient execution of aggregation queries over encrypted databases," in *International Conference on Database Systems for Advanced Applications (DASFAA)*, 2004.
4. E. Mykletun, M. Narasimha, and G. Tsudik, "Authentication and integrity in outsourced databases," in *Symposium on Network and Distributed Systems Security (NDSS'04)*, Feb. 2004.
5. E. Mykletun, M. Narasimha, and G. Tsudik, "Signature 'bouquets': Immutability of aggregated signatures," in *European Symposium on Research in Computer Security (ESORICS'04)*, Sept. 2004.
6. P. Devanbu, M. Gertz, C. Martel, and S. G. Stubblebine, "Authentic third-party data publication," in *14th IFIP 11.3 Working Conference in Database Security*, pp. 101–112, 2000.

7. B. Hore, S. Mehrotra, and G. Tsudik, "A privacy-preserving index for range queries," in *International Conference on Very Large Databases (VLDB)*, 2004.
8. A. Ceselli, E. Damiani, S. Vimercati, S. Jajodia, S. Paraboschi, and P. Samarati, "Modeling and assessing inference exposure in encrypted databases," in *ACM Transactions on Information and System Security*, vol. 8, pp. 119–152, 2005.
9. M. Bellare and P. Rogaway, "Optimal asymmetric encryption," in *Advances in Cryptology - Eurocrypt*, pp. 92–111, 2004.
10. "Public-key cryptosystems based on composite degree residuosity classes," in *99* (P. Paillier, ed.), vol. 1592 of *LNCS*, pp. 206–214, International Association for Cryptologic Research, IEE, 1999.
11. R. Rivest, L. Adleman, and M. Dertouzous, "On data banks and privacy homomorphisms," in *Foundations of Secure Computation*, Academic Press, pp. 169–179, 1978.
12. D. Boneh, C. Gentry, B. Lynn, and H. Shacham, "Aggregate and Verifiably Encrypted Signatures from Bilinear Maps,"
13. A. J. Menezes, P. C. van Oorschot, and S. A. Vanstone, *Handbook of applied cryptography*. CRC Press series on discrete mathematics and its applications, CRC Press, 1997. ISBN 0-8493-8523-7.
14. J. Benaloh, "Dense Probabilistic Encryption," *Proceedings of the Workshop on Selected Areas of Cryptography*, pp. 120–128, 1994.
15. T. ElGamal, "A public key cryptosystem and a signature scheme based on discrete logarithms," *IEEE Transactions on Information Theory*, vol. IT-31, pp. 469–472, July 1985.
16. T. Okamoto and S. Uchiyama, "A New Public-key Cryptosystem as Secure as Factoring," *EUROCRYPT*, pp. 308–318, 1998.
17. C. Castelluccia and E. Mykletun and G. Tsudik, "Efficient Aggregation of encrypted data in Wireless Sensor Networks," *Mobile and Ubiquitous Systems: Networking and Services*, 2005.
18. N. I. of Standards and Technology, "Triple-des algorith," *FIPS 46-3*, 1998.
19. N. I. of Standards and Technology, "Advanced encryption standard," *NIST FIPS PUB 197*, 2001.
20. E. Mykletun and J. Girao and D. Westhoff, "Public Key Based Cryptoschemes for Data Concealment in Wireless Sensor Networks," *International Conference on Communications*, 2006.
21. N. Gura, A. Patel, A. Wander, H. Eberle, and S. Shantz, "Comparing Elliptic Curve Cryptography and RSA on 8-bit CPUs," *Cryptographic Hardware and Embedded Systems (CHES)*, pp. 119–132, 2004.
22. IEEE, "Standard P1363: Standard Specifications For Public-Key Cryptography," *http://grouper.ieee.org/groups/1363/*.
23. E. Mykletun and G. Tsudik, "Incorporating a Secure Coprocessor in the Database-as-a-Service Model," *International Workshop on Innovative Architecture for Future Generation High Performance Processors and Systems*, 2005.
24. J. G. Dyer, M. Lindemann, R. S. R. Perez, L. van Doorn, and S. W. Smith, "Building the IBM 4758 Secure Coprocessor," in *EEE Computer*, pp. 57–66, 2001.

# Policy Classes and Query Rewriting Algorithm for XML Security Views*

Nataliya Rassadko

The University of Trento, via Sommarive 14, 38050 Povo(TN), Italy
rassadko@dit.unitn.it

**Abstract.** Most state-of-the-art approaches of securing XML documents are based on a partial annotation of an XML tree with security labels which are later propagated to unlabeled nodes of the XML so that the resulting labeling is full (i.e. defined for every XML node). The first contribution of this paper is an investigation of possible alternatives for policy definition that lead to a fully annotated XML. We provide a classification of policies using different options of security label propagation and conflict resolution. Our second contribution is a generalized algorithm that constructs a full DTD annotation (from the the partial one) w.r.t. the policy classification. Finally, we discuss the query rewriting approach for our model of XML security views.

## 1 Introduction

In [1], we presented a generalized notion of XML security views. The intuition behind XML security views is similar to that of multi-level security views for a relational database [2]: *views* are virtual tables that are defined by multilevel relational expressions over the multilevel relations and are evaluated each time the view is used; view evaluation yields a derived multilevel relation.

In a hierarchical structure like XML, it is hardly possible to define accessibility via a single query. Thus, for XML, we define a partial assignment of security labels to XML nodes; then, a security policy is applied to these security labels so that the partially annotated XML becomes fully annotated; finally, the latter is "sanitized", i.e. (some) nodes with negative authorizations are hidden (deleted or encrypted), but their permitted children are revealed (e.g., moved up to a permitted ancestor if a forbidden parent is deleted). This approach is used, for example, in [3], [4], [5], [6]. The resulting XML tree is called *authorized* ($T_A$). Another approach to XML view calculation enforces security annotations on the schema level. The result is a DTD schema of the permitted data (or in other words, a DTD view $D_v$) as in [1], [7], [8]. Then, the *materialized* version of XML document ($T_M$) is constructed from the initial XML document by deleting forbidden nodes w.r.t. $D_v$ so that $T_A$ is isomorphic to $T_M$.

* This work has been partially supported by MIUR under the project FIRB-ASTRO, by PAT under the project PAT-MOSTRO and by the EU Commission under the project EU-IST-IP-SERENITY.

E. Damiani and P. Liu (Eds.): Data and Applications Security 2006, LNCS 4127, pp. 104–118, 2006.

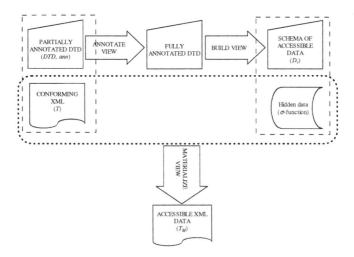

**Fig. 1.** Schema of accessible data materialization

A diagram of the methodology to construct a schema for the accessible data is shown in Fig. 1 (see [1] for details).

The construction of the fully annotated document, in which every node is labeled, depends on the overall *security policy* [9] that is used. The first contribution of this paper is an investigation of different alternatives for policy definition and enforcement at the level of an XML tree. Our analysis shows that not all combinations of policy options satisfy the properties of *completeness* and *consistency*, i.e., result in a single fully annotated tree. We provide a classification of policies using different options of security label propagation and conflict resolution. The second contribution is a generic algorithm that constructs a fully annotated DTD $D_F$ (from the the partial one) according to the policy classification so that $D_F$ reflects a full annotation of a corresponding XML document.

The final phase of XML view construction is a computation of the document $T_M$ which conforms to $D_v$, i.e. materialization of accessible data. However, the user often wants to know only a small part of the materialized view, e.g., an answer on some XPath query expressed in terms of $D_v$. In this case, the materialization of the security view can be avoided by rewriting user queries over $T_M$ conforming to $D_v$ into queries over the original data, and then evaluating this query. The third contribution of this paper is the description of an algorithm for such a query rewriting.

The paper is organized as follows. First, in Sec. 2, we provide a classification of XML security policies that can be used in construction of a fully annotated XML from a partial one. Second, a general algorithm for calculation of a fully annotated DTD is presented in Sec. 3. Next, we discuss query rewriting algorithm in Sec. 4. Finally, Sec. 5 presents related work and concludes the paper.

## 2    Classification of Policies

We can classify security policies by *completeness* and *consistency* [9]. The former handles *unassigned values*, and the latter is to handle *conflicting assignments*.

**Definition 1.** *A policy is* complete *and* consistent *if every partially annotated tree can be extend to a single fully annotated tree.*

We list here several possible policies. These are variations of classical security policies [9]:

**Local Propagation (LP):** "open", "closed", or "none";
**Hierarchy Propagation (HP):** "topDown" (td), "bottomUp" (bu), or "none";
**Structural Conflict Resolution (SC):** "localFirst" (lf), "hierarchyFirst" (hf), or "none";
**Value Conflict Resolution (VC):** "denialTakesPrecedence" (dtp), "permissionTakesPrecedence" (ptp), or "none".

The LP option is similar to traditional policies for access control: in the case of "open" ("closed"), if a node is not labelled then it is labelled by Y (N); with the "none" option, an unlabeled node is not assigned any label.

The HP option specifies annotation inheritance in the tree. In the case of "td" ("bu"), an unlabelled node with a labelled parent (children) inherits the label of the latter; "none" means that no hierarchy propagation is applied. Note that the "bu" case can result in conflicts, and they should be addressed by the VC option.

The SC option specifies whether the local or hierarchy rule takes precedence ("lf" or "hf" respectively); in the case of "none", both kinds of inheritance are applied (if they are not "none") resulting in more than one possible annotations and the "winning" label is defined based on the VC option. The latter specifies how to resolve conflicts for unlabelled nodes that are assigned different labels by the preceding rules: N always has precedence over Y ("dtp"); Y always has precedence over N ("ptp"), and no choice ("none").

Finally, we also use *most-specific-takes-precedence* (MSTP) policy [9] that prohibits propagation of labels on already labeled nodes.

We represent all the possible policy options in Table 1, where symbol "∗" means "any", i.e. any possible value from the appropriate set [1].

**Definition 2.** *The policy is called a* top-down/bottom-up/local/multilabel *policy if it satisfies conditions in lines 1-2/3-4/5-6/7 of Table 1.*

**Proposition 1.** *The top-down, bottom-up, local, and multilabel policies are complete and consistent.*

---

[1] Note that Table 1 indeed shows all 81 possible combination of security options, since symbols ∗ and ≠ mean, respectively, three and two possible values for a corresponding policy option.

**Table 1.** Policy alternatives

|    | HP | LP | SC | VC | additional condition |
|----|----|----|----|----|----------------------|
| 1  | td | ≠none | hf | * | none |
| 2  | td | none | * | * | root is annotated |
| 3  | bu | ≠none | hf | ≠none | none |
| 4  | bu | none | * | ≠none | all leaves are annotated |
| 5  | * | ≠none | lf | * | none |
| 6  | none | ≠none | * | * | none |
| 7  | ≠none | ≠none | none | ≠none | none |
| 8  | none | none | * | * | none |
| 9  | ≠none | ≠none | none | none | none |
| 10 | bu | * | hf | none | none |
| 11 | bu | none | ≠hf | none | none |

All the other policies are classified as *unresolvable* since they do not result in a unique fully annotated tree.

In the next section, we will show how to construct a full DTD annotation (from the the partial one) for every specified policy class.

## 3   Construction of Security View

We start with the definition of a DTD.

**Definition 3.** *A DTD D is a triple (Ele, P, root), where Ele is a finite set of element types; root is the distinguished type in Ele called "root"; P is a function defining element types such that for each A in Ele, $P(A) = \alpha$, where $\alpha$ is a regular expression, defined as follows:*

$$\alpha := \mathtt{str} \mid Ele \mid \epsilon \mid \alpha + \alpha \mid \alpha, \alpha \mid \alpha*$$

*where* str *is a special type denoting PCDATA, $\epsilon$ is the empty word, and "+", ",", and "*" denote disjunction, concatenation, and Kleene star, respectively. We refer to $A \to P(A)$ as the* DTD production rule *of A. For all element types B occurring in $P(A)$, we refer to B as a* subelement type *(or a* child type*) of A and to A as a* superelement type *(or a* parent type*) of B.*

We assume that DTD is finite and non-recursive, i.e., without cycles.

**Definition 4.** *An* authorization specification *is a pair (D, ann), where D is a DTD,* ann *is a partial mapping between adjacent DTD element types A and B:*

$$\mathsf{ann}(A, B) \quad ::= \quad \mathsf{Q}[q] \mid \mathsf{Y} \mid \mathsf{N}$$

*where [q] is a qualifier in some fragment of XPath. A special case is the root of D, for which we define* $\mathsf{ann}(root) = \mathsf{Y}$ *by default.*

*Every* ann(A, B) *defines a* source element type *A denoted as s, a* destination element type *B denoted as d, and a* generator of security label for B *(or simply* generator) $(A, B)$ *denoted as g. A mapping from a source type $A$ to a set of destination types $B$ is called an* annotation production *and is denoted* $P_{\mathsf{ann}}(A)$. *An* annotation production rule *is a mapping between $A$ and $P_{\mathsf{ann}}(A)$ denoted* $A \to P_{\mathsf{ann}}(A)$.

We consider that $A$ and $B$ are adjacent element types, i.e., form a DTD edge [2]. Since we put annotations on DTD edges, the idea behind our algorithm is to "push" security labels from generators to destination types.

**Definition 5.** *If* $\mathsf{ann}(s, d) = a \neq \emptyset$, *we say that $s$* transmits *(or propagates) annotation $a$ to $d$ via $g$.*

After obtaining an annotation, a destination type $d$ becomes a source type and may retransmit its annotation to generators where $d$ is a source.

*Remark 1.* In the local policy, we suppose that $\mathsf{ann}(A, B)$ is an annotation between *parent $A$* and its *child $B$*, i.e., pushing security labels is performed in a top-down manner that assures that there are not any conflicts at tree level since every node $B$ has only one parent $A$, i.e., only one generator. Hence, we consider the *local* policy as a subset of the *top-down* policy.

**Definition 6.** *The DTD document is called* fully annotated *if for every DTD node $A$, there is a function* $\mathsf{ann}_{\mathsf{data}}(A) ::= \mathsf{Y} \mid \mathsf{N}$ *called* full annotation *of the document DTD.*

The notion of a full annotation was defined for XML documents which have a unique full annotation provided a complete and consistent policy is given. At the schema level, however, there may be several "paths" transmitting different annotations to the same element type. Below we show how to resolve this problem.

**Definition 7.** *We denote the set of all generators of $d$ as $G(d)$. An element type $d$ with a generator $g \in G(d)$ such that $\mathsf{ann}(g) = \emptyset$ is called* expecting.

**Definition 8.** *We say that a subset $\overline{G}(d)$ of $G(d)$ has a* simultaneous impact *on $\mathsf{ann}_{\mathsf{data}}(d)$ if there exists an XML instance $T$ conforming to a DTD schema $D$ such that every instance of type $d$ has a set of either outgoing or incoming edges that can be mapped to the set $\overline{G}(d)$. We call $\overline{G}(d)$ a set of simultaneous impact (SSI).*

*Example 1.* Consider a DTD:

$$A \to (B, C); \; B \to (D, E); \; C \to (D|E); \; D \to (\mathtt{str}); \; E \to (\mathtt{str}).$$

Generators $(B, D)$ and $(C, D)$ belong to different SSIs on $\mathsf{ann}_{\mathsf{data}}(D)$ since a node $D$ has either $B$ or $C$ parent in any XML instance. Generators $(D, B)$ and $(E, B)$

---

[2] Note that an annotation production rule in this case $A \to P_{\mathsf{ann}}(A)$ may be either of a *top-down nature* (i.e. every $B \in P_{\mathsf{ann}}(A)$ is a child of $A$ in the DTD schema) or of a *bottom-up nature* (i.e. every $B \in P_{\mathsf{ann}}(A)$ is a parent of $A$ in the DTD schema).

belong to the same SSI on $\text{ann}_{\text{data}}(B)$ because any node $B$ has both $D$ and $E$ children in any XML instance. Generators $(D, C)$ and $(E, C)$ belong to different SSIs on $\text{ann}_{\text{data}}(C)$ as long as node $C$ has either a $D$ or an $E$ child node in any XML instance.

**Definition 9.** *We say that $d$ may obtain a preliminary full annotation (PFA) from SSI $\overline{G}(d)$ denoted as* $\text{ann}_{\text{data}}(d)_{\overline{G}(d)}$, *if for every $g \in \overline{G}(d)$, $\text{ann}(g)$ is the same, non empty, and $\text{ann}(g)$ is not a qualifier.*

If $\text{ann}(g)$ is the same for all $g \in \overline{G}(d)$ then $\text{ann}_{\text{data}}(d)_{\overline{G}(d)} = \text{ann}(g)$. Otherwise, we use the VC resolution option if it is not "none" [3]. From the analysis of policy options follows that value conflict may arise only in the case of the bottom-up policy class, because every XML instance usually has a node with more than one child.

In Def. 9, we required that $\text{ann}(g) \neq Q[q]$. Before explaining the case when $\text{ann}(g) = Q[q]$, we recall the meaning of $\text{ann}(s, d) = Q[q]$: "a node of type $d$ is visible from node of type $s$ via generator $(s, d)$ if $child(s, d)[q]$ holds", where $child(s, d)$ is a function that for generator $(s, d)$ returns a child element type $ch$ (either $s$ or $d$) w.r.t. a DTD structure [4]. At the XML instance $T$ conforming to $D$, it means that condition $q$ may evaluate to *true* for some node instances of type $child(s, d) = ch$, while for the other $ch$ instances, it may evaluate to *false*. In the latter case, a node instance of type $d$ is not visible. Thus, at the schema level, we perform a *splitting* operation for element type $d$ into $d_Y$ (i.e. visible $d$) and $d_N$ (i.e. hidden $d$). Basically, $d_Y$ is the initial element $d$, while $d_N$ is its clone. After that, we substitute $d$ in $P(s)$ with $d_Y + d_N$.

The connection of $d_Y$ and $d_N$ with other (not equal to $s$) sources/destinations and parents/children of $d$ as follows. (1) $d_Y$ ($d_N$) transmits Y (N) to destinations $d'$ of $d$ if $\text{ann}(d, d') = \emptyset$; otherwise, it transmits $\text{ann}(d, d')$. This rule connects $d_Y$ and $d_N$ with all DTD parents (children) of $d$ in the case of bottom-up (top-down) propagation. (2) $d_Y$ ($d_N$) has the same set of children as an element type $d$ had. This rule connects $d_Y$ and $d_N$ with all children in the case of any kind of propagation. (3) After application of steps (1) and (2), the only connection with parents $p \neq s$ in the case of top-down propagation is not defined. Here, $d_Y$ ($d_N$) which is the initial $d$ (the clone of $d$) should be connected with sources of generators transmitting Y or nothing (N and nothing more).

An algorithmic description of the procedure of removing qualifiers is depicted in Fig. 2. Lines 5, 6, 7 represents the rules for connecting $d_Y$ and $d_N$ with non-equal to $s$ sources/destinations and parents/children of $d$.

Having removed qualifiers, we can define SSIs. Obviously, for the top-down propagation, SSI contains only one generator (parent-child DTD edge), and the number of SSIs is equal to the number of parents in DTD graph. However, the situation is more complicated for the bottom-up policy. First of all, every destination element type $d$ may have several children transmitting their security

---

[3] Otherwise, the policy is inconsistent.

[4] In the same way we may introduce function $parent(s, d)$ that returns parent element type w.r.t. DTD structure for a pair $(s, d)$.

**Algorithm:** QUALIFIER REMOVING
**Input:** Partially annotated DTD with qualifiers
**Output:** Partially annotated DTD without qualifiers
1: **for** every generator $(s, d)$ such that $\mathrm{ann}(s, d) = Q[q]$ **do**
2:        Create element types $d_Y$ and $d_N$;
3:        In $s \to P(s)$, substitute $d$ for $d_Y + d_N$;
4:        Set
                $\sigma(parent(s, d_Y), child(s, d_Y)) = child(s, d)[q]; \sigma(parent(s, d_N), child(s, d_N)) = child(s, d)[\neg q];$
                $\mathrm{ann}(s, d_Y) = Y; \mathrm{ann}(s, d_N) = N;$
5:        Connect $d_Y$ and $d_N$ with all destinations $d'$ of $d$:
                $\sigma(parent(d', d_Y), child(d', d_Y)) = \sigma(parent(d', d), child(d', d)) = \sigma(parent(d', d_N), child(d', d_N))$
                $\mathrm{ann}(d_Y, d') = \mathrm{ann}(d, d') = \mathrm{ann}(d, d'), \ if \ \mathrm{ann}(d, d') \neq \emptyset;$
                $\mathrm{ann}(d_Y, d') = Y; \mathrm{ann}(d_N, d') = N, \ if \ \mathrm{ann}(d, d') = \emptyset;$

                // After step 5, the next step has the meaning only for *bottom-up* policy class
6:        Connect $d_Y$ and $d_N$ with all DTD children $ch \neq s$ of $d$ setting:
                $\sigma(d_Y, ch) = \sigma(d, ch) = \sigma(d_N, ch);$
                $\mathrm{ann}(ch, d_Y) = \mathrm{ann}(ch, d) = \mathrm{ann}(ch, d_N);$

                // After step 5, the next step has the meaning only for *top-down* policy class
7:        Connect $d_Y$ $(d_N)$ with other parents $p \neq s$ of $d$ such that $\mathrm{ann}(p, d) = Y|\emptyset$ $(\mathrm{ann}(p, d) = N)$
        setting:                $\sigma(p, d_Y) = \sigma(p, d)$ $(\sigma(p, d_N) = \sigma(p, d));$
                $\mathrm{ann}(p, d_Y) = \mathrm{ann}(p, d)$ $(\mathrm{ann}(p, d_N) = \mathrm{ann}(p, d));$

**Fig. 2.** Algorithm QUALIFIER REMOVING

labels to $d$. Secondly, the number of SSIs and their components depend on the presence of choices $(\alpha + \alpha)$ in $P(A)$ (see Def. 3). The intuition is the following: we present every sequence $(\alpha, \alpha)$ of $P(A)$ as a conjunction $(\alpha \wedge \alpha)$, and every choice $(\alpha + \alpha)$ of $P(A)$ as disjunction $(\alpha \vee \alpha)$ in parenthesis. From the introduced logical expression, we construct formula $\Delta$ by removing parenthesis. The number of SSIs and their configuration is, respectively, the number of disjuncts and configuration of conjuncts in every disjunct in $\Delta$. For example, logical representation of production rule $A \to ((B|C), D)$ is $A = (B \vee C) \wedge D$ which has the following view after parenthesis removing: $B \wedge D \vee C \wedge D$. Therefore, in the case of bottom-up propagation, $A$ has two SSIs: $\{B, D\}$ and $\{C, D\}$.

Next, for every SSI, we calculate the PFA using VC option if necessary.

**Definition 10.** *We say that* $\mathrm{ann}_{\mathsf{data}}(d)$ *is steady if for every* $\overline{G}(d)$, $\mathrm{ann}_{\mathsf{data}}(d)_{\overline{G}(d)}$ *are the same and not empty. Otherwise,* $\mathrm{ann}_{\mathsf{data}}(d)$ *is* alternating.

An alternating annotation means that $d$ may obtain different annotations depending on the SSI at the XML level, while a steady annotation for $d$ means that $d$ always has the same label wherever $d$ occurs in XML document. To deal with alternating annotations, we split node as in QUALIFIER REMOVING connecting $d_Y$ $(d_N)$ with SSI of generators transmitting $Y$ $(N)$.

**Definition 11.** *We say that destination type* $d$, *such that* $\mathrm{ann}_{\mathsf{data}}(d) \neq \emptyset$, *is* closed *if for every destination type* $d' \in P_{\mathsf{ann}}(d)$, $\mathrm{ann}(d, d') \neq \emptyset$. *Otherwise,* $d$ *is* open *and for* $\forall d' \in P_{\mathsf{ann}}(d)$ *such that* $\mathrm{ann}(d, d') = \emptyset$, $d$ *retransmits annotation* $\mathrm{ann}_{\mathsf{data}}(d)$ *to* $d'$ *via generator* $(d, d')$. *Thus, we rename* $d$ *as* $s$ *and* $d'$ *as* $d$.

We assume that every initially annotated DTD element type $e$ (e.g., root or all leaves for bottom-up propagation) automatically retransmits its annotation to all generators $g = (e, d')$ such that $\mathrm{ann}(g) = \emptyset$.

The generic algorithm ANNOTATE VIEW is shown in Fig 4. It starts with a *preprocessing* procedure which is needed only for the local policy to define and

**Algorithm:** SPLIT
**Input:** DTD element type $d$ having generators with different annotations
**Output:** $d_N$
1: Create element types $d_Y$ and $d_N$;
2: **for** every SSI $\overline{G_k}(d)(k = \overline{1, n})$ having sources $\{s_1, \ldots, s_{m_k}\}$ and resulting in a PFA Y (N) of $d$
   **do**
3:     Connect source $s_i$ of every generator $g_i \in \overline{G_k}(d), i = \overline{1, m_k}$ with $d_Y$ ($d_N$) setting:
          $\sigma(parent(s_i, d_Y), child(s_i, d_Y)) = child(s_i, d) = \sigma(parent(s_i, d_N), child(s_i, d_N))$
          $\mathsf{ann}(s_i, d_Y) = \mathsf{ann}(s_i, d)(= \mathsf{Y}); \mathsf{ann}(s_i, d_N) = \mathsf{ann}(s_i, d)(= \mathsf{N});$
4: **for** every generator $g' = (d, d')$ where $d$ is a source **do**
5:     Connect $d_Y$ and $d_N$ with $d'$ setting:
          $\sigma(parent(d', d_Y), child(d', d_Y)) = child(d', d) = \sigma(parent(d', d_N), child(d', d_N))$
          $\mathsf{ann}(d_Y, d') = \mathsf{ann}(d, d') = \mathsf{ann}(d_N, d');$
6: return $d_N$;

**Fig. 3.** Algorithm SPLIT

**Algorithm:** ANNOTATE VIEW
**Input:** Partially annotated annotated DTD $D$
**Output:** Fully annotated DTD
1: Preprocessing;
2: QUALIFIER REMOVING;
3: Create empty *queue*, initialize it with all DTD element types;
4: **while** *queue* is not empty **do**
5:     $d :=$ DEQUEUE($queue$);
6:     **if** $\mathsf{ann}_{\mathsf{data}}(d) = \emptyset$ **then**
7:         **if** $d$ is not *expecting* **then**
8:             Calculate SSIs $\left\{ \overline{G_1}(d), \overline{G_2}(d), \ldots, \overline{G_n}(d) \right\}$;
9:             **for** every $\overline{G_i}(d)$ **do**
10:                Calculate $\mathsf{ann}_{\mathsf{data}}(d)_{\overline{G_i}(d)}$ (applying *value conflict resolution* policy option if
                       not for all $g \in \overline{G_i}(d)$ $\mathsf{ann}(g)$ is the same);
11:            **if** $\mathsf{ann}_{\mathsf{data}}(d)$ is *steady* **then**
12:                Assign any $\mathsf{ann}_{\mathsf{data}}(d)_{\overline{G_i}(d)}$ to $\mathsf{ann}_{\mathsf{data}}(d)$;
13:            **else if** $\mathsf{ann}(d)$ is *alternating* **then**
14:                $d_{clone} :=$ SPLIT($d$);
15:                ENQUEUE($queue, d_{clone}$);
16:            **if** $d$ is not splitted and $d$ is *open* **then**
17:                For every $d' \in P_{\mathsf{ann}}(d)$ such that $\mathsf{ann}(d, d') = \emptyset$, set $\mathsf{ann}(d, d') = \mathsf{ann}_{\mathsf{data}}(d)$;
18:        **else**
19:            ENQUEUE($queue, d$);

**Fig. 4.** Algorithm ANNOTATE VIEW

apply a default labeling for non-annotated generators. After the preprocessing and qualifier removing steps, we invoke labeling iterations via *queue* [10]: if the next considered element type $d$ has a full annotation $\mathsf{ann}_{\mathsf{data}}(d)$, there is no need to process it; otherwise, the **if** clause at line 2. If all generators of $d$ have a defined annotation, then $\mathsf{ann}_{\mathsf{data}}(d)$ is defined. If not, place $d$ back to *queue* (step 19), thus delaying definition of a full annotation of $d$ (i.e. $d$ is *expecting*).

Finally, we remove the N-labeled nodes from the fully annotated DTD. This algorithm is identical to that in [1].

*Example 2.* The left part of Fig. 5 represents an initial annotation of a DTD schema. We use top-down propagation to obtain a full annotation which is shown on the central part of Fig. 5. In particular, solid and dashed lines are generators transmitting Y and N respectively; labels on $(B, C_Y)$ and $(B, C_N)$ generators are corresponding $\sigma$-functions; for the other generators, $\sigma(x, y) = y$. Finally, the

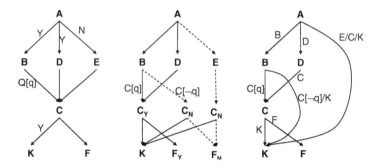

**Fig. 5.** View construction example

right part of Fig. 5 is the DTD after deletion of N-labeled nodes. Labels on edges represent corresponding $\sigma$-functions.

# 4   Query Rewriting Algorithm Description

In this section we show the algorithm for query rewriting. The query language is that of the CoreXPath of Gottlob et al. [11] augmented with the union operator and atomic tests and which is denoted by Benedict et al. [12] as $\mathcal{X}$.

**Definition 12.** *An XPath expression in $\mathcal{X}$ is defined by the following grammar:*

$$
\begin{aligned}
\langle path \rangle &::= \langle step \rangle \; (\text{`/`} \langle remaining\ path \rangle))? \\
\langle remaining\ path \rangle &::= \langle path \rangle \\
\langle step \rangle &::= \theta(\text{`[`} \langle qual \rangle \text{`]`})* \; | \; \langle path \rangle \text{`} \cup \text{`} \langle path \rangle \\
\langle qual \rangle &::= A \; | \; \text{`} * \text{`} \; | \; op\ c \; | \\
&\quad \langle qual \rangle \ and \ \langle qual \rangle \; | \; \langle qual \rangle \ or \ \langle qual \rangle \; | \\
&\quad not \ \langle qual \rangle \; | \; \text{`(`} \langle qual \rangle \text{`)`} \; | \; \langle path \rangle
\end{aligned}
$$

*where $\theta$ stands for an XPath step specification (axis :: label, where label is either label A or symbol $*$), c is a str constant, op stands for one of $=$, $\neq$, $<$, $>$, $\leq$, $\geq$; qual is called* qualifier *(or* filter*) and is denoted by q.*

The algorithm for query rewriting has two phases: query parsing and further translation of the parsed query into $\sigma$-functions. Query parsing phase implies that user query is represented as a tree of subqueries (*parse tree*) according to the grammar that we have shown in Def. 12.

The translation of the parsed query starts from the leaves of the parse tree and moves up to the root $\langle path \rangle$. In particular, for each subquery $p$ and an element $A$, the algorithm calculates $QR_{(p,A)}$ using QUERY REWRITE$(p_i, B_j)$, where $p_i$ is a direct subquery (child in a parse tree) of $p$ and $B_j$ is a node reachable from $A$ via $p_i$ in $D_v$. At the same time, the algorithm calculates $reach(p, A)$ representing the set of nodes reachable from node $A$ via the path $p$. To obtain a rewriting of the initial user query $q$, we invoke QUERY REWRITE$(q, root)$.

**Algorithm:** QUERY REWRITE
**Input:** a subquery $q$ (as a parsed XPath expression), a node $A$ for which query rewriting is carried
**Output:** rewritten subquery $q$ w.r.t. $A$ node
1: **if** $q$ is $\langle path \rangle$ **then**
    // $q = q_1/q_2$ where $q_1 = firstStep, q_2 = remainingSteps$
2:     $QR_{(q,A)} :=$ QUERY REWRITE$(q_1, A)/\bigcup_{v \in reach(q_1,A)}$ QUERY REWRITE$(q_2, v)$;
3:     $reach(q_1/q_2, A) := reach(q_1/q_2, A) \cup \bigcup_{v \in reach(q_1,A)} reach(q_2, v)$;
4: **else if** $q$ is a union of paths $\langle path \rangle$ **then**
    // $q = p_1 \cup p_2 \cup \ldots \cup p_n$
5:     $QR_{(q,A)} := \bigcup_{p_i}$ QUERY REWRITE$(p_i, A)$;
6:     $reach(q, A) = reach(q, A) \cup reach(p_i, A)$;
7: **else if** $q$ is $\theta[\langle qual \rangle]$ **then**
    // $q = q_0[filter_1] \ldots [filter_n]$ where $q_0$ is $nodeTest$
8:     $QR_{(q,A)} :=$ QUERY REWRITE$(q_0, A) \bigcup_{filter_i} [\bigcup_{v \in reach(q_0,A)}$ QUERY REWRITE$(filter_i, v)]$;
9:     $reach(q, A) := reach(q_0, A)$;
10: **else if** $q$ is $\langle qual \rangle$ **then**
    // $q = \langle qual \rangle$ from Def. 12
11:     **if** $q$ has no operands **then**
12:         $QR_{(q,A)} :=$ QUERY REWRITE$(q, A)$; // $q$ is $\langle path \rangle$
13:     **else if** $q$ has one (not) operand **then**
14:         $QR_{(q,A)} = not$ QUERY REWRITE$(q_0, A)$; // where $q_0$ is the operand;
15:     **else if** $q$ has two operands **then**
    // $q_1$ is the first operand, $q_2$ is the second operand; $op_2$ is one of and, or, $=$, $\neq$, $\geq$, $\leq$;
16:         $QR_{(q,A)} :=$ QUERY REWRITE$(q_1, A)$ $op_2$ QUERY REWRITE$(q_2, A)$;
17: **else if** $q$ is $\theta$ **then**
    // $\theta = axis :: label$
18:     **if** $axis$ is 'child' or 'parent' **then**
19:         $QR_{(q,A)} :=$ processChildParent$(label, axis, A)$;// (Fig. 8)
20:     **else if** $axis$ is 'descendant-or-self' or 'ancestor-or-self' **then**
21:         $QR_{(q,A)} :=$ processDescendAncest$(label, axis, A)$;//(Fig. 7)
22:     **else if** $axis$ is 'attribute' **then**
23:         **if** $A$ has attribute $label$ **then**
24:             $QR_{(q,A)} := q$;
25: **else if** ($q$ is literal) or ($q$ is number) **then**
26:     $QR_{(q,A)} = q$;
27: **return** $QR_{(q,A)}$;

**Fig. 6.** Algorithm QUERY REWRITE

The algorithm presented in Fig. 6 shows the translation procedure. Lines 1, 4, 7, 10, 17 distinguish whether the subexpression is $\langle path \rangle$, union of steps, node with qualifiers $\theta[\langle qual \rangle]$, qualifier $\langle qual \rangle$, and node test $\theta$ respectively.

The translation of $\langle path \rangle$, union of steps, $\theta[\langle qual \rangle]$, and $\langle qual \rangle$ is quite straightforward, and we concentrate on a processing of node test $\theta$. Since $\theta$ has a general form $axis :: label[filter_1] \ldots [filter_n]$, we have the following possibilities for rewriting:

1. $label$ is a child of $A$ in $D_v$: $rewrite(q_1, A) = \sigma(A, label)$;
2. $label$ is a parent of $A$: $rewrite(q_1, A) = \sigma^{-1}(label, A)$ (the definition of $\sigma^{-1}(B, A)$ goes below);
3. $label$ is a descendant (ancestor) of $A$: all the paths from $A$ to $label$ (from $label$ to $A$) in $D_v$ should be rewritten w.r.t. $\sigma$ ($\sigma^{-1}$)-function.

We introduce two auxiliary functions: $processChildParent$ (that captures possibilities 1 and 2) in Fig. 8 and $processDescendAncest$ (handling possibility 3) in Fig. 7. The symbol $\downarrow *$ ($\uparrow *$) is used to denote the subquery $q = descendant$-$or$-$self$ ($ancestor$-$or$-$self$).

**Algorithm:** processDescendAncest
**Input:** node $label \in \{str, *\}$, node $axis \in \{descendant\text{-}or\text{-}self, ancestor\text{-}or\text{-}self\}$, element node $A$ of $D_v$
// $p = axis::label$; $reach(\downarrow *, A)$ $(reach(\uparrow *, A))$ contain all descendants (ancestors) of $A$;
1: **if** $axis = descendant\text{-}or\text{-}self$ **then**
2:    $q := `\downarrow *$';
3: **else if** $axis = ancestor\text{-}or\text{-}self$ **then**
4:    $q := `\uparrow *$';
5: $res := \bigcup_{label \in reach(q, A)} preRewrite(q, A, label)$;
6: $reach(p, A) := reach(p, A) \cup \{label \in reach(q, A)\}$
7: **return** $res$;

**Fig. 7.** Algorithm processDescendAncest

**Algorithm:** processChildParent
**Input:** node $label \in \{str, *\}$, node $axis \in \{child, parent\}$, node $A$ of $D_v$
// $q = axis::label$
1: $reach(q, A)$ is a set of nodes that are in relation $axis$ with $A$;
2: $res := \bigcup_{label \in reach(q, A)} \max \{\sigma(A, label), \sigma^{-1}(A, label)\}$;
3: **return** $res$;

**Fig. 8.** Algorithm processChildParent

For rewriting of descendant/ancestor relations, we use the data of the statically precomputed table $preRewrite$ which contains all the rewritten paths from $A$ to all $B$ descendants/ancestors. We use a simple deep-first-search algorithm to find the union $u$ of all paths $p_i$ from $A$ to any $B$. After that, every $p_i$ of $u$ is rewritten by a call of QUERY REWRITE$(p_i, A)$. Thus, $preRewrite(\downarrow *(\uparrow *), A, B)$ is a union of rewritten paths $p_i$.

Now, consider the meaning of $\sigma^{-1}(B, A)$. $\sigma(B, A)$ is a collection of paths from $B$ to $A$ in the initial DTD $D$ such that $B$ is a parent of $A$ in $D_v$: $\sigma(B, A) := \cup_{i=1}^{k} p_i$ where each

$$p_i = c_{i_1}[f_{i_1}]/c_{i_2}[f_{i_2}]/ \ldots /c_{i_{n_i-1}}[f_{i_{n_i-1}}]/c_{i_{n_i}}[f_{i_{n_i}}]$$

with $c_{i_1}$ as the child of $B$ (since $p_i$ is applied to $B$), $c_{i_{n_i}}$ is $A$, each $c_{i_j}$ is a child of $c_{i_{j-1}}$, $f_{i_j}$ is a filter expression for the node $c_{i_j}$. Then $\sigma^{-1}(B, A)$ is defined as follows:

**Definition 13.** *The reversed representation* $\sigma^{-1}(B, A)$ *of non empty* $\sigma(B, A)$ *is* $\sigma^{-1}(B, A) := \cup_{i=1}^{k} p_i^{-1}$ *where each*

$$p_i^{-1} = self :: c_{i_{n_i}}[f_{i_{n_i}}]/parent :: c_{i_{n_i-1}}[f_{i_{n_i-1}}]/ \ldots$$
$$/parent :: c_{i_1}[f_{i_1}]/parent :: B[preRewrite(\uparrow *, B, root)]$$

*is applied to the node* $A$.

An expression $self::c_{i_{n_i}}[f_{i_{n_i}}]$ ensures that $\sigma^{-1}(B, A)$ is applied to a *permitted* $A$ node. Analogously, $parent::B$ is filtered by $[preRewrite(\uparrow *, B, root)]$ to guarantee that the user cannot reveal any additional information like in the following example:

*Example 3.* Suppose, $D_v$ contains a fragment $B \rightarrow (C, A), C \rightarrow (D, A)$; the user has an access to $B$ and $A$, but $C$ and $D$ are visible only under some condition

$Q_C$. The query $//A/parent::C/D$ may leak sensitive information if we do not restrict $C$ with an expression $[Q_C]$.

The algorithm of $\sigma^{-1}(B, A)$ calculation directly follows from Def. 13. We do not show it here for the lack of the space.

The algorithm $processChildParent$ is presented in Fig. 8. The expression $\max\{\sigma(A, B), \sigma^{-1}(B, A)\}$ in line 2 selects the non-empty element from $\sigma(A, B)$ and $\sigma^{-1}(B, A)$ (one of them is always empty, while the other is not).

*Example 4.* We use the security view of Example 2 to demonstrate our query rewriting algorithm.

**Path rewriting** :$A/B/K \rightarrow A/\sigma(A, B)/\sigma(B, K) \rightarrow A/B/C[\neg q]/K$;
**Descendant rewriting** : $A//C \rightarrow A/preRewrite(\downarrow*, A, C) \rightarrow A/(B/C \cup D/C) \rightarrow$
   $\rightarrow A/(\sigma(A, B)/\sigma(B, C) \cup \sigma(A, D)/\sigma(D, C)) \rightarrow A/(B/C[q] \cup D/C)$;
**Filter rewriting** : $A[B]/K \rightarrow A[\sigma(A, B)]/\sigma(A, K) \rightarrow A[B]/E/C/K$;
**Usage of** $\sigma^{-1}$ : $A/B//K/parent::C \rightarrow A/\sigma(A, B)/prerewrite(\downarrow*, B, K)/\sigma^{-1}(C, K) \rightarrow$
   $\rightarrow A/B/(C[q]/K \cup C[\neg q]/K)/self::K/parent::C[preRewrite(\uparrow*, C, A)] \rightarrow$
   the latter filter is rewritten as follows
   $preRewrite(\uparrow*, C, A) \rightarrow$QUERY REWRITE$(parent::B/parent::A \cup parent::D/parent::A, C) \rightarrow$
   $\rightarrow \sigma^{-1}(B, C)/\sigma^{-1}(A, B) \cup \sigma^{-1}(D, C)/\sigma^{-1}(A, D)$
   The last expression is calculated according to Def. 13.

The closest approach to query rewriting is presented by Fan et al. in [8]. The main differences are: the algorithm derives a security view without any dummy element types which may be a source of sensitive information leakage. Therefore, the $\sigma$-function used in our query rewriting has different semantics. An extended XPath fragment has *parent* and *descendant-or-self* axes. Finally, Fan et al. use dynamic programming so that $QR_{(q,A)}$ is calculated for *every* DTD element type $A$; while we perform a rewriting of $q$ w.r.t. to a *subset of relevant element types A of DTD* in a recursive manner.

## 5   Related Work and Conclusion

The mapping between existing policy frameworks and our proposal is summarized in Table 2. Note that our Y(N) label corresponds to "grant" ("deny"), + (−) of other models. The comparison of some other access control parameters is shown in Table 3.

The provisional access control model for XML documents [6] considers both top-down and bottom-up propagation. Since the rule *most specific takes precedence* (MSTP) is not used, arising conflicts are resolved by the VC option. In the case of the presence of unresolved conflicts or unlabeled nodes, a special *default* option (Y or N) is applied. The policy is evaluated at the stage of query answering (we marked it in Table 3 as "policy evaluation" (PE)). If access to the requested node is permitted, the user receives "weak" XML view, where N-labeled nodes having Y-children are revealed without their attributes.

**Table 2.** Existing policy frameworks

| Method | HP | LP | SC | VC | MSTP | default |
|---|---|---|---|---|---|---|
| Kudo et al. [6] | * | none | hf | * | No | Yes ($\neq$none) |
| Murata et al. [13] | td ind. | * ind. | none | dtp | No | Yes (closed) |
| Gabillon et al. [5] | td ind. | * ind. | none | priority, order | No | Yes ($\neq$none) |
| Damiani et al. [3] | td ind. | * ind. | none | dtp | Yes | Yes (closed) |
| Bertino et al. [4] | td ind. | * ind. | none | dtp | Yes | Yes (closed) |
| Cho et al. [14] | td ind. | * ind. | none | dtp | No | Yes (open) |
| Fan et al. [8] | td | none | $\neq$lf | none | Yes | No |
| Our method | * | * | * | * | Yes | No |

**Table 3.** Existing XML access control frameworks

| Method | XML view | DTD view | Query asking over | Query answering by |
|---|---|---|---|---|
| [6] | Yes (weak) | No | initial XML | policy evaluation (PE) |
| [13] | No | No | initial XML/DTD | rewriting, PE |
| [5] | Yes (weak) | No | XML view | XPath evaluation |
| [3] | Yes (weak) | Yes (loosened) | XML/DTD view | XPath evaluation |
| [4] | Yes | No | XML view | XPath evaluation |
| [14] | No | No | initial XML/DTD | rewriting, PE |
| Stoica et al. [7] | No | Yes | - | - |
| [8] | No | Yes | DTD view | safe rewriting |
| Our method | Yes | Yes | DTD/XML view | safe rewriting |

The proposal of Murata et al. [13] defines for every XML node an individual label which is propagated either in hierarchical (td) or in local manner (in the Table 2, it is marked as "ind."). An additional *denial downward consistency* (DDC) policy is introduced: a subtree rooted at N-labeled node has only N-labeled descendants. The method rewrites (using DTD if exists) the query $q$ posed over the initial XML/DTD so that to minimize the need in PE during query answering.

Gabilon et al. [5] differs from [13] in that the VC resolution is based on a *priority* associated with every access control rule. In the case of multiple rules with the same priority, the last rule in *XML Authorization Sheet* (i.e., the list of access rules) is elected. In this method, PE is used to construct an XML view. Thus, the query evaluation is simply an XPath evaluation over the XML view.

Damiani's et al. [3] proposal partially annotates the DTD schema or an XML instance by Y|N labels which are, then, propagated. The notions of *soft* and *hard* authorizations define the precedence of DTD label over XML label and viceversa. However, this subtlety can be captured by qualifiers of our proposal. Next, the fully annotated schema/instance is pruned. The method considers the XML view in "weak" form and the DTD view in "loosened" form, i.e., every forbidden element has cardinality "optional".

A similar policy enforcement mechanism is used in Author-X system [4]. The differences with the previous approach are (i) the absolute precedence of DTD labels over XML labels, (ii) the presence of an additional option ONE_LEVEL of the HP (td), and (iii) the construction of an XML view without any N-labeled nodes. However, the DTD view is not available for user.

In [14], the DTD/XML is annotated by *mandatory* (i.e., all instances of the element in XML tree *must* specify their security level, DTD may specify a default value), *optional* (instances *may* specify their security level) and *forbidden* (instance labeling is inherited or Y) labels. We treat this framework in the following way: mandatory (optional) specification is Y|N (∗, respectively) label with local propagation, forbidden specification is a label defined via HP (td) propagation, and the default policy is "open". Like in [13], the approach minimizes the need in policy evaluation during query answering by a special query rewriting.

The method of Stoica et al. [7] takes as an input a fully annotated DTD from which the DTD view is derived. There is no discussion of policy propagation and conflict resolution in [7], thus we do not introduce this method in Table 2. In addition, neither XML view nor query evaluation is considered.

The proposal of Fan et al. [8] has the similar notion of the initial DTD annotation as in this paper. However, the range of policies is restricted to the *top-down* policy. Moreover, the paper does not consider XML view construction, but discusses a *safe query rewriting* when the query over the DTD view is translated into the equivalent query over the initial DTD and the rewritten query is evaluated over the initial XML data. Hence, policy evaluation is used for DTD view construction instead of query answering. Furthermore, the safe rewriting of queries excludes system answers "access denied" which are presented, for example, in [6], [13], [14]. Thus, the information leakage is diminished.

As it may be seen from Table 3, our proposal comprises both the XML view (not "weak") and the DTD view (not "loosened"). Moreover, we use safe query rewriting to eliminate denial of service. In addition, we provide an extended range of policy classes (see Table 2). However, there are directions for future work. First of all, we plan to investigate the compatibility of our proposal with others. For example, one of the closest policy framework is that of Kudo et al. [6]. Hence, we plan to investigate whether XML security views can be integrated into Provisional Authorization Architecture. Secondly, XML access control models of [13], [5], [3], [4] showed a possibility of an individual policy configuration, i.e. for every node. Next, in this paper, we have introduced a notion of generator, i.e., a DTD edge which, in essence, may by generalized to a path in an undirected graph isomorphic to a given DTD graph. However, we leave this generalization for future work as well. Finally, an extended experimental evaluation is required.

## Acknowledgments

I would like to thank Gabriel Kuper and Fabio Massacci for encouragement and many useful discussions, and Gabriel Kuper, in particular, for checking my English.

# References

1. Kuper, G., Massacci, F., Rassadko, N.: Generalized XML security views. In: SACMAT '05: Proceedings of the tenth ACM symposium on Access control models and technologies, New York, NY, USA, ACM Press (2005) 77–84
2. Lunt, T.F., Denning, D.E., Schell, R.R., Heckman, M., Shockley, W.R.: The SeaView security model. IEEE Trans. Softw. Eng. 16(6) (1990) 593–607
3. Damiani, E., De Capitani di Vimercati, S., Paraboschi, S., Samarati, P.: A fine-grained access control system for xml documents. ACM Trans. Inf. Syst. Secur. 5(2) (2002) 169–202
4. Bertino, E., Braun, M., Castano, S., Ferrari, E., Mesiti, M.: Author-X: A Java-based system for XML data protection. In: Proceedings of the IFIP TC11/WG11.3 Fourteenth Annual Working Conference on Database and Application Security, Deventer, The Netherlands, The Netherlands, Kluwer, B.V. (2001) 15–26
5. Gabillon, A., Bruno, E.: Regulating access to XML documents. In: Proceedings of the IFIP TC11/WG11.3 fifteenth annual working conference on Database and application security, Norwell, MA, USA, Kluwer Academic Publishers (2002) 299–314
6. Kudo, M., Hada, S.: XML document security based on provisional authorization. In: CCS '00: Proceedings of the 7th ACM conference on Computer and communications security, New York, NY, USA, ACM Press (2000) 87–96
7. Stoica, A., Farkas, C.: Secure XML views. In: Proceedings of the IFIP TC11/WG11.3 Sixteenth International Conference on Data and Applications Security. Volume 256., Kluwer (2003) 133–146
8. Fan, W., Chan, C.Y., Garofalakis, M.: Secure xml querying with security views. In: SIGMOD '04: Proceedings of the 2004 ACM SIGMOD international conference on Management of data, New York, NY, USA, ACM Press (2004) 587–598
9. Samarati, P., De Capitani di Vimercati, S.: Access control: Policies, models, and mechanisms. In: FOSAD '00: Revised versions of lectures given during the IFIP WG 1.7 International School on Foundations of Security Analysis and Design on Foundations of Security Analysis and Design, London, UK, Springer-Verlag (2001) 137–196
10. Cormen, T.H., Stein, C., Rivest, R.L., Leiserson, C.E.: Introduction to Algorithms. McGraw-Hill Higher Education (2001)
11. Gottlob, G., Koch, C., Pichler, R.: Efficient algorithms for processing XPath queries. ACM Trans. Database Syst. 30(2) (2005) 444–491
12. Benedikt, M., Fan, W., Kuper, G.M.: Structural properties of XPath fragments. In: ICDT '03: Proceedings of the 9th International Conference on Database Theory, London, UK, Springer-Verlag (2002) 79–95
13. Murata, M., Tozawa, A., Kudo, M., Hada, S.: XML access control using static analysis. In: CCS '03: Proceedings of the 10th ACM conference on Computer and communications security, New York, NY, USA, ACM Press (2003) 73–84
14. Cho, S., Amer-Yahia, S., Lakshmanan, L., Srivastava, D.: Optimizing the secure evaluation of twig queries. In: VLDB '02: Proceedings of the 28th International Conference on Very Large Data Bases. (2002) 490–501

# Interactive Analysis of Attack Graphs
# Using Relational Queries⋆

Lingyu Wang[1], Chao Yao[1], Anoop Singhal[2], and Sushil Jajodia[1]

[1] Center for Secure Information Systems
George Mason University
Fairfax, VA 22030-4444, USA
{lwang3, cyao, jajodia}@gmu.edu
[2] Computer Security Division, NIST
Gaithersburg, MD 20899, USA
anoop.singhal@nist.gov

**Abstract.** Attack graph is important in defending against well-orchestrated net-work intrusions. However, the current analysis of attack graphs requires an al-gorithm to be developed and implemented, causing a delay in the availability of analysis. Such a delay is usually unacceptable because the needs for analyzing attack graphs may change rapidly in defending against network intrusions. An administrator may want to revise an analysis upon observing its outcome. Such an *interactive* analysis, similar to that in decision support systems, is difficult if at all possible with current approaches based on proprietary algorithms. This paper removes the above limitation and enables interactive analysis of attack graphs. We devise a relational model for representing necessary inputs including net-work configuration and domain knowledge. We generate the attack graph from those inputs as relational views. We then show that typical analyses of the attack graph can be realized as relational queries against the views. Our approach elimi-nates the needs for developing a proprietary algorithm for each different analysis, because an analysis is now simply a relational query. The interactive analysis of attack graphs is now possible, because relational queries can be dynamically con-structed and revised at run time. Moreover, the mature optimization techniques in relational databases can also improve the performance of the analysis.

## 1 Introduction

As the result of topological vulnerability analysis, an *attack graph* describes all possible sequences of exploits an attacker can follow to advance an intrusion [16,18,1]. Attack graphs have been explored for different purposes in defending against network intru-sions. First, an attack graph can more clearly reveal the weakness of a network than

---

⋆ This material is based upon work supported by National Institute of Standards and Tech-nology Computer Security Division; by Homeland Security Advanced Research Projects Agency under the contract FA8750-05-C-0212 administered by the Air Force Research Labo-ratory/Rome; by Army Research Office under grants DAAD19-03-1-0257 and W911NF-05-1-0374, by Federal Aviation Administration under the contract DTFAWA-04-P-00278/0001, and by the National Science Foundation under grants IIS-0242237 and IIS-0430402. Any opin-ions, findings, and conclusions or recommendations expressed in this material are those of the authors and do not necessarily reflect the views of the sponsoring organizations.

E. Damiani and P. Liu (Eds.): Data and Applications Security 2006, LNCS 4127, pp. 119–132, 2006.

individual vulnerability does by providing the *context* of attacks. Second, attack graphs can indicate available options in removing identified weaknesses and help administrators to choose an optimal solution. Third, the knowledge encoded in attack graphs can also be used to correlate isolated alerts into probable attack scenarios.

However, many current approaches to the analysis of attack graphs share a common limitation. That is, a proprietary algorithm must be developed and implemented before the corresponding analysis becomes possible. Standard graph-related algorithms usually do not apply here due to unique characteristics of attack graphs. However, the delay in the analysis of attack graphs is usually unacceptable for defending against network intrusions. The needs for analyzing an attack graph usually change rapidly due to constantly changing threats and network configurations. An administrator may need to modify an analysis after the results of that analysis are observed. Such an *interactive analysis*, similar to that in decision support systems, is difficult if at all possible with current approaches based on proprietary algorithms.

In this paper, we provide a solution to the interactive analysis of attack graphs. First, we represent in the relational model the necessary inputs including network configuration and domain knowledge. We then generate the attack graph using relational queries, which can either be materialized as relations or simply left as the definition of relational views. The latter case is especially suitable for large networks where materializing the complete attack graph can be prohibitive. Second, we show how typical analyses of attack graphs can be realized as relational queries. The interactive analysis of attack graphs is now possible, because administrators can immediately pose new queries based on the outcome of previous analyses. Finally, as a side-benefit, the performance of an analysis can usually be transparently improved by the mature optimization techniques available in most relational databases.

The rest of this paper is organized as follows. The next section reviews related work. Section 3 proposes a relational model for representing the attack graph. Section 4 then discusses how typical analyses can be written as relational queries. Section 5 describes our implementation of the proposed methods. Finally, Section 6 concludes the paper and gives future direction.

## 2   Related Work

Attack graphs represent the knowledge about the inter-dependency between vulnerabilities [6,21,14,4,13,16,19,17,1,18,8]. Model checking was first used to decide whether a goal state is reachable from the initial state [16,15] and later used to enumerate all possible sequences of attacks connecting the two states [18,9]. However, the number of attack sequences is potentially exponential, leading to high complexity. A more compact representation was thus proposed based on the *monotonicity assumption* (that is, an attacker never relinquishes an obtained capability) [1]. The new representation keeps exactly one vertex for each exploit or condition, leading to attack graphs of polynomial size.

Analyses of attack graphs have been used for different purposes in defending against network intrusions [18,9,12,11,20]. The *minimal critical attack set* analysis finds a minimal subset of attacks whose removal prevents attackers from reaching the goal state [18,9]. However, the attacks in a minimal critical attack set are not necessarily independent, and a consequence cannot be removed without removing its causes. This observation leads to the *minimum-cost hardening* solution, which is a minimal set of independent security conditions [12]. Finding the minimum set of attacks leading to given goals is computationally infeasible, whereas a minimal set can be found in polynomial time [18,9,1]. All attacks involved in at least one of such minimal sets of attacks can also be enumerated [1]. Finally, in *exploit-centric alert correlation* [11,20], attack graphs assist the correlation of isolated intrusion alerts.

The afore-mentioned analysis of attack graphs is largely based on proprietary algorithms. However, as mentioned earlier, this may delay a new analysis and make interactive analysis impossible. To our best knowledge, our study is the first to remove this limitation and to enable interactive analysis of attack graphs. On the other hand, decision support systems, such as on-line analytical processing (OLAP) [7], have been used for interactive analysis of data for a long time. However, an analyst there is usually interested in generalized data and statistical patterns, which is different from the analysis of attack graphs.

## 3    A Relational Model for Representing Attack Graphs

Section 3.1 reviews the basic concept of attack graph. Section 3.2 then proposes a relational model for representing attack graphs as relational views.

### 3.1    Attack Graph

The attack graph is usually visualized as a directed graph having two type of vertices, *exploits* and *security conditions* (or simply *conditions*). An exploit is a triple $(h_s, h_d, v)$, where $h_s$ and $h_d$ are two connected hosts and $v$ is a vulnerability on the destination host $h_d$. A security condition is a pair $(h, c)$ indicating the host $h$ satisfies a condition $c$ relevant to security (both exploits and conditions may involve more hosts, for which our model can be easily extended).

An attack graph has two types of edges denoting the inter-dependency between exploits and conditions. First, the *require* relation is a directed edge pointing from a condition to an exploit. The edge means the exploit cannot be executed unless the condition is satisfied. Second, the *imply* relation points from an exploit to a condition. This means executing the exploit will satisfy the condition. Notice that there is no edge between exploits (or conditions). Example 1 illustrates the concept of attack graph.

*Example 1.* The left-hand side of Figure 1 depicts our running example of attack graph. The right-hand side shows a simplified version where $x$ denotes the existence of a vulnerability *SADMIND BUFFER OVERFLOW* (Nessus ID 11841), $y$ the user privilege, and $A$ the exploitation of that vulnerability. The attack graph shows an attacker having user privilege on host 3 can exploit the vulnerability on hosts 1 and 2 and obtain user privilege on the hosts.

Two important aspects of attack graphs are as follows. First, the require relation is always *conjunctive* whereas the imply relation is always *disjunctive*. More specifically, an exploit cannot be realized until *all* of its required conditions have been satisfied,

**Attack Graph (Exploits As Ovals)        Simplified Version (Exploits As Triplets)**

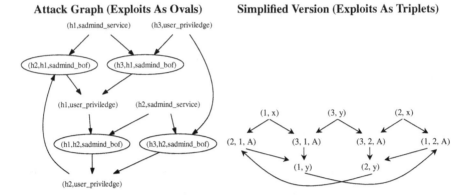

**Fig. 1.** An Example of Attack Graph

whereas a condition can be satisfied by any *one* of the realized exploits. Second, the conditions are further classified as *initial* conditions (the conditions not implied by any exploit) and *intermediate* conditions. An initial condition can be independently disabled to harden a network, whereas an intermediate condition usually cannot be [12].

### 3.2 A Relational Model for Attack Graphs

The complete attack graph is not explicitly represented in our model, but left as the result of a relational query. The result to the query may be materialized, or the query can simply be left as a view. Such flexibility is important to large networks where materializing the complete attack graph may be prohibitive. We model two inputs, the *network configuration* (vulnerabilities and connectivity of the network) and the *domain knowledge* (the interdependency between exploits and conditions), as illustrated in Example 2. The domain knowledge is available in tools like the Topological Vulnerability Analysis (TVA) system, which covers more than 37,000 vulnerabilities taken from 24 information sources including X-Force, Bugtraq, CVE, CERT, Nessus, and Snort [8]. On the other hand, the configuration information including vulnerabilities and connectivity can be easily obtained with tools such as the Nessus scanner [5].

*Example 2.* Figure 2 depicts the network configuration and domain knowledge required for generating the attack graph in Example 1. The left-hand side shows the connectivity between the three hosts, and initially hosts 1 and 2 satisfy the condition $x$ and host 3 satisfies $y$. The right-hand side says that an attacker can exploit the vulnerability $A$ on the destination (denoted by the symbol $D$) host, if it satisfies $x$ and the source host satisfies $y$ at the same time. This exploitation will then satisfy $y$ on the destination host.

Definition 1 defines the schema of our model. The connectivity relation represents the connectivity from each the source host $H_s$ to the destination host $H_d$. The condition relation indicates a host $H$ having an initial condition $C$. The condition-vulnerability dependency relation indicates a condition $C$ is required for exploiting a vulnerability $V$ on the destination host. The attribute $F$ indicates whether the condition $C$ belongs to the source ($S$) or the destination ($D$) host. The vulnerability-condition dependency relation indicates a condition $C$ is satisfied by exploiting a vulnerability $V$.

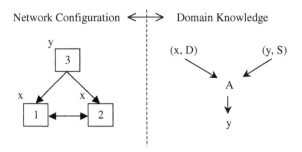

**Fig. 2.** An Example of Network Configuration and Domain Knowledge

The last three relations together with the condition relation are required for representing the complete attack graph (those relations may or may not need to be materialized). The vertices are conditions (the relation $HC$) and exploits (the relation $EX$), and the edges interconnect them are represented by relations $CE$ and $EC$. Each relation has a composite key composed of all the attributes in that relation. Example 3 shows the relational model of Example 2.

**Definition 1.** *Define the following relational schemata:*

**Connectivity** $HH = (H_s, H_d)$
**Condition** $HC = (H, C)$
**Condition-Vulnerability Dependency** $CV = (C, F, V)$
**Vulnerability-Condition Dependency** $VC = (V, C)$
**Exploit** $EX = (H_s, H_d, V)$
**Condition-Exploit** $CE = (H, C, H_s, H_d, V)$
**Exploit-Condition** $EC = (H_s, H_d, V, H, C)$

*Example 3.* Table 1 describes a relational model composed of four relations, which precisely represents Example 2.

**Table 1.** Representing Network Configuration and Domain Knowledge in Relational Model

| hh(HH) | | hc(HC) | | cv(CV) | | | vc(VC) | |
|---|---|---|---|---|---|---|---|---|
| $H_s$ | $H_d$ | H | C | C | F | V | V | C |
| 1 | 2 | 3 | y | x | D | A | A | y |
| 2 | 1 | 1 | x | y | S | A | | |
| 3 | 1 | 2 | x | | | | | |
| 3 | 2 | | | | | | | |

# 4  Analyzing Attack Graphs with Relational Queries

We first show how the complete attack graph can be generated using relational queries based on our model in Section 4.1. We then realize typical analyses of attack graphs as relational queries in Section 4.2.

## 4.1    Generating Attack Graphs Using Relational Queries

We regard the generation of the complete attack graph from given network configuration and domain knowledge as a special analysis, and we show how to conduct this analysis using relational queries. First, Example 4 illustrates a generation procedure similar to that in [1].

*Example 4.* Given the network configuration and domain knowledge in Example 2, the attack graph in Figure 1 can be generated by an iterative procedure as follows. Initially, the attack graph only includes the three initial conditions $(1, x)$, $(3, y)$, $(2, x)$ as vertices. First, domain knowledge implies that the conditions $(1, x)$ and $(3, y)$ jointly imply the exploit $(3, 1, A)$, and $(2, x)$ and $(3, y)$ jointly imply $(3, 2, A)$. Second, the two conditions $(1, y)$ and $(2, y)$ are satisfied. Next, we repeat the above two steps with the two new conditions and insert four more edges between $(1, y)$, $(2, y)$ and the two exploits. The process then terminates because no new conditions are inserted in the second iteration.

The key challenge in realizing the above procedure using relational queries lies in the conjunctive nature of the require relation. More specifically, an exploit cannot be realized unless *all* the required conditions are satisfied. In contrast, the imply relation can be easily realized using a join operation, since a condition can be satisfied by any *one* of the realized exploits. We deal with this issue with two set-difference operations as follows (similar to the division operation in relational algebra). Intuitively, we first subtract (that is, set difference) the satisfied conditions from the conditions required by all possible exploits. The result includes all the unsatisfied but required conditions, from which we can derive the exploits that cannot be realized. Then we subtract the unrealizable exploits from all possible exploits to derive those that can indeed be realized.

Definition 2 states the relational queries corresponding to each iteration of the procedure illustrated in Example 4. In the definition, $Q_1$ and $Q_2$ are intermediate results (we shall use subscripts in numbers to denote intermediate results) of satisfied and unsatisfied conditions up to this iteration, respectively. The vertices of the attack graph are $Q_e$ and $Q_c$, which are realized exploits and satisfied conditions, respectively. The fourth and fifth relation jointly compose the edge set. The set union operations do not keep duplicates, and hence this process always terminates. Example 5 illustrates those queries.

**Definition 2.** *Given $hh(HH)$, $hc(HC)$, $cv(CV)$, and $vc(VC)$, let $Q_c = hc$, and let $Q_e(EX)$, $Q_{ce}(CE)$, $Q_{ec}(EC)$ be empty relations, define queries*

- $Q_1 = \sigma_{H_s=H \vee H_d=H}(hh \times \Pi_V(vc) \times hc)$
- $Q_2 = \Pi_{H_s,H_d,V,H_d,C}(hh \times \sigma_{F=D}(cv)) \cup \Pi_{H_s,H_d,V,H_s,C}(hh \times \sigma_{F=S}(cv)) - Q_1$
- $Q_e = (\Pi_{H_s,H_d,V}(hh \times cv) - \Pi_{H_s,H_d,V}(Q_2)) \cup Q_e$
- $Q_{ce} = \Pi_{H_d,C,H_s,H_d,V}(Q_e \times \sigma_{F=D}(cv)) \cup \Pi_{H_s,C,H_s,H_d,V}(Q_e \times \sigma_{F=S}(cv)) \cup Q_{ce}$
- $Q_{ec} = \Pi_{H_s,H_d,V,H_d,C}(\sigma_{Q_e.V=vc.V}(Q_e \times vc)) \cup Q_{ec}$
- $Q_c = \Pi_{H,C}(Q_{ec}) \cup Q_c$

*Example 5.* Table 2 shows the result to each query in the first iteration in generating the attack graph of Example 1. The relation $Q_1$ are the satisfied conditions and their

**Table 2.** An Example of One Iteration in Deriving the Complete Attack Graph

**$Q_1$**

| $H_s$ | $H_d$ | $V$ | $H$ | $C$ |
|---|---|---|---|---|
| 1 | 2 | A | 1 | x |
| 1 | 2 | A | 2 | x |
| 2 | 1 | A | 1 | x |
| 2 | 1 | A | 2 | x |
| 3 | 1 | A | 1 | x |
| 3 | 1 | A | 3 | y |
| 3 | 2 | A | 2 | x |
| 3 | 2 | A | 3 | y |

**$Q_2$**

| $H_s$ | $H_d$ | $V$ | $H$ | $C$ |
|---|---|---|---|---|
| 1 | 2 | A | 1 | y |
| 2 | 1 | A | 2 | y |

**$Q_e$**

| $H_s$ | $H_d$ | $V$ |
|---|---|---|
| 3 | 1 | A |
| 3 | 2 | A |

**$Q_{ce}$**

| $H$ | $C$ | $H_s$ | $H_d$ | $V$ |
|---|---|---|---|---|
| 1 | x | 3 | 1 | A |
| 2 | x | 3 | 2 | A |
| 3 | y | 3 | 1 | A |
| 3 | y | 3 | 2 | A |

**$Q_{ec}$**

| $H_s$ | $H_d$ | $V$ | $H$ | $C$ |
|---|---|---|---|---|
| 3 | 1 | A | 1 | y |
| 3 | 2 | A | 2 | y |

**$Q_c$**

| $H$ | $C$ |
|---|---|
| 1 | y |
| 2 | y |

related (but not necessarily realizable) vulnerabilities. Subtracting those from the conditions required by all possible exploits yields the two unsatisfied conditions and the unrealizable exploits in $Q_2$. Then, subtracting the unrealizable exploits from all possible exploits gives the two realizable exploits in $Q_e$. The exploits then imply the two conditions in $Q_c$. The edges in $Q_{ce}$ and $Q_{ec}$ interconnect the conditions and exploits.

### 4.2   Typical Analyses of Attack Graphs in Relational Queries

We now turn to typical analyses of attack graphs previously studied in the literature. We show how to rewrite those analyses as relational queries based on our model. In the following discussion, our queries are against the relations (or views) given by Definition 2.

*Vulnerability-Centric Alert Correlation and Prediction.* The alert correlation method first maps a currently received intrusion alert to the corresponding exploit. Then, it reasons about previous exploits (alerts) that prepare for the current one and possible exploits in the future [20]. The key difference between this analysis and the one used to generate the attack graph is that the conjunctive nature of the require relation should be ignored here. The relationship between alerts is usually regarded as *casual* instead of logical [10,3]. Such a conservative approach is more appropriate in this context because alerts may have been missed by intrusion detection systems.

*Example 6.* In Figure 1, suppose the current alert maps to the exploit $(2, 1, A)$. The backward search will first reach conditions $(1, x)$ and $(2, y)$ and then follows $(2, y)$ to $(3, 2, A)$ and $(1, 2, A)$ to find a previous correlated alert if there is any, or to make a hypothesis for a missing alert, otherwise. The search continues from $(1, 2, A)$ to $(1, y)$ and $(2, x)$, then from $(1, y)$ to $(3, 1, A)$ (the branch to $(2, 1, A)$ is a loop and hence ignored) and consequently to $(1, x)$ and $(3, y)$. The search stops when it reaches only initial conditions or if a loop is encountered.

Definition 3 states the relational queries corresponding to the backward search in Example 6. The forward search can be realized in a similar way and hence is omitted. First, the relation $Q_3$ includes the conditions reachable from the current exploits while ignoring the conjunctive relationship between those conditions. Second, subtracting from $Q_3$ the initial conditions in $hc$ and the previously visited conditions in $Q_5$ (to avoid loops) yields the reachable conditions and consequently the exploits in $Q_4$. The above two steps are repeated until no more conditions are left (that is, all the conditions are in $hc$ or in $Q_5$). The exploits encountered in this process are collected in $Q_A$ as the final result. Loops are avoided in this process because the set union operation does not keep duplicates and the relation $Q_5$ ensures each condition to be visited at most once.

**Definition 3.** *Given* $hh(HH)$, $hc(HC)$, $cv(CV)$, $vc(VC)$, *and* $(h_s, h_d, V)$, *let* $Q_3(HC)$, $Q_5$, *and* $Q_A$ *be empty relations and* $Q_4(EX) = \{(h_s, h_d, V)\}$. *Define*

- $Q_3 = \Pi_{h_d,C}(Q_4 \bowtie \sigma_{F=D}(cv)) \cup \Pi_{h_s,C}(Q_4 \bowtie \sigma_{F=S}(cv))$
- $Q_4 = \Pi_{H_s,H_d,V}(\sigma_{H_d=H \wedge Q_3.C=vc.C}(hh \times (Q_3 - hc - Q_5) \times vc))$
- $Q_5 = Q_5 \cup Q_3$
- $Q_A = Q_A \cup Q_4$

*Example 7.* Table 3 shows the three iterations corresponding to the backward search in Example 6. The first iteration starts from the given exploit $(2,1,A)$ and reaches two exploits $(1,2,A)$ and $(3,2,A)$ through the condition $(2,y)$. The second iteration reaches $(3,1,A)$ and $(2,1,A)$ through $(1,y)$. The exploit $(2,1,A)$ leads to two previously visited conditions (that is, a loop) and the other exploit $(3,1,A)$ reaches only initial conditions. Consequently, no new exploit appears in $Q_4$ in this iteration and the search terminates.

*Enumerating Relevant Attacks and Network Hardening.* Enumerating the *relevant* exploits (those appears in at least one sequence of attacks leading to the goal conditions [1]) and finding a *network hardening* solution (given goal conditions represented as a logic formula of initial conditions [12]) share a similar backward search in the attack graph, as illustrated in Example 8 and Example 9, respectively.

*Example 8.* In Figure 1, we start from a given goal condition $(1,y)$ and search backwards in the attack graph. First, the two exploits $(3,1,A)$ and $(2,1,A)$ are reached. The former branch ends at initial conditions, and the latter leads to one initial condition $(1,x)$ and an intermediate condition $(2,y)$. The condition $(2,y)$ then leads to $(3,2,A)$ and $(1,2,A)$. The former ends at initial conditions, and the latter leads to a loop back to $(1,y)$. The relevant exploits with respect to the goal condition $(1,y)$ are thus $(2,1,A)$, $(3,1,A)$, and $(3,2,A)$ (the exploit $(1,2,A)$ is not relevant because it can never be realized before satisfying the goal $(1,y)$ itself).

*Example 9.* With a similar search, we can transform the goal condition $(1,y)$ into a logic formula of initial conditions as follows (by regarding the exploits and conditions as Boolean variables). In the fourth line, the value $FALSE$ replaces the second appearance of the goal condition $(1,y)$, because it is a predecessor of $(1,2,A)$, indicating a loop. The final result says that if any of the two conditions $(1,x)$ and $(3,y)$ is disabled, then the goal can no longer be satisfied.

**Table 3.** An Example of Analyzing Attack Graphs for Alert Correlation and Prediction

First Iteration

$Q_3$

| H | C |
|---|---|
| 1 | x |
| 2 | y |

$Q_4$

| $H_s$ | $H_d$ | V |
|---|---|---|
| 1 | 2 | A |
| 3 | 2 | A |

$Q_5$

| H | C |
|---|---|
| 1 | x |
| 2 | y |

$Q_A$

| $H_s$ | $H_d$ | V |
|---|---|---|
| 1 | 2 | A |
| 3 | 2 | A |

Second Iteration

$Q_3$

| H | C |
|---|---|
| 1 | y |
| 2 | x |
| 3 | y |

$Q_4$

| $H_s$ | $H_d$ | V |
|---|---|---|
| 3 | 1 | A |
| 2 | 1 | A |

$Q_5$

| H | C |
|---|---|
| 1 | x |
| 2 | y |
| 1 | y |
| 2 | x |
| 3 | y |

$Q_A$

| $H_s$ | $H_d$ | V |
|---|---|---|
| 1 | 2 | A |
| 3 | 2 | A |
| 3 | 1 | A |
| 2 | 1 | A |

Third Iteration

$Q_3$

| H | C |
|---|---|
| 1 | x |
| 3 | y |
| 2 | y |

$Q_4 = \phi$

$Q_5$

| H | C |
|---|---|
| 1 | x |
| 2 | y |
| 1 | y |
| 2 | x |
| 3 | y |

$Q_A$

| $H_s$ | $H_d$ | V |
|---|---|---|
| 1 | 2 | A |
| 3 | 2 | A |
| 3 | 1 | A |
| 2 | 1 | A |

$$
\begin{aligned}
(1, y) &\equiv (3, 1, A) \vee (2, 1, A) \\
&\equiv (1, x) \wedge (3, y) \vee (1, x) \wedge (2, y) \\
&\equiv (1, x) \wedge (3, y) \vee (1, x) \wedge ((3, 2, A) \vee (1, 2, A)) \\
&\equiv (1, x) \wedge (3, y) \vee (1, x) \wedge ((3, y) \wedge (2, x) \vee (2, x) \wedge FALSE) \\
&\equiv (1, x) \wedge (3, y)
\end{aligned}
$$

The key differences between the above backward search and that used for correlating alerts are as follows. First, the conjunctive nature of the require relation must be considered. In Example 8, the exploit $(1, 2, A)$ is not relevant, because one of its required conditions $(1, y)$ is not satisfiable, even though the other required condition (that is, $(2, x)$) is already satisfied. Second, duplicate appearances of exploits and conditions must be kept. This is required for obtaining sequences of relevant exploits leading to the goal, as well as for generating the logic formula in network hardening. In the former case, different sequences may share common exploits or conditions, whereas the logic formula in the second case clearly contains duplicates. In order for the search to traverse an exploit or condition for multiple times, the set union operation needs to keep duplicates. Hence, loops must be avoided by maintaining a predecessor list for each vertex as in standard breadth-first search (BFS) [2] (although the search discussed above is different from a BFS).

Definition 4 states the relational queries used to enumerate relevant exploits or to generate the logic formula in network hardening. The two queries simply traverse the attack graph given by Definition 2. The two relations in the definition keep duplicates in set union operations. Notice that the actual construction of the logic formula (adding the *and* and *or* connectives) is external to the relational queries and can easily be incorporated.

**Definition 4.** *Given relations* $hh(HH)$, $hc(HC)$, $cv(CV)$, $vc(VC)$ *and a non-empty relation* $Q_7(HC)$, *let* $Q_6(EX)$ *be an empty relation. Define*

- $Q_6 = \Pi_{H_s,H_d,V}((Q_7 - hc) \bowtie Q_{ec})$
- $Q_7 = \Pi_{H,C}(Q_6 \bowtie Q_{ce})$

*Example 10.* Table 4 shows the iterations corresponding to the procedure in Example 8 and Example 9. Originally, $Q_7 = \{(1,y)\}$.

**Table 4.** An Example of Enumerating Relevant Exploits and Network Hardenning

First Iteration    **Q₆**       **Q₇**

| $H_s$ | $H_d$ | $V$ |
|-------|-------|-----|
| 3 | 1 | A |
| 2 | 1 | A |

| H | C |
|---|---|
| 1 | x |
| 2 | y |
| 1 | x |
| 3 | y |

Second Iteration    **Q₆**       **Q₇**

| $H_s$ | $H_d$ | $V$ |
|-------|-------|-----|
| 3 | 2 | A |

| H | C |
|---|---|
| 3 | y |
| 2 | x |

*Reachability From Subsets of Initial Conditions and Incremental Updates of Attack Graphs.* Many analyses ask a similar question, that is whether the goal condition is still satisfiable, if a given subset of initial conditions are disabled. The question may arise when we need to determine the potential effect of enforcing a security measure (so some initial conditions will be disabled), or when we want to decide whether the goal condition is reachable with only stealthy attacks [18]. The question may also be asked simply because the network configuration has changed and some initial conditions are no longer satisfied (on the other hand, new initial conditions can be easily handled with more iterations of the queries in Definition 2.) In each case, we can certainly recompute the attack graph from scratches, with the given conditions removed from the relation $hc$. However, this is not desired especially when the attack graph is much larger than the set of conditions to be disabled. Instead, we should incrementally update the attack graph by computing the effect of disabling the given conditions. The conjunctive nature of the require relation must be taken into accounts, but in a different way, as illustrated in Example 11.

*Example 11.* In Figure 1, suppose the condition $(2,x)$ is disabled. Then the exploits $(1,2,A)$ and $(3,2,A)$ can no longer be realized. Then the condition $(2,y)$ becomes unsatisfiable, because it can only be implied by the above two exploits. Finally, the exploit $(2,1,A)$ cannot not longer be realized. However, the condition $(1,y)$ is still satisfiable, due to another exploit $(3,1,A)$.

Example 11 shows that such a *negative* analysis is quite different from the previous ones. The previous searches are all unidirectional in the sense that the edges are only followed in one direction (either forwards or backwards). However, the above analysis follows edges in both directions. For example, after the forward search reaches the condition $(1, y)$ from the exploit $(2, 1, A)$, it must go back to see whether other exploits also imply the condition $(1, y)$ (in this case, the exploit $(3, 1, A)$ does so). Definition 5 states the relational queries for this purpose. The first query simply derives unrealizable exploits from unsatisfied conditions. The next three queries use two set difference operations to derive the unsatisfied conditions while taking into accounts the conjunctive nature of the require relation. Finally, the results are collected.

**Definition 5.** *Given relations $hh(HH)$, $hc(HC)$, $cv(CV)$, $vc(VC)$ and a non-empty relation $Q_{11}(HC)$ as a subset of $hc$, let $Q_8(EX)$, $Q_9(EC)$, $Q_{10}(EC)$, $Q_e$, and $Q_c$ be empty relations. Define*

- $Q_8 = \Pi_{H_s, H_d, V}(Q_{11} \bowtie Q_{ce}))$
- $Q_9 = Q_8 \bowtie Q_{ec}$
- $Q_{10} = Q_{ec} \bowtie \Pi_{H,C}(Q_9) - Q_9$
- $Q_{11} = \Pi_{H,C}(Q_9) - \Pi_{H,C}(Q_{10})$
- $Q_e = Q_e \cup Q_8$
- $Q_c = Q_c \cup Q_{11}$

*Example 12.* Table 5 shows the iterations corresponding to the procedure in Example 11. Originally, $Q_{11} = \{(2, x)\}$.

**Table 5.** An Example of Incremental Updates

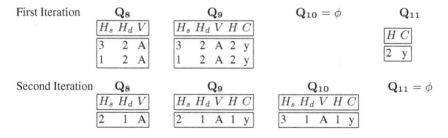

| First Iteration | $\mathbf{Q_8}$ | $\mathbf{Q_9}$ | $Q_{10} = \phi$ | $\mathbf{Q_{11}}$ |
|---|---|---|---|---|
| | $H_s$ $H_d$ $V$ | $H_s$ $H_d$ $V$ $H$ $C$ | | $H$ $C$ |
| | 3    2   A | 3    2   A  2   y | | 2   y |
| | 1    2   A | 1    2   A  2   y | | |

| Second Iteration | $\mathbf{Q_8}$ | $\mathbf{Q_9}$ | $\mathbf{Q_{10}}$ | $Q_{11} = \phi$ |
|---|---|---|---|---|
| | $H_s$ $H_d$ $V$ | $H_s$ $H_d$ $V$ $H$ $C$ | $H_s$ $H_d$ $V$ $H$ $C$ | |
| | 2    1   A | 2    1   A  1   y | 3    1   A  1   y | |

## 5   Empirical Results

As proof of concept, we have implemented the analyses discussed in the previous section. The queries are written in PL/SQL. The queries are tested in Oracle 9i in its default settings on a Pentium IV 2GHz PC with 512MB RAM. In our preliminary experiments, we test the queries against the attack scenario originally studied in [18,1] [1]. The results of the analyses match those in the previous work, which justifies the correctness of our techniques. Next we test the performance of our techniques. We have two main objectives. First, we want to determine whether the running time of the queries is practical for interactive analysis. For most decision support systems, the typical delay to a query

---

[1] Our ongoing work will compare the performance of our approach with that of the proprietary algorithms proposed before.

that is considered as tolerable in interactive analyses is usually in a matter of seconds. Such a short delay is also critical to the analysis of attack graphs, especially when the analysis is used for real-time detection and prevention of intrusions.

Second, we want to determine whether the techniques scale well in the size of attack graphs. Although the attack graph may be very large for a large network, an analysis and its result usually only involves a small part of the attack graph. The running time of an analysis thus depend on how efficiently an analysis searches the attack graph. We expect the mature optimization techniques available in most databases can transparently improve the performance and make the analyses more scalable. To test the queries against large attack graphs in a manageable way, we increase the number of vertices in the original attack graph by randomly inserting new hosts with random connectivity and vulnerabilities. We then execute the same set of analyses in the new network and measure the running time of each analysis. The main results are shown in Figure 3. All the results have 95% confidence intervals within about 5% of the reported values.

The left-hand side shows the running time of generating the attack graph in the size of that attack graph. The attack graph with about 20,000 vertices can be generated in less than seven minutes. The result also shows that our methods scale well in the size of attack graphs. The right-hand side shows the running time of each analysis in the size of the attack graph. The result shows that all the analyses require less than a second, which clearly meets the requirement of an interactive analysis. The analyses all scale well with the size of the attack graph. This proves our conjecture that the optimization techniques in databases such as indexing can transparently help to keep analyses efficient. A closer look at the result reveals that the increase in running time is mainly caused by larger results. This also explains the fact that the incremental update analysis scales differently from the other two (the effect of disabled initial conditions does not change much when the size of the attack graph increases).

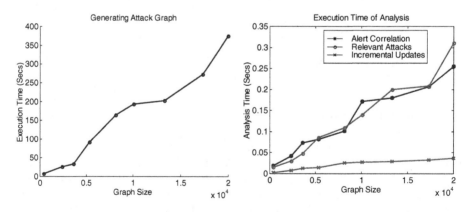

**Fig. 3.** The Performance of Analyzing Attack Graphs Using Relational Queries

## 6    Conclusion

We have proposed a relational model to enable interactive analysis of attack graphs for intrusion detection and prevention. We have shown that the complete attack graph can be generated as relational views. Any analysis of the attack graph are thus relational queries against such views. We have shown how to write relational queries for typical analyses previously studied in the literature. This approach made the analysis of attack graphs an interactive process similar to that in the decision support systems. As a side effect, the mature optimization techniques existing in most relational databases also improved the performance of the analysis.

**Acknowledgements.** The authors are grateful to the anonymous reviewers for their valuable comments.

# References

1. P. Ammann, D. Wijesekera, and S. Kaushik. Scalable, graph-based network vulnerability analysis. In *Proceedings of the 9th ACM Conference on Computer and Communications Security (CCS'02)*, pages 217–224, 2002.
2. T.H. Cormen, C.E. Leiserson, and R.L. Rivest. *Introduction to Algorithms*. MIT Press, 1990.
3. F. Cuppens and A. Miege. Alert correlation in a cooperative intrusion detection framework. In *Proceedings of the 2002 IEEE Symposium on Security and Privacy (S&P'02)*, pages 187–200, 2002.
4. M. Dacier. Towards quantitative evaluation of computer security. Ph.D. Thesis, Institut National Polytechnique de Toulouse, 1994.
5. R. Deraison. Nessus scanner, 1999. Available at http://www.nessus.org.
6. D. Farmer and E.H. Spafford. The COPS security checker system. In *USENIX Summer*, pages 165–170, 1990.
7. J. Gray, A. Bosworth, A. Bosworth, A. Layman, D. Reichart, M. Venkatrao, F. Pellow, and H. Pirahesh. Data cube: A relational aggregation operator generalizing group-by, cross-tab, and sub-totals. *Data Mining and Knowledge Discovery*, 1(1):29–53, 1997.
8. S. Jajodia, S. Noel, and B. O'Berry. Topological analysis of network attack vulnerability. In V. Kumar, J. Srivastava, and A. Lazarevic, editors, *Managing Cyber Threats: Issues, Approaches and Challenges*. Kluwer Academic Publisher, 2003.
9. S. Jha, O. Sheyner, and J.M. Wing. Two formal analysis of attack graph. In *Proceedings of the 15th Computer Security Foundation Workshop (CSFW'02)*, 2002.
10. P. Ning, Y. Cui, and D.S. Reeves. Constructing attack scenarios through correlation of intrusion alerts. In *Proceedings of the 9th ACM Conference on Computer and Communications Security (CCS'02)*, pages 245–254, 2002.
11. S. Noel and S. Jajodia. Correlating intrusion events and building attack scenarios through attack graph distance. In *Proceedings of the 20th Annual Computer Security Applications Conference (ACSAC'04)*, 2004.
12. S. Noel, S. Jajodia, B. O'Berry, and M. Jacobs. Efficient minimum-cost network hardening via exploit dependency grpahs. In *Proceedings of the 19th Annual Computer Security Applications Conference (ACSAC'03)*, 2003.
13. R. Ortalo, Y. Deswarte, and M. Kaaniche. Experimenting with quantitative evaluation tools for monitoring operational security. *IEEE Trans. Software Eng.*, 25(5):633–650, 1999.
14. C. Phillips and L. Swiler. A graph-based system for network-vulnerability analysis. In *Proceedings of the New Security Paradigms Workshop (NSPW'98)*, 1998.
15. C.R. Ramakrishnan and R. Sekar. Model-based analysis of configuration vulnerabilities. *Journal of Computer Security*, 10(1/2):189–209, 2002.

16. R. Ritchey and P. Ammann. Using model checking to analyze network vulnerabilities. In *Proceedings of the 2000 IEEE Symposium on Research on Security and Privacy (S&P'00)*, pages 156–165, 2000.

17. R. Ritchey, B. O'Berry, and S. Noel. Representing TCP/IP connectivity for topological analysis of network security. In *Proceedings of the 18th Annual Computer Security Applications Conference (ACSAC'02)*, page 25, 2002.

18. O. Sheyner, J. Haines, S. Jha, R. Lippmann, and J.M. Wing. Automated generation and analysis of attack graphs. In *Proceedings of the 2002 IEEE Symposium on Security and Privacy (S&P'02)*, pages 273–284, 2002.

19. L. Swiler, C. Phillips, D. Ellis, and S. Chakerian. Computer attack graph generation tool. In *Proceedings of the DARPA Information Survivability Conference & Exposition II (DIS-CEX'01)*, 2001.

20. L. Wang, A. Liu, and S. Jajodia. An efficient and unified approach to correlating, hypothesizing, and predicting intrusion alerts. In *Proceedings of the 10th European Symposium on Research in Computer Security (ESORICS 2005)*, pages 247–266, 2005.

21. D. Zerkle and K. Levitt. Netkuang - a multi-host configuration vulnerability checker. In *Proceedings of the 6th USENIX Unix Security Symposium (USENIX'96)*, 1996.

# Notarized Federated Identity Management for Web Services*

Michael T. Goodrich[1], Roberto Tamassia[2], and Danfeng Yao[2]

[1] Department of Computer Science, University of California
Irvine, CA 92697 USA
goodrich@acm.org
[2] Department of Computer Science, Brown University
Providence, RI 02912 USA
{rt, dyao}@cs.brown.edu

**Abstract.** We propose a *notarized* federated identity management model that supports efficient user authentication when providers are unknown to each other. Our model introduces a notary service, owned by a trusted third-party, to dynamically notarize assertions generated by identity providers. An additional feature of our model is the avoidance of direct communications between identity providers and service providers, which provides improved privacy protection for users. We present an efficient implementation of our notarized federated identity management model based on the Secure Transaction Management System (STMS). We also give a practical solution for mitigating aspects of the identity theft problem and discuss its use in our notarized federated identity management model. The unique feature of our cryptographic solution is that it enables one to proactively prevent the leaking of secret identity information.

## 1 Introduction

Digital identity management is becoming an integral part of our lives, as consumers and businesses rely more and more on online transactions for daily tasks, such as banking, shopping, and bill payment. These transactions crucially depend on networked computer systems to communicate sensitive identity data across personal, company, and enterprise boundaries.

Unfortunately, the overuse of personal information in online transactions opens the door to identity theft, which poses a serious threat to personal finances and credit ratings of users and creates liabilities for corporations. Moreover, the increasing dangers of identity theft are negatively affecting people's collective confidence on the digital world for online financial transactions [10]. Thus, effective solutions for managing digital identity on both the individual and enterprise levels are urgently needed.

---

* This work was supported in part by the National Science Foundation under grants IIS–0324846, CCF–0311510 and CNS–0303577, and by IAM Technology, Inc. The work of the first author was done primarily as a consultant to Brown University.

E. Damiani and P. Liu (Eds.): Data and Applications Security 2006, LNCS 4127, pp. 133–147, 2006.

Additionally, end users are challenged with increasing numbers of websites that require access control and authentication. Studies show that users resort to using weak passwords or writing them down to alleviate the burden of memorizing multiple passwords. One well-known identity management solution that deals with this issue is the *single sign-on (SSO)* technique, which requires the user to authenticate only once to a website, and then automatically authenticates the user to other websites from then on, within a session.

The approach based on cryptographic-enabled assertions is embodied by the *Security Assertion Markup Language (SAML)* [7]. SAML 2.0 is generally believed to support general cross-domain authentication and SAML is quickly becoming the de-facto means for exchanging user credentials between trusted environments. The identity federation architecture of *Liberty Alliance* is compliant with the SAML 2.0 standard [14]. Indeed, SAML is specifically designed to support cross domain single sign-on, which is illustrated in the following example.

A user has a secure logon session to a website, (e.g., Airline.com), and is accessing resources on that site. Airline.com serves as the *identity provider* site. At some point in the session, the user is directed to another web site in a different DNS domain for a related service, and this outside domain is called the *service provider* site (e.g., CarRental.com). The identity provider (Airline.com) asserts to the service provider (CarRental.com) that the user is known to the identity provider and gives to the service provide the user's name and session attributes (e.g., Gold member). Since the service provider trusts the assertions generated by the identity provider, it creates a session for the user based on the information received. The user is not required to authenticate again when directed to the service provider site. Hence, single sign-on is achieved.

The *identity provider (IdP)* in SAML [7] is defined as the system, or administrative domain, that asserts information about a subject. An identity provider asserts that a user has been authenticated and has certain attributes. The *service provider (SP)* is defined as the system, or administrative domain, that relies on the information supplied to it by the identity provider.

## 1.1   Motivation for Notarized ID Federation

In existing federated identity management systems that support SAML, such as the *Liberty Identity Federation Framework (ID-FF)* [8] and *WS-Federation* [24], it is up to the service provider to decide whether it trusts the assertions provided to it. Service providers in SAML are also known as *relying parties* due to the fact that they rely on the information provided by an identity provider. This reliance implies that websites of different administrative domains need to trust each other's access control verdicts on end users. In fact, SAML single sign-on relies on the concept of *identity federation* in order for it to work at all. An identity federation is said to exist between an identity provider and a service provider, when the service provider accepts assertions regarding a user from the identity provider [7].

In fact, most existing SSO solutions assume preexisting trust relationship among providers and do not provide concrete mechanisms for the trust establishment between providers. The WS-Federation specification [24] discusses several trust relationships between identity providers and service providers, including directed trust, indirected brokered trust, and chained trust. However, details on how the trust relationships and identity brokers can be instantiated are not given. This limitation hinders the wide deployment of SSO in web-service environments, because providers may be unknown to each other. Therefore, flexible, reliable, and secure trust establishment mechanisms need to be provided for federated identity management.

## 1.2  Our Contributions

1. We propose a notarized federated identity management model that supports automatic user authentications when the providers are unknown to each other. Our model introduces a *notary server*, which is owned by a trusted third-party to dynamically notarize assertions generated by identity providers. As an extra feature provided by the notary server, our federated identity management model reduces possible collusions between identity providers and service providers, and gives improved privacy protections for users.

2. We describe an efficient implementation of the federated identity management protocol with the existing *Secure Transaction Management System (STMS)* [1,11]. The notary server caches the assertions at a collection of responders deployed in the network. Even when the responders are located in insecure, untrusted locations, a service provider can easily identify a forged or tampered assertion so that the integrity of an assertions is maintained.

   Our protocol is a concrete solution for a trust broker model proposed by existing federated identity management systems [24]. Besides brokering trust, our solution offers additional features. *Accountability* is supported by archiving signatures on requests and assertions. *User privacy* is achieved by encrypting assertions stored by the notary server. *Verification efficiency* is achieved by using the authenticated-dictionary technique (see, e.g., [1,11,18,21]) implemented in STMS.

3. We also give a practical solution for mitigating aspects of the identity theft problem, and discuss how it is used in our federated identity management protocol. Our cryptographic solution is based on the *Identity-Based Encryption (IBE)* scheme [4]. The main feature of our cryptographic solution is that it enables one to proactively prevent the leaking of secret identity information.

**Organization of the paper.** Our model for notarized federated identity management is described in Section 2. The STMS implementation of the notarized federated identity management protocol is presented in Section 3. In Section 4, we give an IBE-based authentication protocol. The security of the federated identity management protocol and the IBE-based authentication protocol is analyzed in Section 5. Related work is given in Section 6.

## 2   Notarized Federated Identity Management

Our notarized federated identity management model introduces a *notary server*, a trusted third-party that dynamically maintains assertions generated by identity providers. Assertions are generated by identity providers and stored by the notary server. When a service provider needs to verify an assertion, it queries the notary server for a *notarized assertion* that shows the trustworthiness of the identity provider generating the assertion.

### 2.1   Notary Server and Notarized Assertion

In a notarized ID federation, a notary server is trusted by both identity providers and service providers. Identity providers that have good internet behavior and reputation are allowed to register with the notary server, and thus are trusted. The notary server stores the assertions generated by registered identity providers. A notary server supports two operations, SUBMIT and QUERY.

- SUBMIT($id, S_{id}, sig$): a registered identity provider *IdP* authenticates itself to the notary server, and submits via a secure channel the tuple (id, assertion, signature), denoted by $(id, S_{id}, sig)$, to the notary server. The assertion $S_{id}$ states the attributes of an identity *id*, and the signature *sig* is signed by *IdP* on the assertion $S_{id}$. The notary server stores the tuple.
- QUERY($id$): a service provider *SP* queries in a *public (insecure)* channel the notary server for assertions associated with identity *id*, and the notary server returns the *notarized assertion(s)*.

A notarized assertion has a proof showing that the assertion is indeed stored by the notary server, which implies that the identity provider that generates the assertion is trustworthy. The reason for not using a secure channel in QUERY is for higher efficiency and scalability in a distributed environment. The challenge, thus, becomes how to efficiently generate and verify the notarized assertion, even when it is transmitted in a insecure channel. Our solution is based on the authenticated dictionary technique [1,11,18,21], which is more scalable than using a signature scheme.

The notary server provides the assurance of the trustworthiness of assertions when identity providers are unknown to the service providers. The notary server is a bridge of trust between providers in web-service transactions. Another advantage of storing assertions on the notary server is the prevention of direct contact between identity providers and service providers. A notarized assertion does not contain the name of the identity provider. This further increases the difficulty of collusions among providers to discover private user information.

We assume that the notary server is trustworthy, and is trusted by all entities (users, identity providers, service providers). The security properties of our notarized federated identity management protocol are summarized below and are analyzed in Section 5.

- *Security* is defined as that no polynomial-time adversary can forge a notarized assertion that can be accepted by a service provider.

– *Secrecy* is defined intuitively as that the protocol does not leak any information about a notarized assertion to a (polynomial-time) adversary. This property provides privacy protection to the users.
– *Accountability* is defined as that identity providers should be held accountable for the assertions generated, and for any unauthorized information disclosure about the users.

Note that the notary server only certifies that the source of an assertion is trustworthy; it is not required to examine and certify the content of an assertion. In fact, our protocol, which is described next, deliberately avoids disclosing assertion contents to the notary server by encrypting the assertions. This feature is for the purpose of user privacy, and prevents the notary server from gaining knowledge of private user information.

## 2.2 Protocol

In this section, we present the protocol for our notarized federated identity management model. The following entities participate in the protocol: a user, an identity provider, a service provider, and a notary server. The protocol gives an instantiation of operations SUBMIT and QUERY. Note that the roles of identity provider and service provider are interchangeable. For example, a bank can be the identity provider in one scenario and the service provider in another scenario.

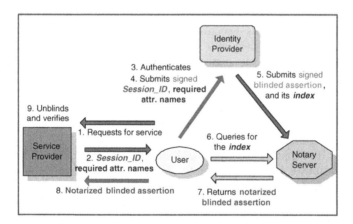

**Fig. 1.** Overview of the notarized federated identity management protocol

We assumes that the notary server knows the public keys of registered identity providers. In addition, the public key of the notary server is known by all of the providers. A schematic drawing of the protocol is shown in Figure 1.

In the protocol, the user only needs to authenticate once to an identity provider. Subsequent requests for service from multiple service providers do not require the user for authentication. Nevertheless, for protecting personal privacy, the user is given the ability to examine the contents of assertions to be given to the service providers in our protocol. If the assertions are generated by the identity provider according to the user's request, then they are passed on to the service providers. We argue that having the user involved in the identity management protocol for privacy purpose is a feasible solution. This concept was also proposed by other federated identity management solution [2]. The process can be automated to minimize the user's manual participation.

Public parameters include a collision-resistant one-way hash function, $H$, that takes a binary string of arbitrary length and hashes to a binary string of fixed length $k$: $H : \{0,1\}^* \rightarrow \{0,1\}^k$. For the blinding purpose, the public parameters also include two public strings $P_1$ and $P_2$. Providers also agree on a symmetric-key encryption scheme for blinding and unblinding assertions. The encryption and decryption of a message $x$ with a secret key $K$ are denoted as $E_K(x)$ and $D_K(x)$, respectively. Our protocol is described as follows.

1. The user requests services from a service provider $SP$. $SP$ requires attribute information of the user needed to complete the service.
2. $SP$ opens a secure communication channel with the user. The user and $SP$ each generate a random integer of the same length. They first exchange the cryptographic hashes of these integers as commitments using the secure channel, and then they exchange the integers using the secure channel. The session_ID $N$ is finally computed as the XOR of the two integers. $SP$ also informs the user of the attribute names that are needed for the service (e.g., billing address and age).
3. The user authenticates to her identity provider $IdP$. If the authentication is successful, the user opens a secure channel with $IdP$, and transmits a *signed* request that contains the session_ID and the required attribute names.
4. $IdP$ verifies and stores the signed request by the user. The signature is for the accountability purpose in case of dispute (see Section 5).
5. $IdP$ then computes the *index* of the assertion as the hash of session_ID concatenated with the public parameter $P_1$: $h = H(N, P_1)$. It then generates an assertion $S_h$ about the user using index $h$. For example, $S_h$ states that $h$ is a university student.
6. To prevent information leaking, $IdP$ blinds the assertion as follows.
   (a) $IdP$ computes the *blinding factor* $K$ as the hash of the session_ID concatenated with the public parameter $P_2$: $K = H(N, P_2)$.
   (b) $IdP$ encrypts $S_h$ with the symmetric encryption scheme, using $K$ as the secret key. This gives the *blinded assertion* $S'_h = E_K(S_h)$.
   The blinded assertion $S'_h$ is signed by $IdP$ with its private key, which gives a signature $sig_h$.
7. $IdP$ runs SUBMIT($h, S'_h, sig_h$) with the notary server to submit tuple $(h, S'_h, sig_h)$ through a secure channel as follows.
   (a) $IdP$ first authenticates to the notary server to establish a secure communication channel.
   (b) $IdP$ then transmits tuple $(h, S'_h, sig_h)$ to the notary server.
   (c) The notary server verifies signature $sig_h$, and stores $(S'_h, sig_h)$ indexed by $h$. The signature is stored for accountability purposes.

8. The user computes the index $h = H(N, P_1)$ from $N$ and $P_1$, and runs QUERY($h$) to obtain the assertion for $h$. The notary server processes the query as follows.
   (a) The blinded assertion $S'_h$ associated with index $h$ is retrieved.
   (b) The notary server *notarizes* the assertion $S'_h$, and returns the notarized assertion. We describe two approaches for the realization of notarized assertion in the following sections. Note that the QUERY operation between the user and the notary server does not require a secure channel.
9. Once the user obtains the returned notarized blinded assertion, she unblinds it with the blinding factor $K = H(N, P_2)$. This is done by decrypting $S'_h$ with $K$, which gives $S_h = D_K(S'_h)$. The user verifies that the assertion does not release any unauthorized personal information about her.
10. The notarized blinded assertion is then relayed from the user to the service provider, who verifies that it is notarized by the notary server. This implies that the identity provider *IdP* is trusted by the notary server. If the verification succeeds, the assertion $S'_h$ is unblinded in the same way as in Step 9. The attribute information is obtained from the assertion, and index $h$ is compared with the hash $H(N, P_1)$ of session_ID $N$ and $P_1$. The user is then granted the service if the verification passes. The service provider also stores the notarized assertion for accountability purposes.

The computation of blinding factor $K$ and index $h$ is equivalent to using two different hash functions on the session_ID $N$, i.e., $h = H_1(N)$ and $K = H_2(N)$, where $H_1$ and $H_2$ are collision-resistant one-way hash functions.

# 3    Realization of Notarized Assertions

Notarized assertions can be realized using simple time-stamped signatures. The notary server individually signs every assertion and the current time-stamp with its private key. The notarized assertion consists of this signature along with the assertion and time-stamp. To verify a notarized assertion, the service provider verifies the signature against the public key of the notary server, which can be obtained through usual means such as a public key certificate.

In the above approach, notarizing assertions can be a performance bottleneck because the notary server needs to sign every individual assertion. To improve the efficiency of the notary server, we give an improved realization of notarized assertions using the secure transaction management system (STMS).

The main advantage of implementing notary assertions with STMS in comparison to the simple time-stamped signature approach is its high efficiency of computation. The notary server only needs to generate one signature as opposed to a signature for each assertion. In addition, STMS also provides a distributed architecture for fast real-time dissemination of assertion updates. STMS has been previously used to build an accredited domainkeys framework for secure e-mail systems [12]. Next, we first introduce the components and algorithms of STMS, then we describe how to use STMS to scale up the notary service.

## 3.1   Secure Transaction Management System (STMS)

The computational abstraction underlying STMS is a data structure called an *authenticated dictionary* (see, e.g., [1,11,17,18,21,22]), which is a system for publishing data and supporting authenticated responses to queries about the data. In an authenticated dictionary, the data originates at a secure central site, called *STMS source* and is distributed to servers scattered across the network, called *STMS responders*. The responders answer queries on behalf of the source about the data made by clients. It is desirable to delegate query answering to the responders for two reasons: (1) the source is subject to risks such as denial-of-service attacks if it provides services directly on the network, and (2) the large volume and diverse geographic origination of the queries require distributed servers to provide responses efficiently.

The STMS source sends real-time updates to the responders together with a special signed time-stamped fingerprint of the database called the *basis*. A user's query to the responder asks whether an element is contained in the authenticated dictionary maintained by STMS source. A responder replies to the query with an authenticated response. This consists of the answer to the query, the proof of the answer, the basis and its signature signed by the STMS source. Informally speaking, the proof is a *partial fingerprint* of the database that, combined with the subject of the query, should yield the fingerprint of the entire database. A proof consists of a very small amount of data (less than 300 bytes for most applications) and can be validated quickly against the signed basis by a client. We refer readers to the authenticated dictionary literature [1,11] for more information.

## 3.2   Realization of Notarized Assertions with STMS

Using STMS, the notary server consists of a *notary source* and several *notary responders*. The notary source needs to be a trusted server that stores assertion inputs from identity providers. Notary responders can be strategically placed in geographically dispersed locations to accommodate fast queries. They obtain real-time updates from the notary source, and answer queries from users. Notary responders do not need to be trusted servers. The notarized assertions returned by them can be authenticated by verifying against the public key of the notary source by anyone.

With STMS, a notarized assertion returned by QUERY operation consists of two parts: assertion itself and a STMS proof. As described in the previous section, the proof is a sequence of hash values of elements in the notary server for proving the existence of the assertion. The size of the proof is quite compact, even for large number of items in the notary server. Therefore, transmitting the proof can be quite fast. The service provider then obtains the signed STMS basis of the current time quantum from the notary responder, if it does not yet have it. The proof of the assertion is verified against the basis, and the signature of the basis is verified against the public key of the notary source. If the verification is successful, the request is granted. The signed basis remains the same for the duration of a time quantum, therefore it only needs to be obtained once for each time quantum. The rest of the notarized federated identity management protocol with STMS follows the protocol in Section 2.2.

Due to page limit, the protocol and security of STMS implemented notarized federated identity management are not presented. The security is based on the security of STMS, which has been previously proved [1].

# 4    Reducing the Risks of Identity Theft

Recently, several practical solutions against on-line identity theft have been proposed [2,16]. In this section, we first analyze causes of a successful identity theft. Then, we give a practical solution, and describe how to use our scheme in our notarized federated identity management protocol.

## 4.1    Identity Theft and Its Causes

Identity theft is a type of crime in which an imposter obtains key pieces of personal information, such as Social Security or driver's license numbers, in order to impersonate someone else. Although an identity thief might crack into a database to obtain personal information, it is believed that a thief is more likely to obtain information using Trojans or even old-fashion methods such as dumpster diving and shoulder surfing.

We observe that the current authentication protocols, both physical and digital ones, are fundamentally susceptible to identity theft, even if an individual is careful in protecting her sensitive information. Physical authentication protocols include the procedures for obtaining a driver's license at a government office, opening a bank account, and applying for mortgage. Digital authentication protocols include the corresponding on-line transactions. In current solutions, key pieces of personal information are usually communicated in the clear or stored in the clear. This makes stealing of information easier for identity thieves. Although the SSL protocol encrypts communications between a user and a server, this does not prevent Trojan keyloggers, or shoulder surfing, because the user still needs to disclose and type over and over sensitive information such as her social security number.

We argue that this fundamental characteristic of the existing authentication protocols is one of the main causes of identity theft, namely using sensitive information in clear form for authentication. We propose a simple and practical cryptographic protocol for authentication. Our solution ties personal information to random secrets, which are used to prove *interactively* the ownership of the personal information but are *never disclosed.*

**Motivation for using IBE.** In public key encryption schemes, the private key information is never disclosed. Yet, a challenge-response process can be used by a user to prove the possession of the private key to an identity provider. The private key is usually protected by encrypting it with a passphrase, and storing it in a portable device, such as a smart card or a USB flash drive. Observe that the private key is never disclosed in clear during transactions, hence it never appears in any printed form or display. Therefore, it is difficult for attackers to retrieve someone's private key using standard identity theft techniques. To steal the private key, an attacker would need to obtain the physical device and know the passphrase. In order to associate identity information with public keys, the only known encryption scheme is the Identity-Based Encryption (IBE) scheme [4,20,25]. A public key in IBE will be the personal information (e.g., the social security number of an individual). For authentication, an individual not only needs to know her personal information (e.g., social security number), but also needs to prove the possession of the corresponding private key for authentication.

## 4.2    A Cryptographic Authentication Protocol

We propose to use ID-based encryption scheme for implementing an authentication protocol for sensitive personal information. Our protocol minimizes the exposure of secret personal information and thus is more robust against identity theft than existing authentication methods. Entities in our protocol include a user, an ID authority, an identity provider, and a revocation server controlled by the ID authority. Our authentication protocol has the following operations: SETUP, REGISTER, AUTHENTICATE, and REFRESH. It requires an on-line revocation server maintained by the ID authority.

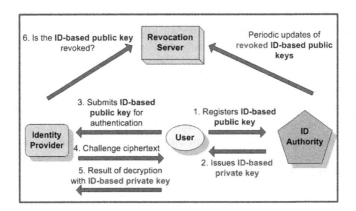

**Fig. 2.** A diagram of the IBE-based authentication protocol

Refreshing the secret key of identity information can be tricky, because the identity information typically does not change, e.g. social security number. We show later how to use multiple pieces of identity information and on-line revocation checking to leverage this. A diagram of the protocol is shown in Figure 2. Here, we describe the realization of the above operations with IBE scheme.

1. SETUP: The ID authority runs the PKG SETUP operation of IBE.
2. REGISTER: A user requests for an *ID-based private key* from an ID authority. The user needs to be physically present in the ID office, for example the

passport office, with paper identifications such as passport, birth certificate. The ID authority authenticates the user's identity.

If the user's identity is verified, the ID authority generates the ID-based private key for the user. The ID authority runs the EXTRACT operation of IBE with the user's *ID-based public key*, which is the user's identity information concatenated with a unique serial number $l$. For example, $l$ can be the driver's license number. $l$ is used for revocation purpose. Because the identity information such as social security number cannot be easily revoked, we need an additional replaceable field $l$. Note that $l$ cannot be any random number, because using a random value as public key requires public-key certification, which defies the purpose of identity-based encryption. In what follows, we use the driver's license number as $l$. The ID-based private key generated by EXTRACT is given to the user. The user's driver's license can be equipped with a smart card chip and store the private key.

3. AUTHENTICATE: The user and the identity provider engage in a challenge-response protocol as follows.

   (a) The user gives his ID-based public key to the identity provider, which is the identity information concatenated with the driver's license number $l$ to the identity provider.

   (b) The identity provider picks a random nonce $m$. It runs ENCRYPT of IBE to encrypt $m$ using the user's ID-based public key.

   (c) The ciphertext is given to the user, who runs DECRYPT of IBE with his ID-based private key. If the user is unable to correctly decrypt the ciphertext, the authentication fails and returns false.

   (d) The identity provider queries the revocation server maintained by the ID authority for the number $l$ in the public key of the user. If $l$ has been revoked, then the authentication fails. Otherwise, the authentication is successful and returns true.

4. REFRESH: The ID authority refreshes the ID-based private key of the user as follows.

   (a) The user authenticates his current ID-based public key to the ID authority.

   (b) The ID authority puts the the driver's license number $l$ on the revocation server to indicate that $l$ has been revoked.

   (c) The ID authority generates a new driver's license number $l'$ for the user. The new ID-based public key of the user associated with his identity information is that identity information concatenated with $l'$. For example, the public key is 999-99-9999 $\circ$ 1234567890, where 999-99-9999 is the social security number and 1234567890 is the new driver's license number $l'$.

   (d) The ID authority runs EXTRACT of IBE to compute a new private key, which is transmitted to the user via a secure channel or in person. The user stores the new ID-based private key in his smart card.

The main advantage of our authentication protocol is that the secret personal information is not released during the transaction, which minimizes identity theft attacks such as dumpster diving and shoulder surfing. Our protocol can be used in any user authentication applications. In particular, it can be used in any federated identity management system when a user authenticates his personal information with an identity provider. For example, a user is required to run the AUTHENTICATE algorithm with the identity provider when his social security number is needed. Without the corresponding private key, it is impossible for an identity thief to accomplish this.

## 5    Security Analysis

In this section, we first analyze the security of the notarized federated identity management protocol, and then analyze the IBE-based authentication protocol.

The security of our notarized federated identity management protocol is analyzed from the perspectives of the user, the identity provider, the service provider, and the notary server, as each of them has different requirements on the security provided by the system. In what follows, we assume the existence of a signature scheme that is secure against existential forgery by polynomial-time adversaries in the security parameter of the signature scheme. Existential forgery means that an adversary forges a signature that the notary server has not signed in the past. An adversary in our protocol can monitor traffics in unsecured channels, request for services, request the identity provider to blind assertions of her choice, and request the notary server to notarize assertions of her choice.

We assume that the notary server is trustworthy, and is trusted by all entities (users, identity providers, service providers). All entities are assumed to follow the federated identity management protocol presented in Section 2. The following theorem states the nonforgeability of a notarized assertion.

**Theorem 1.** *In the notarized federated identity management protocol, no polynomial-time adversary can successfully forge a valid notarized assertion that is not generated by the notary server.*

For the privacy protection of a user, an important privacy requirement is the secrecy of assertions. This is summarized in the following theorem.

**Theorem 2.** *Assume the existence of a collision-resistant one-way hash function, and a secure symmetric key encryption scheme. In the notarized federated identity management protocol, a polynomial-time adversary and untrusted notary responders cannot obtain any information from a blinded assertion.*

For decentralized authorization systems such as the federated identity management, an important security requirement is accountability. To prevent possible disputes, identity providers should be held accountable for the assertions that they have generated. In addition, to prevent unauthorized information exchange among providers, users should be able to dispute any fraudulent assertion requests. These properties are achieved in our protocol.

**Theorem 3.** *In the notarized federated identity management protocol, the identity provider is held accountable for the assertions that it generates.*

**Theorem 4.** *In the notarized federated identity management protocol, providers are held accountable for any unauthorized information exchange among them.*

**Theorem 5.** *The notarized federated identity management protocol is secure against replay attacks.*

The security of the IBE-based authentication protocol is defined as the adversary's inability of impersonating a user, and is based on the security of the identity-based encryption scheme as stated in Theorem 6.

**Theorem 6.** *Given an identity-based encryption scheme that is semantic-secure against an adaptive polynomial-time adversary, the IBE-based authentication protocol is secure.*

The proofs of the above theorems are in the full version of the paper [13].

## 6 Related Work

Our approach of using privacy protection as a means to avoid identity theft is related to anonymous credential systems [5,6,9,15,26]. Anonymous credential systems (a.k.a. pseudonym systems) allow anonymous yet authenticated and accountable transactions between users and service providers. Existing anonymous credential systems are different from our single sign-on system, in that they do not consider a federated identity infrastructure behind the providers. In comparison, our system focuses on how to manage user authentication in the more realistic setting of a federation of providers. Our system achieves simple pseudonym solutions and efficient single sign-on by taking advantages of the federated structure. In particular, we do not need a credential system, because the assertions can be short-lived and generated on-line by identity providers.

The federated identity management solution proposed by Bhargav-Spantzel, Squicciarini, and Bertino [2] emphasizes the need for proving the knowledge of personal information without actually revealing it, in order to help prevent identity theft. In their solution, personal data such as a social security number is never transmitted in the clear. Commitment schemes and zero-knowledge proofs are used to commit data and prove the knowledge of the data. Our identity-based solution has a similar goal to this approach, but there is one important difference. We allow personal data such as social security numbers and credit card numbers to be transmitted in the clear. Yet, every time this information is used, the user needs to prove the possession of corresponding private keys. This requires minimal changes to the existing financial and administrative infrastructure, as personal information in our scheme is stored the same way as it is currently. IBE [4] conveniently makes this possible, and, interestingly, this approach is also more efficient than zero-knowledge proof-of-knowledge protocols.

BBAE is the federated identity-management protocol proposed by Pfitzmann and Waidner [19]. They give a concrete browser-based single sign-on protocol that aims at the security of communications and the privacy of user's attributes. Their protocol is based on a standard browser, and therefore does not require the user to install any program. The main difference with this and our approach is that we provide a notary mechanism for authenticating assertions when *IdP* and *SP* are not previous known to each other.

In the access control area, the closest work to ours is the framework for regulating service access and release of private information in web-services by Bonatti and Samarati [3]. They study the information disclosure using a language and policy approach. We designed cryptographic solutions to control and manage information exchange. Their framework mainly focuses on the client-server model, whereas our architecture include two different types of providers.

A counter measure for identity theft through location cross-checking and information filtering was recently proposed [23]. This paper addresses the identity cloning problem, and proposes to use personal location devices such as GPS and central monitoring systems to ensure the uniqueness of identities. However, the central monitoring system in their solution is likely to be a performance bottleneck. Moreover, because identity thieves are geographically dispersed, distributing the monitoring task into several locations is not feasible. In comparison, our solution is simple and efficient to adopt. Because we tie the secret identification information to a tamper-resistant smart card (e.g., driver's license), card theft can be easily noticed and reported by the card owner.

**Acknowledgements.** The authors would like to thank David Croston for useful comments.

# References

1. A. Anagnostopoulos, M. T. Goodrich, and R. Tamassia. Persistent authenticated dictionaries and their applications. In *Proc. Information Security Conference (ISC 2001)*, volume 2200 of *LNCS*, pages 379–393. Springer-Verlag, 2001.
2. A. Bhargav-Spantzel, A. C. Squicciarini, and E. Bertino. Establishing and protecting digital identity in federation systems. In *Proceedings of the 2005 ACM Workshop on Digital Identity Management*, pages 11–19, November 2005.
3. P. A. Bonatti and P. Samarati. A uniform framework for regulating service access and information release on the web. *Journal of Computer Security*, 10(3):241–272, 2002.
4. D. Boneh and M. K. Franklin. Identity-based encryption from the Weil pairing. In *Advances in Cryptology — Crypto '01*, volume 2139 of *LNCS*, pages 213–229. Springer-Verlag, 2001.
5. J. Camenisch and A. Lysyanskaya. Efficient non-transferable anonymous multi-show credential system with optional anonymity revocation. In B. Pfitzmann, editor, *Advances in Cryptology — EUROCRYPT 2001*, volume 2045 of *Lecture Notes in Computer Science*, pages 93–118. Springer Verlag, 2001.
6. J. Camenisch and E. Van Herreweghen. Design and implementation of the *idemix* anonymous credential system. In *Proceedings of the 9th ACM Conference on Computer and Communications Security (CCS)*, pages 21–30, 2002.
7. S. Cantor, F. Hirsch, J. Kemp, R. Philpott, E. Maler, J. Hughes, J. Hodges, P. Mishra, and J. Moreh. Security Assertion Markup Language (SAML) V2.0. Version 2.0. OASIS Standards.

8. S. Cantor and J. Kemp. Liberty ID-FF Protocols amd Schema Specification. Version 1.2. Liberty Alliance Project. http://www.projectliberty.org/specs/.
9. D. Chaum. Security without identification: transaction systems to make big brother obsolete. *Communications of the ACM*, 28(10):1030–1044, October 1985.
10. Cyber Security Industry Alliance. Internet security national survey, No. 2, December 2005. https://www.csialliance.org/StateofCyberSecurity2006/.
11. M. T. Goodrich, R. Tamassia, and A. Schwerin. Implementation of an authenticated dictionary with skip lists and commutative hashing. In *Proc. 2001 DARPA Information Survivability Conference and Exposition*, volume 2, pages 68–82, 2001.
12. M. T. Goodrich, R. Tamassia, and D. Yao. Accredited DomainKeys: a service architecture for improved email validation. In *Proceedings of the Conference on Email and Anti-Spam (CEAS '05)*, July 2005.
13. M. T. Goodrich, R. Tamassia, and D. Yao. Notarized federated identity management for web services, April 2006. Brown University Technical Report. http://www.cs.brown.edu/cgc/stms/.
14. Liberty Alliance Project. http://www.projectliberty.org.
15. A. Lysyanskaya, R. Rivest, A. Sahai, and S. Wolf. Pseudonym systems. In H. Heys and C. Adams, editors, *Selected Areas in Cryptography*, volume 1758 of *Lecture Notes in Computer Science*. Springer Verlag, 1999.
16. P. Madsen, Y. Koga, and K. Takahashi. Federated identity management for protecting users from ID theft. In *Proceedings of the 2005 ACM Workshop on Digital Identity Management*, pages 77–83, November 2005.
17. C. Martel, G. Nuckolls, P. Devanbu, M. Gertz, A. Kwong, and S. G. Stubblebine. A general model for authenticated data structures. *Algorithmica*, 39(1):21–41, 2004.
18. M. Naor and K. Nissim. Certificate revocation and certificate update. In *Proceedings of the 7th USENIX Security Symposium*, pages 217–228, 1998.
19. B. Pfitzmann and M. Waidner. Federated identity-management protocols. In *Security Protocols Workshop*, pages 153–174, 2003.
20. A. Shamir. Identity-based cryptosystems and signature schemes. In *Advances in Cryptology — Crypto '84*, volume 196 of *LNCS*, pages 47–53. Springer-Verlag, 1984.
21. R. Tamassia. Authenticated data structures. In *Proc. European Symp. on Algorithms*, volume 2832 of *Lecture Notes in Computer Science*, pages 2–5. Springer-Verlag, 2003.
22. R. Tamassia and N. Triandopoulos. Computational bounds on hierarchical data processing with applications to information security. In *Proc. Int. Colloquium on Automata, Languages and Programming (ICALP)*, volume 3580 of *LNCS*, pages 153–165. Springer-Verlag, 2005.
23. P. van Oorschot and S. Stubblebine. Countering identity theft through digital uniqueness, location cross-checking, and funneling. In *Proceedings of Financial Cryptography and Data Security (FC '05)*, pages 31–43, 2005.
24. Web Services Federation Language (WS-Federation), 2003. ftp://www6.software.ibm.com/software/developer/library/ws-fed.pdf.
25. D. Yao, N. Fazio, Y. Dodis, and A. Lysyanskaya. ID-based encryption for complex hierarchies with applications to forward security and broadcast encryption. In *Proceedings of the ACM Conference on Computer and Communications Security (CCS)*, pages 354 – 363. ACM Press, 2004.
26. D. Yao and R. Tamassia. Cascaded authorization with anonymous-signer aggregate signatures. In *Proceedings of the Seventh Annual IEEE Systems, Man and Cybernetics Information Assurance Workshop (IAW '06)*, June 2006.

# Resolving Information Flow Conflicts in RBAC Systems

Noa Tuval[1] and Ehud Gudes[1,2]

[1] Department of Computer Science, Open University, Raanana, Israel
[2] Department of Computer Science, Ben-Gurion University, Beer-Sheva, Israel

**Abstract.** Recently, Role Based Access Control (RBAC) model has taken place as a promising alternative to the conventional access control models, MAC and DAC. RBAC is more general than those traditional models as was shown by Osborn et al. [17], however, mapping a role based system to a valid MAC configuration is not always possible because certain combinations of permissions that are included in a role's effective privileges may cause information flow. Given a role-based graph where role's permissions refer to labeled data objects, Osborn et al. showed how to find conflicts that are resulted from information flow, but they have not suggested a solution for these conflicts and they have not handled user-role assignments, for the solved scheme. In this paper, we assume a more general model of permissions conflicts than MAC. We introduce an algorithm that handles information flow conflicts in a given role-based graph, corrects the Role-based graph if needed, and proposes a consistent users-roles assignment. As RBAC and information flow are becoming extremely important in Web based information systems, this algorithm becomes very relevant.

**Keywords:** Role based access control, role graph consistency, canonical groups.

## 1 Introduction

The RBAC (Role Based Access Control) model [21] has taken place, for several years now, as an alternative to the MAC (Mandatory Access Control) and DAC (Discretionary Access Control) models, as RBAC simplifies the access control management of complex systems, which contain large number of users, objects and applications [10], [17], [19].

According to MAC method, which is more relevant for our discussion – system elements such as data objects, users and sessions are labeled with security labels. The MAC (or LBAC) model can be represented by a lattice of security labels in which information flow is permitted in one direction only – from a low level to a high level [19]. RBAC is more general than the traditional access methods since it can be configured to enforce both MAC and DAC [17], [19]. Recently RBAC has become an important component of many Web systems and various standards specifying it have appeared [8].

E. Damiani and P. Liu (Eds.): Data and Applications Security 2006, LNCS 4127, pp. 148–162, 2006.

An RBAC system can be illustrated as a hierarchial role-based graph, which is composed of a vertex set and an edge set. A vertex indicates a role, which contains certain privileges. An edge connects a role with its direct ancestor. Privileges of a role are of two kinds: *direct privileges* – privileges which are explicitly assigned to this role, and *effective privileges* – which include the role's direct privileges and the inherited effective privileges of all its juniors [15], see Fig. 1.

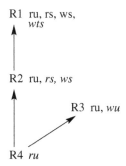

**Fig. 1.** A role-based graph including roles privileges. Direct privileges are marked by italics.

Conflict of interest must be considered while dealing with security. Several kinds of conflicts have been defined and discussed for the role-based graph model [15], of those, role-role conflict and privilege-privilege conflict, are the most relevant here. However, existing algorithms, which support role graph administration, do not try to solve such conflicts. For example, the PrivilegeAddition algorithm execution in [15], [10] aborts when such conflict is detected.

The problem of mapping a given role based system to a valid MAC configuration, was introduced in [17]. Given a role-based graph in which any role contains permissions to data objects that are labeled with security labels, Osborn et al. pointed at conflicts that are resulted from information flow, but they did not suggest any solution for these conflicts. In this paper we handle role-based graph conflicts from the following aspects:

– We address a more general model of information flow and permission conflicts then just MAC.
– We present an algorithm for detecting conflicts in a role-based graph and correcting them by creating new roles or assigning some of the conflicting permissions to existing roles. We then suggest a valid user-role assignment to the corrected graph. This algorithm is also very useful for Role-based administration.
– The resolution of conflicts is based on partitioning the permission-set to *canonical groups* that do not contain conflicts. Such partition raises interesting theoretical issues, which are also discussed.

The above are the main contributions of this paper. The rest of the paper is organized as follows: Section 2 discusses related work and reviews Osborn's work on information flow conflicts for the role-graph model. Section 3 focuses on role-based graph conflicts. We define several constraints, which are more general than those, which have been defined for the MAC model, and we introduce our role-graph consistency verification and correction algorithm. This is followed by a discussion of theoretical issues, which relate to constructing a partition of the role-graph to non-conflicting collections. Finally, in Section 4 we discuss possible applications and future work.

## 2    Related Work

The Role-based model was introduced first by Sandhu et al. [21] and was followed by many papers and standards [1], [11], [19], [20], [8]. An important area in RBAC research is assigning users to roles under various constraints. This was addressed in [4], [12]. Information flow models started with the Bell/Lapadulla model and the MAC methodology, and was followed by work in other directions, such as information flow in object-oriented databases [18], and information flow in distributed systems [14]. The latter works are relevant here, because one can derive from those models sets of permissions, which are in conflict for information flow reasons, and if one assigns such permissions to roles, it will get a role-graph model with possible conflicts. Our work mostly relates to Osborn's work, which investigated several aspects of the RBAC model, using the *role-graph* model. The role-graph model is discussed in [1], [2], [15], [16], [19]. In [17] Osborn et al. show the power of RBAC by configuring RBAC to enforce Mandatory and Discretionary Access control policies. Conflicts of interest and their reflection in a role-based graph are demonstrated in [15]. Role and permission administration for the role graph model are described in [10], [15], [23]. In the next section we briefly review those aspects of Osborn et al. work, which are most relevant to the issues we focus on in this paper.

### 2.1    Osborn's Previous Model

**Mapping Role Hierarchies to LBAC.** LBAC (Lattice Based Access Control) model uses labels to enforce multilevel security. The allowable paths of information flow in an LBAC system, are defined by Mandatory access rules as follows, where $\lambda$ is the security label of the specified entity:

**Definition 1.** *Simple Security Property: Subject $s$ can read object $o$ only if* $\lambda(s) \geq \lambda(o)$.

**Definition 2.** *Liberal (Strict)\* Property: Subject $s$ can write object $o$ only if* $\lambda(s) \leq (=)\lambda(o)$.

In [17] Osborn et al. show how RBAC can be configured to enforce MAC policy. Nevertheless, the structure of role hierarchies that do map to valid LBAC configuration is greatly restricted since several permissions combinations that belong to a role's effective permission-set may cause information flow when assigning the role to a user. Figure 2 illustrates a role-based system, where a role contains permissions to data objects that are labeled with security labels (e.g. **rs** mean "read secret"). All of the roles except the role labeled R7 can be assigned to users without causing any information flow conflict (for example, the roles labeled R1 and R4 can be assigned to unclassified users and the roles labeled R3 and R6 can be assigned to secret users.) Making an assignment of the role labeled R7 to any user is not possible without violating either the Simple Security Property or the Liberal*-Property. Thus, the effective permission-set of R7 is not valid because it can't be assigned to any user without causing information flow.

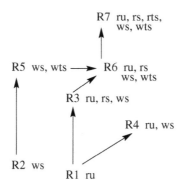

**Fig. 2.** A role-based graph, which includes a role (*R7*) that can't be assigned to any user, since it contains an illegal effective permission set

Osborn introduces two more definitions to capture the maximum read level and the minimum write level (if exists) of objects in a role as follows:

**Definition 3. *The r-level of a role* R *(denoted* r-level(R)*)***
r-level(R) *is the least upper bound (lub) of the security levels of the objects o for which (o, r) is in the permissions of R.*

**Definition 4. *The w-level of a role* R *(denoted* w-level(R)*)***
w-level(R) *is the greatest lower bound (glb) of the security levels of the objects o for which (o, w) is in the permissions of R, if such a glb exists. If the glb does not exist, w-level is undefined.*

Using Definitions 3-4, Osborn defines the following constraint on user/role assignments UA:

**Constraint on UA:**

$$(\text{for every}(u, R)\text{that belongs to } UA[\lambda(u) \geq r\text{-}level(R)])$$

$$(\text{for every}(u, R)\text{that belongs to } UA[\lambda(u) \leq w\text{-}level(R)])$$

**Conflicting Permissions and Conflicting Roles.** As was illustrated in Fig. 2, the pair (rts, ws) creates a *permission-permission conflict*. It obviously violates the constraint above and it means that the two permissions must not appear together. This example demonstrates an *information flow* conflict but there can be other kinds of conflicts among permissions such as *Object-based separation of duty*, or existence of both *positive and negative authorizations* on the same object. The current paper is focused on information flow conflicts. Nevertheless the presented algorithm is general enough to be used on any kind of permission-permission conflicts.

The basic constraint for conflicting permissions states that no role's effective permission-set may contain two permissions, which have been defined to be in conflict. When such a role is discovered it should be modified into one or more consistent roles. This modification is discussed later in the current paper.

Conflicting roles demand even tighter restrictions: If two roles are declared to be in a *Role-role conflict*, then a user authorized to one of the roles, must not be authorized to any of the permissions of the other role. As role-role conflicts apply great limitations on user-role assignments, they induce organizing graph's roles into collections of roles that can be assigned together. Nyanchama and Osborn [15] developed the following technique for partitioning the graph's roles to non-conflicting role collections, using a role-role Matrix $C$, which describes pairs of conflicting roles. For any two roles $r_i$ , $r_j$ that have been defined to conflict – $c_{i,j}$ is set to 1. Next, the dual matrix of $C$ (in which 1's are substituted for 0's vise versa) represents pairs of roles that can be assigned together. The dual matrix is represented by a graph and the cliques in this graph correspond to set of roles, which can be assigned together.

**Role Graph Administration.** Algorithms for manipulating role-based graph are also described in [15]. Graph administration includes role addition, role deletion, permission addition and deletion and edge insertion and deletion. Revised algorithms, which improve the original addition algorithms, are introduced in [10]. While the previous algorithms assume that when a permission $p$ is added to a role, all permissions that might be implied by $p$ are presented in the role automatically, the late addition algorithms actually add those permissions. The role-graph manipulating algorithms that are introduced in [15] and [10] only detect conflicting permissions and roles. The resolving of such conflicts is not dealt with. In case that a permission addition creates a conflict, the permission addition is not performed [10] or the algorithm execution abort [15].

# 3    Resolving Role-Based Graph Conflicts – Our Approach

## 3.1    Assignments Validation Constraints for the MAC Model

We first rewrite Osborn constraints in a slightly more general way, by using the concept of *effective permissions*.

**effective permissions** - the set of permissions assigned directly or inherited via the role-hierarchy.

**Valid effective permission-role constraint:** Effective permission set which is assigned to role $R$ is valid only if: $r\text{-}level(R) \leq w\text{-}level(R)$.

**Valid user-role assignment constraint:** A valid role R can be assigned to user $u$ only if: $\lambda(u) = r\text{-}level(R)$.

The *Valid user-role assignment constraint* satisfies MAC rules, since the minimal write level of objects in a valid role $R$, is greater than the maximal read level of objects in $R$, as the *Valid effective permission set for a role $R$ constraint* assures. Therefore, no information flow occurs while using these assignments constraints. Next we discuss a more general model for permission information flow conflicts.

## 3.2 Assignments Validation Constraints – Extended Model

The model that has been described above is based on the MAC rules, which explicitly determine allowable paths of information flow. In this section we use more general definitions for conflict of interest that may cause information flow. For example Myer's model [14] refers to a system that includes two sets of objects, one that contains objects to which a read operation is defined and the second set contains objects to which a write operation is defined. It also supports multiple independent policies on the same object. The model defines the conditions under which a write operation can be performed on a certain object. When such operations are not allowed then a permission conflict can be defined. Our extended model below can then apply also to Myer's [14] or Samarati et al.[18] models. In the following definitions of the extended model, we use Read and Write operations, but in fact we could have used any conflicting permissions as explained above. Also, in the rest of the discussion we assume the hierarchical model of roles, where a role inherits all permissions of the roles below it.

**Extended model Definitions:**

- *r-set* is a set of objects for which a read permission is defined.
- *r-set(R)*  contains all the read permissions that are assigned to a role $R$, where $r\text{-}set(R) \subseteq r\text{-}set$.
- *w-set*  is a set of objects for which a write permission is defined.
- *w-set(R)* contains the write permissions that are assigned to a role $R$, where $w\text{-}set(R) \subseteq w\text{-}set$.
- *c-set(R)*  is a set of conflicting permissions pairs of the form $(r_i, w_j)$ that can't exist together in a role $R$, where $r_i \in r\text{-}set$ and $w_j \in w\text{-}set$.
- *R-set*  is the set of roles.
- *R-set(u)*  contains the roles that are assigned to a user $u$, where $R\text{-}set(u) \subseteq R\text{-}set$.

Based on the extended model definitions, we can determine the following assignments constraints:

**Valid permission set for a role $R$ constraint – extended model:**
Permission set which is assigned to a role $R$ is valid only if
> for any $r_i \in r\text{-}set(R), w_j \in w\text{-}set(R)$
>> $(r_i, w_j) \notin c\text{-}set(R)$

**Valid user-role assignment constraint – extended model:**
A valid role $R$ can be assigned to a user $u$ only if
> for any $r_i \in r\text{-}set(R), w_j \in w\text{-}set(R)$
>> for any $R_k \in R\text{-}set(u)$ /* already assigned set of roles */
>>> for any $r_m \in r\text{-}set(R_k), w_n \in w\text{-}set(R_k)$
>>>> $(r_i, w_n) \notin c\text{-}set(R) \cup c\text{-}set(R_k)$
>>>> $(r_m, w_j) \notin c\text{-}set(R) \cup c\text{-}set(R_k)$

We like to show now that the above constraints will prevent information flow in the general case. Assume there is information flow from object $X$ to object $Y$. Then there must be a sequence of permissions:

$$P_1(X_1 = X), P_2(X_2), \ldots P_n(X_n = Y)$$

that caused this information flow. In this sequence there must be two permissions in conflict, otherwise there wouldn't be such a flow (proof by induction). Now if these two permissions are assigned to the same role, or to two roles assigned to the same user, the constraint above will detect it, and prevent such assignment. Therefore no information flow is possible. Next we present an algorithm to check the above constraints.

### 3.3    Role Graph Consistency Verification Algorithm

In this section we introduce our resolution, which refers to the model that was described above. It shall be noticed that external regulations as administrative constrains, must be considered before operating the algorithm since such constraints might change the graph's initial configuration.

The purpose of our algorithm is twofold. The first is to check the validity of a given role graph and correct it if needed. The second is to find a valid user-role assignment to the corrected role graph. The algorithm is divided into the following phases:

**a. Creating a consistent graph**
Based on the extended model definitions, the algorithm checks every role's effective permission set for validity, while performing a recursive top-down walk on the role graph $G$. The algorithm's output is $G'$, the corrected role-based graph. The algorithm first phase is presented in Alg. 1.

Since the algorithm descends the graph top-down, it assures that when a role is consistent (or resolved to be consistent), all its sons are already consistent. Therefore, the role-based graph which is output by this algorithm is consistent.

**b. Handling user-role assignments**
The algorithm's second phase handles user assignments to the corrected role graph, and is shown in Alg. 2. This algorithm is very similar to the algorithm

**Algorithm 1** Role graph consistency verification algorithm
**Input** $G(N, \rightarrow)$ a role-based graph possibly containing information flow conflicts.
**Output** $G'(N, \rightarrow)$ a role graph based on $G$, which does not include any information flow conflict.
**Method** Resolving permission assignment conflicts

```
 1: copy G to G'
 2: for every connected component of G' do
 3:     for every root of component of G' do
 4:         if root is consistent then exit
 5:         for every son of root do
 6:             perform a recursive Depth-first walk, in which:
 7:             for every role R do
 8:                 for every r_i , w_j where r_i ∈ r-set(R) , w_j ∈ w-set(R) do
 9:                     if  (r_i, w_j) ∈ c-set(R) then
10:                         create the canonical groups for R effective permission set
11:                     for every canonical group cg  do
12:                         combine cg permissions to an existing role or create a new role
13:                         for cg or for a part of it, according to the system's policy
14: Phase b
```

presented in [15], except that it accepts as input the already modified role-based graph generated by Alg. 1. and in the last step it may handle additional user-user constraints as follows. At the last step one may assign users to the found cliques or to subsets of them. However, when individual users are assigned, additional user-user constraints such as separation of duty constraints may be present. A general scheme for user-role assignment with general constraints was presented in [12] using the techniques of Constraint processing (CSP). This technique is very powerful for solving various types of constraints and can works also in the distributed case as was shown in [13].

Next we discuss in detail the correction of inconsistent roles.

**The Problem of Correcting Role Inconsistency.** Once we find an inconsistent role, we are faced with the problem of correcting it, and create a valid new and consistent role graph. There may be several approaches to solving this problem, And we discuss two of them here.

The first approach tries to locate the permissions, which are most "problematic", and remove them from the checked role. If we represent the permissions and the conflicts between them as a graph, we like to find minimal set of permissions that will remove all conflicts. This problem is equivalent to the Vertex-Cover problem and is known to be NP-hard [7]. For any permission removed from the checked role, we should first check if it already exists in another role, and only if it does not exist, we should create a new role for it. This new role may contain the removed permission plus all consistent permissions with it, which were in the checked role. The problem with this approach is that it tends to split the original permissions to too many groups.

**Algorithm 2** Handling user assignments to the consistent graph
**Input** $G'(N, \rightarrow)$ a role graph based on $G$, which does not include any information flow conflict.
**Output** Legal user-role assignments.

    **Phase1** Performing a search for conflicting permissions that are assigned to separate roles and representing the conflicts by a graph
1: **for** every two roles $R_i$ , $R_j$ such that there exist permissions $p_1$ in $R_i$ and $p_2$ in $R_j$ that are in conflict **do**
2:      add the edge $(R_i, R_j)$ to the role conflict graph $GC$.

    **Phase2** Constructing GC' – GC graph complement and Getting potentially legal user-role assignments
3: **for** every couple of roles $R_i$ , $R_j$ which appear in the role-based graph $G'$: **do**
4:      **if** the edge $(R_i, R_j)$ does not appear in $GC$ **then**
5:          add $(R_i, R_j)$ to $GC'$.
6: find all the cliques in graph $GC'$.         ▷ Get legal user-role assignments
    **Phase3** Perform the actual user-role assignment considering all constraints

Another approach uses the concept of *canonical groups*. A canonical group is a maximal set of permissions with no conflict in it. The problem of finding canonical groups is discussed in Section 3.4. For now we assume that the permission set was divided into a set of canonical groups. Then we suggest the following heuristics: When an inconsistent role $R$ is found, the graph correction has to be performed using the algorithm: Resolve_Using_Canonical_Groups.

**Resolve_Using_Canonical_Groups.** For every canonical group $cg$, which includes permissions that have to be removed from the effective permission set of $R$:

1. In case that there is not any role to which the permissions that are included in $cg$ are assigned – create a new role $R_N$ and assign $cg$ permissions to it. $R_N$ will be put above the role that contains the maximal subset of $cg$, in the role hierarchy.
2. In case that the role graph contains already a consistent role $R'$ to which $cg$ permissions are assigned:
   (a) If $R'$ does not contain any permission except $cg$ permissions – there is no need to perform any change.
   (b) In case that $R'$ – to which $cg$ permissions are assigned, contains additional permissions – the decision whether a creation of a new role for $cg$ permissions is needed – is depended on the system designer policy.
3. In case that the role graph contains a consistent role $R''$ to which only a part of $cg$ permissions are assigned – create a new role, $R_N$ , for those $cg$ permissions that are not included in $R''$. In case $R''$ contains only permissions which are in $cg$, put $R_N$ above $R''$ in the role hierarchy, otherwise perform step 2b above.

*In any case*: Delete $cg$ permissions from the original role's permission set.

**Theorem 1.** *The two algorithms, the verification and the resolving algorithms result with a consistent role-based graph.*

The proof uses mathematical induction and is omitted here for space reasons.

Note that the heuristics above is not necessarily "optimal". One may define optimal by the following criteria: Find a division of the permission set of the checked role, such that the total number of changes (including role addition, permission addition and permission deletion) is minimized. We are still investigating this problem. The other issue is what we called "system policy". it is possible that an organization will have some policy constraints regarding the composition of roles and the hierarchy of roles, e.g. a specific branch of a hierarchy should not be modified. Such constraints should be taken into account when we assign the cannonical groups to roles or create new roles. We plan to investigate this issue too in the future.

Figures 3a, 3b illustrate the algorithm's operation on a given inconsistent role based graph $G$. Note that for this example, we assumed that $R1$ is the only inconsistent role in the graph, therefore the canonical groups can be assigned to existing roles without checking those role's permission sets for consistency. As explained earlier, the general algorithm can handle multiple inconsistent roles. Figure 4a shows the resultant role-conflicts graph and Fig. 4b shows the resultant dual graph $GC'$ and the resulting conflict-free cliques. Finally, as discussed earlier, the actual user/role assignment may be performed using the methods presented in [12].

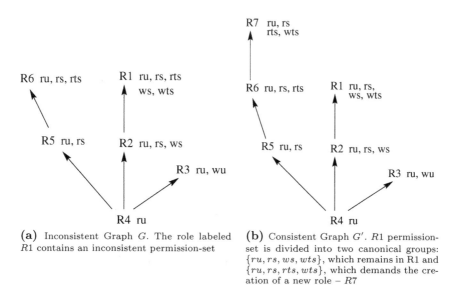

(**a**) Inconsistent Graph $G$. The role labeled $R1$ contains an inconsistent permission-set

(**b**) Consistent Graph $G'$. $R1$ permission-set is divided into two canonical groups: $\{ru, rs, ws, wts\}$, which remains in $R1$ and $\{ru, rs, rts, wts\}$, which demands the creation of a new role – $R7$

**Fig. 3.** Resolving information flow conflicts in a role based graph

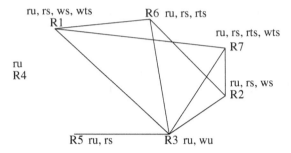

**(a)** $GC$ - the conflicting-roles graph which is derived of $G'$

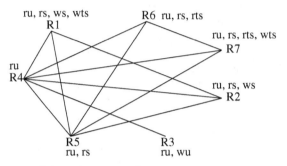

**(b)** $GC'$ - the dual non-conflicting-roles graph

$$G_1 : \{R_1, R_2, R_4, R_5\}$$
$$G_2 : \{R_3, R_4\}$$
$$G_3 : \{R_4, R_5, R_6, R_7\}$$

**Fig. 4.** Finding conflict-free cliques for user-role assignment

### 3.4   The Problem of Finding Canonical Groups

The problematic permission-set which is assigned to the role labeled R7 in Fig. 2, can be divided into non-conflicting groups in several ways, as it is illustrated in Table 1. One possible division is to include the read permissions in one group and the write permissions into another group, as is shown in line 1 of the table. An alternative resolution is to partition the permissions set into canonical groups. Canonical groups are defined to be maximal groups of non-conflicting elements, as is demonstrated in the second line of Table 1. In this case first the two conflicting permissions are divided between the two groups, and then the rest of the permissions can be assigned to both of the groups.

Obviously, not all resolutions can be satisfied by forming only two cannonical groups, but one is usually interested in minimizing the number of such groups in order to minimize the required changes to the role-graph.

**Table 1.** Two optional divisions for the inconsistent permission set (ru, rs, rts, ws, wts) to non-conflicting groups

|   | ru, rs, rts, ws, wts |
|---|---|
| 1. | ru, rs, rts / ws, wts |
| 2. | rts, ru, rs, wts / ws, ru, rs, wts |

The problem of dividing a permission set into a minimal number canonical groups is similar to the problem of finding cliques in an undirected graph. A clique of a graph is a maximal complete sub-graph. Covering vertices by cliques (VERTEX CLIQUE COVER or CLIQUE PARTITION), is an NP-complete problem [7], [22], and is also equivalent to the GRAPH COLORING problem: A graph has a vertex clique cover of size $k$ iff its complement graph can be colored with $k$ colors such that adjacent vertices have different colors [7]. Finding a minimal coloring can be done using brute-force search [6], [22], [24], but more efficient algorithms exist for some special cases. The *four-color theorem* establishes that all *planar graphs* (graphs that can be drawn in a plane without graph edges crossing) are 4-colorable [22].

*Two-colorable* graphs are exactly *bipartite graphs*. A *bipartite graph* is a set of graph vertices decomposed into two disjoint sets such that no two graph vertices within the same set are adjacent. A bipartite graph is a special case of a *k-partite graph* with $k = 2$. A graph is bipartite iff all its cycles are of even length [22]. To determine if a graph $G = (V, E)$ is bipartite, we perform a BFS search on it with a little modification, whose run time is $O(V + E)$ [7].

A related problem is covering the edges of a graph with a minimum number of cliques, which is known as the CLIQUE COVER problem, and is also an NP-complete problem. For CLIQUE COVER there is a solving algorithm, which is polynomial time heuristic from the 1970's. Gramm et al. present an improved version for this heuristic, using data reduction techniques, in [9].

In practice, it may very well be that two cannonical groups will be sufficient for resolving the inconsistency. So it will be worthwhile first to check if the graph is bi-partite, before attempting to use the more complex algorithms for finding more than two cannonical groups.

Note that the second algorithm, the user-role assignment also requires finding cliques, so similar theoretical problems arise. Finally, the actual user-role assignment under user-user constraints also present some theoretical questions, some of them are NP hard and some are polynomial and can be reduced to a network-flow problem. This is discussed in detail in [13].

### 3.5 Extending Administration Algorithms

Nyanchama and Osborn's basic algorithms for adding a permission to a role and for adding a role to the role based graph [15], contain the following lines for conflict of interest detection which checks any role that belongs to the graph's roles, after making the addition:

**If** *effective(r) contains a pair of privileges which is in p-conflicts* **then abort**.

Our solution in this case is to perform the *Role graph consistency verification algorithm*, which checks any role for consistency and makes graph corrections using the algorithms discussed above. Note that the organization (system) policies may be different when a permission is added to a role, or when a role is added to a hierarchy and these should be taken into account.

# 4    Discussion and Future Work

The algorithms above can be useful in several applications and also raise several outstanding issues. These issues and future research are discussed in this section.

1. **User-role assignment and delegation.** As was discussed above the role hierarchy does not limit user-role assignments only to roles along the same hierarchy. However, if we allow delegation of roles from one user to another, the problem becomes more difficult. Such delegation requires running the verification algorithm for each such delegation, which may create considerable overhead. One possible restriction is to allow delegation only along the role hierarchy. Obviously, if a user of role $R_i$ delegates to a user with role $R_j$ where $R_i < R_j$ then no role conflict will occur, since originally the graph is consistent and role $R_i$ has inherited all permissions of $R_j$. Therefore, if users are assigned to roles only along a single hierarchy, delegation will be consistent and no verification will be needed (except for constraints such as SOD). Otherwise, the algorithm needs to be executed for each such delegation.

2. **Dynamic user-role assignment.** The restrictions above on static role assignment (i.e. assigning users only conflict-free cliques) may put heavy restriction on a real life system. Similar to the MAC policy, if we enforce the static * property, then an employee who has a top-secret job cannot write an email to his wife who has a confidential level. The *water-mark* policy used in MAC systems can be used here. Thus, roles can be assigned dynamically to an application based on its dynamic needs, and therefore role conflicts must be checked dynamically. Furthermore, the application may require a temporary assignment of hierarchy between roles. In that case, the verification algorithm will need to be executed as well. Note that even in the dynamic case, to detect the conflicts one does not need to create a log of the operations performed. If we extend the "water-mark" idea to permissions and allow assignment of conflicting roles to the same user, then we just need to create a log of permissions and make sure no conflicting permissions were assigned.

3. **Distributed systems.** The algorithm can be also used in distributed systems. For example, a system composed of two sub-systems, anyone of them contains data-base and files. Suppose that a user gets access to sub-system1, by assigning him to a role $R$ that belongs to sub-system1's roles. In case that the user is also assigned to certain roles in sub-ststem2, the system has to check whether the new permissions he gets are not conflicting with his sub-system2's permissions. This check and the corrections that follow it are made using the *Role graph consistency verification algorithm*.

4. **Integrating multi-domains.** The problem of integrating the security requirements of multiple domains is a serious problem in our cooperative business world (see [3], [5]). The integration of such multiple domains requires the mapping of two separate role hierarchies into a single hierarchy. Such integration will require an algorithm, which is basically a generalization of the single verification and correction algorithm shown here and is a topic of future research

5. **The problem of optimal correction.** As was demonstrated in Section 3, there may be several policies to correct an inconsistency in role definition. The criteria of optimality, is not very obvious, and both the criteria and the algorithm required to satisfy it are a subject for future research. Related to that is the issue of satisfying system policy and organization constraints.

6. **Other kinds of permission-permission conflicts.** Although our model can be implemented on any kind of permission-permission conflicts, it refers mostly to information flow conflicts. Solving other kinds of permission-permission conflicts may force different criteria for division to canonical groups than has been introduced here. This is also a topic for future work.

**Acknowledgement.** We thank Max Binshtok for helping with the editing and LATEX of the manuscript.

# References

1. G. J. Ahn, Specification and Classification of Role-Based Authorization Policies: IEEE Computer Society, 2003.
2. A. Belokosztolszki, D. Eyers, K. Moody, Policy Contexts: Controlling Information Flow in Parameterised RBAC, IEEE Computer Society, 2003.
3. P. Belsis, S. Gritzalis: A scalable Security Architecture enabling coalition formation between autonomous domains. Proceedings of ISSPIT2005, Athens, Greece, 2005.
4. E. Bertino, E. Ferrari, V. Atluri: The Specification and Enforcement of Authorization Constraints in Workflow Management Systems, ACM Trans. Inf. Systems. Security. 2(1): 65-104 (1999).
5. E. Bertino, J. Joshi, R. Bhatti, A. Ghafoor: Access-Control Language for Multidomain Environments. IEEE Internet Computing 8(6): 40-50 (2004).
6. N. Christofides: An Algorithm for the Chromatic Number of a Graph, Computer J. 14, 38-39, 1971.
7. T. Cormen, C. Leiserson, R. Rivest: Introduction to Algorithms, MIT Press, Cambridge, 83, 89 506-539, 1990.
8. D. F. Ferraiolo, R. Sandhu, S. Gavrila, D. Kuhn and R. Chandramouli: Proposed NIST Standard for Role-Based Access Control, ACM Transactions on Information and System Security, Vol. 4, No. 3, August 2001, Pages 224-274.
9. J. Gramm, J. Guo, F. Huffner, R. Niedermeir: Data Reduction, Exact and Heuristic Algorithms for Clique Cover, In Proceedings of the 8th Workshop on Algorithm Engineering and Experiments (ALENEX 2006), Miami, USA, January 2006.
10. C. M. Ionita, S. Osborn: Privilege administration for the role graph model. In Proc.IFIP WG11.3 Working Conference on Database Security, July 2002.
11. J. Joshi, E. Bertino, B. Shafiq, A. Ghafoor: Dependencies and Separation of Duty Constraints in GTRBAC, SACMAT'03 June 2-3, 2003.

12. I. Moodahi, E. Gudes, O. Lavee, A. Meisels: A SecureWorkflow Model Based on Distributed Constrained Role and Task Assignment for the Internet, ICICS 2004: 171-186.
13. I. Moodahi, E. Gudes, A. Meisels: A three tier architecture for Role/User assignment for the Internet, submitted for a journal publication.
14. A. C. Myers, B. Liskov: A Decentralized Model for Information Flow Control (1997) Proceedings of the 16th ACM Symposium on Operating Systems Principles, Saint-Malo, France, October 1997.
15. M. Nyanchama, S. Osborn: The Role Graph Model and Conflict of Interest, ACM Transactions on Information and Systems Security, vol. 2, no. 1, (1999) 3-33.
16. S. Osborn: Information Flow Analysis of an RBAC system, SACMAT02, June 3-4, 2002.
17. S. Osborn, R. Sandhu and Q. Munawer: Configuring Role-Based Access Control to enforce Mandatory and Discretionary access control policies, ACM Trans. Information and system security, 3(2): 1-23, 2000.
18. P. Samarati, E. Bertino, A. Ciampichetti, S. Jajodia: Information Flow Control in Object-Oriented Systems. IEEE Trans. Knowl. Data Eng. 9(4): 524-538 (1997).
19. R. Sandhu: Lattice-based access control models, IEEE Computer 26, 11, 9-19, 1993.
20. R. Sandhu: Role Hierarchies and constraints for lattice-based Access Controls, Proc. Fourth European on Research in Computer Security, Rome, Italy, September 25-27, 1996.
21. R. Sandhu, E. J. Coyne, H. L. Feinstein, C. E. Youman: Role-based access control models, IEEE Computer 29, 2, 38-47, 1996.
22. S. Skiena: Finding a Vertex Coloring, 5.5.3 in Implementing Discrete Mathematics: Combinatorics and Graph Theory with Mathematica, Reading, MA: Addison-Wesley, pp. 141, 214-215, 1990.
23. H. Wang, S. Osborn: An Administrative Model for Role Graphs, Proc. IFIP WG11.3 Working Conference on Database Security, Estes Park, Colorado, 2003.
24. H. Wilf, Backtrack: An O(1) Expected Time Algorithm for the Graph Coloring Problem, Info. Proc. Let. 18, 119-121, 1984.

# Policy Transformations for Preventing Leakage of Sensitive Information in Email Systems

Saket Kaushik[1], William Winsborough[2], Duminda Wijesekera[1], and Paul Ammann[1]

[1] Department of Information & Software Engineering,
George Mason University,
Fairfax, VA 22030, USA
{skaushik, dwijesek, pammann}@gmu.edu
[2] Department of Computer Science,
University of Texas at San Antonio,
San Antonio, TX 78249-0667, USA
wwinsborough@acm.org

**Abstract.** In this paper we identify an undesirable side-effect of combining different email-control mechanisms for protection from unwanted messages, namely, leakage of recipients' private information to message senders. The problem arises because some email-control mechanisms like bonds, graph-turing tests, *etc.*, inherently leak information, and without discontinuing their use, leakage channels cannot be closed. We formalize the capabilities of an attacker and show how she can launch guessing attacks on recipient's mail acceptance policy that utilizes leaky mechanism in an effort to avoid unwanted mail.

The attacker in our model guesses the contents of a recipient's private information. The recipients' use of leaky mechanisms allow the sender to verify her guess. We assume a constraint logic programming based policy language for specification and evaluation of mail acceptance criteria and present two different program transformations that can prevent guessing attacks while allowing recipients to utilize any email-control mechanism in their policies.

**Keywords:** Application layer security, inference attacks, information leakage channels, secrecy.

## 1 Introduction

Email, a widely popular communication medium, is plagued with several problems like delivery of unsolicited commercial or fraudulent messages, lack of authentication of message senders, inability to ensure integrity and secrecy of message content, *etc.* Several solutions have been proposed to counter these problems and many have been incorporated into the delivery mechanisms. However, there exists a class of problems that has not received much attention yet, which is the problem of protection of recipients' sensitive information. It is surprisingly easy to uncover information that recipients may consider sensitive, like recipient maintained *blacklist* or *whitelist*. Not only can this lead to security breaches; it can also jeopardize the defenses against unwanted messages. In this paper, we formalize this problem and a new attack technique on policy based evaluation, which is a counterpart to dictionary attacks on cryptographic protocols [3]. As

E. Damiani and P. Liu (Eds.): Data and Applications Security 2006, LNCS 4127, pp. 163–178, 2006.
© IFIP International Federation for Information Processing 2006

a solution we also provide a policy transformation technique to prevent attacks on sensitive information.

Leakages can occur in many ways. For instance, simple *address harvesting* attacks through the Simple Mail Transfer Protocol (SMTP [16]), the default email delivery protocol, are easy to construct. In this attack, a malicious sender attempts delivery to a preconstructed list of possible recipient addresses, and recipient mail server replies help her to identify which addresses are assigned to users [13]. Contrary to the SMTP protocol recommendations, mail servers can prohibit such feedback, thus implementing a blanket protection policy against harvesting attacks. More fine-tuned, policy-based schemes for feedback control are also possible [8].

Because email-control techniques in use at a mail server can send feedback out of band with SMTP, controlling SMTP feedback to senders is not enough to protect recipient's private data. For example, graph-turing tests for ensuring human-initiation of email messages [12] respond to incoming messages with a puzzle that can only be solved by humans. Senders can, thus, infer that mail address belongs to a real user and being protected against unwanted mail. This signal also informs the sender that the sent message was able to overcome the recipient's Bayesian filters. This knowledge can further help a malicious sender in propagating unwanted emails in future. Apart from the efficacy of filter rules, a recipient or a domain may wish to protect a lot of other private data, like their email behavior, the set of their email acquaintances, *etc.*

In this paper, we identify two types of email-control mechanisms, *viz.*, *leaky mechanisms* like monetary bonds, acknowledgement receipts, *etc.*, and *sensitive mechanisms* like white-lists, *i.e.*, the set of senders from whom a recipient always accepts emails, blacklists, *i.e.*, the set of senders from whom the recipient does not wish to receive messages, filters, *etc.* A leaky mechanism is defined as an email-control mechanism that, when used, informs the sender whether his or her message was accepted by the recipient or not. Whereas, a sensitive mechanism is defined as an email control mechanism that uses recipient's private information to decide whether to accept a message or not, but does not disclose any information to the sender. However, if these two types of mechanisms are used in combination, disclosure of recipient's private information is possible and it is the security goal of this paper to prevent such disclosures. Readers may be familiar with leakages due to well-crafted web addresses and images embedded within a message that provide automatic acknowledgement receipts. In section 2 we provide additional details on such leakages. Mechanisms like blacklists, filters, *etc.*, are sensitive because of the nature of the information they control and because their knowledge can help a malicious sender to bypass the control they provide.

The abundance of email-control solutions and the need for automation of several aspects of user's email agents have led to the use of policies that allow flexible control over the behavior of local email systems. Such policies are easily constructed through end user input (*e.g.*, simple user feedback allows Gmail to display or not display embedded images, *etc.*) and through explicit administrator level policies, leading to considerable automation of repetitive tasks. However, because the email system is highly automated, there exists a potential for confidential information to be leaked unintentionally. Even though it is not guaranteed that using a means to leak information will reveal information, however, the probability of leakage of sensitive information, when using leaky and sensitive mechanisms in combination, is non-zero. In particular, schemes that allow sharing acceptance policies to stop undesirable messages earlier in the transmission process (see [8]) compound the problem. Armed with this knowledge, an attacker can simply send a large volume of messages and extract sensitive information from the behavior of the feedback channel.

Our modeling of an attacker assumes basic capabilities of computing unfold/fold transformations [17], computing Clark completion of predicate definitions, and the ability to generate a large number of messages. Though, in the worst case analysis, the attacker need send only a $O(n)$ number of message, where $n$ is the size of the policy.

## 1.1   Overview of Our Approach

A survey of recent proposals and initiatives for controlling unwanted messages give sufficient evidence of an eventual move towards policy-controlled email systems. Existing implementations exhibit varied policy evaluation strategies, from complete secrecy (like silent dropping of messages identified as unwanted during Bayesian filtering [19]) to requests for additional information (like human verification tests [12]). Bringing all strategies under a single umbrella enables, both, sharing and hiding of acceptance criteria. Clearly, sanitization of acceptance policies is a prerequisite to communicating them upstream. However, it is our view that such a (non-trivial) task cannot be entrusted to end users. The only option that remains is to automatically 'strengthen' or sanitize policies susceptible to leakage; a non-trivial problem addressed here.

Our first step in policy sanitization is to distinguish leaky mechanisms and sensitive information in the policy syntax. Next, we provide a syntactic transformation of the original policy into two zero-information leakage policies and show that they don't leak protected information. The first transformation simply drops all references to sensitive information. The resultant policy, called necessary policy, identifies a set of criteria thus must be satisfied, assuming best case scenario with respect to sensitive information. Similarly, the second transformation constructs a sufficient policy that assumes worst case scenario with respect to sensitive information and identifies messages that can still be accepted. The necessary policy can be shared without risk of leakages, while sufficient policy is designed to be applied at only at the recipient end – thereby achieving complete secrecy in policy evaluation.

## 1.2   Our Contribution

The main contributions of this paper include what is to the best of our knowledge the first formal analysis of confidentiality problems in the context of emails, and a novel solution to protect sensitive information from attacks. In summary:

- We develop a logical formalism for expressing and solving the problem of leakage of private information due to the use of leaky mechanisms.
- We define a new attacker model with the attacker being capable of computing *Clark completion* of programs and applying *unfold/fold transformations* in addition to the ability of generating messages. We show that this is enough to uncover information considered sensitive by the message recipient.

- We describe a new type of information leakage attack on email systems due to the combination of email-control mechanisms.
- We develop two policy transformation schemes, namely, necessary and sufficient policies that, when used in tandem, can prevent the leakage of sensitive email information.

The rest of the paper is organized as follows. In section 2 we provide some motivating examples of information leakage attacks. Formal model of security policies for email are presented in section 3, followed by the attacker model in section 4. In section 5 we discuss the transformation algorithm and necessary and sufficient policy transformations that can prevent leakage of information, followed by the related work (section 6) and the conclusion (section 7).

## 2   Examples

We focus on automatic leakage of information through the email system. A simple leakage scenario is one where specially crafted messages can lead to recipients divulging private financial information to attackers. Such attack techniques are termed as 'phishing' and are beyond the scope of this paper. Several types of information may be regarded as valuable by different classes of message senders. For example, a large set of valid email users or the strength of message filtering rules of an email domain would be valuable to bulk emailers. For these and other reasons senders may want to know if their messages were read by the recipient, even if the recipient does not wish to release an acknowledgment receipt. We provide some basic examples below how the system could be manipulated to yield such confirmations.

### 2.1   Direct Disclosure

SMTP, the default email protocol, allows leakage of information, as discussed earlier. In table 1 we list some of the reply codes that can be used for gaining confirmation of valid/invalid email addresses and is an example of direct leakage. In addition, email-control schemes using protocols layered on top of the SMTP protocol can also result in leakage of information. For instance, graph-turing tests [12] generate a human-solvable challenge for incoming messages, and accept messages only if the answer is correct. However, issuing a challenge confirms that the recipient address is in use. As these disclosures are made through feedback provided in the protocol, they can be prevented by modifying the behavior of SMTP state machine. In the rest of the paper, we assume that these disclosures can be prevented using policy-based control schemes for feedback control [8] and don't investigate them further.

### 2.2   Disclosure Through Leaky Mechanisms

Mechanisms that provide feedback beyond the SMTP reply codes are called leaky as they can reveal information even if all SMTP feedback is prevented. For instance, bond seizure [10] is one such means. We characterize these leakages as follows:

- **Confirmation of email address:** Confirmation of email addresses is desired (usually by bulk emailers) for increased 'viewership'.

**Table 1.** Leakage through SMTP reply codes

| Reply Code | Meaning | Confirmation provided |
|---|---|---|
| 251 | User not local; will forward to ⟨email address⟩ | Forwarding address |
| 450 | Mailbox unavailable | Invalid address |
| 452 | Insufficient system storage | Valid address |
| 550 | Mailbox unavailable | Invalid address |
| 551 | User not local; try ⟨email address⟩ | Forwarding address |
| 553 | Mailbox name not allowed | Invalid address |

- **Leakage of sensitive information:** Validity of address is known by sender; additional private information, like contents of filter rules, reputation lists are sought.

**Example 1 (Leakage through monetary bonds).** *Consider a simple recipient policy that allows messages from people not on her blacklist if they attach a bond valued at least at $ a; for all other users, a bond worth $ b ($b > a$) is required. We represent this policy informally next. A formal definition of syntax is presented later.*

$$accept \; -if- \; some \; 'allow' \; rule \; is \; true \; and \; all \; 'disallow' \; rules \; are \; false \quad (1)$$

$$allow \; -if- \; sender \; is \; not \; blacklisted \; and \; message \; is \; bonded \; with \; value \; a \quad (2)$$

$$allow \; -if- \; for \; all \; other \; senders \; message \; is \; bonded \; with \; value \; b > a \quad (3)$$

$$disallow \; -if- \; if \; message \; has \; an \; attachment \; with \; extension \; .scr \quad (4)$$

*First, assume the sender knows that an acceptance policy uses blacklists and bonds together, but doesn't know the values a and b. The sender can send a large number of messages with different bonds and analyze seizure information to deduce a and b. If on the other hand, policies are shared, the values are already known. With this information, the sender can easily verify if an email address he can send mail from is in the recipient's blacklist or not – by sending as little as only one email message with bond of value $ c, $c \in (a,b)$ attached. Assuming that the targeted recipient seizes bonds for all commercial mail delivered, no seizure or seizure of bond will prove to the sender that he is not on the blacklist or not, respectively.*

## 3   Formal Model

We assume that each message is evaluated by a single evaluation engine, unlike other proposals [8]. We reconcile this design decision with existing proposals by admitting a syntax that is more general, and can be specialized according to the needs.

### 3.1   Syntax

**Definition 1 (Constraint domain).** *We use finite integer domain as the constraint domain, represented by $\mathcal{R}$, that supports standard interpretation of the symbols $=$, $\neq$, $\leq$ and $\geq$. We assume that non-numeric constants can be encoded in finite integer domain.*

**Definition 2 (Terms).** *Terms consist of only variables and constants. Constants are from the set $\mathcal{R}$. Tuples of terms $t_1, \ldots, t_N$ may be represented by $\overrightarrow{t}$.*

**Definition 3 (Primitive constraint).** *A primitive constraint is of the form $q(t_1, t_2)$ where q is a symbol from the set $\{=, \neq, \leq, \geq\}$ and $t_1$, $t_2$ are terms such that $t_1$ is a variable and $t_2$ is a constant. We use infix notation to represent primitive constraints.*

**Definition 4 (Constraint).** *A constraint is conjunction ($\wedge$) of primitive constraints.*

**Definition 5 (Predicates).** *Predicate symbols are partitioned into three sets: $R_D$, which are the user defined predicates, $R_U$, which are the system defined predicates, and $R_A$ is the set of predicates that are guesses for predicates in $R_D$. In particular, we assume that top level predicate symbols* allow *and* disallow $\in R_D$ *and* accept $\in R_U$. .

We treat a message as a set of facts that constrain email message headers and content to sender supplied values. For instance, `Mail From: abc@xyz` is encoded as $atrb_{\text{From}}(abc@xyz.com)$ where $atrb_{\text{From}}$ is an $R_D$ predicate. Example $R_D$ predicates include $atrb_{\text{Bond}}$ – representing attached bonds, $atrb_{\text{Attachment}}$ representing attachments, *etc*. Predicates required for defining *allow, disallow* predicates are included in $R_D$, as discussed in the definition of clauses below.

**Definition 6 (Private and Sensitive Predicates).** *Subsets of $R_D$ predicates, represented by $\mathcal{P}$ and $\mathcal{L}$, form the set of private and sensitive predicates, respectively.*

**Definition 7 (System-defined Predicates $R_U$).** *$R_U$ predicates are further partitioned into following sets:*

**Mch.** *For each predicate $p_i \in \mathcal{P}$, two predicate symbols, $matchP_i$ and $matchNotP_i$ of same arity as $p_i$, are reserved to be defined by the program. In addition for every predicate $Q_j \notin \mathcal{P}$, the program reserves predicate symbols $Q_j MatchP_i$ and $Q_j MatchNotP_i$.*

**Pes.** *For every predicate Q, such that $Q \notin \mathcal{P}$, the program reserves a predicate symbol 'pesQ', Q's pessimistic version (defined in section 5).*

**Opt.** *For every predicate Q, such that $Q \notin \mathcal{P}$, the program reserves a predicate symbol 'optQ', Q's optimistic version (defined in section 5).*

**Definition 8 (Atom and Literal).** *An atom is of the form $q(t_1, \ldots, t_n)$ where q is a symbol from $R_D \cup R_U \cup \{=, \neq, \leq, \geq\}$ and $t_1, \ldots, t_n$ are terms. A literal is an atom (called a positive literal) or its negation (called a negative literal).*

**Definition 9 (Clause, Fact and Rule).** *A clause is of the form $H \leftarrow B$ where H is an atom, and B is a list of literals. A fact is a clause in which B is an empty list or a list of literals with predicate symbols from the set $\{=, \neq, \leq, \geq\}$. A clause is called a rule otherwise.*

**Definition 10 (CLP Program).** *A CLP Program (simply a program) is a set of clauses. For a program $\Pi$ and a predicate P, $P \propto \Pi$ if for any rule $H \leftarrow B_1, \ldots, B_n$ in $\Pi$, P = $H\theta$ or $P = B_i\theta$ ($i \in [1,n]$) for some $\theta$.*

**Definition 11 (Message).** *A message is a set of facts.*

**Definition 12 (Mail Acceptance Policy).** *A mail acceptance policy, or simply, a policy is a pair* $\Pi = \langle \Pi_R, \Pi_D \rangle$ *where* $\Pi_R$ *is a set of rules (ruleset) and* $\Pi_D$ *is a set of facts. The program* $\Pi_R$ *is required to be stratified and contain definitions of top level predicate accept and at least one of the predicates: allow, disallow. The predicate symbol accept is always defined as*

$$accept(\overrightarrow{msg}) \leftarrow allow(\overrightarrow{msg}), \neg disallow(\overrightarrow{msg})$$

Here $\overrightarrow{msg}$ tuple represents all the variables and their bindings derived from a message, e.g., *From, To, Time, Bond, etc.*, would all be included in the tuple. Predicates other than *allow, disallow* may have single variables from $\overrightarrow{msg}$ tuple as arguments.

### 3.2 Semantics

We reuse the three-valued semantics (with constructive negation) used in [8], which is Fages' fully abstract semantics $(T_P(I) = \langle T_P^+(I), T_P^-(I) \rangle)$ where symbols are as defined in [6], P = $\Pi \cup$ M where M is a message and $I = \langle I^+, I^- \rangle$ in which $I^+$ and $I^-$ are disjoint sets of constrained atoms, defined next.

**Definition 13 (Constrained atom).** *A constrained atom is a pair* $c|A$ *in which c is a solvable constraint, A is an atom and free variables occurring in c also occur as free in A. The set of all constrained atoms is denoted by* $\mathcal{B}$.

**Definition 14.** *Immediate consequence function*
$T_P^+(I) = \{c|p(X) \in \mathcal{B} \mid$ *there exist a* $p(X) \leftarrow d|A_1, \ldots, A_m, \neg A_{m+1}, \ldots, \neg A_n \in P$ *with local variables Y,* $c_i|A_i \in I^+$ *for* $i \in [1,m]$ *and* $c_j|A_j \in I^-$ *for* $j \in [m+1,n]$ *such that* $c = \exists Y(d \wedge \bigwedge_{i=i}^n c_i)$ *is satisfiable* $\}$ $T_P^-(I) = \{c|p(X) \in \mathcal{B} \mid p(X) \leftarrow d_k|A_{k,1}, \ldots, A_{k,m_k}, \neg A_{k,m_k+1}, \ldots, \neg A_{k,n_k}$ *for every clause with head* $p \in P$ *and local variables* $Y_k$, *there exist* $e_{k,1}|A_{k,1}, \ldots, e_{k,m_k}|A_{k,m_k} \in I^-$ *and* $e_{k,m_k+1} \mid A_{k,m_k+1}, \ldots, e_{k,n_k}|A_{k,n_k} \in I^+$, *such that* $c = \bigwedge_k \forall Y_k(\neg d_k \vee \bigvee_{i=i}^{n_k} e_{k,i})$ *is satisfiable* $\}$.

**Definition 15.** *Ordinal powers of* $T_P$
$T_P \uparrow 0 = \emptyset$; $T_P \uparrow \beta = T_P(T_P \uparrow \beta - 1)$, $\beta$ *is a successor ordinal;* $T_P \uparrow \alpha = \bigsqcup_{\beta < \alpha} T_P \uparrow \beta$, *in which* $\alpha$ *is a limit ordinal and* $\bigsqcup_{\beta < \alpha} T_P \uparrow \beta = \langle \bigcup_{\beta < \alpha}(T_P \uparrow \beta)^+, \bigcup_{\beta < \alpha}(T_P \uparrow \beta)^- \rangle$.

A message is accepted if $c| \, accept(\overrightarrow{msg}) \in T_P^+ \uparrow \omega$ where $\overrightarrow{msg}$ is a tuple of headers and content supplied in the message. The authors show that the decision procedure using the presented semantics is complete [8].

**Definition 16 (Extension of a predicate).** *Extension of a predicate p is the set ext(p)* $\subset T_P^+(I)$ *such that each constrained atom in ext(p) is of the form* $c| \, p(\overrightarrow{x})$.

Space constraints prohibit us from defining Clark completion here, so we refer the reader to Jaffar and Maher's survey on CLP [7]; later examples can help unfamiliar readers understand the concept better. We represent completion of a predicate p by p*.

## 4 Attacker Model

An attacker is constrained to unlimited, but legal runs of the SMTP protocol. We make following (worst-case) assumptions:

- Form of policies used at an email domain may be known, *e.g.*, use of blacklists, whitelists, filters, *etc.* In particular $\Pi_R$ (rule set) may be known but not $\Pi_D$ (set of facts) where contains definitions of private predicates.
- By observing protocol runs alone an attacker cannot conclude if a message was delivered. (Recipient may silently drop messages.)
- Recipient acts on every delivered message, like, seizes bond for unwanted message, *etc.*

### 4.1 Capabilities

Given a set of rules $\Pi = \{\pi_1, \ldots, \pi_n\}$, and the set P = {q | q $\propto$ $\Pi$}, an attacker has following capabilities:

1. **Capability of computing Clark completion:** For all $q \in P$, the attacker can compute $q^*$, q's Clark completion with respect to $\mathcal{P}$.
2. **Capability of unfold transformation [15, 17]:** Given a rule $\pi_k$: H $\leftarrow$ A, B, C where A, C $\subset$ P and B $\in$ P is a positive literal such that for some rule $\pi_i$ and some $\theta$ where B = head$(\pi_i)\theta$, the attacker can transform $\pi_k$ to H $\leftarrow$ A, body$(\pi_i)\theta$, C (here *head* and *body* functions map a rule to the atom in its head and literals in its body, respectively). Note that variables in $\pi_i$ and $\pi_k$ are renamed apart. We represent the fully unfolded form of a program $\Pi$ by $\Pi^\omega$.
3. **Capability of fold transformation [15, 17]:** Given a rule $\pi_k$: H $\leftarrow$ A, B, C where A, B, C $\subset$ P such that for some rule $\pi_i$ and some $\theta$ such that B = body$(\pi_i)\theta$, the attacker can transform $\pi_k$ to H $\leftarrow$ A, head$(\pi_i)\theta$, C.
4. **Capability of message generation:** An attacker can generate any number of messages $(M_i, \ldots, M_n)$ of her choice.

(For additional information on unfold/fold transformation of logic programs the reader is referred to [15, 17]).

### 4.2 Scripting an Attack

Next we show how an attack can be effected using capabilities defined above. Essentially, the steps to an attack involve computing the fully unfolded form of *accept* predicate, followed by computing its Clark completion. With this computed predicate an attacker can design messages effectively, to verify her guesses. A sample attack is shown next. The unfold/fold transformation belongs to NP complexity class [2], as does the Clark completion operation. Overall, the complexity of policy attack is NP.

**Example 2.** *We provide the formal syntax of policy in example 1 and show how an attack can be orchestrated against it. Here,* blacklist *is a private predicate, whose definition (or extension) is hidden from the attacker and* atrb$_{bond}$ *is a leaky predicate. The rules (2), (3) and (4) from example 1 written in the above syntax are as follows:*

$$allow(\overrightarrow{m}) \leftarrow \neg blacklist(Y), atrb_{bond}(X), X \geq 5$$
$$allow(\overrightarrow{m}) \leftarrow blacklist(Y), atrb_{bond}(X), X \geq 10$$
$$disallow(\overrightarrow{m}) \leftarrow atrb_{ext}('.scr')$$

*Similarly, rule (1) in example 1 is encoded as:*

$$accept(\overrightarrow{m}) \leftarrow allow(\overrightarrow{m}), \neg disallow(\overrightarrow{m})$$

*Using the unfolding capability, accept predicate definitions can be transformed to (for simplicity, we ignore disallow clause):*

$$accept(\overrightarrow{m}) \leftarrow \neg blacklist(Y), atrb_{\text{bond}}(X), X \geq 5$$
$$accept(\overrightarrow{m}) \leftarrow blacklist(Y), atrb_{\text{bond}}(X), X \geq 10$$

*Next the attacker can compute Clark completion of accept definition:*

$$\forall \overrightarrow{m} \; accept(\overrightarrow{m})^* \leftrightarrow \exists Y_1, X_1 \; \neg blacklist(Y_1), atrb_{\text{bond}}(X_1), X_1 \geq 5$$
$$\vee$$
$$\exists Y_2, X_2 \; blacklist(Y_2), atrb_{\text{bond}}(X_2), X_2 \geq 10$$

*An attacker is now in a position to guess parts of the extension of blacklist using following rule:*

$$blacklist'(Y_g) \leftarrow \neg accept(\overrightarrow{m_1}), accept(\overrightarrow{m_2}), atrb_{\text{bond}}(X_1),$$
$$atrb_{\text{bond}}(X_2), X_1 \in [5, 10], X_2 > 10$$

*Here blacklist' $\in R_A$, is defined by the attacker. The attacker can send two messages with all facts same except the bond values. The first message ($m_1$) is bonded with a value $v \in (5,10)$ and second one ($m_2$) bonded with a value greater than 10. It is easy to see that if $Y_g \in ext(blacklist)$, then the sender will get one negative and one positive verification – $c|accept(\overrightarrow{m_1}) \in T_P^-(I)$ and $c|accept(\overrightarrow{m_2}) \in T_P^+(I)$; otherwise both verifiers are positive.*

## 5    Policy Transformations for Privacy

To prevent an attacker from deducing subsets of recipient maintained set(s) of private information, we propose to transform the evaluation policy such that leakage signals are rendered useless. There are two flavors of transformation that we propose: *the sufficient policy* and *the necessary policy* transformation. Intuitively, the sufficient policy should accept a message just in case the message is accepted by the original policy under *all* possible definitions of the private predicates. On the other hand, the necessary policy accepts a message for *some* definition of the private predicates in the original policy, hence ensuring that only messages satisfying the necessary policy can satisfy the original policy. These policies are designed to be used in tandem, *i.e.*, single evaluation of original policy is replaced by the evaluation of necessary and sufficient policies.

### 5.1    Transformation Algorithm

Transformation algorithm is discussed next. Since only those rules that use private literals in their bodies can leak private information, the algorithm applies to such rules and

$$Q_u(\overrightarrow{Y_u}): - Q_1(\overrightarrow{Y_1}), \ldots, \neg Q_v(\overrightarrow{Y_v}), p_1(\overrightarrow{X_{1,1}}), \ldots, p_1(\overrightarrow{X_{m_1,1}}), \neg p_1(\overrightarrow{X_{m_1+1,1}}), \ldots,$$
$$\neg p_1(\overrightarrow{X_{m_1+n_1,1}}), \ldots, p_{t'}(\overrightarrow{X_{t',1}}), \ldots, \neg p_{t'}(\overrightarrow{X_{m_{t'}+n_{t'},t'}}), c.$$

For each clause in $\Pi_R$ as shown above, add create following clauses, for each k and u, if not already present: (with $i \in [1, m_{k'}]$, $j \in [1, n_{k'}]$, $k' \in [1, t']$)

$$pesQ_u(\overrightarrow{Y_u}): -Q_umatchP_1(\overrightarrow{X_1}, \overrightarrow{m}), Q_umatchNotP_1(\overrightarrow{X_1}, \overrightarrow{m}).$$

$$\vdots$$

$$pesQ_u(\overrightarrow{Y_u}): -Q_umatchP_{t'}(\overrightarrow{X_{t'}}, \overrightarrow{m}), Q_umatchNotP_{t'}(\overrightarrow{X_{t'}}, \overrightarrow{m}).$$

$$Q_umatchP_k(\overrightarrow{X_{m_k+j}}, \overrightarrow{m}): -pesQ_1(\overrightarrow{Y_1}), \ldots, \neg optQ_v(\overrightarrow{Y_v}), Q_umatchP_1(\overrightarrow{X_{1,1}}, \overrightarrow{m}), \ldots,$$
$$Q_umatchP_1(\overrightarrow{X_{m_1,1}}, \overrightarrow{m}), \ldots, Q_umatchP_k(\overrightarrow{X_{1,k}}, \overrightarrow{m}), \ldots, Q_umatchP_k(\overrightarrow{X_{m_k,k}}, \overrightarrow{m}),$$
$$Q_umatchNotP_k(\overrightarrow{X_{m_k+1,k}}, \overrightarrow{m}), \ldots, Q_umatchNotP_k(\overrightarrow{X_{m_k+(j-1),k}}, \overrightarrow{m}),$$
$$Q_umatchNotP_k(\overrightarrow{X_{m_k+(j+1),k}}, \overrightarrow{m}), \ldots, Q_umatchNotP_k(\overrightarrow{X_{m_k+n_k,k}}, \overrightarrow{m}), \ldots,$$
$$Q_umatchP_{t'}(\overrightarrow{X_{1,t'}}, \overrightarrow{m}), \ldots, Q_umatchNotP_{t'}(\overrightarrow{X_{m_{t'}+n_{t'},t'}}, \overrightarrow{m}), \overrightarrow{X_{i,k'}} \neq \overrightarrow{X_{m_{k'}+j,k'}}, c.$$
$$Q_umatchNotP_k(\overrightarrow{X_i}, \overrightarrow{m}): -pesQ_1(\overrightarrow{Y_1}), \ldots, \neg optQ_v(\overrightarrow{Y_v}), Q_umatchP_1(\overrightarrow{X_{1,1}}, \overrightarrow{m}), \ldots,$$
$$Q_umatchP_1(\overrightarrow{X_{m_a,1}}, \overrightarrow{m}), \ldots, Q_umatchP_k(\overrightarrow{X_{1,k}}, \overrightarrow{m}), \ldots, Q_umatchP_k(\overrightarrow{X_{i-1,k}}, \overrightarrow{m}),$$
$$Q_umatchP_k(\overrightarrow{X_{i+1,k}}, \overrightarrow{m}), \ldots, Q_umatchP_k(\overrightarrow{X_{m_k,k}}, \overrightarrow{m}), Q_umatchNotP_k(\overrightarrow{X_{m_k+1,k}}, \overrightarrow{m}), \ldots,$$
$$Q_umatchNotP_k(\overrightarrow{X_{m_k+n_k,k}}, \overrightarrow{m}), \ldots, Q_umatchP_{t'}(\overrightarrow{X_{1,t'}}, \overrightarrow{m}), \ldots,$$
$$Q_umatchNotP_{t'}(\overrightarrow{X_{m_{t'}+n_{t'},t'}}, \overrightarrow{m}), \overrightarrow{X_{i,k'}} \neq \overrightarrow{X_{m_{k'}+j,k'}}, c.$$
$$optQ_u(\overrightarrow{Y_u}): -optQ_1(\overrightarrow{Y_1}), \ldots, \neg pesQ_v(\overrightarrow{Y_v}), \overrightarrow{X_{i,k'}} \neq \overrightarrow{X_{m_{k'}+j,k'}}, c.$$

**Fig. 1.** Transformation algorithm

leaves others unchanged. The transformation algorithm is shown in figure 1 and consists of two transformations for each rule containing sensitive predicates and is described in detail next.

Figure 1 begins with a general Horn clause representation of rules in $\Pi_R$ with meta-variables $Q_u$, $Q_v$ and $p_k$ and $\overrightarrow{m}$ is the tuple of all variables used in $\Pi_R$. $Q_u(\overrightarrow{y})$ represents a non-sensitive literal at the $u^{th}$ position in a rule, and can also appear in the head of the rule. The rule is shown to have $v$ non-sensitive predicates in its body and some sensitive predicates $p_k$, for $k \in [1, t']$, each used positively $m_k$ times and negatively $n_k$ times. In other words, recursive calls and multiple calls to the same predicate may be made in a rule, i.e., $Q_u$ may be in $[Q_1, Q_v]$ or $Q_{u_1} = Q_{u_2}$ for $u_1, u_2 \in [1, v]$, $u_1 \neq u_2$. However, $Q_u$ cannot make recursive calls to itself through negation or include calls such that the program dependency graph includes negative cycles, the stratification restriction. Also, each $p_k$ literal need not appear in the body of every $Q_u$ clause, i.e., both $m_k$ and $n_k$ can be equal to zero.

As shown in the figure, each $Q_u$ definition is transformed to two related predicates, viz., $pesQ_u$ and $optQ_u$, where $pesQ_u$ is the 'pessimistic' version of $Q_u$, independent of the definition of any private predicate used in the definition of $Q_u$, and $optQ_u$ is the 'optimistic' version of $Q_u$ predicate, which holds for 'some' definition of private predicates. More precisely, $optQ_u$ will hold if there exists *some* definition of private predicates used in the definition of $Q_u$, such that $Q_u$ can be shown to hold in $\Pi$, whereas $pesQ_u$ will only hold if for all definitions of private predicates, $Q_u$ can be shown to hold true in $\Pi$.

It must be noted that the algorithm, as presented, does not include the details of how transformed and non transformed rules are linked. Suppose there is a predicate $Q(\overrightarrow{x})$ in the body of a transformed clause that does not use any sensitive literals. The transformation still renames it as $pesQ(\overrightarrow{x})$ whenever it is used positively, and $optQ(\overrightarrow{x})$ when it is used negatively. However, the transformed versions of the definition of $Q(\overrightarrow{x})$ are not created since it does not use any sensitive predicates in the body. Hence we add two rules for each such predicate, which are, $pesQ(\overrightarrow{x}) \leftarrow Q(\overrightarrow{x})$ and $optQ(\overrightarrow{x}) \leftarrow Q(\overrightarrow{x})$. In example 3 we present a concrete example of this transformation.

**Example 3.** *Pessimistic and optimistic transformations.*
*Consider the $\Pi_R$ definition of predicate trusted(x,...,z) that uses non sensitive predicates professor(Profile), student(Profile) and bonded(B, minValue) and private predicate blacklist($X_{From}$) defined in $\Pi_D$ (ignore the distinction between 'atrb' and other predicates):*

$$trusted(\overrightarrow{x}) \leftarrow professor(X_{From})$$
$$trusted(\overrightarrow{x}) \leftarrow student(X_{From}), \neg blacklist(X_{From})$$
$$trusted(\overrightarrow{x}) \leftarrow blacklist(X_{From}), bonded(X_{X\text{-}Bnd}, 5)$$

*The optimistic and pessimistic forms of the predicate trusted in $\Pi_{suf}$ are as follows. For simplicity we retain the names of other predicates (i.e., student, professor, bonded are unchanged), however, in reality, their pessimistic and optimistic versions coincide. Also, we use trustedMB symbol for trustedMatchBlacklist and trustedMNB for trusted-MatchNotBlacklist predicate due to space constraints:*

$$pesTrusted(\overrightarrow{x}) \leftarrow professor(X_{From})$$
$$pesTrusted(\overrightarrow{x}) \leftarrow trustedMB(\overrightarrow{y_1}),$$
$$trustedMNB(\overrightarrow{y_2})$$
$$trustedMB(\overrightarrow{y_1}) \leftarrow student(X_{From})$$
$$trustedMNB(\overrightarrow{y_2}) \leftarrow bonded(X_{X\text{-}Bnd}, 5)$$
$$optTrusted(\overrightarrow{x}) \leftarrow student(X_{From})$$
$$optTrusted(\overrightarrow{x}) \leftarrow bonded(X_{X\text{-}Bnd}, 5)$$

### 5.1.1  Necessary Policy

Intuitively, the necessary policy, $\Pi_{nec}$, strips away sensitive predicates from the original policy. The basic idea is to generate a policy where satisfaction requirements are in terms of non-sensitive literals, while assuming the best possible scenario with respect to the definition of sensitive predicates. This aim is achieved by the following definition of top-level accept predicate (accept$_{nec}(\overrightarrow{msg})$ for clarity) and while example 4 illustrates the basic idea:

$$accept_{nec}(\overrightarrow{m}) \leftarrow optAllow(\overrightarrow{m}), \neg pesDisallow(\overrightarrow{m})$$

**Example 4 (Illustration of necessary policy).** *Consider a ruleset $\Pi_R$ where $B_1$ and $B_2$ are a list of positive literals with no literal belonging to $\mathcal{P}$. Hence their 'opt' and 'pes' versions coincide. Also, $p \in \mathcal{P}$*

$$allow(\overrightarrow{msg}) \leftarrow B_1, p(X) \tag{5}$$
$$allow(\overrightarrow{msg}) \leftarrow B_2, \neg p(X) \tag{6}$$

*Applying the necessary transformation we get:*

$$accept_{nec}(\overrightarrow{m}) \leftarrow optAllow(\overrightarrow{m}), \neg pesDisallow(\overrightarrow{m})$$
$$optAllow(\overrightarrow{m}) \leftarrow B_1$$
$$optAllow(\overrightarrow{m}) \leftarrow B_2$$

*By unfolding and completing the definition of $accept_{nec}$ we get ($\overrightarrow{y_1}$ and $\overrightarrow{y_2}$ are free variables in $B_1$ and $B_2$ respectively)*

$$\forall \overrightarrow{m} \ accept_{nec}^{\omega*}(\overrightarrow{m}) \leftrightarrow \exists \overrightarrow{y_1} \ B_1 \vee \exists \overrightarrow{y_2} \ B_2$$

*This policy accepts messages depending upon the clauses of the original policy, with the change that sensitive predicate is dropped from rules 5,6.*

### 5.1.2  Sufficient Policy

The basic idea behind this transformation is to syntactically match the uses of sensitive literals in the body of rules with *allow* head, *e.g.*, use $pesAllow(\overrightarrow{m})$ in place of $allow(\overrightarrow{m})$. In other words, we wish to *resolve away* the uses of sensitive literals, akin to the predicate elimination strategy proposed by Reiter [14]. The following top-level predicate accept ($accept_{suf}$ for clarity) achieves this aim:

$$accept_{suf}(\overrightarrow{m}) \leftarrow pesAllow(\overrightarrow{m}), \neg optDisallow(\overrightarrow{m})$$

**Example 5 (Illustration of sufficient policy).** *Consider the ruleset given by rules 5 and 6. The sufficient transformation of rules yields the following ruleset*

$$accept_{suf}(\overrightarrow{m}) \leftarrow pesAllow(\overrightarrow{m}), \neg optDisallow(\overrightarrow{m})$$
$$pesAllow(\overrightarrow{m}) \leftarrow matchP(X), matchNotP(X)$$
$$matchP(X, \overrightarrow{m}) \leftarrow B_1$$
$$matchNotP(X, \overrightarrow{m}) \leftarrow B_2$$

*By unfolding and completing the definition of $accept_{suf}$ we get*

$$\forall \overrightarrow{m} \ accept_{suf}^{\omega*}(\overrightarrow{m}) \leftrightarrow \exists \overrightarrow{y_1}, \overrightarrow{y_2} \ B_1, B_2$$

*This policy accepts messages that simultaneously satisfy the bodies of clauses 5 and 6, with private predicate stripped off from the rules.*

### 5.2  Syntactic Properties

The syntactic properties of necessary and sufficient policies essentially state that the predicates identified as private in the original policy do not occur in transformed policies. These follow in a straightforward manner from the transformation algorithm.

**Lemma 1.** *Given $P \subseteq \mathcal{P}$ such that if $p_i \in P$ and $p_i \propto \Pi_R$ then $p_i \not\propto \Pi_{nec}$ (resp. $\Pi_{suf}$) where $\Pi_{nec}$ (resp. $\Pi_{suf}$) is necessary (resp. sufficient) transformation of $\Pi_R$.*

**Corollary 2.** *Given $P \subseteq \mathcal{P}$ such that if $p_i \in P$ and $p_i \propto \Pi_R$ then $p^{\omega *}$ or $p$ do not occur in $\Pi_{nec}^{\omega *}$ (resp. $\Pi_{suf}^*$).*

## 5.3   Semantic Properties

To show how evaluation of $\Pi_{nec}$ and $\Pi_{suf}$ instead of $\Pi_R$ prevents sensitive leakages, we need to show some semantic properties of the transformed rulesets. However, space constraints don't allow us to go into the full details of our claims, the theorems and their proofs. Hence, we briefly describe the results informally and refer the interested reader to a technical report [9] with complete results. However, here we state our main theorem without its proof.

We use the following notations. The program corresponding to the original policy is represented by P, where $P = \Pi_R \cup \Pi_D \cup M$, in which $M$ is the message being evaluated, $\Pi_D$ is the set of private facts and $\Pi_R$ is a ruleset. The sufficient transformation yields a set of rules represented by $\Pi_{suf}$, whereas the necessary ruleset is represented by $\Pi_{nec}$. Assuming $\Pi_D$ contains only facts constructed from private predicates, we denote the program corresponding to $\Pi_{suf}$ by $P_S$, where $P_S = \Pi_{suf} \cup M$ and the program corresponding to $\Pi_{nec}$ by $P_N$, where $P_N = \Pi_{nec} \cup M$. Both these programs are independent of the definitions of the sensitive predicates.

The main theorem involves a general relation between satisfaction of 'optimistic' and 'pessimistic' versions of any literal and the satisfaction of the literal itself. Intuitively, this means that whenever the pessimistic version of a predicate is true, then the original predicate is also true, irrespective of the truth values of the sensitive predicates. Similarly, 'optimistic' version being satisfied implies that there is a possible definition of private predicates (in the set of program facts, $\Pi_D$), such that the original predicate is satisfied.

**Theorem 3.** *Given a program $P = \Pi_R \cup \Pi_D \cup M$, in which $\Pi_R \cup \Pi_D$ is a policy that includes sensitive predicates $p_1$ to $p_t$ defined in $\Pi_D$ and $M$ is a set of facts, any literal $pesQ_u(\overrightarrow{y})$ in the program $P_S = \Pi_{suf} \cup M$ or $P_N = \Pi_{nec} \cup M$, apart from the $accept(\overrightarrow{msg})$ atom, is satisfied if and only if for all definitions of $p_1, \ldots, p_t$ $Q_u(\overrightarrow{y})$ is satisfied in P, and $optQ_u(\overrightarrow{y})$ is satisfied if and only if there exists some definition of $p_1, \ldots, p_t$ such that $Q_u(\overrightarrow{y})$ is satisfied.*

With the help of the theorem above, semantic closeness of transformations to the original policy can be shown in a straightforward manner. That is, transformed policies are closest, semantically, to the original policy compared to any other policy that protects recipient's private information. Based on semantic closeness, email policies can be partially ordered (additional details can be found in [9]) and it can be shown that the necessary policy is the least upper bound for all policies that protect recipient's sensitive information, while the sufficient policy the greatest lower bound.

**Protection against attacks.** Under the assumed capabilities of the attacker, the above results enable us to prove certain results regarding the protection offered by the transformations. We summarize when an attacker can gain sensitive information and when the information is protected, next. (For proofs see [9]).

- The attacker can gain knowledge of sensitive information (*i.e.*, portions of $\Pi_D$) if she knows the original ruleset (*i.e.*, $\Pi_R$) and messages (*i.e.*, $M_i$) are evaluated by the original policy (*i.e.*, the program $\Pi_R \cup \Pi_D \cup M_i$).
- Attacker's knowledge of necessary and sufficient policy and evaluation of messages by these policies does not lead to leakage of sensitive information.
- Attacker's knowledge of original policy and evaluation of messages by sufficient and necessary policies will not lead to leakage of sensitive information.

## 6   Related Work

Cryptanalysis of private-key cryptosystems through statistical attacks, like correlation attacks [11], aim to determine the statistical relationship between outputs and inputs of cryptographic transformations. Zhang, Tavares *et al.* [20] describe a zero information leakage between the change of output(s) and prescribed change patterns in the inputs for protecting against correlation attacks. Our approach resembles this information theoretic model of protection against information leakage, however, we describe how correlation-like attacks can be mounted against sets of Horn clauses and present a transformation that can prevent against such attacks.

Our transformation procedure resembles the predicate elimination strategy, a complete resolution proof strategy for multi-predicate formulas, proposed by Reiter [14]. Essentially, this strategy involves rewriting the theory with a predicate P 'resolved away'. Subsequently, a set of unsatisfiable P-independent clauses can be derived if the original set of clauses were unsatisfiable. In our approach, we propose a strategy for 'resolving away' the private predicates in a given set of rules. However, our aim here is not to detect unsatisfiability. Instead, we construct new clauses that do not leak any discernible information to guessing attacks.

The third closely related work is of Delaune and Jacquemard [3], who give a theory of dictionary attacks against cryptographic protocols. In their work, they claim that if the set of possible values of the input is finite (and small), then a dictionary attack (guessing attack) is only PTIME complex. They go on to give a theory of dictionary attack by extending the classic Dolev-Yao intruder model for statistical inferences. In our work, we adopt their attack model, and even though we require the attacker to be able to handle a greater degree of computational complexity, the basis of launching attacks remains the same.

Relational databases have mature techniques for both access control and inference control. Access control protects direct access to sensitive information. In our case, we assume that this is possible by policy specification and enforcement. Inference control has been extensively studied in statistical databases and census data [4, 18, 1]. These approaches can be classified into *restriction-based*, or restricting queries, or *perturbation-based*, *i.e.*, addition of random noises to source data. Our approach is closer to the restriction based techniques.

In restriction based inference control schemes, one of the concerns is of an attacker deriving protected information through aggregation of separate queries. In other words, the protected information cannot be queried directly, but deducible from the results of other queries. In the email domain, a query can be replaced by a message, and the result of a query by a yes or no decision (*i.e.*, accept or a reject). Even with a boolean response, attackers can deduce relevant information. This is the reason why we claim that inference attacks are easier to construct. Similar to their response, we transform the evaluation policies, and thus reduce attacker's capabilities to run some queries.

In summary, we have applied a well-studied problem to the context of email messages and showed that important information can be lost due to the current email delivery protocols and deployed mechanisms. Solutions applied to other domains are not directly applicable to our domain, and therefore we provide a custom solution based on program transformations, using ideas developed by researchers who have studied similar problems in other domains.

## 7  Conclusion

In this paper we have identified an undesirable side effect of combining different email-control mechanisms, namely, the leakage of sensitive information. Even though confidentiality of sensitive information has been widely studied as a research problem, it assumes a different form in the email context, because of the ease with which sensitive information is leaked. We provide example scenarios where leakage is made possible in two ways – using the message delivery protocol itself and using leakage channels beyond the mail delivery protocol. Based on how these leakages may be used by an attacker, we categorize them into two classes – automatic generation of acknowledgement receipts for validating an email address and automatic generation of acknowledgments for inferring private information about the recipient. As leakage channels beyond the control of the delivery protocol can't be closed by modifying email delivery protocol alone, preventing leakages is hard to achieve. In particular, we investigate in detail the second class of attacks where a victim's sensitive information is leaked.

As opposed to the classical Dolev-Yao attacker [5], we define a new attacker model and a new attack technique. In the worst case scenario, we assume that the attacker knows recipient's mail acceptance criteria, but not the sensitive information maintained by the recipient. With the abilities of computing Clark completion of normal Horn clauses, unfold/fold transformations and generating messages, the attacker can mount attacks such that sensitive information is leaked. As a solution, we provide an algorithmic transformation which can sanitize the combination of email-control mechanisms, so that the leakage is plugged, while being 'closest' semantically to the original policy.

## References

[1] N. R. Adam and J. C. Worthmann. Security-control methods for statistical databases: a comparative study. *ACM Computing Surveys*, 21(4):515–556, 1989.
[2] E. Dantsin, T. Eiter, G. Gottlob, and A. Voronkov. Complexity and expressive power of logic programming. *ACM Computing Surveys*, 33(3):374–425, 2001.
[3] S. Delaune and F. Jacquemard. A theory of dictionary attacks and its complexity. In *Proceedings of the 17th IEEE Computer Security Foundations Workshop (CSFW'04)*, pages 2–15, 2004.

[4] D. E. Denning and J. Schlrer. Inference control for statistical databases. *IEEE Computer*, 16(7):69–82, 1983.

[5] D. Dolev and A. Yao. On the security of public-key protocols. *IEEE Transaction on Information Theory*, 29:198–208, 1983.

[6] F. Fages. Constructive negation by pruning. *Journal of Logic Programming*, 32/2, 1997.

[7] J. Jaffar and M. J. Maher. Constraint logic programming: A survey. *Journal of Logic Programming*, 19/20:503–581, 1994.

[8] S. Kaushik, W. Winsborough, D. Wijesekera, and P. Ammann. Email feedback: A policy-based approach to overcoming false positives. In *3rd ACM Workshop on Formal Methods in Security Engineering: (FMSE 2005)*, pages 73–82, Fairfax, VA, November 2005.

[9] S. Kaushik, W. Winsborough, D. Wijesekera, and P. Ammann. Policy transformation for preventing leakage of sensitive information in email systems. Technical Report ISE-TR-06-05, ISE Dept, George Mason University, Fairfax, VA, May 2006.

[10] T. Loder, M. V. Alstyne, and R. Wash. An economic solution to the spam problem. In *ACM E-Commerce*, 2004.

[11] W. Meier and O. Staffelbach. Fast correlation attacks on certain stream ciphers. *Journal of Cryptology*, 1(3):159–176, 1989.

[12] M. Naor. Verification of a human in the loop or identification via the turing test. http://www.wisdom.weizmann.ac.il/ñaor/ PAPERS/human_abs.html, 1996.

[13] S. Petry. Port 25: The gaping hole in the firewall. In *Proceedings of ACSAC'02 Annual Computer Security Applications Conference*, Dec 2002.

[14] R. Reiter. The predicate elimination strategy in theorem proving. In *Proceedings of the second annual ACM symposium on Theory of computing*, pages 180–183, Northampton, Massachusetts, 1970.

[15] T. Sato. Equivalence-preserving first-order unfold/fold transformation systems. *Theoretical Computer Science*, 105(1):57 – 84, October 1992.

[16] Simple Mail Transfer Protocol. RFC 2821, Apr 2001.

[17] H. Tamaki and T. Sato. Unfold/fold transformation of logic programs. In S.-A. Tarnlund, editor, *Proceedings of the Second International Conference on Logic Programming*, pages 127–138, Uppsala, 1984.

[18] L. Willenborg and T. de Waal. *Statistical disclosure control in practice*. Springer Verlag, New York, 1996.

[19] W. S. Yerazunis. Sparse binary polynomial hashing and the CRM114 discriminator. In *2003 Cambridge Spam Conference Proceedings*, 2003.

[20] M. Zhang, S. Tavares, and L. Campbell. Information leakage of boolean functions and its relationship to other cryptographic criteria. In *Proceedings of the 2nd ACM Conference on Computer and Communications Security (CCS'94)*, pages 156–165, Fairfax, 1994.

# Term Rewriting for Access Control

Steve Barker and Maribel Fernández

King's College London,
Dept. of Computer Science,
Strand, London WC2R 2LS, U.K.

**Abstract.** We demonstrate how access control models and policies can be represented by using term rewriting systems, and how rewriting may be used for evaluating access requests and for proving properties of an access control policy. We focus on two kinds of access control models: discretionary models, based on access control lists (ACLs), and role-based access control (RBAC) models. For RBAC models, we show that we can specify several variants, including models with role hierarchies, and constraints and support for security administrator review querying.

## 1 Introduction

Access control has long been recognised as being of fundamental importance in computer security. In early work on access control models, Lampson [27] described the use of a matrix for describing the access privileges that users may exercise on system resources. Variations of the access matrix, typically *Access Control Lists (ACLs)*, are still very much in use today (see, for example, [16]). In recent years, *Role-Based Access Control (RBAC)* [32,9] has emerged as *the* principal form of access control model in theory and practice.

For all types of access control models, from the access matrix to RBAC, researchers have recognised the importance of applying formal techniques to define access control models, access policies and the operational methods used for access request evaluation. Formal specification makes it possible to, for instance, compare policies rigorously, to understand the consequences of modifying policies, and to prove properties of policies.

In this paper, we demonstrate how *term rewriting* [15,24,5] may be profitably used in the formalisation of ACL and RBAC models and policies, and we demonstrate the use of rewriting for access request evaluation with respect to policies that are defined in terms of these models.

Term rewriting systems are usually defined by specifying a set of terms, and a set of rewrite rules that are used to "reduce" terms. This simple idea is very powerful: term rewriting techniques have been successfully applied to many domains in the last 20 years. They have had deep influence in the development of computational models, programming and specification languages, theorem provers and proof assistants. More recently, rewriting techniques have been fruitfully exploited in the context of security protocols (see, for instance, [10]) and security policies for controlling information leakage (see, for example, [17]).

E. Damiani and P. Liu (Eds.): Data and Applications Security 2006, LNCS 4127, pp. 179–193, 2006.
© IFIP International Federation for Information Processing 2006

Although rewriting is widely applicable, its application to problems in access control has hitherto been quite restricted (albeit [26], which uses graph transformations, is a notable exception). Instead, the emphasis in the literature, on the formalisation of access control, has been on the use of logic languages for (i) the specification of access control requirements [9,22,12], and (ii) sound, complete and PTIME operational methods for evaluating access control requests with respect to policy requirements (see, for example, [8]). Nevertheless, there are several reasons to consider the use of term rewriting approaches for ACL and RBAC model definition, policy specification and access request checking. The expressivity of term rewriting is an important reason for applying rewrite techniques to access control: in the past, rewriting systems have been used to specify, in a uniform way, several computational paradigms, including functional, logic, imperative and concurrent ones (see, for example, [4,18,21]); in this paper we will show that rewriting can also be used to define ACL and RBAC policies in a uniform and formal way. Another important reason to use rewrite-based languages to specify access control policies is that we can then apply rewriting techniques, and use tools such as ELAN [13,23], MAUDE [14] and CiME (www.lri.fr), to study properties of the policies (for instance, to check confluence and termination of the reduction relation induced by the rewrite rules), to test, compare and experiment with evaluation strategies, to automate equational reasoning, and also for rapid prototyping of access policies. Rewriting systems can provide a formal basis for the study of a broad range of security issues (e.g., authentication [1,20] and intrusion detection [2]). In this paper we will use term rewriting systems for the specification, implementation and validation of ACL and RBAC policies that are used to protect resources in centralised computer systems from pre-authenticated system users.

The rest of this paper is organised as follows. In Section 2, some preliminary notions are briefly described. Discretionary access control models are studied in Section 3, where we show how to specify ACLs as rewrite systems and how properties of ACL policies may be proven. In Section 4, we describe a variety of RBAC policies as rewrite systems, and we demonstrate how properties of these policies may be proven. In Section 5, we discuss related work. Finally, in Section 6, we draw conclusions and make suggestions for further work.

## 2    Preliminaries

We begin by describing the principal components of ACLs and RBAC. We then describe some basic notions on term rewriting. We refer the reader to [16,9,5] for additional information on ACLs, RBAC and term rewriting, respectively.

### 2.1    The Access Matrix and Access Control Lists

The language of the access matrix [27] includes a finite set $\mathcal{U}$ of *users* (e.g., human users and software agents), a finite set $\mathcal{O}$ of *objects* (e.g., files and directories), and a finite set $\mathcal{A}$ of *access privileges* (e.g., read, write and execute privileges).

The access matrix [27] itself includes a row for each subject, and a column for each object in the system. Each cell of the matrix describes the set of access privileges that a subject may exercise on an object. An access matrix is usually implemented as an ACL, which records for each subject the privileges on objects that are assigned to the subject. A *reference monitor* is used to evaluate requests by subjects to exercise access privileges on an object. A user $u \in \mathcal{U}$ is authorised to exercise an access privilege $p \in \mathcal{P}$ on an object $o \in \mathcal{O}$ if and only if the access matrix/access control list includes an entry that specifies that $u$ is assigned the $p$ privilege on $o$.

## 2.2  Role-Based Access Control

In very simple terms, the fundamental idea of RBAC is that:

- a user $u$ of a resource $o$ may be assigned to a set of roles $\{r_1, \ldots, r_n\}$ (usually as a consequence of the user performing a job function in an organisation e.g., *doctor*, *CEO*, etc);
- access privileges on resources are also assigned to roles;
- a user $u$ may exercise an access privilege $p$ on a resource $o$ if and only if $u$ is assigned to a role $r$ to which the privilege $p$ on $o$ is also assigned.

It follows, from the discussion above, that RBAC models/policies are specified with respect to a domain of discourse that includes the sets $\mathcal{U}$ of users, $\mathcal{O}$ of objects, and $\mathcal{P}$ of access privileges, together with a (finite) set $\mathcal{R}$ of *roles*.

The capability of assigning users to roles and permissions (i.e., access privilege assignments on objects) to roles are primitive requirements of all RBAC models. The most basic category of RBAC model, flat RBAC [32] (or $RBAC_F$ for short), requires that these types of assignment are supported. The $RBAC_{H2A}$ model extends $RBAC_F$ to include the notion of an RBAC role hierarchy (see below) in addition to user-role and permission-role assignments. The $RBAC_{C3A}$ model extends $RBAC_{H2A}$ by allowing constraints on policies to be represented, and the $RBAC_{S4A}$ model extends $RBAC_{C3A}$ by allowing administrator queries to be evaluated with respect to an RBAC policy specification. The flat RBAC, $RBAC_{H2A}$, $RBAC_{C3A}$ and $RBAC_{S4A}$ models from [32] are referred to, respectively, as $RBAC_F, RBAC^P_{H2A}, RBAC^P_{C3A}$ and $RBAC^P_{S4A}$ logic theories in the formal representation of RBAC models in [9]. In the remainder of the paper, we will refer to $RBAC_F, RBAC^P_{H2A}, RBAC^P_{C3A}$ and $RBAC^P_{S4A}$ theories rather than models.

In the $RBAC^P_{H2A}$ theory, the semantics of user-role assignment may be defined in terms of a 2-place *ura* predicate (where *ura* is short for "user role assignment") and permission-role assignment can be defined in terms of a 3-place predicate *pra* (where *pra* is short for "permission role assignment"). The extensions of these predicates define role and permission assignments in a world of interest.

**Definition 1.** *Let $\Pi$ be an $RBAC^P_{H2A}$ theory. Then,*

- *$\Pi \models ura(u, r)$ if and only if user $u \in \mathcal{U}$ is assigned to role $r \in \mathcal{R}$;*
- *$\Pi \models pra(a, o, r)$ if and only if the access privilege $a \in \mathcal{A}$ on object $o \in \mathcal{O}$ is assigned to the role $r \in \mathcal{R}$.*

An $RBAC_{H2A}^P$ *role hierarchy* is defined as a (partially) ordered (and finite) set of roles. The ordering relation is a role seniority relation. In an $RBAC_{H2A}^P$ theory $\Pi$, a 2-place predicate $senior\_to(r_i, r_j)$ is used to define the seniority ordering between pairs of roles i.e., the role $r_i \in \mathcal{R}$ is a more senior role (or more powerful role) than role $r_j \in \mathcal{R}$. If $r_i$ is senior to $r_j$ then any user assigned to the role $r_i$ has at least the permissions that users assigned to role $r_j$ have. Role hierarchies are important for specifying implicitly the inheritance of access privileges on resources.

The semantics of the $senior\_to$ relation may be expressed, in terms of an $RBAC_{H2A}^P$ theory $\Pi$, thus:

- $\Pi \models senior\_to(r_i, r_j)$ if and only if the role $r_i \in \mathcal{R}$ is senior to the role $r_j \in \mathcal{R}$ in an $RBAC_{H2A}^P$ role hierarchy.

The $senior\_to$ relation may be defined as the reflexive-transitive closure of an irreflexive-intransitive binary relation $ds$ (where $ds$ is short for "directly senior to"). The semantics of $ds$ may be expressed, in terms of an $RBAC_{H2A}^P$ theory $\Pi$, thus:

- $\Pi \models ds(r_i, r_j)$ iff $r_i \neq r_j$, the role $r_i \in \mathcal{R}$ is senior to the role $r_j \in \mathcal{R}$ in an $RBAC_{H2A}^P$ role hierarchy defined in $\Pi$, and there is no role $r_k \in \mathcal{R}$ such that $[ds(r_k, r_j) \wedge ds(r_i, r_k)]$ holds where $r_k \neq r_i$ and $r_k \neq r_j$.

*Remark 1.* In RBAC, users activate and deactivate roles in the course of session management. Session management is an implementation issue, the details of which will be the subject of future work.

*Example 1. Suppose that the users $u_1$ and $u_2$ are assigned to the roles $r_2$ and $r_1$ respectively, and that write (w) permission on object $o_1$ is assigned to $r_1$ and read (r) permission on $o_1$ is assigned to $r_2$. Moreover, suppose that $r_1$ is directly senior to $r_2$ in an $RBAC_{H2A}^P$ role hierarchy. Then, using the notation introduced above, this $RBAC_{H2A}$ policy is represented by the relations:*

$$ura(u_1, r_2), ura(u_2, r_1), pra(w, o_1, r_1), pra(r, o_1, r_2), ds(r_1, r_2).$$

User-role and permission-role assignments are related via the notion of an *authorisation*. An authorisation is a triple $(u, a, o)$ that expresses that the user $u$ has the $a$ access privilege on the object $o$. Given an $RBAC_{H2A}^P$ theory $\Pi$, the set of authorisations $\mathcal{AUTH}$ defined by $\Pi$ may be expressed thus:

$$(u, a, o) \in \mathcal{AUTH} \Leftrightarrow \exists r_1, r_2.ura(u, r_1) \wedge senior\_to(r_1, r_2) \wedge pra(a, o, r_2)$$

According to the definition of the set $\mathcal{AUTH}$ above, a user $u$ may exercise the $a$ access privilege on object $o$ if:

$u$ is assigned to the role $r_1$,[1] $r_1$ is senior to a role $r_2$ in an $RBAC_{H2A}^P$ role hierarchy, and $r_2$ has been assigned the $a$ access privilege on $o$.

---

[1] Here we assume that $u$ is also active in $r_1$ at the time of any access request.

*Example 2. By inspection of the user-role assignments, permission-role assignments, and the role seniority relationships that are specified in Example 1, it follows that the set of authorisations that are included in $\mathcal{AUTH}$ is:*

$$\{(u_2, w, o_1), (u_2, r, o_1), (u_1, r, o_1)\}.$$

To extend $RBAC_{H2A}$ theories to $RBAC_{C3A}$ theories, *separation of duties constraints* must be supported. The *static separation of duties (ssd)* constraint is used to specify that a user cannot be assigned to a pair of mutually exclusive roles [9]. The *dynamic separation of duties (dsd)* constraint is used to prevent a user simultaneously activating a pair of roles that are specified as being dynamically separated [9].

To extend $RBAC_{C3A}$ programs to $RBAC_{S4A}$ theories, *permission-role review* must be possible in addition to *user-role reviews*, the latter being a requirement of $RBAC_F$ theories (see [32,9]). That is, it must be possible for security administrators to pose queries on RBAC policy specifications to determine (i) the set of roles a user is assigned to, and (ii) the permissions that are assigned to roles.

### 2.3   Term Rewriting

Term rewriting systems can be seen as programming or specification languages, or as formulae manipulating systems that can be used in various applications such as operational-semantics specification, program optimisation or automated theorem proving. We recall briefly the definition of first-order terms and term rewriting systems, and refer the reader to [5] for further details and examples.

A *signature* $\mathcal{F}$ is a finite set of *function symbols* together with their (fixed) arity. $\mathcal{X}$ denotes a denumerable set of *variables*, and $T(\mathcal{F}, \mathcal{X})$ denotes the set of *terms* built up from $\mathcal{F}$ and $\mathcal{X}$.

Terms are identified with finite labeled trees, as usual. The symbol at the root of $t$ is denoted by $root(t)$. *Positions* are strings of positive integers. The *subterm* of $t$ at position $p$ is denoted by $t|_p$ and the result of replacing $t|_p$ with $u$ at position $p$ in $t$ is denoted by $t[u]_p$.

$\mathcal{V}(t)$ denotes the set of variables occurring in $t$. A term is *linear* if variables in $\mathcal{V}(t)$ occur at most once in $t$. A term is *ground* if $\mathcal{V}(t) = \emptyset$. Substitutions are written as in $\{x_1 \mapsto t_1, \ldots, x_n \mapsto t_n\}$ where $t_i$ is assumed different from $x_i$. We use Greek letters for substitutions and postfix notation for their application.

**Definition 2.** *Given a signature $\mathcal{F}$, a* term rewriting system *on $\mathcal{F}$ is a set of* rewrite rules $R = \{l_i \rightarrow r_i\}_{i \in I}$*, where $l_i, r_i \in T(\mathcal{F}, \mathcal{X})$, $l_i \notin \mathcal{X}$, and $\mathcal{V}(r_i) \subseteq \mathcal{V}(l_i)$. A term $t$ rewrites to a term $u$ at position $p$ with the rule $l \rightarrow r$ and the substitution $\sigma$, written $t \rightarrow_p^{l \rightarrow r} u$, or simply $t \rightarrow_R u$, if $t|_p = l\sigma$ and $u = t[r\sigma]_p$. Such a term $t$ is called* reducible. *Irreducible terms are said to be in* normal form.

We denote by $\rightarrow_R^+$ (resp. $\rightarrow_R^*$) the transitive (resp. transitive and reflexive) closure of the rewrite relation $\rightarrow_R$. The subindex $R$ will be omitted when it is clear from the context.

*Example 3. Consider a signature for lists of natural numbers, with function symbols:*

- Z *(with arity 0) and* S *(with arity 1, denoting the successor function) to build numbers;*
- nil *(with arity 0, to denote an empty list),* cons *(with arity 2, to construct non-empty lists), and* append *(also with arity 2, to represent the operation that concatenates two lists).*

*We can specify list concatenation with the following rewrite rules:*

$$\mathsf{append}(\mathsf{nil}, x) \to x$$
$$\mathsf{append}(\mathsf{cons}(y, x), z) \to \mathsf{cons}(y, \mathsf{append}(x, z))$$

*Then we have a reduction sequence:*

$$\mathsf{append}(\mathsf{cons}(\mathsf{Z}, \mathsf{nil}), \mathsf{cons}(\mathsf{S}(\mathsf{Z}), \mathsf{nil})) \to^* \mathsf{cons}(\mathsf{Z}, \mathsf{cons}(\mathsf{S}(\mathsf{Z}), \mathsf{nil}))$$

Let $l \to r$ and $s \to t$ be two rewrite rules (we assume that the variables of $s \to t$ were renamed so that there is no common variable with $l \to r$), $p$ the position of a non-variable subterm of $s$, and $\mu$ a most general unifier of $s|_p$ and $l$. Then $(t\mu, s\mu[r\mu]_p)$ is a *critical pair* formed from those rules. Note that $s \to t$ may be a renamed version of $l \to r$. In this case a superposition at the root position is not considered a critical pair.

A term rewriting system $R$ is:

- *confluent* if for all terms $t$, $u$, $v$: $t \to^* u$ and $t \to^* v$ implies $u \to^* s$ and $v \to^* s$, for some $s$;
- *terminating* (or *strongly normalising*) if all reduction sequences are finite;
- *left-linear* if all left-hand sides of rules in $R$ are linear;
- *non-overlapping* if there are no critical pairs;
- *orthogonal* if it is left-linear and non-overlapping;
- *non-duplicating* if for all $l \to r \in R$ and $x \in \mathcal{V}(l)$, the number of occurrences of $x$ in $r$ is less than or equal to the number of occurrences of $x$ in $l$.

For example, the rewrite system in Example 3 is confluent, terminating, left-linear and non-overlapping (therefore orthogonal), and non-duplicating.

A *hierarchical union* of rewrite systems consists of a set of rules defining some basic functions (this is called the *basis* of the hierarchy) and a series of *enrichments*. Each enrichment defines a new function or functions, using the ones previously defined. Constructors may be shared between the basis and the enrichments.

We recall a modularity result for termination of hierarchical unions from [19] (Theorem 14), which will be useful later:

If in a hierarchical union the basis is non-duplicating and terminating, and each enrichment satisfies a general scheme of recursion, where each recursive call in the right-hand side of a rule uses subterms of the left-hand side, then the hierarchical union is terminating.

## 3   Access Control Lists as a Rewrite System

In this section, we illustrate the use of rewriting systems to specify ACL policies with an example. We do not claim that this is the only way to formalise an ACL policy as a rewrite system. Instead, our goal is to give an executable[2] specification of an ACL policy, to show some basic properties, and to address, using rewriting techniques, the problem of checking that the specification is consistent, correct, and complete (that is, no access can be both granted and denied, no unauthorised access is granted and no authorised access is denied).

## 3.1   Rewrite Rules

Consider a set of objects, and a set of user-identifiers: $\mathcal{U} = \{u_1, \ldots, u_n\}$, such that each user has a certain number of access privileges on those objects. For simplicity, assume that user identifiers are natural numbers, and to make the example more concrete, assume that the objects are files and the access privileges are read $(r)$, write $(w)$ or execute $(x)$. For simplicity, we will only consider one file (the generalisation to many files is straightforward). The policy that we will model specifies that a user with an even identifier has $rw$ rights (i.e., can read and write on the file), whereas users with odd numbers can only read, and users whose identifier is a multiple of 4 can read, write and also execute the file.

Users will request access to the file by using the function access, which will grant or deny the access depending on the user and the operation requested. Requests will be expressed as access$(u, req)$ where $u$ is a user-identifier and $req$ is either $r$, $w$ or $x$. The request will be evaluated using the rewrite system $R_{ACL}$ given below; the result will be either grant or deny.

In the rewrite rules below, we denote variables with capital letters (e.g., $U$ is a variable), and function symbols (including constants) with lower-case letters (e.g. $r, w, x$ are constants). We use rem$(n, m)$ to compute the remainder of the division of $n$ by $m$.

$$\mathsf{access}(U, R) \rightarrow \mathsf{acl}(\mathsf{rem}(U, 2), R, U)$$

$$\mathsf{acl}(1, r, U) \rightarrow \mathsf{grant}$$
$$\mathsf{acl}(1, w, U) \rightarrow \mathsf{deny}$$
$$\mathsf{acl}(1, x, U) \rightarrow \mathsf{deny}$$

$$\mathsf{acl}(0, r, U) \rightarrow \mathsf{grant}$$
$$\mathsf{acl}(0, w, U) \rightarrow \mathsf{grant}$$
$$\mathsf{acl}(0, x, U) \rightarrow f(\mathsf{rem}(U, 4))$$

$$f(0) \rightarrow \mathsf{grant}$$
$$f(1) \rightarrow \mathsf{deny}$$
$$f(2) \rightarrow \mathsf{deny}$$
$$f(3) \rightarrow \mathsf{deny}$$

For example, with these rewrite rules a request from user 101 to write on the file is denied, whereas a request from user 20 to execute it is granted, since:

---

[2] For instance, the language MAUDE [14] can be used to execute rewrite-based specifications.

$$\mathsf{access}(101, w) \to^*_{R_{ACL}} \mathsf{deny}.$$
$$\mathsf{access}(20, x) \to^*_{R_{ACL}} \mathsf{grant}.$$

$R_{ACL}$ provides an executable specification of the policy (the rewrite rules are both a specification *and* an implementation of the access control function).

## 3.2 Properties of the Policy

In order for an access policy to be "acceptable", it is necessary that the policy satisfies certain acceptability criteria. As an informal example, it may be necessary to ensure that an access policy formulation does not specify that any user is granted and denied the same access privilege on the same data item (i.e., that the policy is consistent).

The following properties of $R_{ACL}$ are easy to check, and will be used to prove that the policy specified is consistent, correct, and complete.

*Property 1.* The rewrite system $R_{ACL}$ is terminating and confluent.

> *Proof.* Termination is trivially obtained, since $R_{ACL}$ is a first-order system, and there are no recursive or mutually recursive functions.
>
> To prove confluence, first note that there are no critical pairs, therefore the system is locally confluent. Termination and local confluence imply confluence, by Newman's Lemma [30].

**Corollary 1.** *Every term has a unique normal form in $R_{ACL}$.*

As a consequence of the unicity of normal forms, our specification of the access control policy is *consistent*.

*Property 2 (Consistency).* For any user $u$ and request $req$, it is not possible to derive both **grant** and **deny** for a request $\mathsf{access}(u, req)$.

We can give a characterisation of the normal forms:

*Property 3.* The normal form of a ground term of the form $\mathsf{access}(u, req)$ where $u$ is a number and $req \in \{r, w, x\}$ is either **grant** or **deny**.

As a consequence, our specification of the access control policy is *total*, in the sense that any valid request (i.e., a request from a valid user to perform a valid operation on an existing object) produces a result (a denial or an acceptance).

*Property 4 (Totality).* Each access request $\mathsf{access}(u, req)$ from a valid user $u$ to perform a valid operation $req$ is either denied or granted.

*Correctness* and *Completeness* are also easy to check:

*Property 5 (Correctness and Completeness).* For any user $u$ and request $req$:

- $\mathsf{access}(u, req) \to^*$ **grant** if and only if $u$ has the access privilege $req$ on the file.
- $\mathsf{access}(u, req) \to^*$ **deny** if and only if $u$ does not have the access privilege $req$ on the file.

*Proof.* Since we have consistency and totality, it is sufficient to show:

$$\mathsf{access}(u, req) \to^* \mathsf{grant} \text{ if and only if } u \text{ has the access privilege } req.$$

This is shown by inspection of the rewrite rules.

# 4  RBAC Policy Specifications as Rewrite Systems

In this section, we specify RBAC policies in terms of a rewrite system that is confluent and terminating. The normal forms of access requests are grant/deny i.e., each access request is reducible to grant or deny but not both.

## 4.1  Rewrite Rules

As indicated in Section 2, RBAC policies are specified with respect to: a set $\mathcal{U}$ of users, a set $\mathcal{O}$ of objects, a set $\mathcal{A}$ of access privileges, and a set $\mathcal{R}$ of roles.

We will use the function roles : $\mathcal{U} \to List(\mathcal{R})$ to represent the assignment of roles to users (note that a user may be assigned to several roles). Lists will be built from constructors nil and cons (see Example 3), and we will write $[e_1, \ldots, e_n]$ as an abbreviation for the list constructed from the elements $e_1, \ldots, e_n$. It is worth noting that a predicate $ura$, as discussed in Section 2, can also be specified with rewrite rules, since predicates are boolean functions (in this case we could define a function from pairs $(u, r) \in (\mathcal{U} \times \mathcal{R})$ to booleans True, False). However, we prefer to model $ura$ as a function from users to lists of roles because of the additional advantages this provides. In particular, modelling $ura$ as a function makes it easy to obtain all of the roles that a specific user is assigned to. This is an essential requirement of $RBAC_F$ theories, which emphasise the importance of performing administrative checks of user-role assignments from an RBAC policy specification. The following rewrite rules specify a function roles, where we assume $\mathcal{U} = \{u_1, \ldots, u_n\}$ and each $r_{ij} \in \mathcal{R}$.

$$\mathsf{roles}(u_1) \to [r_{11}, \ldots, r_{1i}]$$
$$\vdots$$
$$\mathsf{roles}(u_n) \to [r_{n1}, \ldots, r_{nk}]$$

To represent the assignment of privileges to roles (called *pra* in Section 2), we have again two design choices: we could use a boolean function (i.e., , a predicate) with three arguments (role, access privilege, object) or we can use a function priv from roles to lists of pairs $(a, o) \in (\mathcal{A} \times \mathcal{O})$, priv : $\mathcal{R} \to List(\mathcal{A} \times \mathcal{O})$. The second approach has advantages from a security administrator's point of view, since a function priv, to compute the set of access privileges assigned to a role, can be used to perform checks on the access policy specification (as required for $RBAC_{S4A}^P$ policies). We define priv by the following set of rules, where $r_i, \ldots, r_n \in \mathcal{R}$, $a_{ij} \in \mathcal{A}$, and $o_{ij} \in \mathcal{O}$.

$$\mathsf{priv}(r_1) \to [(a_{11}, o_{11}), \ldots, (a_{1i}, o_{1i})]$$
$$\vdots$$
$$\mathsf{priv}(r_n) \to [(a_{n1}, o_{n1}), \ldots, (a_{nk}, o_{nk})]$$

*Example 4. The user-role and permission-role assignments described in Example 1 may be expressed by the following rewrite rules:*

$$\mathsf{roles}(u_1) \rightarrow [r_2]$$
$$\mathsf{roles}(u_2) \rightarrow [r_1]$$
$$\mathsf{priv}(r_1) \rightarrow [(w, o_1)]$$
$$\mathsf{priv}(r_2) \rightarrow [(r, o_1)]$$

Access requests from users can be evaluated by using a rewrite system to grant or deny the request according to the user-role and permission-role assignments that are included in an RBAC policy specification. For that, we may use the following rules, where $U, A, O, R, L$ are variables and the operators member and $\cup$ are the standard membership test and union operators.

$$\mathsf{access}(U, A, O) \rightarrow \mathsf{check}(\mathsf{member}((A, O), \mathsf{privileges}(\mathsf{roles}(U))))$$
$$\mathsf{check}(\mathsf{True}) \rightarrow \mathsf{grant}$$
$$\mathsf{check}(\mathsf{False}) \rightarrow \mathsf{deny}$$

$$\mathsf{privileges}(\mathsf{nil}) \rightarrow \mathsf{nil}$$
$$\mathsf{privileges}(\mathsf{cons}(R, L)) \rightarrow \mathsf{priv}(R) \cup \mathsf{privileges}(L)$$

For example, with the assignment shown in Example 4, we have a reduction sequence: $\mathsf{access}(u_1, r, o_1) \rightarrow^* \mathsf{grant}$.

In the discussion that follows, we will use $R_{RBAC}$ to refer to the rewrite system that contains the set of rules that we have defined in this section.

## 4.2   Properties of the RBAC Policy

The following properties of $R_{RBAC}$ are easy to check and will be used to show that the specification is consistent, correct and complete:

*Property 6.* The rewrite system $R_{RBAC}$ is terminating and confluent.

> *Proof.* To prove termination, we use a modularity result for hierarchical unions (see Section 2 and [19]). First, observe that the system $R_{RBAC}$ is hierarchical: the rules defining roles, priv and check form the basis of the hierarchy, they are trivially terminating since the right-hand sides of rules are normal forms, and they are non-duplicating because the right-hand sides contain no variables. The rules defining privileges are recursive, but the recursive call is made on a subterm of the left-hand side argument. The rule defining access is not recursive. Therefore, the rules defining privileges and access satisfy the recursive scheme and the full system is terminating.
>
> To prove confluence, first note that there are no critical pairs, therefore the system is locally confluent. Termination and local confluence imply confluence, by Newman's Lemma [30].

**Corollary 2.** *Every term has a unique normal form in $R_{RBAC}$.*

As a consequence of the unicity of normal forms, our specification of the RBAC policy $R_{RBAC}$ is *consistent*.

*Property 7 (Consistency).* For any $u \in \mathcal{U}$, $a \in \mathcal{A}$, $o \in \mathcal{O}$: it is not possible to derive, from $R_{RBAC}$, both grant and deny for a request access($u, a, o$).

We can give a characterisation of the normal forms:

*Property 8.* The normal form of a ground term of the form access($u, a, o$) where $u \in \mathcal{U}$, $a \in \mathcal{A}$ and $o \in \mathcal{O}$ is either grant or deny.

As a consequence, our specification of the access control policy is *total*.

*Property 9 (Totality).* Each access request access($u, a, o$) from a valid user $u$ to perform a valid action $a$ on the object $o$ is either granted or denied.

*Correctness* and *Completeness* are also easy to check:

*Property 10 (Correctness and Completeness).* For any $u \in \mathcal{U}$, $a \in \mathcal{A}$, $o \in \mathcal{O}$:

- access($u, a, o$) $\rightarrow^*$ grant if and only if $u$ has the access privilege $a$ on $o$.
- access($u, a, o$) $\rightarrow^*$ deny if and only if $u$ does not have the access privilege $a$ on $o$.

*Proof.* Since the specification is consistent and total, it is sufficient to show that access($u, a, o$) $\rightarrow^*$ grant if and only if $u$ is assigned the access privilege $a$ on the object $o$. By inspection of the rewrite rules:

$$\text{access}(u, a, o) \rightarrow \text{check}(\text{member}(a, o), \text{privileges}(\text{roles}(u)))$$

Therefore, the result is grant if and only $(a, o) \in$ privileges(roles($u$)) if and only if $(a, o) \in$ priv($r$) for some $r \in$ roles($u$).

It is important to note that the proofs above do not have to be generated by a security administrator; rather, the proofs demonstrate that an RBAC policy $R_{RBAC}$ satisfies the properties described above. A security administrator can simply base an RBAC policy on the term rewrite system that we have defined and can be sure that the properties of $R_{RBAC}$ hold.

## 4.3   RBAC with a Hierarchy of Roles: $RBAC_{H2A}^P$ Policies

It is easy to accommodate a notion of seniority of roles where a role inherits, via a role hierarchy, the privileges of its subordinate roles (as explained in Section 2). For that, we just add rules of the form dsub($r_i$) $\rightarrow [r_1, \ldots, r_j]$ to specify a function dsub : $\mathcal{R} \rightarrow List(\mathcal{R})$, where dsub($r_i$) $= [r_1, \ldots, r_j]$ means that $r_1, \ldots, r_j$ are direct subordinate roles of $r_i$ (hence $r_i$ is directly senior to $r_1 \ldots r_n$). Then, we redefine the privileges of a role as its privileges plus the privileges of its direct subordinate roles. We use the functions dp to compute direct privileges (which corresponds to the previously defined priv) and the function privileges defined above:

$$\text{priv}(r) \rightarrow \text{dp}(r) \cup \text{privileges}(\text{dsub}(r))$$

Note that we do not need to change the definition of access (see Section 4.1) to accommodate hierarchies of roles, and we do not need to impose conditions on the form that a role hierarchy takes (apart from an acyclicity condition, which is a natural requirement for RBAC role hierarchies).

There are obvious optimisations that could be made if the hierarchy contains sharing (i.e., we should avoid computing twice the privileges of a role if it appears as a subordinate role of several of a user's roles). For instance, we may want to compute first all the roles of a user, including subordinate ones, and then the privileges of this set of roles. Efficiency considerations will be addressed in future work.

### 4.4    RBAC with Constraints and Reviews

For RBAC policies beyond $RBAC_{H2A}^P$ policies, separation of duties constraints must be supported and it must be possible for security administrators to review policy specifications (beyond simple user-role reviewing). We can implement several administrative checks on an RBAC policy, again as rewrite rules.

*Separation of Duties* is the property that specifies that roles assigned to a user cannot be mutually exclusive. To ensure that a specification of an RBAC policy satisfies the separation of duties property, we will erase conflicting roles assigned to a user (producing a list of roles without mutually exclusive pairs). This is obtained by evaluation of clean(roles($u$)) in a rewrite system containing the rules:

$$\begin{aligned}
\text{clean(nil)} &\rightarrow \text{nil} \\
\text{clean(cons}(R, L)) &\rightarrow \text{cons}(R, \text{clean(eraseclash}(R, L))) \\
\text{eraseclash}(R, \text{nil}) &\rightarrow \text{nil} \\
\text{eraseclash}(R, \text{cons}(R', L)) &\rightarrow \text{cons}(R', \text{eraseclash}(R, L)) \qquad (R, R' \text{ do not clash}) \\
\text{eraseclash}(R, \text{cons}(R', L)) &\rightarrow \text{eraseclash}(L) \qquad\qquad\qquad\quad (R, R' \text{ clash})
\end{aligned}$$

*Reviews.* We can add to the specification $R_{RBAC}$ the rules given below. Then, to check that every user has been assigned a role, an administrator could simply evaluate the term RolesDefined?($u$).

$$\begin{aligned}
\text{RolesDefined?}(u) &\rightarrow \text{review(roles}(u)) \\
\text{review(nil)} &\rightarrow \text{"error: user without a role"} \\
\text{review(cons}(r, lr)) &\rightarrow \text{"OK"}
\end{aligned}$$

## 5    Related Work

In terms of security applications, we note that the SPI-calculus [1] was developed as an extension of the $\pi$-calculus for proving the correctness of authentication protocols. In [3], the $\pi$-calculus is applied to reason about a number of basic access control policies and access mechanisms. However, the work described in [3] does not treat RBAC models and policies as rewrite systems. The work most closely related to ours is Koch et al's proposal [26]. In [26], RBAC is formalised by using a graph-based approach, with graph transformation rules used for describing the effects of actions as they relate to RBAC notions. This formalisation is used by Koch et al as a basis for proving properties of RBAC specifications, based on the categorical semantics of the graph transformations. Our work addresses similar issues to Koch et al's work but provides a different formulation of RBAC policies, and focuses on operational aspects. We use rewrite rules both as a specification and an implementation of an access control policy. To obtain efficient evaluators for request evaluation, sharing of computations is an important issue; for that, we note that graph-based rewriting may be used to devise efficient evaluation strategies.

In recent years, researchers have developed some sophisticated access control models in which access control requirements may be expressed by using rules that are employed to reason about authorised forms of access (see, for example, [22], [11], and [9]). In these approaches, the requirements that must be satisfied in order to access resources are specified by using rules expressed in (C)LP languages and access request evaluation may be viewed as being performed by rewriting, using, for example, SLG-resolution [33] or constraint solvers [28]. Our term rewriting approach offers similar attractions to the (C)LP approaches. We envisage term rewriting, or more generally, equational specifications, being used as an alternative to (C)LP. Term rewriting offers an algebraic approach to specification, where functional definitions can be easily accommodated. In this paper we have used first-order rewriting system; we could also consider a more restricted framework, for instance, orthogonal rewrite systems (in which case the confluence property is guaranteed). On the other hand, we could also consider more general rewriting frameworks, such as higher-order rewriting systems [25,29], to gain expressivity: we could then use higher-order functions in our policy specifications.

# 6  Conclusions and Further Work

In this paper, we have described the representation of ACL policies and RBAC policies as term rewrite systems. In particular, we have shown how different access control models may be flexibly defined in a completely uniform way. We also demonstrated how access requests may be evaluated with respect to an access policy specification by term rewriting, and how (static) properties of policies may be proven of ACL and RBAC policy specifications.

We have argued that term rewriting is particularly attractive in allowing multiple access control models and policies to be defined in a uniform way. In future work, we intend to consider the use of term rewriting for the specification of access control models other than ACL and RBAC. In particular, we wish to consider the specification of usage control models [31] as term rewrite systems, and access control models that may be used in a distributed computing environments. We also intend to apply our term rewriting approach to problems relating to the administration of RBAC policies (e.g., issues of administrative delegation), and to the specification of RBAC policies that allow conditional user-role, permission-role and denial-role assignments to be specified (see, for example, [6] and [9]). We also propose to investigate the use of policy materialisation [22] and policy specialisation methods [8] for the optimisation of access request evaluation with respect to the formulation of ACL and RBAC policies as rewrite systems.

# References

1. M. Abadi and A. Gordon. A calculus for cryptographic protocols: The spi calculus. In *Proc. 4th ACM Conf. on Computer and Communication Security*, pages 36–47, 1997.
2. T. Abbes, A. Bouhoula, and M. Rusinowitch. Protocol analysis in intrusion detection using decision tree. In *Proc. ITCC'04*, pages 404–408, 2004.
3. J. Abendroth and C. Jensen. A unified security mechanism for networked applications. In *SAC2003*, pages 351–357, 2003.
4. E. Albert, M. Hanus, F. Huch, J. Oliver, and G. Vidal. Operational semantics for declarative multi-paradigm languages. *Journal of Symbolic Computation*, 2004.
5. F. Baader and T. Nipkow. *Term rewriting and all that*. Cambridge University Press, 1998.
6. S. Barker. Data protection by logic programming. In *Proc. 1st International Conference on Computational Logic*, volume 1861 of *LNAI*, pages 1300–1314. Springer-Verlag, 2000.
7. S. Barker. Protecting deductive databases from unauthorized retrieval and update requests. *Journal of Data and Knowledge Engineering*, 23(3):231–285, 2002.
8. S. Barker, M. Leuschel, and M. Varea. Efficient and flexible access control via jones optimality logic program specialisation. *HOSC, To Appear*, 2006.
9. S. Barker and P. Stuckey. Flexible access control policy specification with constraint logic programming. *ACM Trans. on Information and System Security*, 6(4):501–546, 2003.
10. G. Barthe, G. Dufay, M. Huisman, and S. Melo de Sousa. Jakarta: a toolset to reason about the JavaCard platform. In *Proceedings of e-SMART'01*, volume 2140 of *Lecture Notes in Computer Science*. Springer-Verlag, 2002.
11. E. Bertino, B. Catania, E. Ferrari, and P. Perlasca. A system to specify and manage multipolicy access control models. In *Proc. IEEE 3rd International Workshop on Policies for Distributed Systems and Networks (POLICY 2002)*, 2002.
12. E. Bertino, B. Catania, E. Ferrari, and P. Perlasca. A logical framework for reasoning about access control models. In *SACMAT*, pages 41–52, 2001.
13. P. Borovansky, C. Kirchner, H. Kirchner, and P-E. Moreau. ELAN from a rewriting logic point of view. *Theoretical Computer Science*, 285:155–185, 2002.
14. M. Clavel, F. Durán, S. Eker, P. Lincoln, N. Martí-Oliet, J. Meseguer, and C. Talcott. The Maude 2.0 system. In *Rewriting Techniques and Applications (RTA 2003)*, number 2706 in Lecture Notes in Computer Science, pages 76–87. Springer-Verlag, 2003.
15. N. Dershowitz and J.-P. Jouannaud. Rewrite Systems. In J. van Leeuwen, editor, *Handbook of Theoretical Computer Science: Formal Methods and Semantics*, volume B. North-Holland, 1989.
16. S. De Capitani di Vimercati, S. Paraboschi, and P. Samarati. Access control: principles and solutions. *Softw., Pract. Exper.*, 33(5):397–421, 2003.
17. R. Echahed and F. Prost. Security policy in a declarative style. In *Proc. 7th ACM-SIGPLAN Symposium on Principles and Practice of Declarative Programming (PPDP'05)*. ACM Press, 2005.

18. M. Fernández. *Programming Languages and Operational Semantics: An Introduction.* King's College Publications, 2004.
19. M. Fernández and J.-P. Jouannaud. Modular termination of term rewriting systems revisited. In *Recent Trends in Data Type Specification. Proc. 10th. Workshop on Specification of Abstract Data Types (ADT'94)*, number 906 in LNCS, 1995.
20. G. Feuillade, T. Genet, and V. Viet Triem Tong. Reachability Analysis over Term Rewriting Systems. *JAR*, 33 (3-4):341–383, 2004.
21. M. Hanus. A unified computation model for functional and logic programming. In *Proc. 24st ACM Symposium on Principles of Programming Languages (POPL'97)*, ACM Press, 1997.
22. S. Jajodia, P. Samarati, M. Sapino, and V.S. Subrahmaninan. Flexible support for multiple access control policies. *ACM TODS*, 26(2):214–260, 2001.
23. C. Kirchner, H. Kirchner, and M. Vittek. *ELAN user manual.* Nancy (France), 1995. Technical Report 95-R-342, CRIN.
24. J.-W. Klop. Term Rewriting Systems. In S. Abramsky, Dov.M. Gabbay, and T.S.E. Maibaum, editors, *Handbook of Logic in Computer Science*, volume 2. Oxford University Press, 1992.
25. J.-W. Klop, V. van Oostrom, and F. van Raamsdonk. Combinatory reduction systems, introduction and survey. *Theoretical Computer Science*, 121:279–308, 1993.
26. M. Koch, L. Mancini, and F. Parisi-Presicce. A graph based formalism for rbac. In *SACMAT*, pages 129–187, 2004.
27. Butler W. Lampson. Protection. *SIGOPS Oper. Syst. Rev.*, 8(1):18–24, 1974.
28. K. Marriott and P.J. Stuckey. *Programming with Constraints: an Introduction.* MIT Press, 1998.
29. Richard Mayr and Tobias Nipkow. Higher-order rewrite systems and their confluence. *Theoretical Computer Science*, 192:3–29, 1998.
30. M.H.A. Newman. On theories with a combinatorial definition of equivalence. *Annals of Mathematics*, 43(2):223–243, 1942.
31. J. Park and R. Sandhu. The uconabc usage control model. *ACM Trans. Inf. Syst. Secur.*, 7(1):128–174, 2004.
32. R. Sandhu, D. Ferraiolo, and R. Kuhn. The NIST model for role-based access control: Towards a unified standard. In *Proc. 4th ACM Workshop on Role-Based Access Control*, pages 47–61, 2000.
33. *The XSB System Version 2.7.1, Programmer's Manual*, 2005.

# Discretionary and Mandatory Controls
# for Role-Based Administration

Jason Crampton

Information Security Group, Royal Holloway, University of London
jason.crampton@rhul.ac.uk

**Abstract.** Role-based access control is an important way of limiting the access users have to computing resources. While the basic concepts of role-based access control are now well understood, there is no consensus on the best approach to managing role-based systems. In this paper, we introduce a new model for role-based administration, using the notions of discretionary and mandatory controls. Our model provides a number of important features that control the assignment of users and permissions to roles. This means that we can limit the damage that can be done by malicious administrative users. We compare our approach to a number of other models for role-based administration, and demonstrate that our model has several advantages.

## 1 Introduction

Role-based access control (RBAC) is an increasingly popular model for limiting the access users have to resources provided by a computer system. A role provide a means of associating a group of users (typically corresponding to some particular job within an organization) to some set of permissions (corresponding to the functions and duties performed by users with that particular job).

"Administration" in the context of access control is a generic term that is taken to mean the management of the sets and relations underpinning the access control model. Adding users or changing the access rights associated with those users are part of the administrative process, for example. The administration of role-based systems using role-based principles has been less widely studied than RBAC itself, although some important progress has been made [1,2,3]. A number of important ideas have emerged from this work: RBAC96 introduces the idea of administrative permissions [3]; ARBAC97 requires that the parameters of administrative operations should satisfy certain conditions [2]; the RHA model introduces the idea of administrative scope which divides the role hierarchy into a number of different administrative domains [1].

The ANSI-RBAC standard was released in 2004 [4]. It is very strongly influenced by the RBAC96 model [3] and the NIST proposal for an RBAC standard [5]. It states the administrative functions that must be supported by an RBAC system that is compliant with the standard. However, it provides no model for administration, nor does it specify how those functions should be implemented.

E. Damiani and P. Liu (Eds.): Data and Applications Security 2006, LNCS 4127, pp. 194–208, 2006.
© IFIP International Federation for Information Processing 2006

We believe, therefore, that there is a pressing need for a comprehensive model for administration in role-based systems, and it is this need that we address in this paper. Moreover, we believe that existing models for administration each have certain limitations: primarily, the assignment of administrative permissions to roles in RBAC96 is insufficiently structured and leads to a lack of control over the propagation of permissions, while the highly structured approaches of ARBAC97 and RHA are insufficiently flexible.

In this paper, we construct a general model for role-based administration that takes advantage of some of the features of existing models and introduces some new features. That is, we employ administrative permissions, divide the role hierarchy into different administrative domains, and require that the parameters of an administrative operation meet certain conditions. In particular, we will show that this approach provides far more control over which roles can perform different administrative operations and provides stronger control over which operations are permitted. We can insist that only a human resources role can update the assignment of users to roles, for example, and that the assignment of a user to a role only succeeds if the user, the role and the administrative role performing the assignment satisfy certain conditions. Our approach also means that we are able to require that different roles perform different types of operations within each administrative domain; what we call *administrative separation of duty*.

In the next section we introduce our model for administration. We introduce some prerequisite concepts from mathematics and RBAC, and then define administrative permissions, domains and commands. We then define the extensions to RBAC96 that are required to support role-based administration. In Sect. 4 we introduce the use of separation of duty constraints for administration. In Sect. 5 we illustrate our approach using an example from the literature. In this section we also compare our approach to related work. We conclude the paper in Sect. 6 by summarizing our contribution and suggesting some ideas for future work.

## 2   Foundations for a New Model for Administration

### 2.1   Mathematical Preliminaries

Let $\leqslant$ be a reflexive, anti-symmetric, transitive binary relation on $X$. Then we say $(X, \leqslant)$ is a *partially ordered set* or *poset*. When the order relation is obvious from context we will simply write "$X$ is a poset". We may write $y \geqslant x$ whenever $x \leqslant y$.

Let $Y \subseteq X$: we say $y \in Y$ is a *maximal element* in $Y$ if $y \leqslant x$ implies that $x = y$ for all $x \in Y$. Informally, there is no element bigger than $y$ in $Y$. A *minimal element* of $Y$ is defined analogously. We write $\max(Y)$ (respectively $\min(Y)$) to denote the set of maximal (minimal) elements in $Y$. Let $x, y \in X$: we say $y$ is the *parent* of $x$ if for any $z \in X$ such that $x < z \leqslant y$, $y = z$. In other words, $y$ is the parent of $x$ if there is no element of $X$ that can "fit between" $x$ and $y$ in the ordering. Given $Y \subseteq X$, we use the following notation:

$\downarrow Y = \{x \in X : x \leqslant y, y \in Y\}$; $\uparrow Y = \{x \in X : x \geqslant y, y \in Y\}$. We write $\downarrow x$ rather than $\downarrow \{x\}$ and $\uparrow x$ rather than $\uparrow \{x\}$.

## 2.2   RBAC Preliminaries

A hierarchical role-based access control model[1] has the following features [3,4]: a partially ordered set of roles $(R, \leqslant)$; a set of permissions $P$ and a permission-role assignment relation $PA \subseteq P \times R$; a set of users $U$ and a user-role assignment relation $UA \subseteq U \times R$. The set of roles available to a user $u \in U$ is defined to be $\{r \in R : r \leqslant r', (u, r') \in UA\}$, and the set of permissions available to $u$ is defined to be $\{p \in P : (p, r) \in PA, r \leqslant r', (u, r') \in UA\}$.

## 2.3   Administrative Permissions

In the early RBAC literature, permissions were simply "uninterpreted symbols", because the precise nature of permissions is "implementation and system dependent" [3]. In the ANSI-RBAC standard, which is based on the RBAC96 model, permissions are defined by an object and an action (or operation). In the context of administrative permissions, it is instructive to actually specify the object and action for each permission.

The RBAC96 model defines five sets, $P$, $U$, $(R, \leqslant)$, $UA \subseteq U \times R$, and $PA \subseteq P \times R$, and we require administrative permissions that can update each of these sets. We assume that the partially ordered set of roles is implemented by a role hierarchy relation $RH \subseteq R \times R$. We assume that there are two generic (primitive) actions add and delete, and that either of these actions may be applied to one of the objects that define the role-based model. In other words, we may add or delete entries from each of $P$, $U$, $RH$, $UA$, and $PA$. We will write addX to denote the permission $(\text{add}, X)$ and delX to denote the administrative permission $(\text{delete}, X)$, where $X \in \{P, U, RH, UA, PA\}$.

## 2.4   Administrative Commands

A request to invoke an administrative permission is made by an administrative role. The request will specify a number of parameters, determined by the permission requested. For example, the parameters required when invoking the addUA permission, which is a request to assign a user $u$ to a role $r$, will obviously be $u$ and $r$, as well as the administrative role $a$ in which the requesting user is acting. In this paper, we will write parameterized administrative requests as function calls and refer to them as *administrative commands* (in the style of Harrison-Ruzzo-Ullman commands [6]).

Table 1 summarizes the ten administrative commands. It should be noted that we have only stated the immediate effect of an administrative command. In general, additional changes may need to be made: in particular, when a role

---

[1] Both RBAC96 [3] and the ANSI-RBAC standard [4] distinguish between flat RBAC (RBAC$_0$ [3]) and hierarchical RBAC (RBAC$_1$ [3]). This distinction is unnecessary as an unordered set is a partially ordered set with an empty order relation.

**Table 1.** Administrative commands

| Command | Effect | Description |
|---|---|---|
| $\mathtt{addU}(a,u)$ | $U \leftarrow U \cup \{u\}$ | Create a new user account |
| $\mathtt{addP}(a,p)$ | $P \leftarrow P \cup \{p\}$ | Create a new permission |
| $\mathtt{addR}(a,r,C,P)$ | $R \leftarrow R \cup \{r\}$ | Add role with children $C$ and parents $P$ |
| $\mathtt{addE}(a,c,p)$ | $RH \leftarrow RH \cup \{(c,p)\}$ | Add edge $(c,p)$ |
| $\mathtt{addUA}(a,u,r)$ | $UA \leftarrow UA \cup \{(u,r)\}$ | Create a new user-role assignment |
| $\mathtt{addPA}(a,p,r)$ | $PA \leftarrow PA \cup \{(p,r)\}$ | Create a new permission-role assignment |

is added or deleted, the set of edges ($RH$) will also need to be updated. We have
omitted these changes in order to simplify the presentation. We assume each
command is initiated by an administrative role $a$. For each add command, there
is a corresponding delete command; these commands are not shown in the table.

## 2.5 Administrative Domains

A fundamental part of our model is the concept of an *administrative domain*.
Intuitively, an administrative domain is a set of roles within the role hierarchy
that can be administered by the same role. Given a role hierarchy, we would
expect that an appropriate choice of domains would be quite apparent. However,
formalizing the notion of an administrative domain is rather more difficult.

In fact, it is easier to consider the set of administrative domains. This is
because it seems reasonable that there should be no overlap between different administrative domains. The justification for this lies in the notions of "ownership"
and "responsibility". Suppose that role $r$ belongs to two different administrative
domains $D_1$ and $D_2$ and each domain is associated with an administrative role $a_1$
and $a_2$. Then if $a_1$ assigns a user $u$ to $r$, $u$ may acquire certain roles and permissions within $D_2$ without $a_2$'s knowledge or approval. This suggests that the set
of roles should be partitioned (in a mathematical sense) into different domains.

There is, however, one situation where overlapping domains would be intuitively reasonable, particularly within the context of RBAC. That is, when one
domain $D_2$ is completely contained within a second $D_1$. In this case, when $a_1$
assigns $u$ to a role within $D_1$, any roles that $u$ obtains in $D_2$ through inheritance
are also contained within $D_1$. Hence, we define the notion of a nested partition
of a set and use this to define an administrative partition of a set of roles.

**Definition 1.** *Let $X$ be a set. A family of sets $\mathcal{Y} = \{Y_1, \ldots, Y_n\}$, $\emptyset \subset Y_i \subseteq X$,
is a* nested partition *of $X$ if $X = \bigcup_{i=1}^{n} Y_i$, and for all $Y_i, Y_j \in \mathcal{Y}$, one of the
following conditions holds:* (i) $Y_i \cap Y_j = \emptyset$ (ii) $Y_i \subseteq Y_j$ (iii) $Y_j \subseteq Y_i$.

Let $(R, \leqslant)$ be a set of roles and let $\mathcal{D} = \{D_1, \ldots, D_n\}$, $D_i \subseteq R$. We say $\mathcal{D}$ is an
*administrative partition* of $R$ if $\mathcal{D}$ is a nested partition of $R$. Each element of an
administrative partition is called an *administrative domain*. In other words, $\mathcal{D}$
is an administrative partition if every role is contained in at least one domain
and every pair of domains either has empty intersection or one is completely

contained in the other. Clearly, $\mathcal{D} = \{R\}$ is a (trivial) set of administrative domains. At the other extreme, $\mathcal{D} = \{\{r_1\}, \ldots, \{r_n\}\}$, where $R = \{r_1, \ldots, r_n\}$, is a set of administrative domains. Note that a set of administrative domains is partially ordered by subset inclusion. In fact, we have the following two results.

**Proposition 2.** *Let $\mathcal{D}$ be a set of administrative domains. Then for any $D \in \mathcal{D}$, $D$ has at most one parent.*

*Proof.* We need to show that if a domain $D$ has a parent $D'$, then $D'$ is unique. Suppose, in order to obtain a contradiction, that there exist two distinct domains $D'$ and $D''$ that are both parents of $D$. Now $D' \cap D'' \neq \emptyset$, since $D \subseteq D' \cap D''$. Hence, since $D'$ and $D''$ are distinct administrative domains, either $D' \subset D''$ or $D'' \subset D'$. We can assume without loss of generality that $D' \subset D''$ and hence $D''$ is not a parent of $D$ (since we have $D \subset D' \subset D''$). This is the required contradiction and the result now follows.

**Corollary 3.** *Let $\mathcal{D}$ be an administrative partition of $R$. Then the graph of the reflexive transitive reduction of the poset $(\mathcal{D}, \subseteq)$ is a forest.*

# 3    A New Administrative Model for RBAC96

We augment the standard RBAC96 model with a set of administrative domains $\mathcal{D}$ and a domain-role assignment relation $DA \subseteq \mathcal{D} \times R$. We say $r$ has *administrative control* over $D$ if $(D, r) \in DA$. We say $r$ is an *administrative role* if $(D, r) \in DA$, for some $D \in \mathcal{D}$. (If $\mathcal{D} = \{R\}$, we do not require the $DA$ relation.) Let $D, D' \in \mathcal{D}$ and $D \subseteq D'$. If $r$ has administrative control over $D'$ then we assume that $r$ also has administrative control over $D$. Hence, the ordering on the set of domains induces an ordering on the set of administrative roles.

We define a new relation assigning administrative permissions to roles $APA \subseteq AP \times R$, where $AP$ is the set of administrative permissions. An administrative command is issued by (a user acting in) an administrative role $a$ and is interpreted as an attempt to invoke an administrative permission with particular parameters (chosen by the requesting user). An administrative command is permitted if the *discretionary administrative property* and the *mandatory administrative property* are satisfied:

**Property 1.** *The administrative command* cmdX$(a, \ldots)$ *satisfies the discretionary administrative property if* $(a, (\text{cmd}, X)) \in APA$, *where* cmd $\in \{\text{add}, \text{delete}\}$.

**Property 2.** *The administrative command* cmdX$(a, \ldots)$ *satisfies the mandatory administrative property if the role parameters of the command belong to a domain over which $a$ has administrative control. In particular:*

- *for* addR$(a, r, C, P)$ *to succeed, there must exist a domain $D$ over which $a$ has administrative control and $C, P \subseteq D$;*
- *for* addE$(a, c, p)$ *and* delE$(a, c, p)$ *to succeed, there must exist a domain $D$ over which $a$ has administrative control and $c, p \in D$;*

- *for* delR($a, r$), addUA($a, u, r$), addPA($a, p, r$), delUA($a, u, r$), *and* delPA($a, p, r$) *to succeed, there must exist a domain* $D$ *over which* $a$ *has administrative control and* $r \in D$.

Note that if $r$ has administrative control over $D'$ then $r$ also has administrative control over every domain $D \in \mathcal{D}$ such that $D \subseteq D'$. In other words, the mandatory administrative property is similar to the simple security property of the Bell-LaPadula model [7], which states that a subject $s$ can read any object $o$ with a security label that is less than or equal to that of $s$.

## 3.1   User-Role Assignment

It is fairly easy to see that the existence of a role hierarchy means that administrative commands could affect more than one administrative domain. In this section we introduce a further mandatory control on the execution of user-role assignment commands.

This control is motivated by the following observation: the assignment of a user $u$ to a role $r$ results in $u$ being implicitly assigned (via inheritance in the role hierarchy) to all roles $r' < r$. In other words, if an administrative role assigns $u$ to a role $r$ within its domain $D$, it may have an impact on the roles available to $u$ in an administrative domain $D' \supset D$. Hence, a very natural (mandatory) requirement on user-role assignment should be that $u$ is already assigned to more junior roles that are not in the administrative domain of the role to which $u$ is to be assigned. More formally, we have the following security property for user-role assignment.

**Property 3.** *The command* addUA($a, u, r$) *satisfies the* mandatory *UA property if there exists a domain* $D$ *over which* $a$ *has administrative control such that* $r \in D$ *and* $u$ *is already assigned to all roles in* $\max(\downarrow r \setminus D)$.

Let us assume that an administrative role $a$ has the permission to create new user accounts. An important consequence of the mandatory *UA* property is that an administrative role assigned to domain $D$ cannot assign a new user to a role $r \in D$ unless $\downarrow r \subseteq D$. This means that it is impossible for an administrative user (assigned to some administrative role), by virtue of the mandatory restrictions on user-role assignment, to assign users to roles over which he has no control. In other words, the damage that a malicious administrative user can do is limited to the domain(s) he controls.

## 3.2   Permission-Role Assignment

Just as the act of assigning a user to a role $r$ may have an impact outside the domain controlled by the administrative role performing the assignment, the act of assigning a permission to a role may also have undesirable consequences. Consider the command addPA($a, p, r$). If $r$ belongs to a domain controlled by $a$ then we might expect that this command should be permitted. However, consider the case when $r < r'$, $p$ is not currently assigned to $r'$, and $r'$ does not belong to any domain controlled by $a$. In this case, $a$ is "giving away" the permission $p$ and the permission leaks from the domain(s) to which it has previously been confined. Hence we introduce a mandatory security property for permission-role assignment.

**Property 4.** *The command* addPA$(a, p, r)$ *satifies the* mandatory *PA property if there exists a domain $D$ over which $a$ has administrative control such that $r \in D$ and $p$ is already assigned to all roles in $\min(\uparrow r \setminus D)$.*

An important consequence of the mandatory *PA* property is that an administrative user cannot downgrade permissions, by assigning them to less senior roles in the domain(s) he controls, beyond a certain level. As with the mandatory *UA* property, the mandatory *PA* property limits the damage that a malicious administrative user can do.

### 3.3   Automatic Assignment of Domains

Note that the union of the set of administrative domains is $R$. Therefore, we need to specify which domain a newly created role should belong to. Intuitively, we wish to assign the role to the most appropriate domain automatically. More formally, we can specify that a newly created role $r$ should belong to the smallest domain $D$ that contains $P$, where $P$ is the set of parents of $r$.[2] (Note that "smallest domain" is well defined since the set of administrative domains can be represented as a forest.)

### 3.4   Choosing Administrative Domains

Of course, the choice of appropriate administrative domains is an important practical aspect of the model proposed in this paper. In fact, the notion of administrative scope, introduced in the RHA model, can be particularly useful in choosing administrative domains.

**Definition 4 (Crampton [1]).** *The* administrative scope *of a role $r$, denoted $\sigma(r)$, is defined in the following way: $\sigma(r) = \{r' \leqslant r : \uparrow r' \subseteq \downarrow r \cup \uparrow r\}$.*

In other words, $r' \in \sigma(r)$ if any role bigger than $r'$ is comparable to $r$ in the role hierarchy. The intuition is that if $r' \in \sigma(r)$, then $r$ "knows about" all the upward inheritance from $r'$, and hence it is appropriate for $r$ to be able to administer $r'$. However, the reason that administrative scope is particularly useful in the context of this paper is that it can be used to define a nested partition of $R$.

**Lemma 5 (Crampton [8, Lemma 2]).** *Let $r, r' \in R$. Then*

$$\sigma(r) \cap \sigma(r') = \begin{cases} \sigma(r) & \text{if } r \in \sigma(r'), \\ \sigma(r') & \text{if } r' \in \sigma(r), \\ \emptyset & \text{otherwise.} \end{cases}$$

---

[2] Note also that if role $r$ is deleted, every domain to which $r$ belongs has $r$ removed from it.

**Corollary 6.** $\Sigma(R) = \bigcup_{r \in R} \sigma(r)$ *defines a nested partition of* $R$.

*Proof.* For all $r \in R$, $r \in \sigma(r)$. Hence $\Sigma(R) = R$. The remaining condition for $\Sigma(R)$ to be a nested partition follows from Lemma 5.

Let $R' \subseteq R$ and write $\Sigma(R')$ for $\bigcup_{r \in R'} \sigma(r)$. Then any $R' \subseteq R$ such that $\Sigma(R') = R$ can be used to define a set of administrative domains. Figure 1 illustrates the non-trivial domains (cardinality greater than 1) identified using administrative scope. Each domain is enclosed by a broken line. $\{\sigma(a), \sigma(b), \sigma(c), \sigma(d)\}$ would be a suitable choice of administrative domains; each of these domains is enclosed by a heavier broken line. The domain forest in this example is simply a root node for $\sigma(a)$, and three child nodes, one for each of the domains determined by the administrative scope of $b$, $c$ and $d$.

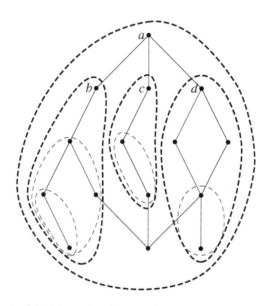

**Fig. 1.** Administrative domains from administrative scope

### 3.5   Checking Access Requests Using the Domain Forest

Given an administrative command with administrative role parameter $a$ and role parameters $X$, we can check whether the mandatory administrative properties are satisfied by considering the sub-tree of the domain forest rooted at $a$. We simply check whether each role in $X$ is contained in one of the domains in the sub-tree. The simplicity with which the satisfaction of mandatory properties can be checked contrasts sharply with the difficulty of checking whether an administrative command is permitted in the ARBAC97 model [1].

Of course, additional resources are required to store and maintain the domain forest. In particular, the domain forest will need to be updated following an addR or delR command. Nevertheless, we believe that the benefits that are obtained by using the domain forest more than offset this disadvantage.

# 4    Administrative Separation of Duty

We now introduce a second facet of our model for administration. We have already seen that the mandatory *UA* and *PA* properties can prevent certain types of administrative abuse. We now consider the use of separation of duty constraints to further reduce the possibility that a single malicious user can compromise the security of a system through a sequence of administrative commands.

Separation of duty is an important control principle in management whereby sensitive combinations of duties are partitioned between different individuals in order to prevent the violation of business rules. The research community has taken an active interest in incorporating separation of duty controls into computer systems since the late 1980s. One of the rules of the Clark-Wilson model [6] requires that separation of duty requirements must be met. In recent years, a number of papers have studied separation of duty in the context of RBAC [9,10,11,12,13,14].

Many of these papers have considered rather complex separation of duty requirements. In the context of role-based administration, we claim that the requirements are rather simple, so we will confine our attention to a very simple model for separation of duty. The model is based on the RBAC96 notion of mutually exclusive roles. However, in our case we will consider mutually exclusive permissions.

**Definition 7.** *An* administrative separation of duty (ASD) constraint *is a set of administrative permissions. An ASD constraint $C$ is* satisfied *provided no user is assigned to all the permissions in $C$. An* ASD policy *is a family of ASD constraints.*

As a motivating example, let us assume that we wish to separate the following functions: the creation of new user accounts (or simply users) and the assignment of users to roles. We might wish to do this so that one user cannot create a new user account and assign it to roles, preferring instead that a user acting in some IT support role is responsible for creating users and a user acting in some human resources role is responsible for deciding which roles are relevant to a user's job. In order to realize this requirement, we specify the separation of duty constraint {addU, addUA}. This constraint is satisfied provided no user is assigned to both permissions (via the *UA* and *APA* relations).

In the case when $|C| = 2$, we can ensure the satisfaction of $C$ by assigning each permission to different administrative roles $a_1$ and $a_2$, and ensuring that no user is assigned to both roles. In other words, we can convert the ASD constraint on administrative permissions into an ASD constraint on administrative roles. In fact, we can ensure the satisfaction of any ASD constraint $\{p_1, \ldots, p_n\}$ by re-writing it as a set of ASD constraints on administrative roles. Specifically, we ensure that each permission $p_i$ is assigned to a different administrative role $a_i$ and define the constraints $\{\{a_i, a_j\} : 1 \leqslant i < j \leqslant n\}$. Now we can be assured that the ASD constraint on administrative permissions is satisfied provided the ASD policy on administrative roles is satisfied. It is quite straightforward to ensure that this policy is always satisfied:

- at system initialization we simply check each user's administrative role assignments;
- before allowing any command of the form $\mathtt{addUA}(a, u, a')$, where $a'$ is an administrative role, we must check that, if there exists an ASD constraint of the form $\{a', a''\}$, then $u$ is not already assigned to $a''$.

Suppose, for example, that $\{a_1, a_2\}$ is an ASD constraint on administrative roles and $u$ is already assigned to $a_1$. Then the command $\mathtt{addUA}(a, u, a_2)$ must fail, because allowing it to succeed would violate the ASD constraint.

Another constraint that is likely to be useful in practice is $\{\mathtt{addUA}, \mathtt{addPA}\}$, which would prevent any administrative role from establishing a link between a user and a particular permission by assigning them to the same role. In practice, we might assign $\mathtt{addUA}$ to human resources and $\mathtt{addPA}$ to senior operational roles within each domain. Clearly, the set of constraints that will be used in practice will vary depending on the environment and on the personnel available.

## 5   Related Work

As we noted in the introduction, there have been two generic approaches to administration of role-based systems. We now consider these approaches in more detail and compare them to our approach. In order to provide a concrete basis for this discussion, we introduce an example from the literature. This also provides an opportunity to illustrate the use of our model.

Figure 2(a) shows a typical role hierarchy that has been used as an illustrative example by Sandhu [2]. The hierarchy should be considered in the context of a software engineering company, with two projects under the leadership of roles PL1 and PL2. All employees are assigned to the E role and all software engineers are assigned to the ED (engineering department) role. Each project has its own security officer role (PSO1 and PSO2); the engineering department has a security officer role (DSO); and the company has a senior security officer (SSO).

It is clear that there are four main administrative domains, one corresponding to each of the projects, one corresponding to the department (which incorporates both project teams) and one corresponding to the whole role hierarchy. These domains (sets of roles) are enclosed by dashed lines in Fig. 2. The PSO roles have control over their respective projects, while the DSO and SSO roles have control over the department and organization domains. Hence we would suggest the following administrative configuration: we define the set of administrative domains to be $\{D_{P_1}, D_{P_2}, D_{Eng}, R\}$, where $D_{P_i} = \{\mathtt{ENGi}, \mathtt{PEi}, \mathtt{QEi}, \mathtt{PLi}\}$[3] and $D_{Eng} = \{\mathtt{ED}\} \cup D_{P_1} \cup D_{P_2}$; and we define the domain assignment relation to be $\{(D_{P_1}, \mathtt{PSO1}), (D_{P_2}, \mathtt{PSO2}), (D_{Eng}, \mathtt{DSO}), (R, \mathtt{SSO})\}$. Note that $D_1, D_2 \subseteq D_{Eng} \subseteq R$ induces the following partial order on the set of administrative roles: $\mathtt{PSO1}, \mathtt{PSO2} < \mathtt{DSO} < \mathtt{SSO}$. In addition we would need to assign administrative permissions to each administrative role.

The mandatory $UA$ property allows the PSO roles to assign $u$ to a role in their respective domains if $u$ is already assigned to ED; DSO can assign $u$ to a role in

---

[3] Note that $\sigma(\mathtt{PLi}) = \{\mathtt{ENGi}, \mathtt{PEi}, \mathtt{QEi}, \mathtt{PLi}\}$.

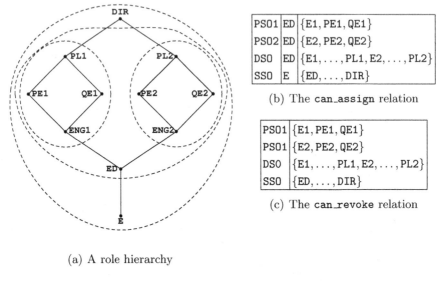

(a) A role hierarchy

(b) The can_assign relation

| PSO1 | ED | {E1, PE1, QE1} |
|---|---|---|
| PSO2 | ED | {E2, PE2, QE2} |
| DSO | ED | {E1, ..., PL1, E2, ..., PL2} |
| SSO | E | {ED, ..., DIR} |

(c) The can_revoke relation

| PSO1 | {E1, PE1, QE1} |
|---|---|
| PSO1 | {E2, PE2, QE2} |
| DSO | {E1, ..., PL1, E2, ..., PL2} |
| SSO | {ED, ..., DIR} |

**Fig. 2.** An ARBAC97 example [2]

$D_{Eng}$ if $u$ is already assigned to E; and SSO can assign any user to any role in $R$. In other words, the larger the domain controlled by an administrative role, the more trust is placed in that role regarding administrative operations.

### 5.1 "Mandatory" Approaches

The ARBAC97 model was designed specifically as a management model for RBAC96. It includes three sub-models URA97, PRA97, and RRA97, for managing user-role assignment, permission-role assignment and role-role assignment (the role hierarchy), respectively.

Each of the three sub-models uses relations that control what administrative roles are permitted to do. Each of these relations (can_assign and can_revoke in URA97, can_assignp and can_revokep in PRA97, and can_modify in RRA97) define sets of roles that each administrative role is permitted to change. An element $(a, q, R') \in$ can_assign, for example, means that an administrative role $a$ can assign any user who is assigned to the "prerequisite" role $q \in R$ to any role in the set $R' \subseteq R$.

Figure 2 shows examples of the two URA97 relations. The project security officers (PSO1 and PSO2), for example, can assign a user to roles in their respective projects, provided the user is already assigned to ED. The departmental and senior security officer roles (DSO and SSO) have greater powers to assign users to roles. Similarly, the different security officer roles can revoke roles from different sets of roles in the hierarchy, as specified by the can_revoke relation.

Note that our model for administration is very much simpler than ARBAC97. We only require a domain-role assignment relation and the *APA* relation.

Indeed, Fig. 2 omits the other ARBAC97 relations, `can_assignp`, `can_revokep` and `can_modify`.

The ARBAC97 approach mixes the definition of administrative domains with administrative rights. Our proposed approach to role-based administration separates the specification of administrative domains and the assignment of administrative rights. One useful consequence of this is that we only need to specify a set of administrative domains and a domain-role assignment relation.

The ARBAC97 model assumes that `can-assign` and the other relations in the model are static. This means that if a new role is added to the hierarchy, for example, no constraints can be imposed on the assignment of users (and permissions) to that role. We believe that the static nature of ARBAC97 relations is a considerable disadvantage.

The role sets specified in ARBAC97 relations are always expressed as ranges within the partially ordered set of roles. Moreover, it is impossible to delete a role that is the end-point of a range in an ARBAC97 relation. A particularly significant limitation of ARBAC97 is the requirement in RRA97 that all ranges in the `can_modify` relation are encapsulated [2] and that all hierarchy operations should preserve the encapsulation of ranges defined in the `can_modify` relation. One side effect of this requirement is that the creation of a role with either no parent or no child will violate the encapsulation of some encapsulated range in the hierarchy and hence such operations are prohibited. In addition, encapsulated ranges are actually quite rare in partially ordered sets.[4] In short, the use of ranges leads to significant usability problems for the ARBAC97 model.

The ARBAC02 model extends ARBAC97 by introducing organizational units [15]. The main motivation for this seems to be to reduce the number of steps that are required when assigning users (and permissions) to roles. This problem arises as a consequence of the use of prerequisite roles in the `can_assign` and `can_assignp` relations. Organizational units are nothing more than groups of roles and hence can be thought of as administrative domains. The designers of ARBAC02 do not impose any structure on organizational units. Can one role belong to two different organizational units, for example? Organizational units are only used to simplify the prerequisite conditions in the assignment relations `can_assign` and `can_assignp`, which seems a wasted opportunity.

The RHA family of models defines the notion of administrative scope. Whether a request to perform an administrative action is permitted is defined in terms of administrative scope. In this respect, administrative scope is similar to the different role ranges that are defined in each of the ARBAC97 relations. The big advantage of RHA over ARBAC97 is that a single set of roles (namely administrative scope) is used to determine the success or otherwise of administrative commands. In many ways, the RHA family of models is simpler and more versatile than ARBAC97 [1].

However, RHA shares one weakness with ARBAC97: it is vulnerable to changes in the role hierarchy, because the administrative domains are defined in terms of the role hierarchy structure itself. In ARBAC97, domains are defined

---

[4] A comprehensive analysis of the shortcomings of ARBAC97 can be found in [1].

by encapsulated ranges; in RHA, domains are defined by administrative scope. Hence, it is necessary to perform some additional checks before allowing hierarchy operations, in order to check that administrative domains are preserved by the operation. Again, it turns out that this is easier to check whether domains are preserved in RHA than in ARBAC97, but it is still an overhead [8]. In other words, we believe the approach advocated in this paper, in which domains are simply specified by the system administrator and then left to evolve according to the successful execution of commands by administrative roles, is likely to lead to more useable systems.

### 5.2 "Discretionary" Approaches

The RBAC96 family of models does not explicitly include administrative functionality. The original paper on RBAC96 suggests that the model can be augmented by administrative permissions and roles, as well as an administrative role hierarchy and an administrative permission-role assignment relation. This approach assumes that there is a single administrative domain $D$.

There are two significant disadvantages to this approach. Firstly, it is rather difficult to provide fine-grained administrative control: an administrative role either has an administrative permission or it doesn't. Secondly, it is difficult to reason about the propagation of permissions to users, for reasons similar to those that make it difficult to reason about the propagation of access rights in a protection matrix [6].

X-GTRBAC is an XML-based RBAC model that includes temporal constraints on the activation of roles. Bhatti *et al* have proposed an administrative model for X-GTRBAC based on the use of administrative permissions [16]. The interesting aspect of X-GTRBAC Admin is its introduction of administrative domains and the association of administrative permissions with administrative domains. However, X-GTRBAC Admin simply defines domains and associates roles and permissions with each domain. Like ARBAC02, it makes no attempt to impose any structure on administrative domains or to exploit the existence of domains in any way. As such, X-GTRBAC Admin simply extends the administrative model of RBAC96 by the introduction of administrative domains, but does not take advantage of the additional possibilities that this provides.

## 6    Conclusion

In this paper we have introduced a new model for role-based administration. To our knowledge, this is the first model to combine the use of administrative permissions and conditions on the parameters of an administrative command. These requirements are characterized as discretionary and mandatory administrative controls, respectively. The mandatory controls limit the extent to which administrative users can propagate user- and permission-role assignments, making it more difficult for an administrative user to compromise or damage the access control system (either deliberately or accidentally).

We believe that our model offers a number of advantages over existing approaches to role-based administration. In particular, it is more flexible than approaches such as ARBAC97 and RHA because it does not require administrative domains to have a particular structure (beyond requiring that the set of domains forms a nested partition of $R$). Nevertheless, it does incorporate mandatory controls, which means it provides greater control over the evolution of the access control system than unstructured approaches such as RBAC96 and X-GTRBAC Admin.

One obvious aspect of future work will be the development of a prototype implementation. On a more theoretical level, it would be interesting to see whether further mandatory properties are required for hierarchy operations. For example, should we limit the ability of a senior administrative role to add an edge between roles in two different domains? Our recent paper considers what conditions need to be placed on hierarchy operations in order to preserve administrative scope in the RHA model and encapsulated ranges in ARBAC97 [8]. It will be interesting to investigate whether analogous conditions are required or can be used for the less structured model described in this paper.

*Acknowledgements.* I would like to thank the anonymous referees for their comments, which have helped to improve the final version of the paper.

# References

1. Crampton, J., Loizou, G.: Administrative scope: A foundation for role-based administrative models. ACM Transactions on Information and System Security **6**(2) (2003) 201–231
2. Sandhu, R., Bhamidipati, V., Munawer, Q.: The ARBAC97 model for role-based administration of roles. ACM Transactions on Information and System Security **1**(2) (1999) 105–135
3. Sandhu, R., Coyne, E., Feinstein, H., Youman, C.: Role-based access control models. IEEE Computer **29**(2) (1996) 38–47
4. American National Standards Institute: ANSI INCITS 359-2004 for Role Based Access Control. (2004)
5. Ferraiolo, D., Sandhu, R., Gavrila, S., Kuhn, D., Chandramouli, R.: Proposed NIST standard for role-based access control. ACM Transactions on Information and System Security **4**(3) (2001) 224–274
6. Harrison, M., Ruzzo, W., Ullman, J.: Protection in operating systems. Communications of the ACM **19**(8) (1976) 461–471
7. Bell, D., LaPadula, L.: Secure computer systems: Mathematical foundations. Technical Report MTR-2547, Volume I, Mitre Corporation, Bedford, Massachusetts (1973)
8. Crampton, J.: Understanding and developing role-based administrative models. In: Proceedings of the 12th ACM Conference on Computer and Communications Security. (2005) 158–167
9. Ahn, G.J., Sandhu, R.: Role-based authorization constraints specification. ACM Transactions on Information and System Security **3**(4) (2000) 207–226

10. Crampton, J.: Specifying and enforcing constraints in role-based access control. In: Proceedings of the 8th ACM Symposium on Access Control Models and Technologies. (2003) 43–50
11. Gligor, V., Gavrila, S., Ferraiolo, D.: On the formal definition of separation-of-duty policies and their composition. In: Proceedings of the 1998 IEEE Symposium on Security and Privacy. (1998) 172–183
12. Jaeger, T., Tidswell, J.: Practical safety in flexible access control models. ACM Transactions on Information and System Security 4(2) (2001) 158–190
13. Nyanchama, M., Osborn, S.: The role graph model and conflict of interest. ACM Transactions on Information and System Security 2(1) (1999) 3–33
14. Simon, R., Zurko, M.: Separation of duty in role-based environments. In: Proceedings of 10th IEEE Computer Security Foundations Workshop. (1997) 183–194
15. Oh, S., Sandhu, R.: A model for role administration using organization structure. In: Proceedings of the Seventh ACM Symposium on Access Control Models and Technologies. (2002) 155–162
16. Bhatti, R., Joshi, J., Bertino, E., Ghafoor, A.: X-GTRBAC Admin: A decentralized administration model for enterprise-wide access control. In: Proceedings of the 9th ACM Symposium on Access Control Models and Technologies. (2004) 78–86

# A Distributed Coalition Service Registry for Ad-Hoc Dynamic Coalitions: A Service-Oriented Approach[*]

Ravi Mukkamala[1], Vijayalakshmi Atluri[2], Janice Warner[2], and Ranjit Abbadasari[1]

[1] Old Dominion University, Norfolk, VA 23528, USA
mukka@cs.odu.edu
[2] Rutgers University, Newark NJ 07012, USA
{atluri, janice}@cimic.rutgers.edu

**Abstract.** It is often necessary for organizations to come together in a coalition to share services, without prior planning, to accomplish certain tasks. The *dynamic coalition-based access control* (DCBAC) model facilitates the formation of dynamic coalitions through the use of a registry service, where available services can be advertised by potential coalition members. The central component of the DCBAC model is the *distributed coalition service registry* (DCSR). Depending upon the levels of service needed by the service providers and requesters, DCSR provides different functionality. We define three levels of DCSR services: (i) Registry Service (ii)Authenticator Service, and (iii) Query Service. For the last service, DCSR answers a specific question directly by using the information resources of service providers, when the requester has needed credentials. No direct interactions are needed between the coalition members in this level of service. In this paper, we describe our service-oriented approach to DCSR design and show the flexibility that it offers. The design features are tested through a prototype DCBAC system built using the .Net framework.

## 1 Introduction

It is often necessary for organizations to come together to share resources without prior planning to accomplish a certain task. This is driven by a number of applications including emergency and disaster management, peace keeping, humanitarian operations, or simply virtual enterprises. Typically, resource sharing is done by establishing alliances and collaborations, also known as *coalitions*. Secure sharing methods, typically used in an intra-organizational setup, may incur significant administrative overhead since they may require access identification for each user who requests resource access. Such methods do not suit the needs of a dynamic coalition where entities may join or leave the coalition in an ad-hoc manner or where they need to be formed without warning. As an example, in a natural disaster scenario such as Hurricane Katrina in 2005, government agencies (e.g. FEMA, local police and fire departments), non-government organizations (e.g., Red Cross) and private organization (e.g., local hospitals, suppliers of emergency provisions) needed to share information about victims, supplies and logistics. While they may have had some on-going information sharing, increased resource

---

[*] The work of Atluri and Warner is supported in part by the National Science Foundation under grant IIS-0306838.

E. Damiani and P. Liu (Eds.): Data and Applications Security 2006, LNCS 4127, pp. 209–223, 2006.

sharing was needed to directly address the situation and they could have benefited from an automated coalition establishment.

In an earlier work [11], we proposed a *dynamic coalition-based access control* (DCBAC) model that enables coalitions to be formed dynamically. Its central component is a coalition service registry (CSR) similar to the model adopted for web service through which services are offered to potential collaborators. Such a model mitigates the need to negotiate and establish collaboration policies among coalition entities. Any entity can set its own sharing policies, describe the types of services that it is willing to share, and specify the required organizational credentials needed to access these services. Any coalition entity with rights to the CSR can search the CSR to find relevant resources. Once found, a coalition entity can obtain a ticket to request the resource from its owner by submitting its entity's credentials and having them evaluated by the CSR. In a later work [6], we extended the concept of a centralized registry to a distributed CSR (DCSR) in order to promote improved availability, higher concurrency, better response times and enhanced flexibility. In a distributed DSCR architecture as seen in Figure 1, several service registry agents cooperate to provide controlled access to resources.

In this paper, we extend our previous work to suit situations where not all coalitions need the same level of service. At one extreme, we may have a coalition of members who simply want a service registry to provide registry service and nothing more (e.g., UDDI, DNS, LDAP, etc.). At the other extreme, we may have a coalition where members need the service registry to provide credential checking or to even act as the entity that retrieves and processes the information needed. We examine these two ends of the spectrum as well as a level in between. Specifically, we consider the following three service levels:

1. Information Resource Registry Service: Here, DCSR service is simply a registry - a place for potential coalition members to locate resources that might be of use. Members themselves perform all needed authorizations and interact directly with one another.
2. Authenticator Service: Besides performing the registry service, DCSR also performs organizational authentication for requesters. Thus, service providers will only get requests from the types of organizations with which they are willing to share their resources. Resource providers need only check individual credentials to ensure that the individual making the request should have the right to access the resource.
3. Query Service: Here, DCSR acts as a portal for all shared coalition services. The coalition members trust the portal to check all credentials. The portal has access to all information that the resource providers are willing to share and can combine the information to provide the resource requester with more than simple access to relevant resources.

These levels of service depend upon four characteristics of coalition membership: (i) the level of trust amongst coalition members; (ii) the level of trust that the members have towards DCSR; (iii) the level of processing and security capabilities of the coalition members; and (iv) the level of desire for anonymity.

**Table 1.** Summary of DSCR Service Characteristics

| Service Level | Level of Trust Control in DCSR | Level of Access Left to Members | Coalition Member Anonymity |
|---|---|---|---|
| Registry | Low | High | Low |
| Authenticator Service | Med | Med | Low |
| Query Service | High | Low | Med |

Functions provided by DCSR depend upon the level of service required by the coalitions. We group them into the following four categories: Authentication, Registration, Querying, and Routing. For the first level of service, only registration functions are needed to register organizations and the services they provide. For the second level of service, both registration and authentication functions are needed to authenticate the organizational level credentials of service requesters on behalf of the resource providers. For the third level of service, all four categories – registration, authentication, routing, and querying – are needed.

Access control research in the area of dynamic coalitions is relatively new. Philips et al. [9] described the dynamic coalition problem by providing several motivating scenarios in a defense and disaster recovery settings. They have developed a prototype that controls access to APIs and software artifacts [8]. Cohen et al. [3] proposed a model that captures the entities involved in coalition resource sharing and identifies the interrelationships among them. In [1,5], the researchers addressed the issue of automating the negotiation of policy between coalition members in a dynamic coalition. Finally, in [12], Yu et al proposed automated mechanisms for trust building between entities using digital credentials Our research complements these works by addressing the issue of automatic translation of coalition level policies to the implementation level policies, and vice versa. Our approach [11,6] concentrated on enabling coalitions to be formed dynamically through a coalition service registry. In this paper, we expand our ideas on the functionality of the coalition service registry to meet the needs of various types of coalitions and we provide our initial results in implementing these ideas.

This paper is organized as follows. In section 2, we describe the proposed service-level architecture of DCSR. In section 3, we provide details of DCSR design. Section 4 describes the prototype implementation that serves as a proof-of-concept. Finally, section 5 summarizes the contributions and describes future work.

## 2   DCSR: Functions and Services

Depending upon the service level, the DCSR provides a subset of the following functions as shown in Table 2: Registration, Authentication, Authorization, Query Processing, Request Routing.

The **Registration** function is used whenever a member intends to share its local services with the coalition. The registration process is as follows.

1. The member (or service provider) sends a service registration request to DCSR. The request consists of details such as API (methods), key terms, service policy (e.g.,

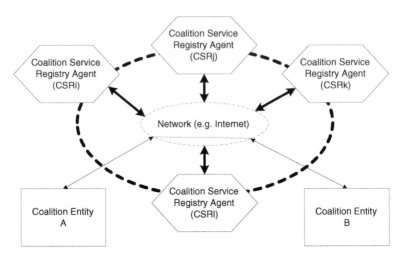

**Fig. 1.** Distributed Coalition-based Access Control: Architecture

**Table 2.** Summary of DSCR Functions Used Per Service

| Service Level | Registration | Authentication | Authorization | Query Processing | Request Routing |
|---|---|---|---|---|---|
| Registry | X | | | X | |
| Authenticator Service | X | X | | X | |
| Query Service | X | X | X | X | X |

WS-Policy), service location, etc. It is also possible to register a service proxy (e.g., Jini's proxy service or stub [7]). The API describes the service being offered, the inputs, and the outputs. The key terms are useful when a non-local user is searching for a service (e.g., yellow pages). The service policy (e.g., WS-policy) describes the service policy. This includes the credentials needed to execute the service, any special security parameters such as encryption algorithms, authentication schemes, etc. The location field indicates the web location where the service is available (e.g., URL address). In cases where a service proxy is registered, the proxy would be downloaded by the non-local members to access the service. Once again, following the philosophy of the naming services (e.g., DNS) and service providers such as Jini, the service registration is only for a limited time (e.g., lease) after which the service is either automatically revoked or renewed by the provider.

2. On receiving the service registration request, DCSR authenticates the service provider organization. The authentication process may use any standard protocol such as the ones using public key cryptography or secret key cryptography. In addition to authentication, if other security methods such as encryption and digital signatures are used, then DCSR validates the received request using appropriate methods.

3. DCSR checks the request for completeness and its compliance with the coalition policies. For example, there may be a coalition policy in which only certain

members are allowed to register services or there may be restrictions on the type of services they offer.

4. Optionally, DCSR could be provided with the ability to test the registered services. While DCSR will not be able to check the correctness of the semantics, it may be able to check some syntactic checks and the location information.
5. DCSR makes the service available to the coalition by publishing it in its service directory. The associated service policy is stored in the policy database.
6. DCSR sends an acknowledgment to the service provider.
7. Optionally, it may inform (advertise) the new service to the coalition members.

The **authentication** function is needed for interaction between a coalition member and the DCSR. The DCSR interacts with coalition members during initial joining of the coalition, service registration, service access, etc. When a member first joins a coalition, it establishes an authentication policy such as shared key for challenge, credentials, certificates, login/password, etc. This procedure may have been established using an out-of-band channel. For example, the DCSR administrator could directly interact with the new member's administrator to establish the authentication procedure and keys. Alternatively, they may use other in-band channels such as SSL to first establish a secure channel and then mutually agree on the authentication procedure an keys to be used henceforth. To limit the damage in case of compromised nodes, the authentication procedure may include limited time keys which need to be renewed or changed prior to their lapse.

Once a member joins a coalition, DCSR authenticates it using the established procedure in all its interactions.

The **authorization** function decides what service are to be made available to which users. Here, we use credential-based authorization where authorization policies are specified in terms of policies at different levels: coalition-level, organization-level, and service-level. The authorization function is initially enforced by the DCSR in showing only permissible services to a specific user. Service-lvele enforcement is done by the service provider.

The **Query** function identifies whether a resource request can be met by a registered service. As stated above, this requires the resolution of policies at the coalition, member, and service levels, and determining which services are to be made available to the specified user (with given credentials).

The **Routing** function is responsible for routing member service requests to the service provider and sending back the reply to the requester. As shown in Figure 2, there are three options for DCSR in handling service requests. According to the option specified, (or implemented), DCSR routes the requests and replies.

## 2.1 Registry Service

For the *registry service* (Figure 2a), the DCSR simply acts as a service directory responding with one of the following options from general to specific:(a) A list of services offered (b) A list of services (API) as well as the associated WS-policies (c) WS-policy only when the query is for a specific service. After responding, it has no role to play in terms of the service access request from a member. However, in the case where a member registers a service proxy with the DCSR, it could send the proxy to the requester. A member can send two types of queries to the DCSR.

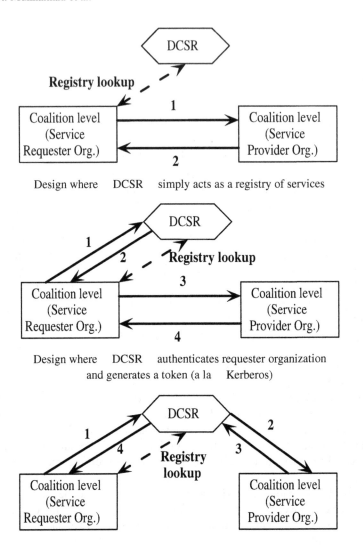

Design where    DCSR    simply acts as a registry of services

Design where    DCSR    authenticates requester organization
and generates a token (a la    Kerberos)

Design where    DCSR    acts as the only interface to the    coalition  members

**Fig. 2.** Three Modes of Operation of DCSR

## 2.2  Authenticator Service

Under the *authenticator service* (Figure 2b), the DCSR receives the service request and
generates a token to be submitted to the service provider. Under this option, the DCSR is
also acting as a trusted third party. This is similar to the role of Kerberos in establishing
a secure session between two untrusted parties. The steps under this role are as follows.

   (i) Authenticate the requesting organization.
  (ii) Extract the requester credentials from the request (e.g., decrypt the message, ver-
       ify the digital signature, etc.).

(iii) Check the coalition policy as well as WS-policy of the service being requested for acceptance of the service request.

(iv) If all checks are successful, generate a token (similar to Kerberos tokens) with the submitted credentials. In addition, as in Kerberos, it may generate a session key to be shared between the requester and the provider and include it in the token. The token itself is signed and encrypted. Features such as nonces and validity periods may be included to limit the possible damage due to requester compromise and to avoid replay attacks.

(v) The token is sent to the requester along with the generated shared key.

Once the requester receives the token, it can directly establish a connection with the service provide and get services using the token.

### 2.3 Query Service

For the **query service** (Figure 2c), DCSR does it all. In particular, it follows the following steps.

(i) Authenticate the requesting organization.

(ii) Extract the requester credentials from the request (e.g., decrypt the message, verify the digital signature, etc.).

(iii) Check the coalition policy as well as service policy of the service being requested for acceptance of the service request.

(iv) Invoke the services at the service provider (using whatever agreed upon protocol), submitting the requester credentials.

(v) Receive result/reply from the service provider.

(vi) Forward the result/reply to the requester.

In the above steps, we implicitly assume that the messages between the requester and the DCSR as well as the ones between DCSR and service provider are signed and encrypted. Under this option, first DCSR acts as a server to the requester. Next, it acts as a client to the service provider.

In fact, under this role, DCSR's functionality may be extended to that of a service provider that provides new aggregation services that are themselves built using the services registered by the members.

## 3  DCSR Design

In the above section, we have described the services offered by DCSR. We now look at a way to design DCSR so as to achieve the service objectives set for DCSR. In particular, we have the following goals for the DCSR design.

1. Customizability. It should be possible to customize the services offered by DCSR for a specific coalition.

2. Extendibility. It should be possible to add new functionalities to DCSR within an established DCSR in a coalition.

3. Scalability. It should be possible to use the same design framework for small, medium, and large coalitions
4. Performance. It should offer good performance in terms of low overhead, expected response time, and good throughput.

Keeping these goals in mind, we propose a service-oriented design (SOD) that offers all functionality (internal and external) as a service [4]. The proposed design has seven components. Following is a brief description of each of these components.

*User interface* is the primary gateway into DCSR. It receives all requests, makes the necessary checks, and invokes other required services.

*Security services* is part of infrastructure services needed by all other components and higher level services. It services include authentication, authorization (e.g., issue of tokens), encryption and decryption, digital signatures and MAC, key management (e.g., key generation, key distribution, key storage), and certificate management (e.g., certificate validation, certificate storage, certificate generation). Almost all DCSR services use these services.

*Communication services* is another infrastructure service and hence used by other services. It offers both unicast (one-to-one communication) and multicast (one-to-many) options. *DCSR management* is a key component that manages the set of agents that represent distributed DCSR as one logical unit. These services are primarily used by DCSR agents, and not by the users. Agent registration management, agent monitoring, consistency management, and load balancing (among agents) are part of this component.

*Policy management* component offers services that are used by other DCSR components (e.g., member services, membership management, and DCSR management) to register and retrieve policies. These policies may correspond to the services, to the members, or to the DCSR agents themselves. It would also include coalition policies. In fact, components such as security services may register its own policies for key management here.

*Member management* component provides several services for the coalition members (i.e., organizations). Whenever a new members intends to join a coalition, it uses the registration services. In addition to join operation, it also handles the leave operations. In case the join operation is only on a lease basis (as in Jini [7]), it also provides means to renew the membership.

*Member services* registers services for sharing offered by the coalition members. A member may register its services using the service registration function. As before, the module also handles withdrawal of services as well as renewal of services when they are made available only on a lease (e.g., Jini [7]). A member also registers a service policy along with the registered service. When a member intends to search for a service, it uses this service. The service returns a set of services that satisfy the query criteria.

## 3.1 SOD: An Example

To illustrate how our design follows service-oriented approach (SOD), consider the service registration function of the DCSR service architecture. Figure 3 illustrates how this function is implemented by composing several DCSR services. Here are a few instances of how it uses these services.

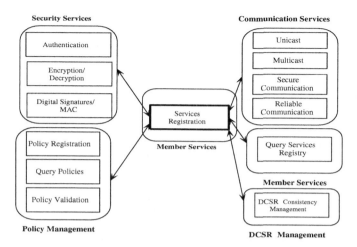

**Fig. 3.** Service-oriented design: An example

- Authenticate the coalition member who is requesting service registration using Authentication service (of Security Services component).
- Decrypt the service request and parameters with Decryption service.
- Check request validity using Digital Signature service.
- Verify coalition's policy of registration (e.g., which members are allowed to register services) by means of Query Polices service (of Policy Management).
- Check if this is a duplicate request using Query Service Registry service (of Member Services).
- Register the service policy (e.g., WS-policy) of the new service using Policy Registration (of Policy Management).
- Check the validity of the registered policy (with coalition policies as well as the requesting member's policies) using Policy Validation service (of Policy Management).
- Propagate the service registration information to other DCSR agents using DCSR Consistent management service (of DCSR Management).
- Send a reply to the requester using Unicast service and Secure Communication service (of the Communication Services).
- Alternately, it could use the Multicast service, Secure Communication service, and Reliable Communication service to reliably propagate the service registration information to other DCSR agents. Optionally, in a publish/subscribe paradigm, it could send the same information to the subscriber coalition members.

### 3.2   Meeting the Design Goals

We will now briefly analyze as to how the proposed design satisfies its goals. Clearly, the proposed DCSR design satisfies the customizability goal as it is modular in structure. For example, if a coalition with minimal trust on DCSR intends to use DSCR only as a registry, then the member services module can be simplified to offer only service registration and query service functions. If there is a single DCSR agent, then much of the communication services module can be simplified to offer only unicast services. Similarly, the DCSR management services module can be eliminated. Policy validation service of the Policy Management component can also be eliminated.

Similarly, suppose a coalition has initially settled with level 1 service (i.e., DCSR as registry only). If it now decides to extend the functionality to level 2 service, then using our design one simply needs to add additional service blocks into DCSR components. For example, if initially there was a single DCSR agent, and if it is to be extended to have multiple agents, then one simply needs to add the DCSR Management component. Thus, extendability goal is achieved.

The scalability goal is achieved through the ability to have multiple DCSR agents and the ability to add/remove agents using DCSR Management services. Thus, as a coalition grows or shrinks, the number of DCSR agents also can grow or shrink. The load balancing service helps balance the load at an agent. The addition of new coalition members is handled by the Membership Management.

The final goal of performability can only be verified through prototype building and further analysis. So we can't yet claim that this design goal is achieved.

## 4   DCSR Implementation

As a proof-of-concept, we have currently implemented a DCSR prototype using .Net framework. The primary reason for the choice, in addition to its being a service-oriented architecture, is the flexibility it offers in the creation and the use of services [10]. For example, by declaring every service as a web service, it is very easy to create and refer to these services in .Net. In fact, due to this flexibility, every service, whether offered to coalition members by DCSR, or offered to processes within DCSR itself, is implemented as a web service. We now describe the implementation.

The current prototype structure is shown in Figure 4. Here, we have implemented the security layer as the bottom most layer. This layer handles both secure communication

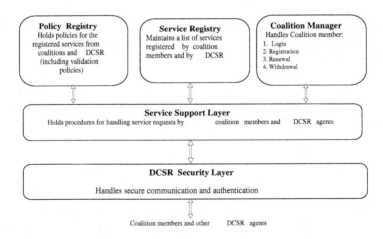

**Fig. 4.** DCSR: Prototype Implementation

and authentication functions. Once a message (request/reply) has been validated, it is forwarded to the service support layer. This has procedures that handle the incoming requests from other DCSR agents and coalition members. These procedures make use of the service registry, policy registry, and coalition manager. For example, when a member registers a service, the request is handled by a registration procedure that calls services of policy registry and service registry. Similarly, coalition member management procedures use services of the policy registry and coalition registry. In the current prototype, we assume a static set of DCSR agents and hence we have not implemented the DCSR management component.

Since we are using .Net framework, several of the services proposed in the DCSR design are already available. For example, consider .Net cryptography module. It offers a variety of hashing algorithms, symmetric and asymmetric encryption algorithms, and digital signatures. The .Net cryptography service hierarchy is described under System.Security.Cryptography. The available asymmetric algorithms are DSA and RSA, both available under System.Security.Cryptography.DSA and System.Security. Cryptography.RSA. Similarly, under the hashing algorithms, .Net offers SHA1, SHA256, SHA 384, SHA 512, DES, Triple DES, and RC2. The prototype makes extensive use of these services.

While .Net does provide services for expressing policies, we feel that they are inadequate for DCSR needs. Accordingly, we built our own policy management services. We express our policies in XML. This even makes communication with web services natural and platform independent.

The DCSR member management is completely specific to our application domain and hence is being implemented completely by us. Similarly, member management is also being implemented by us with help from other .Net infrastructure services.

It is interesting to note that the implementation issues for DCSR are equally applicable at the coalition member but at a smaller scale. For example, a coalition member also offers services (for local and non-local users). It also needs to maintain policies and let its own users register services, etc. While in the real world, each coalition member may be implementing their system independently and probably using legacy systems, the prototype design tries capture the similarity by having similar structures for DCSR and coalition members.

We now describe the prototype through several interfaces made available to member organizations and their users. First, as shown in Figure 5, Organization 1 registers itself with DCSR. At this time, it creates a new username and a password for future authentications (here, username and password alone are used for member authentication). In addition, it also specifies its organizational policy. For simplicity, the organizational policy simply describes the type of accesses it is prepared to offer for coalition users with different credentials. In this prototype, a level number alone is considered as a user credential. There is also an option for a coalition member to choose to override the policy at the coalition level (not shown here). For example, the coalition may have a policy that level 1 users have no access to any service. But a specific coalition member may choose to override this policy by specifying a read access. The coalition policy is stored in XML format at DCSR. The coalition policy is itself stored in an XML file at DCSR.

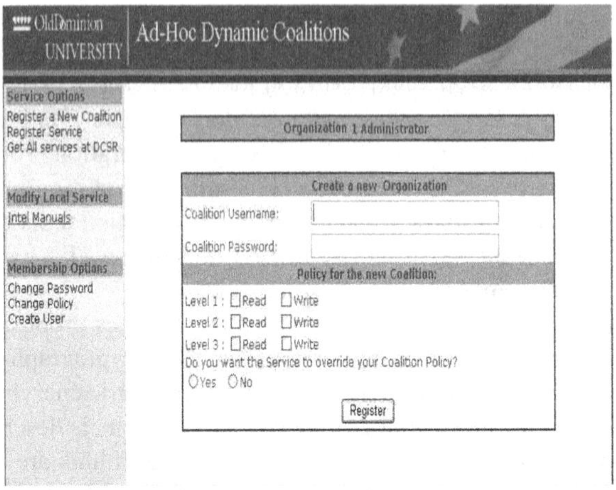

**Fig. 5.** Registration of a Coalition Member

Second, a coalition member intending to share a service, registers the service with DCSR. For example, in Figure 6, organization 2 registers a service, Dell Drivers, at DCSR. As part of the registration, it also indicates its service policy. In this example, it provides read access for level 1 users of the coalition and read/write access for both level 2 and level 3 users. Once again, an XML file is created and stored at DCSR as a service policy for each service. At the time of service registration, a member has the choice of the service to be made accessed directly (using the URL of the service as in Figure 2a) or indirectly via DCSR (Figure 2c). In the former case, at the time of service request, DCSR authenticates the requesting member (via login name and password) and generates a signed token. The token contains the coalition member credentials as well as the requesting user's credentials. For simplicity, we have used only the name of the organization as the coalition member's credential. Similarly, a level number is used as a user's credential. Accordingly, the signed token would also contain the level of the service requester as indicated by its coalition layer. In the latter case, DCSR sends the token directly to the service provider to get the reply. The reply is then displayed to the user. In Figure 6, the latter choice of service via DCSR was made.

Third, a user at a coalition member wants to access a service. After a successful local login, a user is presented with links to both local services and global services (Figure 7). What is presented to a user, on clicking each link, depends on the local user's own level (or credential). In fact the list is presented by DCSR only after it applies the coalition policy, the service provider policy, and the service policy with the user's level. In Figure 7, the logged in user (from Organization 2) is presented with two services: Dell drivers at the global level (non-local services) and intel manuals locally. When a user clicks on a specific service, that service is invoked. The actions that take place on an invocation depend on the choice of the registered service.

Fourth, when a user clicks on a service link, the request (in the form of an XML) is sent to the DCSR by the coalition layer. After DCSR performs the member authentication and other authorization checks, depending on the choice made by the service provider (i.e., direct or via DCSR) for this particular service, DCSR takes different

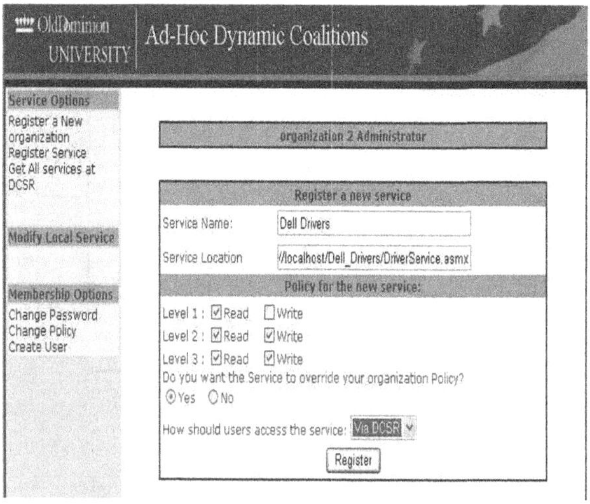

**Fig. 6.** Registration of a Service

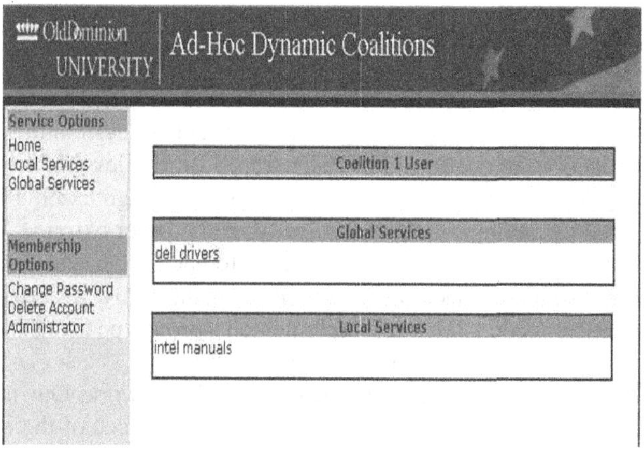

**Fig. 7.** Services offered to a User

actions. In the case of direct option, DCSR forwards an encrypted token to the coalition layer of the user along with an URL for the service. The coalition layer uses the service at that link and supplies the provided token. The service provider checks for the validity of the token and performs its own authorization checks before making the service available. In the case where the services are for read access of pdf files, the files are sent to the member who in turn displays them to the user. In case, the option is via DCSR, DCSR forwards the service request (in XML) along with user level to the service provider. It provides the same service as above but sends it to DCSR who in turn forwards it to the member. In Figure 7, the user has selected one of the drivers and clicked on it. He is now provided with the option of executing the file or saving the file locally. These options depend on DCSR and the underlying policies.

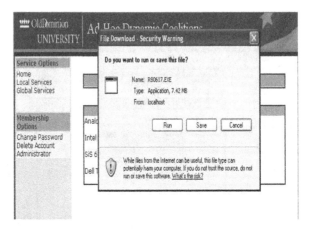

**Fig. 8.** Invocation of a service

Due to limited space, we could not illustrate other features of our prototype such as coalition member validation, local user validation, the token generation, etc.

## 5  Conclusion and Future Work

In this paper, we have presented a distributed service registry system that offers different levels of services to its coalition members, based on the level of trust among the members, level of desired anonymity by a member and the degree of the knowledge of the services offered by the members. Specifically, at the other extreme, we may have a coalition where members are generally strangers to each other and need the service registry to provide credential checking or to even act as the entity that retrieves and processes the information needed. We have implemented a prototype using .Net framework to test the features of our proposed DCBAC system.

We have prototyped our DCSR design using .Net framework. Our next step is to study the impact of different design choices on the performance of the overall DCSR system and the services it offers to the coalition members. We also plan to measure the cost (if any) due to the service-oriented approach. To achieve these objectives, we plan to implement extend our current DCSR prototype with several different types of options. In particular, we are interested in measuring the impact on performance (e.g., response time to user) due to the overhead imposed by the service-oriented architecture and different CSR options.

## References

1. V. Bharadwaj and J. Baras. A framework for automated negotiation of access control policies. *Proceedings of DISCEX III*, 2003.
2. K. Birman. Reliable distributed systems. Springer, 2005.
3. E. Cohen, W. Winsborough, R. Thomas, and D. Shands. Models for coalition-based access control (cbac). *SACMAT*, 2002.

4. T. Erl. *Service-oriented Architecture*. Prentice Hall, 2004.
5. H. Khurana, S. Gavrila, R. Bobba, R. Koleva, A. Sonalker, E. Dinu, V. Gligor, and J. Baras. Integrated security services for dynamic coalitions. *Proc. of the DISCEX III*, 2003.
6. R. Mukkamala, V. Atluri, and J. Warner. A distributed service registry for resource sharing among ad-hoc dynamic coalitions. In *Lecture Notes in Computer Science*. IFIP, December 2005.
7. S. Oaks and H. Wong. *Jini in a Nutshell*. O'Reilly, 2000.
8. C. Philips, E. Charles, T. Ting, and S. Demurjian. Towards information assurance in dynamic coalitions. *IEEE IAW, USMA*, February 2002.
9. C. Philips, T.C. Ting, and S. Demurjian. Information sharing and security in dynamic coalitions. *SACMAT*, 2002.
10. D. Reilly. *Designing Microsoft ASP.Net applications*. Microsoft Press, 2002.
11. J. Warner, V. Atluri, and R. Mukkamala. A credential-based approach for facilitating automatic resource sharing among ad-hoc dynamic coalitions. In *IFIP*, 2005. To be published - August 2005.
12. T. Yu, M. Winslett, and K.E. Seamons. Supporting structured credentials and sensitive policies through interoperable strategies for automated trust negotiation. *ACM Transactions on Information and System Security*, 6(1):1–42, February 2003.

# Enhancing User Privacy Through Data Handling Policies

C.A. Ardagna, S. De Capitani di Vimercati, and P. Samarati

Dipartimento di Tecnologie dell'Informazione
Università degli Studi di Milano – 26013 Crema - Italy
{ardagna, damiani, decapita, samarati}@dti.unimi.it

**Abstract.** The protection of privacy is an increasing concern in today's global infrastructure. One of the most important privacy protection principles states that personal information collected for one purpose may not be used for any other purpose without the specific *informed consent* of the person it concerns. Although users provide personal information for use in one specific context, they often have no idea on how such a personal information may be used subsequently.

In this paper, we introduce a new type of privacy policy, called *data handling policy*, which defines how the personal information release will be (or should be) dealt with at the receiving party. A data handling policy allows users to define simple and appropriate levels of control over who sees what information about them and under which circumstances.

## 1 Introduction

Privacy is repeatedly identified as one of the main concern that prevents users from using the Internet for transactions. Information technology gives organizations the power to gather and disclose vast amounts of personal information and therefore those who collect and disseminate data should be responsible for maintaining privacy. A number of useful *privacy enhancement technologies* (PETs) have been developed for dealing with the privacy issue such as a variety of anonymizing and de-identifying mechanisms [10]. One of the most important privacy protection principles (see http://ohsr.od.nih.gov/guidelines/belmont.html) states that personal information collected for one purpose may not be used for any other purpose without the specific *informed consent* of the person it concerns. However, although the informed consent is intended to prevent inappropriate use of the data, it represents an important problem involving PETs because users provide personal information for use in one specific context, but they often have no idea on how a such personal information may be used subsequently. In other words, users do not always realize that the information they disclose for one purpose (e.g., name, date of birth, and address within an on-line transaction) may also have secondary uses (e.g., access to existing data for purposes of grouping together users on the basis of common characteristics such as age or geographic

E. Damiani and P. Liu (Eds.): Data and Applications Security 2006, LNCS 4127, pp. 224–236, 2006.

location). Therefore, even if users consent to the initial collection of their personal information, they must also be given a mechanism to specify whether or not to consent to the future use of that information in secondary applications.

In this paper, we focus on a new type of privacy policy, called *data handling policy*, that regulates the secondary use of a user's personal data. In particular, a data handling policy regulates how Personal Identifiable Information (PII) will be used (e.g., information collected through a service will be combined with information collected from other services and used in aggregation for market research purposes), how long PII will be retained (e.g., information will be retained as long as necessary to perform the service), and so on. Users can therefore use these policies to define how their information will be used and processed by the counterpart.

## 2    Related Work

Previous work on privacy protection has focused on a wide variety of issues [4,9,14,18,21]. The work most directly related to ours is in the area of access control and privacy-aware languages and models [2,7,13,8,12,20]. In [8] the authors propose a policy language for regulating service access and information disclosure in an open, distributed network system. Access regulations are specified as logical rules, where some predicates are explicitly identified. Besides certificates, the proposal also allows to reason about declarations (i.e., unsigned statements) and user-profiles that the server can maintain and exploit for taking the access decision. PeerTrust [12] defines a logic syntax used to automate trust establishment. Trust is established gradually by disclosing certificates and requests for certificates. Each party can define access control policies to protect their sensitive resources. PROTUNE (PROvisional TrUst NEgotiation) [7] is a policy specification language that provides a powerful declarative metalanguage for driving critical negotiation decisions such as the specification of what certificates are needed to gain an access, where certificates can be retrieved, and so on. In [2], the authors propose an XML-based privacy preference expression language, called *PReference Expression for Privacy* (PREP), for storing the user's privacy preferences with Liberty Alliance. PREP allows users to specify, for each attribute, a *privacy label* that is characterized by a purpose, type of access, recipient, data retention, remedies, and disputes.

P3P (Platform for Privacy Preferences) [20] is an XML-based language that addresses the need of a user to assess whether the privacy practices adopted by a server provider comply with her privacy preferences. Users specify their privacy preferences in term of a policy language, called APPEL [19], and enforce privacy protection through a user agent. The user agent compares the users' privacy policy with the service provider P3P policy and checks whether the P3P policy conforms to the user privacy preferences. Although P3P is a good starting point, it has some drawbacks as the lack of a technical mechanism to verify that Web sites respect and enforce users policies, and a process to negotiate the privacy practices between the interacting parties. Also, P3P presents some

limitations on the user side [1]: users can only accept or deny the privacy practices defined by a service provider. We believe that a better way to enforce the
privacy practices is to offer users a richer, more active role in establishing how
their personal data should be used. Two relevant XML-based languages designed
to enforce privacy policies are XACML (eXtensible Access Control Markup Language) with a privacy policy profile [11,15] and EPAL (Enterprise Privacy Authorization Language) [5]. They allow the definition of powerful and expressive
access control languages but do not regulate the use of personal information in
secondary applications.

# 3   Data Handling Policy Specification

We consider a scenario that involves three main entities: *users* are human entity
that present requests to the service provider; a *service provider* provides services and collects personal information from users; and *third parties* are external
organizations to which the service provider can disclose personal information.
We assume that the service provider collects personal data that are necessary
to provide access to services. In particular, when a user decides to use a service,
she needs to complete a registration process. Information collected from a given
user is then stored into *profiles* associated with the user. Registered users are
characterized by a unique *user identifier* (user id). Users may also choose not to
become registered users. In this case, the service provider can generate a *persistent user identifier* (pseudonym) that is associated with the user who requires
the service. The pseudonym is automatically sent by the Web browser to the
service provider whenever the user submits a request to the service provider.[1]
In this case, personal information is stored under pseudonyms and not users'
real names. Users can require access to data about themselves. Other access
to personal data by the employees of the service provider (internal users) and
third parties who are granted access by the service provider (external users)
should also be supported. For simplicity, we assume that the server collecting
the users data and the third parties accessing them are trusted entities. Personal
data collected by the service provider should be managed in accordance with the
informed consent principle stating that personal information will not be made
available for secondary uses without notice to the subjects of the information.
However, there are situations where the strictly application of this principle can
be impracticable to enforce (e.g., in the context of large studies on population
health). A possible approach to solve this problem consists in giving the users
the possibility to specify a policy, called *data handling policy*, which defines how
their data can be subsequently used by the service provider and/or third parties.
The data handling policy follows the data when they are manipulated by different applications and transferred between different systems. A data handling
policy should be simple and expressive enough to support the following privacy
requirements.

---

[1] This features can be implemented using different strategies (e.g., cookies). However,
this implementation issue is outside the scope of our paper.

- *Individual control.* Users should be able to specify who can see what information about them and when.
- *Consent.* Users should be able to give their explicit consent on how to use their personal data.
- *Correction.* Users should be able to access their personal information to modify it when needed.
- *Security.* Adequate security mechanisms have to be applied, according to the sensitivity of the data collected.

Data handling policies can be pre-defined by service providers (and possibly by users) or can be defined at access time. These different strategies require different levels of negotiation between a user and a service provider. In particular, we identify the following three strategies: *server-side* strategy, where a service provider defines its data handling policies and a user can accept or reject these policies according to her privacy preferences; *customized*, where a user requires a service and a predefined policy template is provided by the service provider as a starting point for creating data handling policies; *user- and server-side*, where both a user and a service provider define their data handling policies and a negotiation process between them starts. This negotiation process can be initiated either by the service provider or the user. The negotiation process ends when the involved parties have reached an agreement. The user then provides her personal data attached to the data handling policy on which the user and the service provider agree.

Another aspect that has to be investigated is how data handling policies can be integrated with traditional *access control policies* [17]. Intuitively, if an access request satisfies at least one access control policy, the service provider has to verity whether there exists at least one data handling policy attached to the requested data. In particular, there may exist one or more data handling policies and each of them can impose different restrictions on how such data can be used in secondary applications. Since, as we will see in Section 4.1, a data handling policy establishes which party (*subject*, in the access control terminology) can execute which *actions* on which *resources* and under which circumstances (*conditions*), it is easy to see that access control and data handling policies are similar in syntax but they are conceptually different. Data handling policies allow the users to define restrictions on their PII management when data are received at server-side (e.g., retention, notification, and so on), while access control policies protect access to data. At evaluation-time, data handling policies are evaluated together with the access control policies, but at disclosure time they are attached to the released data, building a chain of control coming from the data owner. The similarity with access control policies introduces two different ways for defining a data handling policy: it can be an extension of traditional access control policies or it can be defined as a *stand-alone* policy. In the first case, the authorization rules should be extended by adding a *DHP component*. This approach has the main disadvantage that whereas including a DHP component within an access control rule simplifies the policy specification at first sight, it also makes the policy less clear. Stand-alone definition means that data handling policies are

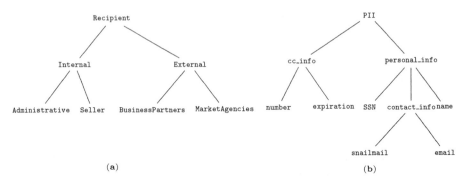

**Fig. 1.** An example of recipient hierarchy (a) and data type hierarchy (b)

defined as independent rules. Therefore, a data handling policy should represent the users' privacy preferences and should then include different components that allow to define how the third parties can use personal data. Personal data are then *tagged* with such data handling policies. Although the stand-alone option can introduce some redundancy in policy definition, choosing the stand-alone representation provides a good separation between policies that are used with different purposes. This clear separation makes data handling policies more intuitive and user-friendly, and implicitly suggests the differences with access control policies.

## 4 DHP Language

We now introduce a language for the specification of data handling policies on the data. We start by describing the basic constructs of the language and then we illustrate the syntax of the language together with some examples.

### 4.1 Elements of a Data Handling Policy

To illustrate what kinds of privacy requirements our solution supports, in the following we will consider an e-commerce scenario where company **ACME** provides a set of services such as *rent-a-car*, *book-a-flight*, and *flight+hotel*.

*Recipients.* It is a third party to which PII can be disclosed. Since we work in an open environment, the third parties may be unknown a-priori and therefore the user should also have the ability to define to which entities her data may be disclosed without knowing their identity. Our approach supports then the definition of the recipient according to one of the following three options: *identity-based*, where the third parties may be identified by their unique identities; *category-based*, where the third parties are grouped into different categories, which represent recipients of different domains; and *attribute-based*, where an *attribute expression* allows the definition of a recipient in term of the properties that it has to satisfy, instead of its identity.

Categories can be hierarchically organized and within the hierarchy, a category inherits from its ancestors all their permissions. For instance, Figure 1(a) illustrates a recipient hierarchy where the third parties are partitioned into two main domains: `Internal` and `External`. Also, the attributes that characterize a recipient can be *certified* by given authorities or can be simply *declared* by the recipient itself. At an abstract level, an attribute certificate is characterized by the following elements: the certificate's *name*, the *issuer*'s public key, the *subject*'s public key, a *validity period*, a list (possibly empty) of pairs ⟨*attribute_name*, *attribute_value*⟩ representing the subject'attributes, and a *signature*. For simplicity, we assume that the service provider maintains a binding between the public key of the authority trusted for asserting a specific set of attributes and an authority name. For instance, *InternationalMarketBoard* is the name of the authority whose public key is `00:b4:31...:7e:41:8f`. Note that in case of certified attributes, the user can then define the authorities trusted for asserting those attributes. For instance, a user can decide to disclosure her personal information only to a company of the `MarketAgencies` category specialized for distribution of computers and such that its attribute specialization has been certified by the *InternationMarketBoard* authority.

*Actions.* The term *action* is used to denote privacy-relevant operations (e.g., `read`, `disclose`, and `modify`) that recipients can require on personal data.

*Privacy profiles.* Users interacting with a service provider are required to provide a significant amount of PII, which is stored within a set of *privacy profiles*. A privacy profile can be seen as a container of pairs of the form ⟨*attribute_name*, *attribute_value*⟩, where *attribute_name* is the name of the attribute provided by the user and *attribute_value* is the value. Each privacy profile, uniquely identified by the user id or pseudonyms together with a *profile number*, is characterized by a specific set of privacy preferences expressed via data handling policies. For instance, suppose that `Alice` is a registered user of company `ACME` and that she requires service *book-a-flight*. To book a flight, `Alice` must provide her `name`, `credit card number` and `expiration date`, `telephone number`, `e-mail address`, and `frequent traveler number` (if any). Since `Alice` requires different levels of privacy according to her perception of the information sensitivity, her PII is partitioned into two privacy profiles: profile `p1` stores the `credit card number` and `expiration date`, and the `telephone number`; profile `p2` stores the `name`, `e-mail address`, and the `frequent traveler number`. Intuitively, the first profile includes information with a high level of sensitivity and the second profile stores information with a lower level of sensitivity. A data handling policy can be defined on a whole privacy profile and/or can be associated with a specific attribute in a privacy profile. Data types can be introduced as abstractions on single PII and therefore privacy preferences may be expressed in terms of data types. Data types can be organized into a hierarchy (we assume that users know the data type hierarchy defined by a server). Figure 1(b) illustrates an example of data type hierarchy, where PII has been partitioned into two data types: `cc_info` is an abstraction for the credit card information and `personal_info` is an abstraction for the personal information. According to the *correction* principle mentioned in Section 3, users can view, update, or delete their personal information (i.e., the information stored in all privacy profiles associated with them).

*Restrictions.* A privacy statement specifies restrictions that have to be satisfied before access to personal data is granted and such that, if at least one condition is not satisfied, the access should not be granted. One of the most important restrictions is the *purpose* for which the information will be used. Abstractions can be defined within the domain of purposes, which allow grouping together purposes with common characteristics and referring to the whole group with a name (e.g., `pure research` and `applied research` can be seen as a specialization of `research`). We distinguish between two kinds of conditions: *provisions* and *obligations*. Provisions represents actions that have to be performed before a decision can be rendered [6]. For instance, a data handling policy can state that a business partner can read the email address of the users provided that it has *paid a fee*. Obligations represents actions that have to be performed after an access has been granted [6]. For instance, a data handling policy can state that users will be notified whenever their personal information is disclosed. In addition, *generic* conditions evaluate membership of requesters and personal data into classes or properties in their profiles or can represents conditions that can be brought to satisfaction at run-time processing of the request.

Conditions on properties of a party are specified via a set of predicates based on the attribute certificates above-mentioned. Let $\mathcal{C}$ and $\mathcal{P}$ be a set of certificates' names and predicates, respectively. We first need to introduce the concept of *certificate expression* as follows.

**Definition 1 (Certificate expression).** Given a certificate name $c \in \mathcal{C}$, a *certificate expression* over $c$ is a boolean formula of terms of the form $c.attr\_name$ *math-op value*, where $c.attr\_name$ denotes attribute *attr_name* within certificate $c$, *math-op* is a standard binary built-in mathematic operator (i.e., $=, \neq, >, \geq, <, \leq$), and *value* is a constant or an attribute.

A binary predicate `certificate`$(ce,A) \in \mathcal{P}$, where $ce$ is a certificate expression and $A$ is the name or the public key of a trusted authority is evaluated to true if and only if there exists a certificate $c$ issued by authority $A$ and such that certificate expression $ce$ is evaluated to true. Provisions and obligations are represented by two disjoint sets of non predefined predicates $\mathcal{PR} \subseteq \mathcal{P}$ and $\mathcal{O} \subseteq \mathcal{P}$, respectively. Examples of provision predicates are `fill_in_form()` and `log_access()`. Examples of obligation predicates are `notify()` and `delete_after`(*num_days*).

## 4.2   Syntax

Syntactically, a data handling policy has the form:

⟨*recipients*⟩ CAN ⟨*actions*⟩ FOR ⟨*purpose*⟩ ON ⟨*PII*⟩ [ IF ⟨*gen_conditions*⟩]
[PROVIDED ⟨*prov*⟩] [FOLLOW ⟨*obl*⟩],

where *recipients* identifies the parties to which the policy refers; *actions* is the action (or class of actions) to which the policy refers; *PII* identifies the personal data to which the policy refers; *gen_conditions* is an optional boolean expression of conditions that every request to which the policy applies must satisfy; *prov* is an optional boolean expression of provisions; and *obl* is an optional boolean expression of obligations that the server must follow when manages the PII.

A data handling policy specifies that *recipients* can execute *actions* on *PII* for *purpose* provided that *prov* is satisfied, *gen_conditions* are satisfied, and with obligations *obl*. The *actions* field in the policy is simply the identifier of an action or group thereof. Data handling policies referred to groups of actions are considered applicable to all actions in the set. We now look at the different components in the rule.

*Recipients.* The field *recipients* can be an identifier, a recipient category, or a *recipient expression* of terms that evaluate conditions on the requester. A recipient expression is a boolean formula of terms of the form:

- `certificate(`*ce*`,`*A*`)`, where *ce* is a certificate expression over certificate *c* and *A* is the authority that must have issued certificate *c*. The requester and the subject of certificate *c* have to be the same.
- *attr_name math_op attr_value*, where *attr_name* is an attribute, *math_op* is a standard binary built-in mathematic operator, and *attr_value* is a constant or an attribute. Intuitively, this formula is evaluated to true whenever the requester presents property *attr_name* which satisfies the specified condition.

Since it may be necessary to refer to the user of the request being evaluated, we introduce the keyword **requestor**, which is intended to be substituted with the actual parameters of the request in the evaluation at access control time. For instance, recipient **requestor.country** = 'EU' indicates that property **country** provided by the party whose request is being processed has to be equal to 'EU'.

*PII.* The field *PII* can be the name of an attribute, the name of a data type, the identifier of a privacy profile, or a specific attribute stored within a privacy profile, which is specified by means of the usual dot notation (e.g., `Alice.p2.email`).

*Prov, Gen_conditions, Obl.* These fields contain conditions that are syntactically similar and correspond to a boolean formula of terms of the form:

- `predicate_name(`*arguments*`)`, where *arguments* is a list, possibly empty, of arguments on which predicate `predicate_name` is evaluated.

From the evaluation point of view, however, *gen_conditions*, *prov*, and *obl* are different: provisions are preconditions that need to be evaluated as prerequisites before a decision can be taken; generic conditions specify conditions of different type (e.g., trusted-based, location-based [3], and so on); obligations are additional steps that must be taken in account after the policy evaluation.

As an example of data handling policies, consider the following rules that regulate the secondary use of personal information stored by the `ACME` organization.

**Rule 1.** The business partners of ACME can read for market purpose the **name** of the ACME's users provided that they have paid a fee.

BusinessPartners CAN read FOR market ON name PROVIDED pay_a_fee()

**Rule 2.** The credit card information of Alice can be read by the business partners of ACME for service release purpose and must be deleted at the end of the service.

BusinessPartners CAN read FOR service_release ON Alice.p1 FOLLOW delete_after_service()

**Rule 3.** The market agencies specialized for distribution of computers and whose specialization has been certified by the *International Market Board* (IMB) authority can read the snailmail information for market purpose.

MarketAgencies AND certificate(speciality.category = 'computer',IMB) CAN read FOR market ON snailmail

**Rule 4.** The seller of ACME can read the personal information of their clients for statistical purpose during the working hours (i.e., from 8:30 am to 6:00 pm) provided that the access is logged.

Seller CAN read FOR statistical ON personal_info IF time(8:30,6:00) PROVIDED log_access()

**Rule 5.** The e-mail address of Alice can be released for market purpose to European business partners of organization ACME with the obligation of notify Alice.

BusinessPartners AND requestor.country = 'EU' CAN read FOR market ON Alice.p2.e-mail FOLLOW notify()

**Rule 6.** The administrative staff of ACME can read the contact information of their clients for market purpose only if they are in the building of ACME.

Administrative CAN read FOR market ON contact_info IF inarea(requestor, ACMEBuilding)

Rule 1, Rule 3, Rule 4, and Rule 6 are associated with the privacy profiles of the ACME's users that store property **name**, properties of data type snailmail, properties of data type personal_info, and properties of data type contact_info, respectively. Rule 2, and Rule 3 are associated with and protect the privacy profiles (p1, p2) of user Alice.

## 5   The Privacy Architecture

We are currently developing a privacy-aware architecture (see Figure 2) in the framework of the European PRIME project [16]. The architecture is composed of three main components: a *Privacy Control Module*, a *Policy Repository*, and a *Context Manager*.

The Policy Repository contains the policies, both access control and data handling policies, used to protect the data/services. It provides functionalities for administering policies such as search, modify, insert, and delete.

The Privacy Control Module operates on top of the context manager and contains two sub-modules: a *Policy Decision Point* (PDP) and a *Policy Enforcement Point* (PEP). PDP is responsible for taking an access decision for all

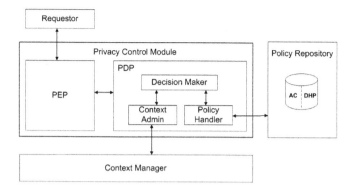

**Fig. 2.** Privacy-aware access control architecture

access requests directed to data/services. It retrieves and evaluates all policies (both access control and data handling) applicable to a request and includes: a *Decision Maker* that produces the final response possibly combining different access decisions coming from different evaluation of different policy types; a *Policy Handler* that is in charge of managing all communications with the *Policy Repository* to retrieve all policies applicable to an access request; and a *Context Administrator* that manages the access and the communication with the *Context Manager* component, which contains the information associated with the requestor during a session. PEP is responsible for the enforcing of access control decisions by intercepting accesses to resources and granting them only if they are part of an operation for which a positive decision has been taken.

The Context Manager is the component that keeps track of all contextual information and combines information from various context sources and deducts new contextual information from this aggregation. The main task of the Context Manager is to provide contextual information from various sources in a standardized way.

## 5.1   Access Request Enforcement

We now discuss how our system evaluates an access request and we start by characterizing the requests to which the system will have to respond. Each request is characterized by three elements: the *requestor* that makes the request; the *action* that is being requested; and the *target* on which the requestor wishes to perform the action. We assume that the *requestor* element contains the identity of the requestor (if any) plus additional contextual information such as the purpose for which the access is requested and certificates that can be used to verify whether the requestor has some properties. Such an information provided by the requestor is then managed by the Context Manager. We assume that the target of an access request can be a service or some personal data associated with a specific user. The access request is first received by the PEP module that sends it to the PDP module. The evaluation process is now composed of two main steps.

**Step 1.** The access request is evaluated against the applicable access control policies. Note that, if no policy is selected the access is denied meaning that the default access decision is "no". The discussion on how this step is performed is outside the scope of this paper and we simply assume that at the end of this first step the system has reached a "yes" or "no" access decision.[2] In case of a negative (no) access decision, the access request is denied and the process terminates. In case of a positive (yes) access decision, the system has to verify whether there exists some restrictions on the secondary use of the requested target.

**Step 2.** The PDP module asks the Policy Repository to retrieve all the applicable data handling policies. This selection is performed by using the requestor, action, and target specified in the access request. For each applicable data handling policy, the system evaluates the conditions specified in the *gen_conditions* field, when possible. Indeed, field *gen_conditions* can contain conditions that have to be brought to satisfaction at run-time, while processing the request. For each of them, we require the existence of an interface function that performs the control and possibly triggers the necessary actions. The corresponding procedure returns either a true or a false value depending on whether or not the implemented condition was or has been brought to satisfaction. Then, the *gen_conditions* are simplified using the usual boolean laws for true and false and the corresponding policy is taken into consideration if and only if the *gen_conditions* would be simplify to true. At this point of the evaluation process, there may exists different data handling policies with different sets of provisions and obligations. The system now should select the most convenient combination of provisions and obligations for the requestor.[3] As an example, suppose that `Alice` requests service *rent-a-car* and that she has to provide her `name`, `credit card number`, and `expiration date`. Suppose also that `ACME` collaborates with company `BestCar.com` which is a business partner. To make a reservation and rent a car, company `BestCar.com` requires access to the credit card information of `Alice`. By considering the data handling policies in Section 4.2, it is easy to see that Rule 2 applies to the access request submitted by `BestCar.com`. According to this policy, `BestCar.com` can use the credit card information of `Alice` but such an information has to be deleted at the end of the transaction.

# 6   Conclusions

Privacy is one of the most important issue for electronic commerce. In this paper, we introduce the definition of data handling policies, that is, policies regulating the use of personal information in secondary applications. This paper is only the first step towards the definition of such a language and leaves space for further work. Future work to be carried out includes investigation of the negotiation

---

[2] Note that a yes/no access decision can be the result of a multi-step process where the requestor and the system interact thus introducing possible forms of negotiation between them.

[3] The development of an efficient technique used to make such a selection will be part of future work.

process between a user and a service provider needed to reach an agreement on the data handling policies; techniques for linking data handling policies with the corresponding personal information; and the implementation of a proof-of-concept prototype, which is under development, to assess the real applicability of the proposed model.

## Acknowledgements

This work was supported in part by the European Union within the PRIME Project in the FP6/IST Programme under contract IST-2002-507591 and by the Italian MIUR within the KIWI and MAPS projects.

## References

1. R. Agrawal, J. Kiernan, R. Srikant, and Y. Xu. An xpath based preference language for P3P. In *Proc. of the 12th International World Wide Web Conference*, Budapest, Hungary, May 2003.
2. Gail-J. Ahn and J. Lam. Managing privacy preferences in federated identity management. In *Proc. of the ACM Workshop on Digital Identity Management (In conjunction with 12th ACM Conference on Computer and Communications Security)*, Fairfax, VA, USA, November 2005.
3. C.A. Ardagna, M. Cremonini, E. Damiani, S. De Capitani di Vimercati, and P. Samarati. Supporting location-based conditions in access control policies. In *Proc. of the ASIACCS'06*, Taipei, Taiwan, March 2006.
4. C.A. Ardagna, E. Damiani, S. De Capitani di Vimercati, and P. Samarati. Towards privacy-enhanced authorization policies and languages. In *Proc. of the 19th Annual IFIP WG 11.3 Working Conference on Data and Applications Security (IFIP)*, Nathan Hale Inn, University of Connecticut, Storrs, USA, August 2005.
5. P. Ashley, S. Hada, G. Karjoth, and M. Schunter. E-p3p privacy policies and privacy authorization. In *Proc. of the ACM workshop on Privacy in the Electronic Society (WPES 2002)*, Washington, DC, USA, November 2002.
6. C. Bettini, S. Jajodia, X. Sean Wang, and D. Wijesekera. Provisions and obligations in policy management and security applications. In *Proc. of the 28th VLDB Conference*, Hong Kong, China, August 2002.
7. P.A. Bonatti and D. Olmedilla. Driving and monitoring provisional trust negotiation with metapolicies. In *Proc. of the IEEE 6th International Workshop on Policies for Distributed Systems and Networks (POLICY 2005)*, Stockholm, Sweden, June 2005.
8. P.A. Bonatti and P. Samarati. A unified framework for regulating access and information release on the web. *Journal of Computer Security*, 10(3):241–272, 2002.
9. R. Chandramouli. Privacy protection of enterprise information through inference analysis. In *IEEE 6th International Workshop on Policies for Distributed Systems and Networks (POLICY 2005)*, Stockholm, Sweden, June 2005.
10. L.F. Cranor. *Web Privacy with P3P*. O'Reilly & Associates, 2002.
11. *eXtensible Access Control Markup Language (XACML) Version 2.0*, February 2005.    http://docs.oasis-open.org/xacml/2.0/access_control-xacml-2.0-core-spec-os.pdf.

12. R. Gavriloaie, W. Nejdl, D. Olmedilla, K. Seamons, and M. Winslett. No registration needed: How to use declarative policies and negotiation to access sensitive resources on the semantic web. In *Proc. of the 1st First European Semantic Web Symposium*, Heraklion, Greece, May 2004.

13. International security, trust, and privacy alliance (istpa). `http://www.istpa.org/`.

14. G. Karjoth and M. Schunter. Privacy policy model for enterprises. In *Proc. of the 15th IEEE Computer Security Foundations Workshop*, Cape Breton, Nova Scotia, Canada, June 2002.

15. OASIS. *Privacy Policy Profile of XACML*, September 2004. http://docs.oasis-open.org/xacml/access_control-xacml-2_0-privacy_profile-spec-cd-01.pdf.

16. Privacy and identity management for europe (PRIME). http://www.prime-project.eu.org/.

17. P. Samarati and S. De Capitani di Vimercati. Access control: Policies, models, and mechanisms. In R. Focardi and R. Gorrieri, editors, *Foundations of Security Analysis and Design*, LNCS 2171. Springer-Verlag, 2001.

18. B. Thuraisingham. Privacy constraint processing in a privacy-enhanced database management system. *Data & Knowledge Engineering*, 55(2):159–188, November 2005.

19. World Wide Web Consortium. *A P3P Preference Exchange Language 1.0 (APPEL1.0)*, April 2002. http://www.w3.org/TR/P3P-preferences/.

20. World Wide Web Consortium. *The Platform for Privacy Preferences 1.1 (P3P1.1) Specification*, July 2005. http://www.w3.org/TR/2005/WD-P3P11-20050701.

21. M. Youssef, V. Atluri, and N.R. Adam. Preserving mobile customer privacy: An access control system for moving objects and customer profiles. In *Proc. of the 6th International Conference on Mobile Data Management*, Ayia Napa, Cyprus, May 2005.

# Efficient Enforcement of Security Policies Based on Tracking of Mobile Users*

Vijayalakshmi Atluri and Heechang Shin

MSIS Department and CIMIC, Rutgers University, USA
{atluri, hshin}@cimic.rutgers.edu

**Abstract.** Recent advances to mobile communication, Global Positioning System (GPS) and Radio Frequency Identification (RFID) technologies have propelled the growth of a number of mobile services. These
require maintaining mobile object's location information and efficiently
serving access requests on the *past, present* and *future* status of the moving objects. Moreover, these services raise a number of security and privacy challenges. To address this, security policies are specified to ensure
controlled access to the mobile user's location and movement trajectories,
their profile information, and stationary resources based on the mobile
user's spatiotemporal information. Considering the basic authorization
specification ⟨*subject, object, privilege*⟩, in a mobile environment, a moving object can be a subject, an object, or both. Serving an access request
requires to search for the desired moving objects that satisfy the query,
as well as enforce the security policies.

Often, enforcing security incurs overhead, and as a result may degrade
the performance of a system. To alleviate this problem, recently Atluri
and Guo have proposed an unified index structure, $^S$TPR-tree, to organize both the moving objects and authorizations specified over them.
However, the $^S$TPR-tree is not capable supporting security policies based
on *tracking* of mobile users. In this paper, we present an index structure,
called $S^{PPF}$-tree, which maintains past, present and future positions of
the moving objects along with authorizations by employing *partial persistent storage*. We demonstrate how the $S^{PPF}$-tree can be constructed
and maintained, and provide algorithms to process two types of access
requests, including moving object requests by stationary subjects such
as *locate* and *track*, and stationary object requests by moving subjects.

## 1 Introduction

Recent advances to mobile communication, Global Positioning System (GPS)
and Radio Frequency Identification (RFID) technologies have propelled the
growth of a number of mobile services. Location-based service is one such example, which aims at delivering personalized services to mobile customers. These
include: providing nearby points of interest based on the real-time location of
the mobile customer, advising of current conditions such as traffic and weather,

---

* This work is supported in part by the National Science Foundation under grant
IIS-0242415.

E. Damiani and P. Liu (Eds.): Data and Applications Security 2006, LNCS 4127, pp. 237–251, 2006.

deliver personalized, location-aware, and context-sensitive advertising based on mobile customer profiles and preferences, or provide routing and tracking information. Delivery of these services requires maintaining mobile object's location information as well as the preference profiles of the customers carrying these mobile objects. In addition, it requires efficient processing of access requests to find the *past, present* and *future* status of the moving objects.

Since effective delivery of a mobile service may need to locate and track a mobile customer, and gain access to his/her profile, it raises a number of security and privacy challenges. Location information has the potential to allow an adversary to physically locate a person. As such, wireless subscribers carrying mobile devices have legitimate concerns about their personal safety, if such information should fall into the wrong hands. Moreover, services such as targeted advertising may deliver the service based on the mobile customers' profile and preferences. As such, privacy of mobile users can be compromised if the sensitive profile information of the mobile users is revealed to unintended users. Therefore, it is important that the sensitive profile information is revealed only on the need-to-know basis. In addition to the privacy concerns mentioned above, there are a number of applications that call for securing resources based on the criteria of mobile objects. These include context (location)-sensitive access control, and ubiquitous computing environment, where access is permitted based on the location of the subjects/objects during a specific time.

In summary, in a mobile environment, there are a number of applications that require enforcing security policies to provide controlled access to the mobile user profiles, to their current location and movement trajectories, to mobile resources, stationary resources based on the user's spatiotemporal information. Thus, an appropriate access control mechanism must be in place to enforce the authorization specifications reflecting the above security and privacy needs.

Traditionally, access policies are specified as a set of authorizations, where each authorization states if a given subject possesses privileges to access an object. Considering the basic authorization specification $\langle subject, object, privilege \rangle$, in a mobile environment, a moving object can be a subject, an object, or both. Access requests in such an environment can typically be on *past, present* and *future* status of the moving objects [1,2]. Serving an access request requires to search for the desired moving objects that satisfy the query, as well as enforce the security policies.

Often, enforcing security incurs overhead, and as a result may degrade the performance of a system. One way to alleviate this problem and to effectively serve access requests, is to efficiently organize the mobile objects as well as authorizations. Towards this end, recently Atluri and Guo [3] have proposed a unified index structure called $^S$TPR-tree in which authorizations are carefully overlaid on a moving object index structure (TPR-tree), based on their spatiotemporal parameters. One main limitation of the $^S$TPR-tree is that it is not capable of maintaining past information. As a result, it cannot support queries based on past location and security policies based on *tracking* of mobile users.

In this paper, we present an index structure, called $S^{PPF}$-tree, which maintains past, present and future positions of the moving objects along with authorizations by employing the *partial persistent storage*. In particular, we build on the concepts of the $R^{PPF}$-tree [4] and overlay authorizations suitably on the nodes of the index tree. Essentially, a partial persistent structure keeps all past states of the data being indexed, but updates only the newest version. We demonstrate how the $S^{PPF}$-tree can be constructed and maintained, and provide algorithms to process access requests. Specifically, we support two types of access requests: requests for moving objects by stationary subjects and requests for stationary objects by moving subjects. The first type of requests, in addition to retrieving the moving objects in a specific spatiotemporal region, allow retrieving the location of the moving objects as well as their trajectories. As such our model would support security policies based on tracking of moving objects.

This paper is organized as follows. In section 2, we present our moving object authorization model. We present the preliminaries in section 3. In section 4, we present our proposed novel unified index structure, the $S^{PPF}$-tree and illustrate our approach and strategy to overlay authorizations on top of the $R^{PPF}$-tree. In this section, we also describe how access requests are evaluated. Related work is presented in section 5. In section 6, we conclude the paper by providing some insight into our future research in this area.

## 2   Moving Object Authorization Model

In this section, we introduce an authorization model for moving object data, which is an extension of the model proposed in [3]. In a moving object environment, authorization specifications should be capable of expressing access control policies based on spatiotemporal attributes of both subjects and objects.

**Definition 1 (Authorization).** *An authorization $\alpha$ is a 4 tuple $\langle ce, ge, p, \tau \rangle$, where ce is a credential expression denoting a set of subjects, ge is a object expression denoting a set of objects, p is a set of privilege modes, and $\tau$ is a temporal term.*

The formalism to specify $ce, ge$ and $\tau$ has been developed in [5]. Credential expression $ce$ can be used to specify a set of subjects such that they are associated with (i) a set of spatiotemporal and/or other traditional credential attributes, (ii) a set of subject identifiers, or (iii) a combination of both. In the same way, object expression $ge$ can be used to specify a set of objects such that they (i) are associated with a set of spatiotemporal and/or other types of attributes, (ii) a set of object identifiers, or (iii) a combination of both. Note that the set of subjects and objects denoted by $ce$ and $ge$ can be moving objects. To avoid confusion, from now on, we denote the objects specified in the authorization as *auth-objects* (stands for authorization objects). $\tau$ can be a time point, a time interval or a set of time intervals.

Our model supports not only *read, write*, and *execute* privileges for traditional auth-objects but also *viewing* and *compose* for moving objects. We support three viewing privileges: *View, Locate,* and *Track* privileges allow subjects

to access a moving object(s), to read the location or trajectory information of
a moving object(s) in the authorized spatiotemporal region, respectively. Compose privileges allow subjects to write information on the auth-objects. In the
following, we present some examples of security policies.

- **Policy 1:** A mobile customer is willing to reveal his personal profile information to a merchant only during the evening hours, and while he is close to
  the shopping mall. In this case, only the auth-object (customer) is a moving
  object and this policy is based on auth-object's spatiotemporal attributes.
- **Policy 2:** An employee is allowed to update certain company data only
  during "office hours" and while "in the office." Note that only the subject
  (employee) is a moving object. Also note that the policy is based on the
  subject's spatiotemporal attributes.
- **Policy 3:** An airport security official can access the trajectory information
  of travelers in the airport only while he is on-duty (i.e., during 11pm-7am).
  In this case, both the subject and the auth-objects are moving objects, and
  the policy is based on the spatiotemporal attributes of both subject and
  auth-object.
- **Policy 4:** A FBI agent can access the current location and trajectory information of a truck with id 325. Note that although the subject and the
  auth-object are moving objects, the subject is allowed to access the information regardless of his location and time. In this case, the policy is based on the
  identifiers of both subject (FBI agent) and auth-object (truck with id 325).
- **Policy 5:** A police office in Newark, NJ can access only the dispatched patrol
  cars from the Newark area. Note that only auth-objects are moving objects.
  Also, the policy is specified on two types of auth-objects: object identifiers
  (patrol cars from Newark police station) and spatiotemporal region.

The above policies can be specified as the following authorizations.

- $\alpha_1 = \langle \text{merchant}(i), \{\text{profile}(i) \wedge \text{rectangle}(j) = (5,6,1,2) \wedge [5\text{pm},9\text{pm}]\}, \text{locate}\rangle$
- $\alpha_2 = \langle \{\text{emp}(i) \wedge \text{rectangle}(j) = (3,5,1,5) \wedge [9\text{am},5\text{pm}]\}, \{\text{profile}(j)\}, \text{update} \rangle$
- $\alpha_3 = \langle \{\text{security\_official}(i) \wedge \text{rectangle}(j) = (1,4,3,4) \wedge [9\text{am}, 5\text{pm}]\},$
  $\{\text{travelers}(i) \wedge \text{rectangle}(j) = (100,50,30,30) \wedge [\text{current time}]\}, \text{track} \rangle$
- $\alpha_4 = \langle \text{FBI\_agent}(i), \text{truckid}(j) = 325, \text{track} \rangle$
- $\alpha_5 = \langle \{\text{dispatch\_department}(i) \wedge \text{office\_location}(j) = '\text{Newark}'\}, \{\text{patrol\_cars}$
  $(k) \wedge \text{rectangle}(l) = (10,50,30,30) \wedge \text{dispatched\_from}(k) = '\text{Newark}'\}, \text{track} \rangle$

## 3    Preliminaries

In this section, we present the partial persistence framework and review the
$R^{PPF}$-tree [4], a moving object index that maintains not only the *present* and
anticipated *future* positions of moving objects, but also their *past* positions.

**Representation of Moving Objects:**    Let the set of moving objects be
$O = \{o_1, \ldots, o_n\}$. In the $d$-dimensional space, objects are specified as points
which move with constant velocity $\bar{v} = \{v_1, v_2, \ldots, v_d\}$ and initial location

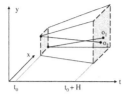

**Fig. 1.** The Time Parameterized
Bounding Rectangle (*tpbr*)

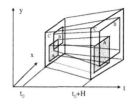

**Fig. 2.** The *tpbr* Hierarchy

$\bar{x} = \{x_1, x_2, \ldots, x_d\}$. The position $\bar{x}(t)$ of an object at time $t(t \geq t_0)$ can be computed through the linear function of time, $\bar{x}(t) = \bar{x}(t_0) + \bar{v}(t - t_0)$ where $t_0$ is the initial time, and $\bar{x}(t_0)$ the initial position. Considering a two-dimensional space, a moving object $o_i$ moving in $\langle x, y \rangle$ space can be represented as $o_i = ((x_i, v_{i_x}), (y_i, v_{i_y}))$.

**Time Parameterized Bounding Rectangle (*tpbr*):** Given a set of moving objects $O = \{o_1, \ldots, o_n\}$ in the time interval $[t_0, t_0 + \delta t]$ in $\langle x, y, t \rangle$ space, the *tpbr* of $O$ is a 3-dimensional bounding trapezoid which bounds all the moving objects in $O$ during the entire time interval $[t_0, t_0 + \delta t]$: $tpbr(O) = \{(x^\vdash, x^\dashv, y^\vdash, y^\dashv), (v_x^\vdash, v_x^\dashv, v_y^\vdash, v_y^\dashv)\}$ where $\forall i \in \{1, 2, \ldots, n\}$, $x^\vdash = min_i\{x_i(t_0)\}$, $x^\dashv = max_i\{x_i(t_0)\}$, $y^\vdash = min_i\{y_i(t_0)\}$, $y^\dashv = max_i\{y_i(t_0)\}$, $v_x^\vdash = min_i\{v_{i_x}\}$, $v_x^\dashv = max_i\{v_{i_x}\}$, $v_y^\vdash = min_i\{v_{i_y}\}$, $v_y^\dashv = max_i\{v_{i_y}\}$.

**Time Horizon (H):** Given a moving object, it is unrealistic to assume that its velocity remains constant. Therefore, the predicted future location of a object specified as a linear function of time becomes less and less accurate as time elapses [6]. To address this issue, a *time horizon H* is defined, which represents the time interval during which the velocities of the moving objects assumed to be the same. Figure 1 shows how *tpbr* bounds the trajectory of two moving objects $o_1$ and $o_2$ in $[t_0, t_0 + H]$.

**The Tree Structure:** Given a set of *tpbrs*, they can be organized in a hierarchical structure. In figure 2, *tpbr* C encloses *tpbrs* A and B. These three can be organized as a hierarchical structure with A and B being the children of C. Essentially, at the bottom-most level of the hierarchy, a set of moving objects could be grouped to form *tpbrs*. Each *tpbr* of the next higher level is the bounding *tpbr* of the set of *tpbrs* of all of its children. The root of the hierarchy is thus the bounding *tpbr* covering all its lower level *tpbrs* in a recursive manner.

**The Partial Persistence Framework:** Partial persistence is a data structure that keeps all past states of the data being indexed, but applies updates only to the newest version. It is based on the following important concepts.

-- **Evolution of Index Nodes and Data Entry:** In order to be transformed to a partially persistent structure, each index (leaf or index) node and data entry (moving object) include two additional fields for maintaining the evolution of the index records: *insertion time* and *deletion time*. These are denoted as $N.insertionTime$ and $N.deletionTime$ for node $N$. If a new moving object is available and captured at time $t_0$, its insertion time is set to $t_0$ and deletion time is set to $\infty$. When the object is logically deleted from the index at time $t_d$, its deletion time is changed from $\infty$ to $t_d$. The same rule applies to index nodes. A node or a data entry is said to be *dead* if its deletion time is less than $\infty$, otherwise it is said to be *alive*.

- **Time Split:** When an update (insertion or deletion) occurs at a node $N$, it may result in structural changes if it becomes underfull or overfull. If this is the case, a *time-split* occurs to $N$. The time-split on $N$ at time $t$ is performed by copying all alive entries in $N$ at $t$ to a new leaf node $L$ and timestamp of both $L$ and those copied entries are set to $[t, \infty)$. In addition, the deletion time of $N$ is set to $t$, and $N$ is considered dead. Then, the new node $L$ is investigated further in order to incorporate it into the tree. Essentially, three different cases may arise: (i) split: If $L$ is overfull, split it into two nodes and then insert these two nodes into the tree. (ii) merge: If $L$ is underfull, merge it with another alive node. (iii) no change: If $L$ is neither overfull or underfull, insert it directly into the tree. After the structural change, the *tpbr* of the parent node may need to be updated accordingly and the described process may be repeated up to the root node. If the root node is time-split at time $t$, a pointer to the new alive node together with timestamp $[t, \infty)$ is added to a special root array that is stored in the main memory [4].

Note that if the tree is constructed at $t_0$ and time split for the alive root element of the root array occurs at $\{t_1, t_2, \ldots, t_n\}$, each root element in the root array is associated with time interval $[t_0, t_1), [t_1, t_2), \ldots, [t_{n-1}, t_n)$, and $[t_n, \infty)$. The associated time interval for each root element represents the valid structure of the tree during those time intervals. Thus, if we want to know the status of the tree at time $t$, we simply need to find a root element $r$ from the root array such that the time interval of $r$ includes $t$.

In the following, we explain the concept of time-split, root array, dead and alive nodes by taking a concrete example. Consider a tree with a node that can hold 5 data entries. Obviously, the node is considered underfull if the number of data entries is less than 2, and overfull if the number of data entries is more than 5. Observe that the dead nodes are shaded in figures.

- **Time interval** $t = [0, 4]$: Moving objects $o_1$, $o_2$, and $o_3$ are inserted into the root node at $t=0$: the insertion time and deletion time of all these objects are set to $[0, \infty)$. Then at $t = 2$ and 3, $o_4$ and $o_5$ are inserted, and, thus, their insertion time and deletion times are $[2, \infty)$ and $[3, \infty)$, respectively. At $t = 4$, $o_6$ is inserted to the root node $N$, which becomes overfull. So, time split occurs. A new leaf node $L$ with insertion and deletion time $[4, \infty)$ is created and all the alive data entries $(o_1, \ldots, o_6)$ in the root node are copied there with insertion and deletion times as $[4, \infty)$. Because $L$ is also overfull, it is split into two nodes, which are inserted into the tree. A new root entry is added, forming a root array. The previous root's deletion time is set to 4, representing it as a dead node, and the time interval of the newly created root is set to $[4, \infty)$, as shown in Figure 3.

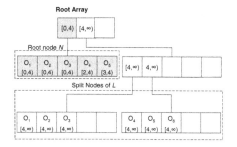

**Fig. 3.** The Index Structure at time 4

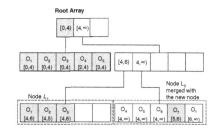

**Fig. 4.** The Index Structure at time 6

– **Time interval** $t = [\mathbf{5, 6}]$: At $t = 5$, $o_2$ is deleted and $o_7$ is inserted. Thus, the deletion time of $o_2$ is set to 5, and $o_7$ is inserted in the tree with the insertion and deletion times $[5, \infty)$. Then, at $t = 6$, $o_3$ and $o_7$ are deleted. So, deletion time of these objects are set to 6. Because the deletion of $o_3$ results in the underfull of the node $L_1$ that stores $o_3$, a time split occurs: another new node $K$ is created and alive entry $o_1$ is copied there. Since newly created node $K$ is underfull, it is merged with its neighboring alive node $L_2$. The deletion time of the node $L_1$ is set to 6, representing that $L_1$ is dead. The resultant data structure is shown in figure 4.

When update occurs, the resulting trajectory of a moving object may consist of disconnected and slightly incorrect segments because at the insertion of the object, the predicted future positions can be different from the actual positions. Therefore, during update, the last-recorded trajectory segment of an object needs to be updated. It may be stored in more than one leaf node because the leaf node in question may have been time split a number of times since the previous updates [4]. $\mathrm{R}^{PPF}$-tree corrects the last-recorded trajectory segment by visiting all leaf nodes that contain copies of the segment and also tightens the *tpbr* accordingly. For example, in figure 4, suppose the actual location of $o_3$ turns out to be different from the predicted location during update (deletion). Then, after setting the deletion time of $o_3$ as 6, all the nodes that include the trajectory of $o_3$ since the last update (insertion of $o_3$ at $t = 3$) are updated to point the actual location of $o_3$ correctly. The first root element and the node $L_1$ is such a case.

## 4 The $\mathbf{S}^{PPF}$-Tree

In this section, we present our proposed unified index, the $\mathrm{S}^{PPF}$-tree that indexes authorizations as well as the moving objects by capturing their past, present, and future locations. As a result, we can support authorizations based on *locate* and *track* privileges.

### 4.1 Authorization Overlaying

Our approach is to first construct a $\mathrm{R}^{PPF}$-tree index for moving objects, and then overlay authorizations on top of each node of the index by carefully examining the spatiotemporal extents of both the node and the authorizations. The resulting tree is the $S^{PPF}$-tree. We denote the spatiotemporal extent of an authorization $\alpha$ by $\alpha^{\square}$. In other words, $x$-axis interval $= [\alpha.x_b, \alpha.x_e]$, $y$-axis interval $= [\alpha.y_b, \alpha.y_e]$, and $t$-axis interval $= [\alpha.\tau_b, \alpha.\tau_e]$ where $\alpha.x_b$, $\alpha.x_e$, $\alpha.y_b$ and $\alpha.y_e$ denote the spatiotemporal extent specified by $ce$ or $ge$ represented by the lower and upper bounds in the $x$ and $y$ axes, respectively, and $[\alpha.\tau_b, \alpha.\tau_e]$ denote the time interval during which $\alpha$ is valid. Also, we denote the spatiotemporal extent ($tpbr$) of a node $N$ by $N^{\square}$.

An authorization $\alpha$ is said to be *subject-based authorization*, if $\alpha^{\square}$ is computed from $\alpha.ce$. Similarly, if $\alpha^{\square}$ is from $\alpha.ge$, it is said to be an *object-based authorization*. In other words, in the former case, subjects are the moving objects and in the latter case, objects are the moving objects. In our tree, we are capable of overlaying only if the authorization is specified based on the spatiotemporal extent of $ce$ or $ge$, but not both. In addition, we assume that $\alpha^{\square}$ is a contiguous spatiotemporal region without losing any generality because each non-continuous spatiotemporal region can be sliced to form a single contiguous region.

A node of $S^{PPF}$-tree is similar to that of $R^{PPF}$-tree except that it includes two pointers that point to a set of subject-based authorizations ($\alpha_S$) and a set of object-based authorizations ($\alpha_O$) overlaid on the node.

The overlaying strategy first selects the root nodes from the root array such that the root node's alive time interval is overlapped with the authorization's time interval. Then, for each selected root node $r$, it traverses the tree recursively starting from the root node $r$ to the leaf level in a way that for each node $N$ in the traversal path, $\alpha^{\square}$ is compared with $N^{\square}$. All the possible scenarios for this comparison are as follows:

- **Case 1:** If the spatiotemporal extent of $\alpha$ fully encloses that of the node $N$, we will stop traversing and overlay $\alpha$ on $N$. This is because, if a subject is allowed to access objects within a certain spatiotemporal region, it is allowed to access objects in the *subregion* of that [3]. (If $alphas_S.ce$ ($alpha_O.ge$) points to a combination of spatiotemporal region and a set of subjects (auth-objects), we can exclude unauthorized subjects (auth-objects) by post-processing the query result when we evaluate the query.) After overlaying an authorization on a node, it is not necessary to overlay the same authorization on any of its descendents.

- **Case 2:** If the spatiotemporal extent of $\alpha$ overlaps with that of the node $N$, the level of the node decides where it is overlaid.
  - If $N$ is a non-leaf node, each of $N$'s children is traversed and the algorithm repeats the comparison between $\alpha^{\square}$ and each child$^{\square}$. The goal here is to check if there exist a child of $N$ whose spatiotemporal extent is enclosed by that of $\alpha$.
  - If the node $N$ is a leaf node, we overlay $\alpha$ on the leaf node $N$. This is because, when the spatiotemporal extent of the authorization $\alpha^{\square}$ does not enclose, but overlaps with that of the leaf node $N^{\square}$, we need to ensure that no relevant authorizations are discarded. Also, note that only part of the spatiotemporal extent of $N^{\square}$ is in the authorized region. The

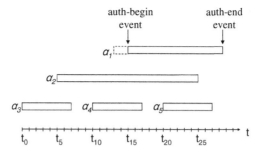

**Fig. 5.** Authorization Time Line

moving objects from the remaining unauthorized spatiotemporal region $N^\square - \alpha^\square$ must be removed from the user's output, if the user request includes this region.

- **Case 3:** Else, which implies the spatiotemporal extent of the authorization, $\alpha^\square$ is disjoint with that of the node $N^\square$, we stop the overlaying process. This is because, if $\alpha.ce$ does not have privilege to the region covered by $N^\square$, then $\alpha$ is not applicable to that region. Also, since $N^\square$ includes spatiotemporal extent of all of its children nodes, $\alpha^\square$ is disjoint with the spatiotemporal extent of each child. Thus, there is no need to traverse further to the leaf level.

### 4.2   Maintenance of the $S^{PPF}$-Tree

One main challenge of the $S^{PPF}$-tree is to maintain the overlaid authorizations as the tree evolves. Changes to the $S^{PPF}$-tree are needed due to the following two reasons:

- **Updates to the moving object:** It is important to note that, while the spatiotemporal region of an overlaid authorization is static in nature, the *tpbr* of each node in the tree changes over time. Therefore, it is possible that certain overlaid authorizations may no longer satisfy the conditions. As a result, it may be necessary to reposition the existing overlaid authorization.
- **Change of applicable authorizations:** If the overlaid authorizations are valid only during a certain time interval, as time elapses, they are no longer applicable. Therefore, these need to be removed from the overlaid set. Also, certain new authorizations may become applicable, which need to be overlaid appropriately.

Because the $S^{PPF}$-tree is an unified index that maintains not only moving objects but also authorizations, we need to pay attention to how updates of one type can be performed without hampering the properties of the $S^{PPF}$-tree.

### 4.2.1   Handling Updates due to Change of Applicable Authorizations
To handle this issue, we introduce the notion of *Authorization Log*, described below.

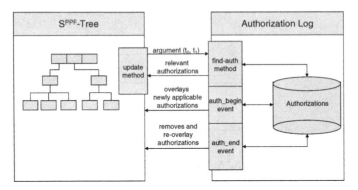

**Fig. 6.** Relationship of Authorization Log and $S^{PPF}$-Tree

**Authorization Log:** An authorization log is nothing but a data structure constructed by spreading all the authorizations on the time line. For each authorization, we consider the following two events: (1) **auth-begin** event and (2) **auth-end** event. These two are nothing but $[\tau.t_b, \tau.t_e]$ specified in the authorization specification. (Note that each authorization will have only two such events since we are not considering periodic authorizations. However, our proposed solution can be easily extended to handle periodic authorizations.) For example, in figure 5, the auth-begin event of the authorization $alpha_1$ occurs at time $t_1 3$, and the auth-end event will occur at time $t_2 8$.

Essentially, as time elapses, new authorizations may become applicable and we do not want to miss overlaying these authorizations on the $S^{PPF}$-tree. An authorization $\alpha$ is said to be applicable to the tree constructed at $t$, if the two time intervals $[\alpha.\tau_b, \alpha.\tau_e]$ and $[t, t+H]$ overlap. For example, suppose the $S^{PPF}$-tree is constructed at $t = t_{10}$, which is valid until $t_{10} + 2$ (assuming $H = 2$). Referring to figure 5, only $\alpha_2$, $\alpha_3$, and $\alpha_4$ are overlaid on the tree. Since valid intervals of $\alpha_1$ and $\alpha_5$ are outside $[t_{10}, t_{10} + 2]$, they are applicable now and therefore are not overlaid on the tree. On the other hand, at $t_{20}$, both $\alpha_1$ and $\alpha_5$ must have been overlaid on the tree. However, the tree has no capability to keep track of newly applicable authorizations that need to be overlaid on the appropriate nodes of the tree. An auth-begin event triggers the overlay procedure to take care of this issue. For example, $\alpha_1$ in figure 5 will be overlaid on the tree at $t_{13}$ because the tree is valid up to the current time + time horizon.

Also, after some time later, certain overlaid authorizations become invalid and therefore must be removed from the tree. This is taken care by the auth-end event to trigger such removals. The removed authorization needs to be re-overlaid on the $S^{PPF}$-tree because it may satisfy the overlaying conditions of another node in the tree.

In addition to triggering the overlaying and deletion of authorizations, update must take care of the cases when the time-split occurs. In this case, an entirely new node will be created for which there exist no overlaid authorizations. The *find-auth* method computes all the authorizations overlapping with the interval of the newly created nodes. Figure 6 depicts the relationship between the

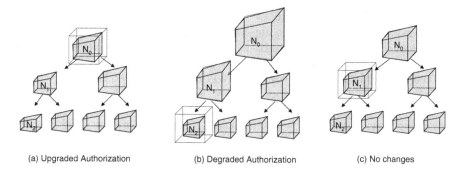

(a) Upgraded Authorization          (b) Degraded Authorization          (c) No changes

**Fig. 7.** Re-overlaying of authorizations due to updates to moving objects

authorization log and the $S^{PPF}$-tree along with the auth-begin and auth-end events, and the find-auth method.

### 4.2.2 Handling Updates due to Changes to Moving Objects

Updates to moving objects may cause a structural change to the $S^{PPF}$-tree. When update (insertion/deletion) occurs on the $S^{PPF}$-tree, all the access nodes, which are ancestors of the leaf node which the update is applied to, need to be checked because the overlaid authorizations in the nodes may either be degraded authorizations (authorizations which were originally overlaid on the access nodes, but no longer fit in their original positions due to the spatiotemporal enlargement of the nodes by updates) or upgraded authorizations (authorizations which were originally overlaid on the access nodes, but able to fit in an ancestor of their original positions due to spatiotemporal shrinkage of the nodes by updates). This procedure is even more complicated if the update process results in the structural changes due to time-split. The details are summarized below.

1. **Update authorizations on the adjusted nodes:** Based on the periodic updates on the position of the moving objects, the *tpbr* of each node in the $S^{PPF}$-tree will be adjusted; they may either shrink or expand. Moreover, adjustments to the *tpbr* of a node may trigger adjustments to the *tpbr*s of its ancestor nodes. For each adjusted node $N$, every overlaid authorization $\alpha$ on it can fall into one of the three categories: (i) degraded authorization, (ii) upgraded authorization, (iii) no changes. The algorithm checks first if it is an upgraded authorization and attempts to overlay it as high in the tree as possible. Else, the same overlaying strategy is used to find the appropriate position for $\alpha$. Figure 7 shows these three different cases. Suppose $N_2$ is the adjusted leaf node. Figure 7 (a) shows the shrinkage of the *tpbr* for $N_2$ and its parents. The authorization initially overlaid on $N_1$ is now repositioned to $N_0$: it can enclose $N_1^\square$ as well as $N_0^\square$ spatiotemporally and therefore becomes an upgraded authorization. On the other hand, the *tpbr* of $N_2$ may be expanded due to the adjustment. Figure 7 (b) shows this expanded case, and that the overlaid authorization does not enclose $N_1^\square$ spatiotemporally any more. It becomes a downgraded authorization. Therefore, it is repositioned to the

child of $N_1$, i.e., $N_2$. In addition, it may be possible that the shrinkage or expansion of the corrected node does not affect the overlaid authorizations if the overlaid authorization still encloses $N_1^{\square}$ but does not enclose its parent $N_0$ spatiotemporally. Figure 7 (c) presents this case.

2. **Overlay authorizations on the newly created node:** The newly created node due to a time-split does not have any authorizations overlaid on it. Therefore, all the authorizations whose valid time intervals are overlapped with the interval of this node are overlaid on the alive root node from the root array.

### 4.3   Access Request Evaluation

In this section, we present the different types of access requests and how these are evaluated against the specified authorizations to retrieve the information that satisfies the user request. Two types of user requests are possible under our framework.

– *Moving Object Request (MOR):* A subject who is stationary may wish to access moving objects that fall within a spatiotemporal region. This can be a *locate*, a *track* or a *view* request on a moving object.
– *Stationary Object Request (SOR):* A subject who is within a spatiotemporal region may wish to access objects that are stationary.

**Definition 2 (Moving Object Request).** *A moving object request (MOR), denoted as a triple* $U = \langle s, Q, m \rangle$, *where $s$ is the subject of the user request, $Q$ is a spatiotemporal region, and $m$ is a track, a locate, or a view access mode.*

The result of a MOR would be one of the trajectory of an object(s), the position of an object(s), or the identifier of an object(s). A trajectory is of the form $\langle o, \{loc_1, loc_2 \ldots, loc_n\} \rangle$, where $o$ is the object, and $loc_i$ is the $i^{th}$ location information of $o$ in the $x, y, t$ dimensional space. In case of locate, the result would be of the form $\langle o, loc \rangle$. The result of a view access mode would be a set of object ids. We use $U^{\square}$, $U.s$, $U.mode$, $U.\tau_b$, and $U.\tau_e$ to denote the spatiotemporal extent, the subject, the access mode, effective time interval $[U.\tau_b, U.\tau_e]$ of the access request $U$ respectively.

**Definition 3 (Stationary Object Request).** *A stationary object request (SOR), denoted as a triple* $V = \langle s, loc, o \rangle$, *where $s$ is the subject of the user request, loc is the current locations of the subject in the $x, y, t$ dimensional space, and $o$ is an auth-object that the subject $s$ tries to gain access to.*

The spatiotemporal query evaluation is based on the overlaying procedure that is introduced in the section 4.1. For a given user request $U$, the procedure first locates a set of roots from the root array of $S^{PPF}$ such that the alive time interval of the root is overlapped with $[U.\tau_b, U.\tau_e]$. Then, for each located root $r$, the procedure traverses the subtree under this root $r$ until it reaches the leaf level During this traversal, it compares the spatiotemporal extent of user request with that of each node in the search path. One would encounter three different cases:

- **enclosing:** If there exists any $\alpha$ such that the set of subjects evaluated by $ce$ contains $U.s$, then return all the moving objects that are overlapped with $(N^\square \cap \alpha^\square)$. In the case of the *locate* access mode, return the location information of those objects at time $= U.\tau_b$. $U.\tau_e$ is ignored if it is different from $U.\tau_b$ because, if we allow time interval, the trajectory information between the time interval $[U.\tau_b, U.\tau_e]$ is rather revealed to the user instead of the location information. If it is a *track* access mode, return the trajectory information of those objects. The trajectory of each object $o$ in the result set is traced back by using the pointer $N.ptr$ where $N$ is the leaf node that stores $o$. Whenever a node $L$ is time split, $ptr$ of newly created node is set to point back to the original node $L$. Thus, all the past location information of $o$ can be reached by following the $ptr$ created each time a node is split. This tracking is processed within the spatiotemporal region $U^\square \cap \alpha^\square$ where $\alpha^\square$ is the spatiotemporal region of all the authorizations with track privilege that are applicable to $U.s$.
- **overlapping:** If there exists any $\alpha$ such that the set of subjects evaluated by $ce$ contains $U.s$, return the objects overlapping with $U^\square$ only. However, we still need to check authorizations overlaid for the descendents of the node $N$ because authorizations overlaid for the descendents may include another spatiotemporal region that $\alpha^\square$ does not cover. In the case of the leaf node, return all the moving objects that are overlapped with $(N^\square \cap \alpha^\square \cap U^\square)$. Again, if it is a *track* access mode, return the trajectory information of those objects. If it is a *locate* access mode return the location information.
- **disjoint:** Stop the evaluation process because no relevant authorizations can be found in the descendents of the node $N$ to satisfy the request.

In SOR, we use $V.s$, $V.o$, and $V^{point}$ to denote the subject, the requested auth-object and the spatiotemporal position of $V$, respectively. Only the alive root node among the root array is traversed because the access control request is evaluated only by the $V.s$'s location at $t_c$. The algorithm traverses the alive tree from the alive root node until it reaches the leaf level. During the traversal, it checks if the spatiotemporal extent of each node in the search path includes the $V^{point}$. If so, the procedure collects all the auth-objects contained in the set of $ge$ such that $V.s$ is in the set of subjects evaluated by $ce$. If $o$ is among this auth-objects set, stop traversing and return true, which means that the user $s$ is allowed to get access to $o$. Otherwise, continue traversing. In case $N$ is a leaf node, for each authorization $N$ in $\alpha_S$, include the auth-objects of $\alpha$ if $N^\square \cap \alpha^\square$ encloses $V^{point}$ since we do not want to get the false positive result for the area $N^\square - \alpha^\square$.

## 5   Related Work

Recently, there has been some endeavors to support effectively evaluating queries of *past, present* and *future* locations of moving objects. Patel et al. [7] index the positions that result from the dual data transformation. Lin et al. [8] propose the $BB^x$-index structure that inherits the ability to index present and future positions from the $B^x$-tree [9], and it extends this ability with support for also past positions. However, $BB^x$-index does not correct trajectory segments and therefore, the index may include disconnected trajectories. Pelanis et al. [4] address this problem by applying partial persistence to the TPR-tree [6] and correcting the last-recorded prediction of moving object.

An index scheme for moving object data and user profiles has been proposed by Atluri et al. [10], but this does not consider authorizations. Beresford et al. [11], [12] have proposed techniques that let users benefit from location-based applications, while preserving their location privacy. Mobile users, in general, do not permit the information shared among different location based services. Primarily, the approach relies on hiding the true identity of a customer from the applications receiving the user's location, by frequently changing pseudonyms so that users avoid being identified by the locations they visit. A system for delivering permission-based location-aware mobile advertisements to mobile phones using Bluetooth positioning and Wireless WAP Push has been developed [13]. An index structure has been proposed to index authorizations ensuring that the customer profile information be disclosed to the merchants based on the choice of the customers [14]. However, this provides separate index structures for data and authorizations, and therefore is not a unified index.

Atluri and Guo have proposed a unified indexing scheme for moving objects and authorizations, called $^S$TPR-tree. However, because $^S$TPR-tree does not maintain historical information on moving objects, it does not support security policies based on tracking of mobile users. The focus of this paper is to provide persistence for unified indexing scheme for mobile objects and authorizations.

## 6   Conclusions

A number of services in the area of mobile commerce environment require maintaining mobile object's location information and efficiently serving access requests on *past, present* and *future* status of the moving objects. Proper access control policies must be enforced to address the security and privacy concerns in this environment. Recently, Atluri and Guo have proposed an unified index structure, $^S$TPR-tree, to organize both the moving objects and authorizations specified over them. However, the $^S$TPR-tree is not capable of answering queries based on the past information, and therefore cannot support security policies based on *tracking* of mobile users. In this paper, we have proposed an index structure, called the $S^{PPF}$-tree, which maintains past, present and future positions of the moving objects along with authorizations by employing the *partial persistent storage*, and therefore can support authorizations based on tracking of mobile objects. Currently, we are conducting a performance evaluation to demonstrate that our uniform indexing scheme indeed has significant impact on the response time.

In our proposal, an authorization is based on the spatial and temporal attributes of either subjects or objects. Thus, we are not capable of overlaying authorizations that cannot be represented with spatiotemporal region. Also, our overlaying strategy cannot accommodate authorizations whose subjects and objects are both moving at the same time. As a result, supporting such authorizations overlaying may require splitting the subject and object components. We will enhance our $\mathrm{S}^{PPF}$-tree to address these issues. Support for negative authorizations require significant changes to the overlaying of authorizations as well as evaluating access requests. In this paper, we do not consider negative authorizations; we will extend our work to support negative authorizations.

# References

1. Wolfson, O., Xu, B., Chamberlain, S., Jiang, L.: Moving objects databases: Issues and solutions. In Rafanelli, M., Jarke, M., eds.: 10th International Conference on Scientic and Statistical Database Management, Proceedings, Capri, Italy, July 1-3, 1998, IEEE Computer Society (1998) 111-122
2. Moreira, J., Ribeiro, C., Abdessalem, T.: Query operations for moving objects database systems. In: Proceedings of the eighth ACM international symposium on Advances in geographic information systems, ACM Press (2000) 108-114
3. Atluri, V., Guo, Q.: Unied index for mobile object data and authorizations. In: ESORICS. (2005) 80-97
4. Pelanis, M., Saltenis, S., Jensen, C.S.: Indexing the past, present and anticipated future positions of moving objects. a TIMECENTER Technical Report TR-78 (2004)
5. Atluri, V., Chun, S.A.: An authorization model for geospatial data. IEEE Trans. Dependable Sec. Comput. 1(4) (2004) 238-254
6. Saltenis, S., Jensen, C.S., Leutenegger, S.T., Lopez, M.A.: Indexing the positions of continuously moving objects. In: SIGMOD Conference. (2000) 331-342
7. Patel, J.M., Chen, Y., Chakka, V.P.: Stripes: an efficient index for predicted trajectories. In: Proceedings of the 2004 ACM SIGMOD International conference on Management of data, New York, NY, USA, ACM Press (2004) 635-646
8. Lin, D., Jensen, C.S., Ooi, B.C., Saltenis, S.: Efficient indexing of the historical, present, and future positions of moving objects. In: Mobile Data Management. (2005) 59-66
9. Jensen, C.S., Lin, D., Ooi, B.C.: Query and Update Efficient B+-Tree Based Indexing of Moving Objects. In: VLDB. (2004) 768-779
10. Atluri, V., Adam, N.R., Youssef, M.: Towards a unied index scheme for mobile data and customer proles in a location-based service environment. In: Workshop on Next Generation Geospatial Information (NG2I'03). (2003)
11. Beresford, A., Stajano, F.: Mix zones: User privacy in location-aware services. In: PerCom Workshops. (2004) 127-131
12. Scott, D., Beresford, A., Mycroft, A.: Spatial security policies for mobile agents in a sentient computing environment. In: FASE. (2003) 102-117
13. Aalto, L., Gthlin, N., Korhonen, J., Ojala, T.: Bluetooth and wap push based location-aware mobile advertising system. In: MobiSYS '04: Proceedings of the 2nd international conference on Mobile systems, applications, and services, New York, NY, USA, ACM Press (2004) 49-58
14. Youssef, M., Adam, N.R., Atluri, V., eds.: Preserving Mobile Customer Privacy: An Access Control System for Moving Objects and Customer Information. In 6th International Conference on Mobile Data Management. Lecture Notes in Computer Science, Springer (2005)

# A Framework for Flexible Access Control in Digital Library Systems*

Indrajit Ray and Sudip Chakraborty

Colorado State University
Fort Collins, CO 80523, USA
{indrajit, sudip}@cs.colostate.edu

**Abstract.** Traditional access control models are often found to be inadequate for digital libraries. This is because the user population for digital libraries is very dynamic and not completely known in advance. In addition, the objects stored in a digital library are characterized by fine-grained behavioral interfaces and highly-contextualized access restrictions that require a user's access privileges to be updated dynamically. These motivate us to propose a trust-based authorization model for digital libraries. Access privileges can be associated with both objects and content classes. Trust levels associated with these specify the minimum acceptable level of trust needed of a user to allow access to the objects. We use a vector trust model to calculate the system's trust about a user. The model uses a number of different types of information about a user, for example, prior usage history, credentials, recommendations etc., to calculate the trust level in a dynamic manner and thus achieve a fine-grained access control.

## 1  Introduction

Access control is one of the major concerns for content-providers on the Internet. Without a proper access control mechanism confidentiality and integrity of information cannot be guaranteed. Different models exist for specifying access control policies like discretionary access control, mandatory access control and role-based access control. However, with increasing complexity of systems and security concerns, a single model does not suffice to provide access control in all systems. In this work we address the problem of access control in digital libraries.

Conventional access control models specify an access control policy as a triple ⟨*subject, object, permission*⟩. This states that that a subject (user) is authorized to exercise some permission on an object. The traditional models implicitly assume that the user population is known a-priori. In a digital library system (DLS) the user population is vast and dynamic. It is almost next to impossible to know all the users before hand. Thus traditional access control mechanisms that rely on knowing the user and associating permissions with them fail significantly in digital libraries. A digital library

---

* This work was partially supported by the U.S. Air Force Research Laboratory (AFRL) and the Federal Aviation Administration (FAA) under contract F30602-03-1-0101 and by the National Science Foundation (NSF) of the USA under grant IIS-0242258. Any opinions, findings, and conclusions or recommendations expressed in this publication are solely those of the authors and do not necessarily represent those of the AFRL, the FAA, or the NSF.

E. Damiani and P. Liu (Eds.): Data and Applications Security 2006, LNCS 4127, pp. 252–266, 2006.

environment poses some additional challenges for access control [1]. The users of a digital library often need access from remote locations or by following links from remote documents. Thus it does not suffice to merely control access to documents local to the digital library. The access control policies are often based on user qualifications and characteristics. For example, a user can be given access to R-rated movies only if she is older than 18 years. Last, but not the least, a digital library needs to support access control to its objects based on the object content in addition to object identity. For example, high resolution satellite images of nuclear power plants can be made available only to citizens of the country.

In one of the early works on access control in digital libraries, Gladney [2] proposes a scheme called DACM (Document Access Control Methods). The basic idea is geared toward discretionary access control with some extensions to handle mandatory access control. Though it is a scalable mechanism, it does not have the provision to dynamically change user privileges. Researchers have also proposed credential-based access control [3,4,5], to address the problem of unknown users. In these models a user has to produce one or more credentials that have been certified by one or more third parties. The credential provides information about the rights, qualifications, responsibilities and other characteristics attributable to its bearer by the third parties. These third parties need to be trusted by the service provider. Bertino et al [1] develops a credential based system for enforcing access control in digital library system. Winslett et al. [6] also propose a credential-based mechanism to assure security and privacy for digital library transactions. Skogsrud et al. [7] introduce a model-driven trust negotiation framework called Trust-Serv for digital library environments. It uses credentials for establishing trust relationships. Ryutov et al. [8] present a framework named ATNAC (Adaptive Trust Negotiation and Access control) to protect sensitive resources in e-commerce. It is designed by integrating two existing systems – Trust-Builder with an adaptive access control API called, GAA-API (Generic Authorization and Access control). In [9], Adam et. al propose a content-based authorization model for digital library environments. Authorization is specified based on positive and negative qualifications and characteristics of the user which are expressed using credentials. Bonatti and Samarati [10] propose a uniform formal framework to regulate service access and information disclosure on the Internet. The regulation is based on credentials.

As is evident from the above discussion most access control methodologies for digital libraries use credential in one form or the other. Credential based access control, however, is not completely satisfactory. For one, a credential based system implements a binary notion of trust. If a user's credentials are accepted the corresponding privileges are allowed; if the credentials are not successfully validated the user is denied access. There is no way to implement fine-grained access control without requiring a large set of credentials. Additionally, reasoned decisions cannot be made in the face of incomplete, insufficient or inconclusive information. For example, let us assume that to validate a particular user credential three different credential certifying authorities need to be consulted. If, for any reason, one of these trusted authorities is not reachable and could not validate the credential, while the other two successfully validated the credential, the access will still be denied. Current credential based systems cannot implement a notion of limited access. Third, the objects stored in a digital library are characterized by fine-grained behavioral interfaces and highly-contextualized access restrictions that require a user's access privileges to be updated dynamically. Credential based access control models do not keep track of a user's behavior history. Access is provided based solely on the credentials presented during the specific access request. Thus, a user's access privileges cannot be updated dynamically under this model.

Note that a basic requirement of any access control mechanism is to determine if a user can be trusted with the access privileges. The notion of *trust* thus plays a crucial role. Classical access control models establish trust in the user based on the user's identity. Credential based access control does this by means of attestations from a-priori trusted authorities. Thus, using trust relationships to enable secure interactions among computational agents or to enforce proper policy seems appropriate. This motivates us to propose a new trust-based access control framework in this work. It is based on the vector model of trust that we had proposed earlier [11]. We use a prototype digital library system – called the DLS system – that we are developing at our institution as the testbed for the new access control framework. In the DLS system the digital library contents are classified into a number of content type categories. Each content type category is associated with a trust level. A user who is trusted to the trust level of the content category or higher can access the contents. The trust level of the user can be established via a number of different means. For example, the trust level can be determined based on past interactions with the user. It can be established based on some credentials presented by the user. It can also be established by virtue of recommendations provided by a partner digital library.

The rest of the paper is organized as follows. Section 2 provides an overview of access control in the DLS digital library system. In particular, it talks about how a notion of trust is used in access control decisions. Section 3 describes the access control model. In section 4 we outline how trust relationships are established between the DLS system and its user population. Section 5 gives the architecture of the DLS access control framework. Finally, we conclude our discussion in section 6 with a summary for future work.

## 2   Digital Library Access Control Model

Access control in the DLS digital library system is implemented using a multi-level trust model. For a digital library, access privileges to a particular category content is restricted to the users with a certain trust level. This trust level can be determined from many different pieces of information available about the user. For example, trust level can be determined from the credentials presented during an access request. Trust levels can be established based on previous behavior of the user. Trust levels can be established from certain physical properties of the user. Changes to the 'trust-level' changes the access privileges of the user. Our model allows access privileges to be updated dynamically during a user's access session. How this change is going to affect user's authorization level depends on the digital library's policy. Similarly what information will be used in determining the trust level and how the information will be used, also depend on the digital library's policy.

Unlike other access control models, our framework keeps track of the behavior of a user. Access privileges are not assigned forever. The user may be denied access to the same resource for which she used to have access, if her trust level detoriates. If a user performs malicious task (e.g., forging credential), her trust level decreases and she gets a reduced set of privileges. In this case the user is not able to access previously accessible contents even if she presents necessary credentials. The digital library system allows the user to access those contents again after the necessary level of trust about the user is reached. Another advantage of this type of multi-level trust-based authorization is it provides finer control over specifying access privileges. The system can define as many trust levels as it wants and can assign each level to specific set of resources tied with a specific set of access privileges. The association of trust levels with set of contents defines the access control policy for the digital library system. The digital library system needs only compute and monitor the trust level of the user and the regulation of access is automatically achieved.

To achieve these goals we adapt the trust model we have proposed earlier [11]. Unlike binary trust models, trust in this new model has different degrees and is computed based on aspects of social interactions in addition to exchange of credentials rather than on just exchange of credentials. The idea is that each interaction that a user performs with the digital library system, the server discloses some portion of the resources. The digital library should have a comfort level with this disclosure. Before giving the access permission to the user for a particular category of content, the digital library needs to determine to what degree it trusts or distrusts the user to have access to those contents. We discuss how access privileges for a portion of the content can be controlled using trust levels. We propose mechanisms by which the system collects, stores, and manages information about the user. The information collected allows the system to compute a trust value for the user. The computed trust value acts as a confidence level for the digital library system for disclosing its resources to that user. Note that, we envision this system to be used in a membership based system that allows monitoring of user access and activities. Thus privacy issues related to this is not addressed in this work. The proposed scheme provides a flexible and powerful approach for the proper disclosure of contents. It offers the digital library system considerable control over how it wishes to disseminate its contents.

## 3  Content Dependent Access Control in DLS

The DLS supports content dependent as well as content independent access control. The basic idea of content dependent access control in DLS is that a user's trust level determines which portion of content she can access with the allowed privileges on that portion. To do this DLS classifies its entire content into sub-categories.

**Definition 1.** *Each DLS object $o_k \in O$ (where $O$ is the set of DLS objects, and $o_k$ is the identity of the $k^{th}$ object) has a set $\mathscr{P}_o^k = \{p_o^1, p_o^2, \ldots, p_o^k\}$ of properties that specifies the content characteristics of the object. These properties are drawn from a larger set of (potentially hierarchically organized) concepts called* object properties.

Some examples of object properties are "journal articles", "magazines", "free content", "premium content", "fiction", "non-fiction", "drama", "comedy", "adult", "mp3-music" etc. The DLS defines a set $CC$ of *content classes* for classifying its objects. A subset of properties from the set of object properties define a content class. Every DLS object is assigned to one or more content classes.

**Definition 2.** *Let $prop(cc_i) = \{p_k, \dots, p_n\}$ be the object properties corresponding to the content class $cc_i$. An object $o_k$ is classified to the content class $cc_i$ if $prop(cc_i) \subseteq \mathscr{P}_o^k$.*

The function $OC : O \to \mathbb{P}(CC)$ maps an object to some subset of content classes. The function $OC^{-1} : CC \to \mathbb{P}(O)$ gives the objects that belong to any content class in $CC$.

**Definition 3.** *Two objects $o_i$ and $o_j$ belong to the same content class $cc_n$ if and only if $\mathscr{P}_o^i \cap \mathscr{P}_o^j \neq \varnothing$ and $\mathscr{P}_o^i \cap \mathscr{P}_o^j = \{p_{n_k} \dots p_{n_m}\}$ contains all the properties for $cc_n$ i.e., $prop(cc_n) \subseteq \mathscr{P}_o^i \cap \mathscr{P}_o^j$.*

The content classes are organized in a hierarchy. Figure 1 gives an example of content classes in the DLS system. We define the *content class hierarchy* as follows.

**Definition 4.** *Content class hierarchy $CCH \subseteq CC \times CC$ is a partial order on $CC$. For any two content classes $(cc_1, cc_2) \in CCH$, we say $cc_1$ dominates $cc_2$, denoted by $cc_1 \succeq cc_2$ if all the object properties that are in $cc_2$ are also in $cc_1$.*

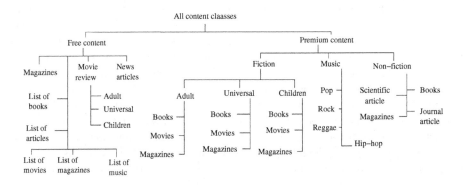

**Fig. 1.** Example of content class hierarchy in DLS system

Access privileges are associated with content classes. We formally define an access privilege as follows.

**Definition 5.** *An access privilege, $ap_i$, is specified as the tuple ⟨ action, sign, constraints, exceptions ⟩, where*

1. action *is a set of possible operations on digital library objects such as browsing, authoring, retrieving, etc,*
2. sign $\in (+,-)$, *denotes whether the privilege is positive or negative,*
3. constraints *define a set of pre-conditions for the actions; the pre-conditions can include spatial and temporal conditions,*
4. exceptions *define conditions under which the constraints can be overridden.*

The access privilege "deny browsing if age less than 18 years unless supervised by adult" will be expressed as ⟨ browse, -, age < 18, adult-supervision ⟩. The set APC defines the set of all possible access privileges for the DLS. What type of access privileges would be associated with which content class depends on the *content class access policy* of the DLS.

**Definition 6.** *The* content class access policy *is a function CCSP : CC → P(APC) that maps a content class in CC to a set of access privileges in APC. The inverse function $CCSP^{-1}$ defined as $CCSP^{-1} : APC → P(CC)$ maps an access privilege to a set of content classes.*

The set of access privileges corresponding to the content class $cc_i$ is represented by $cc_i{}^{ap}$. Objects of the DLS are also associated with access privileges. Thus we define the *object access policy* as follows.

**Definition 7.** *The* object access policy *is a function OAP : O → P(APC) that maps an object in O to a set of access privileges in APC. The inverse function $OAP^{-1}$ defined as $OAP^{-1} : APC → P(O)$ maps an access privilege to a set of objects.*

In DLS, users get different access privileges to different resources on the basis of their 'trust-level' with DLS during access request. Before presenting the authorization framework, we would like to define what we mean by trust.

**Definition 8.** *Trust is defined to be the firm belief in the competence of an entity to act according to some specific rules within a specific context.*

**Definition 9.** *Distrust is defined as the firm belief in the competence of an entity to act contrary to some specific rules within a specified context.*

Although we define trust and distrust separately, we allow neutrality in the belief about competence of the entity. Neutrality represents a position where there is neither trust that the entity will act according to the specified rules nor distrust that the entity will act contrary to those rules.

Trust (distrust) is specified as a relationship between the DLS system – the truster that trusts the target entity – and a user (or an agent working on behalf of the user) – the trustee that is trusted. We use the following notation to specify a trust relationship – $(DLS \xrightarrow{c} U)_t^N$ where $U$ is a specific user of DSL. This expression specifies $DLS$'s *normalized* trust on $U$ at a given time $t$ for a particular context $c$. The normalized trust relationship is obtained from the simple trust relationship – $(DLS \xrightarrow{c} U)_t$ – by combining the latter with a normalizing factor. This trust is always related to a particular context $c$.

**Definition 10.** *A context $c_i$ of a trust relation in DLS is defined as a set of actions $a_1, \ldots, a_n$ from the set of all possible actions that can be defined on objects. The context is interpreted as the conjunction of all these actions, that is $c_i \equiv a_1 \wedge \ldots \wedge a_n$.*

**Definition 11.** *A trust context $c_i$ covers another context $c_j$ if $c_j \subseteq c_i$. A trust relation $(DLS \xrightarrow{c_i} U)_t^N$ is useful in context $c_j$ if $c_i$ covers $c_j$.*

If a trust relationship is *useful* in a context other than the one it was specified for, then the trust relationship can be used to make access control decisions for the different context. Next we introduce a concept called the *value* of a trust relationship. This is denoted by the expression $\mathbf{v}(DLS \xrightarrow{c} U)_t^N$ and is a number in $[-1,1] \cup \{\bot\}$ that is associated with the normalized trust relationship. A user is completely trusted (or distrusted) if the value of the trust relationship is 1 (-1). If the value is in the range $(0,1)$ the user is *semi-trustworthy*; if the value is in the range $(-1,0)$ the user is *semi-distrustworthy*. The 0 value represents trust neutrality that is, the user is neither trustworthy nor untrustworthy. The special symbol $\bot$ is used to denote the value when there is not enough information to decide about trust, distrust, or neutrality. The whole range of trust values are sub-divided into some non-overlapping intervals. Each interval represents a set of trust levels. We use the symbol $\mathscr{I}$ to represent a set of trust-intervals $int_k$ with the properties: $\bigcup_k int_k = [-1,1] \cup \{\bot\}$ and $int_j \cap int_k = \varnothing$, $\forall j \neq k$. The function $TI : \mathbf{v}(DLS \xrightarrow{c} U)_t^N \to int_k$ maps a trust value to a trust interval.

**Definition 12.** *A trust-based access control policy of a digital library system, is defined as one of either $\langle CC, \mathscr{I}, \mathcal{A} \rangle$ or $\langle O, \mathscr{I}, \mathcal{A} \rangle$ or both where CC is the set of content-classes, $\mathscr{I}$ is a set of trust-intervals with each interval being a set of trust levels, and a trust association function $\mathcal{A} : CC \cup O \to \mathscr{I}$ which defines the association between a content-class or an object and a trust-interval. Formally, the association is represented as:*

$$\mathcal{A}(cc_k) = int_j \quad where \ \forall k, \ cc_k \in CC, \ and \ \forall j, \ int_j \in \mathscr{I}. \tag{1}$$

$$\mathcal{A}(o_k) = int_j \quad where \ \forall k, \ o_k \in O, \ and \ \forall j, \ int_j \in \mathscr{I}. \tag{2}$$

This mapping actually defines the access control policy of the system. The policy specifies what trust-level allows a user to access a specific object or a set of objects. If a user's trust level is in the interval $int_j$, she can access any object belonging to the class $cc_k$ with all the privileges tied to this class, provided no exception is defined on the access privilege. Decreasing the trust level beyond this interval $int_j$ results in a change in access privileges of the user; the user may no longer have the same access rights for the same information. The system may also choose to tie special condition(s) (e.g., a mandatory credential) to allow access to a particular content-class $cc_j$, where $\mathcal{A}(cc_j) = int_k$. In this case, the user needs to have her trust level in $int_k$ as well as has to satisfy the mandatory condition in order to have access to the content-class. Figure 2 gives the conceptual model of access control in the DLS.

## 4    Establishing Trust Relationship Between DLS and a User U

To gain access to DLS resources, a user U first needs to register. The user signs in as a 'new user' and the system asks U to choose a 'username' and 'password'. Even if the user U chooses not to provide any information about herself (including name, address, phone number etc.), the registration is successful. The DLS builds a trust relationship $(DLS \xrightarrow{c} U)_t^N$ with each registered user U. The underlying context $c$ for the trust relationship is set to the most basic action that is possible as defined in DLS (log-in, for

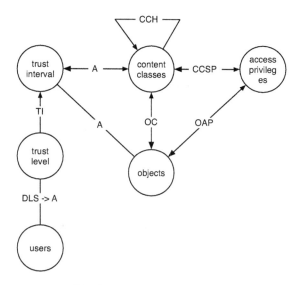

**Fig. 2.** DLS access control model

example). Depending partly on DLS's policy on registration information required, an initial trust level is set for the user. Typically it will be neutral. As the user continues to interact with DLS the trust level changes.

The vector trust model defines three different parameters that influences the computation of a trust level – *experience*, *knowledge* and *recommendation*.

**Definition 13.** *The* experience *of a truster about a trustee is defined as the cumulative effect of a number of events that occurred between the truster and the trustee over a specific period of time in the given context.*

DLS categorizes each experience as *trust-positive*, *trust-negative* or *trust-neutral* experience. A trust-positive experience increases trust degree whereas a trust-negative experience diminishes trust degree. A trust-neutral event contributes neither way.

**Definition 14.** *The* knowledge *of the truster regarding a trustee for a particular context is defined as a measure of the characteristic attributes or information of the trustee for which the truster can have some assertion to be truly related to the trustee.*

The trust value of DLS on a user can change because of some *knowledge* that the DLS possesses about the user. Information about the user may be obtained by the DLS in some earlier time for some purpose or, it may be a piece of information about the user for which the DLS can have a proof to be true. As with interactions, we have *trust-positive*, *trust-negative*, and *trust-neutral* knowledge.

**Definition 15.** *A* recommendation *about a trustee is defined as a measure of the subjective or objective judgment of a recommender about the trustee to the truster.*

It is important to note that the importance of the judgment of the third entity depends on how much the DLS trusts the third person's ability to judge others. As before we can have a *trust-positive*, *trust-negative*, and a *trust-neutral* recommendation. Finally, recommendations can be obtained by the DLS from more than one source and these together will contribute to the final trust relationship.

To compute a trust relationship we assume that each of these three factors is expressed in terms of a numeric value in the range $[-1, 1]$ and a special value $\perp$. A negative value for the component is used to indicate the *trust-negative* type for the component, whereas a positive value for the component is used to indicate the *trust-positive* type of the component. A 0 (zero) value for the component indicates *trust-neutral*. To indicate a lack of value due to insufficient information for any component we use the special symbol $\perp$. Properties of $\perp$ are: If $\mathbb{R}$ is the set of real numbers, then (i) $a \cdot \perp = \perp \cdot a = \perp$, $\forall a \in \mathbb{R}$; (ii) $a + \perp = \perp + a = a$, $\forall a \in \mathbb{R}$; (iii) $\perp + \perp = \perp$ and $\perp \cdot \perp = \perp$. We now discuss how values will be assigned to each of these components.

**Evaluation of knowledge.** The parameter "knowledge" is difficult to compute and is, to some extent, subjective. To begin with, the DLS must define its own criteria for gradation of information (or, properties) regarding any user. After the user U registers with DLS, the system asks for several specific information from U. The user can disclose those at once or she can choose to disclose them gradually at later times. For every piece of information that DLS receives from the user, a value between $[-1, 1]$ is assigned. How the values are assigned, depends on the scheme and policy (called, *knowledge evaluation policy*) of the DLS. Also the DLS solely is responsible for assigning the relative weights to different attributes or information. At any time $t$, the average of those values gives the value of knowledge about U. If the DLS is aware of $k$ attributes of the user, then knowledge of user $U$ according to the DLS in context $c$ is evaluated as $_{DLS}K_U^c = \frac{\Sigma_{i=1}^{k} v_i}{k}$, where $v_i \in [-1, 1]$ $\forall i = 1, 2, \ldots, k$. User's personal as well as professional information constitute the 'knowledge'. For example the following can constitute 'knowledge' about a user U:

- Personal information: Name, Address, Home phone number, Work phone number, Cell number etc.
- Financial Account information: Credit card number, validity period, credit card security code, Bank name, Bank routing number, Checking account number, etc.
- Affiliation: Name of the organization, Branch location, Organization accreditation, Designation of U in the organization, Proofs/Certificates related to affiliation, Designation of certifying authority (like, manager, CEO, advisor, department-chair, dean-of-studies) etc.

It is possible that the DLS has insufficient information to assign a value to knowledge. For these types of cases, it assigns $\perp$ to the component. Note, $_{DLS}K_U^c = \perp$ is different from $_{DLS}K_U^c = 0$. Value 0 implies that after evaluating the information according to trust policy, the DLS's decision is neutral. But the value '$\perp$' implies "lack of information", that is there is not enough data to determine 'knowledge' about the user.

**Evaluation of experience.** Most of the information that goes toward the forming the 'knowledge' of DLS about U in context $c$ does not necessarily enhance or degrade the system's trust on U. This is because all the above information are provided voluntarily by the user U. There is no guarantee that U discloses all information correctly. More useful, is perhaps, the interactions between the user and DLS. The user's behavior manifests in the form of *events*. We model experience in terms of the number of events encountered by the DLS regarding a user U in the context $c$ within a specified period of time $[t_0, t_n]$. Like knowledge, an event can be trust-positive, trust-negative or, trust-neutral. If there are events that conforms to the knowledge that the system has gathered then these events will be termed trust-positive. Every successful verification of information or every successful transaction with U can be considered as a trust-positive event. If the events are contrary to the knowledge then they are trust-negative. Otherwise they are trust-neutral. In fact, negative outcome of a verification procedure or failure of verification of a piece of information results in a trust-negative event. Every time the user logs in, the system tries to verify the information about the user that is stored in the system. The user may accept all information as correct or can edit them. The system verifies the validity of those information. If verification fails or any anomaly is found, it is considered a negative event. Note that all information may not be verifiable at once. Results of those information have the impact on the next transaction. For that instance, user U's trust level is calculated on the basis of the current available results. Some examples of events are as follows. The list is not exhaustive.

- Every successful transaction is considered to be a positive event.
- Providing invalid e-mail id, wrong home address or, wrong contact numbers are considered as negative events. Correct informations are trust positive events.
- Providing wrong credit card or invalid credit card details is a negative event. Similarly, wrong checking account information (either false routing number or account number or combination of these results in a trust-negative event). Correct information results in a trust-positive event.
- Purchase request with stolen or forged credit card/account number is a negative event. Successful purchase is a positive event.
- Forging a credential is a negative event while providing a valid credential generates a positive event.
- Posting improper, objectionable, or irrelevant remarks through *review center* is considered to be negative events.

Events far back in time does not count as strongly as very recent events for computing trust values. Hence we introduce the concept of *experience policy*. It is defined as follows.

**Definition 16.** *An* experience policy *specifies a totally ordered set of non-overlapping time intervals together with a set of non-negative weights corresponding to each element in the set of time intervals.*

Recent intervals in the experience policy are given more weight than those far back. The whole time period $[t_0, t_n]$ is divided in such intervals and the DLS keeps a log of events occurring in these intervals.

If $e_k^i$ denote the $k^{th}$ event in the $i^{th}$ interval, then we denote the value associated with $e_k^i$ as $v_k^i$. This value is assigned according to relative importance of the event $e_k^i$. $v_k^i \in [-10, 0)$ if $e_k^i \in Q$, $v_k^i \in (0, 10]$ if $e_k^i \in P$ and $v_k^i = 0$ if $e_k^i \in \mathcal{N}$ where, $P$ = set of all trust-positive events, $Q$ = set of all trust-negative events and $\mathcal{N}$ = set of all trust-neutral events. The system assigns different weights to different events on a 10-point scale depending on the seriousness or effect of the event. For example, providing a wrong telephone number by a user may not be as serious offense as forging a credit card number. So the system assign two different negative values for these two trust-negative events.

The *incidents* $IN_j$, corresponding to the $j^{th}$ time interval is the normalized sum of the values of all the events, trust-positive, trust-negative, or neutral for the time interval. The normalization is done in such a way that $IN_j \in [-1, 1]$. If $n_j$ is the number of events that occurred in the $j^{th}$ time interval, then

$$IN_j = \begin{cases} \bot & \text{, if } \not\exists\, e_k \in [t_{j-1}, t_j] \text{ for any } k \\ \frac{\sum_{k=1}^{n_j} v_k^j}{\sum_{k=1}^{n_j} |v_k^j|} & \text{, otherwise} \end{cases}$$

The *experience* of DLS with regards to U in the context $c$ is given by, $_{DLS}E_U^c = \sum_{i=1}^{n} w_i IN_i$, where, $w_i \in [0, 1]$ is a non-negative weight assigned to $i^{th}$ interval.

**Evaluation of recommendation.** In our modified trust model [12] recommendation is evaluated on the basis of a *recommendation value* returned by a recommender to the truster about the trustee. A truster will, most likely, have a trust relationship with the recommender, which is different from a trust relationship between truster and trustee and is formulated as specified by the trust model in [12]. The context of this trust relationship will be to act "reliably to provide a service (recommendation, in this case)" and it can be established parallelly or prior to the establishment of current trust relationship. This trust relationship will affect the score of the recommendation provided by the recommender. Therefore, *recommendation* of the DLS with regards to a user $U$ for a context $c$ is given by $_\Psi R_U^c = \frac{\sum_{j=1}^{n} (\mathbf{v}(DLS \xrightarrow{rec} j)_t^N) \cdot V_j}{\sum_{j=1}^{n} (\mathbf{v}(DLS \xrightarrow{rec} j)_t^N)}$, where $\Psi$ is a group of $n$ recommenders, $\mathbf{v}(DLS \xrightarrow{rec} j)_t^N) =$ trust-value of $j^{th}$ recommender and $V_j = j^{th}$ recommender's recommendation value about the user $U$.

Recommendation plays a role in the evaluation of trust level of a user when the DLS is a member of a consortium of digital libraries. In such cases, a member of the consortium should be able to provide information about certifiable behavior at resource pool boundaries. Also recommendations play a role in the process of delegation. Delegations are task oriented relationships that recur within a community. A delegation is a set of privileges required to accomplish related task.

We next observe that given the same set of values for the factors that influence trust, two different DLS may come up with two different trust values for the same user. During evaluation of a trust value, one DLS may assign different weights to the different factors that influence trust. For example, the DLS may choose to emphasize more on its experience about the user than some knowledge about the user. Which particular component of the trust vector needs to be emphasized more than other is a matter of the *normalization policy* of the DLS.

**Definition 17.** *The* normalization policy *for a trust relationship* $(DLS \xrightarrow{c} U)_t$ *is a vector of same dimension as of* $(DLS \xrightarrow{c} U)_t$*; the components are weights in the range* $[0, 1]$ *with their sum being equal to 1 and assigned to experience, knowledge, and recommendation components of* $(DLS \xrightarrow{c} U)_t$.

We use the notation $(DLS \xrightarrow{c} U)_t^N$, called *normalized* trust relationship to specify a trust relationship between the DLS and the user $U$. This relationship is obtained from the simple trust relationship after combining the former with the normalizing policy. It is derived as, $(DLS \xrightarrow{c} U)_t^N = \mathbf{W} \odot (DLS \xrightarrow{c} U)_t$. The $\odot$ operator represents the normalization operator. Let $(DLS \xrightarrow{c} U)_t = [{}_{DLS}E_U^c, {}_{DLS}K_U^c, \psi R_U^c]$ be a trust vector such that ${}_{DLS}E_U^c, {}_{DLS}K_U^c, \psi R_U^c \in [-1,1] \cup \{\bot\}$. Let also $\mathbf{W} = [W_E, W_K, W_R]$ be the corresponding trust policy vector such that $W_E + W_K + W_R = 1$ and $W_E, W_K, W_R \in [0,1]$. The $\odot$ operator generates the normalized trust relationship as $(DLS \xrightarrow{c} U)_t^N = \mathbf{W} \odot (DLS \xrightarrow{c} U)_t = [W_E, W_K, W_R] \odot [{}_{LS}E_U^c, {}_{DLS}K_U^c, \psi R_U^c] = [W_E \cdot {}_{DLS}E_U^c, W_K \cdot {}_{DLS}K_U^c, W_R \cdot \psi R_U^c] = [{}_{DLS}\hat{E}_U^c, {}_{DLS}\hat{K}_U^c, \psi \hat{R}_U^c]$.

We next introduce a concept called the *value* of a trust relationship. This is denoted by the expression $\mathbf{v}(DLS \xrightarrow{c} U)_t^N$ and is a number in $[-1,1] \cup \{\bot\}$ that is associated with the normalized trust relationship $(DLS \xrightarrow{c} U)_t^N$. It is defined as $\mathbf{v}(DLS \xrightarrow{c} B)_t^N = {}_{DLS}\hat{E}_U^c + {}_{DLS}\hat{K}_U^c + \psi \hat{R}_U^c$.

Trust (and distrust) changes over time. We claim that even if the underlying parameters do not change between times $t_i$ and $t_n$ at which a trust relationship is being evaluated, the trust relationship will change. To model this *trust dynamics* (i.e., the change of trust over time) we observe that the general tendency is to forget about past happenings. This leads us to argue that trust (and distrust) tends toward neutrality as time increases. Initially, the value does not change much; after a certain period the change is more rapid; finally the change becomes more stable as the value approaches the neutral (value = 0) level. The idea is captured by the equation $\mathbf{v}(T_{t_n}) = \mathbf{v}(T_{t_i})e^{-(\mathbf{v}(T_{t_i})\Delta t)^{2k}}$ where, $\mathbf{v}(T_{t_i})$, be the value of a trust relationship, $T_{t_i}$, at time $t_i$ and $\mathbf{v}(T_{t_n})$ be the decayed value of the same at time $t_n$. The effect of time is captured by the parameter $k$ which is determined by the truster's *dynamic policy* regarding the trustee in context $c$.

The trust model also has a method to obtain a vector of same dimension as of $(DLS \xrightarrow{c} U)_t^N$ from this value $\mathbf{v}(T_{t_n})$. The current normalized vector together with this time-affected vector are combined according to their relative importance. Relative importance is determined by the DLS's *history_weight policy* which specifies two values $\alpha$ and $\beta$ in $[0,1]$ (where, $\alpha + \beta = 1$) as weights to current vector and the vector obtained from previous trust value. The new vector thus obtained gives the actual normalized trust vector at time $t$ for the trust relationship between the DLS and a user $U$ in context $c$. This is represented by the following equation.

$$(DLS \xrightarrow{c} U)_{t_n}^N = \begin{cases} [{}_{DLS}\hat{E}_U^c, {}_{DLS}\hat{K}_U^c, \psi \hat{R}_U^c] & \text{if } t_n = 0 \\ [\frac{\mathbf{v}(\hat{T})}{3}, \frac{\mathbf{v}(\hat{T})}{3}, \frac{\mathbf{v}(\hat{T})}{3}] & \text{if } t_n \neq 0 \text{ and } {}_{DLS}\hat{E}_U^c = {}_{DLS}\hat{K}_U^c = \psi \hat{R}_U^c = \bot \\ \alpha \cdot [{}_{DLS}\hat{E}_U^c, {}_{DLS}\hat{K}_U^c, \psi \hat{R}_U^c] + \beta \cdot [\frac{\mathbf{v}(\hat{T})}{3}, \frac{\mathbf{v}(\hat{T})}{3}, \frac{\mathbf{v}(\hat{T})}{3}] \\ \qquad \text{if } t_n \neq 0 \text{ and at least one of } {}_{DLS}\hat{E}_U^c, {}_{DLS}\hat{K}_U^c, \psi \hat{R}_U^c \neq \bot \end{cases}$$

$$(3)$$

where $[\frac{\mathbf{v}(\hat{T})}{3}, \frac{\mathbf{v}(\hat{T})}{3}, \frac{\mathbf{v}(\hat{T})}{3}]$ is the time-effected vector and $\mathbf{v}(\hat{T}) = \mathbf{v}(T_{t_n})$.

Note, for DLS, it may not be reasonable to decrease (increase) the trust (distrust) level of a user at a faster rate. Because that will result in reduction (enhancement) in her access privileges with duration of time. For example, let a user with trust value, say 0.4 stop interacting with the DLS. At this point she is cleared to say, $cc_i$. After a long time, the user again interacts with DLS and finds her trust level goes down to, say 0.25 and she can not access all of $cc_i$ anymore and is restricted to a content class, say $cc_j$ where $cc_i \succeq cc_j$. This issue can be solved in one or both of the following ways: (i) Choose the value for $k$ in the *dynamic policy* to ensure a very slow decay in trust values, or (ii) Assign a very small value for $\beta$ in *history-weight-policy* thereby putting very less importance on the time-affected vector.

Sometimes it may not be possible to obtain a non null value for any of the trust parameters. In such cases the DLS system tries to determine if it is aware of a trust relationship for the same user in a related context that *covers* the current context. Recall from section 3 that if such a trust relationship exist it is *useful* in the given context. In such cases, the trust level established for the related context is used by the DLS system to determine access.

## 5    Architecture of the DLS Access Control Module

The high level system architecture of the DLS access control module consists of the components as shown in figure 3. The two main components are *authorization controller* and *trust engine*. The authorization controller interacts with the *content-server* and the trust engine.

**Access specification module.** This module defines the classification of resources into content classes and objects. That is, the module defines $CC$ and $\mathscr{P}_o$s for each object. It also defines the content class hierarchy $CCH$. Types of access privileges

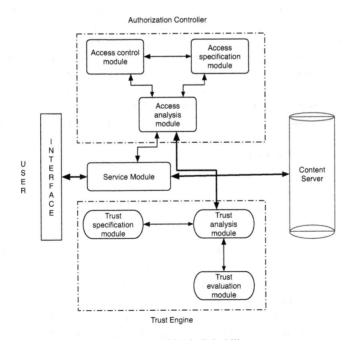

**Fig. 3.** Architecture of DLS digital library system

that are to be tied to each content class or object is also specified here. This module is also responsible for specifying any special constraint (other than trust level) or an exception that has to be satisfied to allow access to a content class or to an object. In other words, the module is responsible for definitionning the functions $OC, CCSP, CCSP^{-1}, OAP$, and $OAP^{-1}$.

**Access control module.** This module is responsible to classify trust levels into different sub-intervals i.e., defines the set $\mathscr{I}$. It also defines the *association function* $\mathscr{A}$.

**Access analysis module.** This module has a user database. It receives the user's information and user's request through a *Service module*. It passes user information to trust engine and receives trust related result from it. Consulting with the access specification module and access policy module, it takes the decision about the specific request of the user and pass it to the service module. It also verifies user information and checks for special constraints and exceptions.

**Service module.** The service module is an independent module outside the authorization controller as well as trust engine. Its job is to interact with the user through an interface. It collects user input and sends it to access analysis module of authorization controller. According to the decision it receives from access analysis module about the request it interacts with the content-server and provides the requested service to the user.

**Trust specification module.** It is responsible for definitionning and managing trust relationships. It creates database entries corresponding to a specific user when a new trust relationship is established. It codifies general trust evaluation policies (for example policy for trust dynamics). The specification module conveys this information to the analysis module and the evaluation module as and when needed.

**Trust analysis module.** The analysis module processes trust queries from access analysis module of authorization controller. It obtains trust vectors from the evaluation module.

**Trust Evaluation module.** This module retrieves information about experience, knowledge, and recommendation from the database and also other pertinent information from the trust specification module to compute trust vector according to the theory specified in this paper. It also stores back resulting values in the database kept in trust specification module.

## 6  Conclusion and Future Work

In this work we develop a flexible access control framework for digital library systems. The framework is based on the vector trust model that we had proposed earlier. We show how a digital library system can specify access control policies by associating a set of objects and access privileges with a set of trust levels. The underlying trust model evaluates a user's trust level with respect to the system using knowledge about the user. The system also considers its experience with the user to evaluate trust. This is a major contribution of the scheme where history of user's behavior is used to control her access clearance. A lot of work, however, still remains to be done. The scheme is proposed with a server-side approach. Extending the underlying trust model to a mutual trust negotiation model, we plan to design a two-way scheme to include client-side access control. Designing such a scheme would help to solve the issues like disclosure of policies, especially privacy protection policies, in online transactions. We also plan to develop efficient methods of interaction between an authorization controller and a trust engine.

# References

1. Bertino, E., Ferrari, E., Perego, A.: Max: An access control system for digital libraries and the web. In: Proceedings of the 26th IEEE International Computer Software and Applications Conference, Oxford, UK (2002)
2. H.M.Gladney: Access Control for Large Collections. ACM Transactions on Information Systems **15** (1997) 154–194
3. Blaze, M., Feigenbaum, J., Lacy, J.: Decentralized Trust Management. In: Proceedings of the 1996 IEEE Symposium on Security and Privacy, Oakland, CA (1996)
4. Blaze, M., Feigenbaum, J., Ioannidia, J.: The KeyNote Trust Management System Version 2. Internet Society, Network Working Group. RFC 2704 (1999)
5. Li, N., Mitchell, J.: Datalog with Constraints: A Foundation for Trust-management Languages. In: Proceedings of the 5th International Symposium on Practical Aspects of Declarative Languages, New Orleans, Louisiana (2003)
6. Winslett, M., Ching, N., Jones, V., Slepchin, I.: Assuring security and privacy for digital library transactions on the Web: client and server security policies. In: Proceedings of the IEEE international forum on Research and Technology Advances in Digital Libraries, Washington, DC, USA (1997) 140–151
7. Skogsrud, H., Benatallah, B., , Casati, F.: A Trust Negotiation System for Digital Library Web Services. Journal of Digital Libraries, Special Issue on Security **4** (2004)
8. Ryutov, T., Zhou, L., Neuman, C., Leithead, T., Seamons, K.: Adaptive Trust Negotiation and Access Control. In: Proceedings of the 10th ACM Symposium on Access Control Models and Technologies, Stockholm, Sweden (2005)
9. Adam, N.R., Atluri, V., Bertino, E., Ferrari, E.: A Content-Based Authorization Model for Digital Libraries. IEEE Transactions on Knowledge and Data Engineering **14** (2002) 296–315
10. Bonatti, P., Samarati, P.: Regulating Service Access and Information Release on the Web. In: Proceedings of the 7th ACM COnference on Computer and Communication Security, Athens, Greece, ACM Press (2000) 134–143
11. Ray, I., Chakraborty, S.: A Vector Model of Trust for Developing Trustworthy Systems. In: Proceedings of the 9th European Symposium of Research in Computer Security (ESORICS 2004). Volume 3193 of Lecture Notes in Computer Science., Sophia Antipolis, France, Springer-Verlag (2004) 260–275
12. Ray, I., Chakraborty, S., Ray, I.: VTrust: A Trust Management System Based on a Vector Model of Trust. In Jajodia, S., Mazumdar, C., eds.: Proceedings of 1st International Conference on Information Systems Security (ICISS 2005). Volume 3803 of Lecture Notes in Computer Science., Kolkata, India, Springer-Verlag GmbH (2005) 91–105

# Authrule: A Generic Rule-Based Authorization Module

Sönke Busch[1], Björn Muschall[2], Günther Pernul[2], and Torsten Priebe[3]

[1] Booz Allen Hamilton GmbH, Zollhof 8, D-40221 Düsseldorf, Germany
[2] Department of Information Systems, University of Regensburg,
D-93040 Regensburg, Germany
[3] Capgemini Consulting Österreich AG, Lassallestrae 9b,
A-1020 Vienna, Austria

**Abstract.** As part of the access control process an authorization decision needs to be taken based on a certain authorization model. Depending on the environment different models are applicable (e.g., RBAC in organizations, MAC in the military field). An authorization model contains all necessary elements needed for the decision (e.g., subjects, objects, and roles) as well as their relations. As these elements are usually inherent in the software architecture of an access control module, such modules limit themselves to the use of a certain specific authorization model. A later change of the model consequently results in a substantial effort for revising the software architecture of the given module. Rule-based systems are well suited to represent authorization models by mapping them to facts and rules, which can be modified in a flexible manner. In this paper we present a generic authorization module, which can take authorization decisions on the basis of arbitrary models utilizing rule-based technology. The implementation of the popular RBAC and ABAC (attribute-based access control) models is demonstrated.

## 1 Introduction and Motivation

Depending on the environment of an IT system, there are varying requirements for its access control mechanism. These requirements determine which authorization model is adequate. For instance, for military purposes, the mandatory access control model (MAC) is favourable as it supports information flow control. This model is however inadequate for commercial purposes—in business IT systems, the mostly used authorization model is role-based access control (RBAC). For information services on the Internet, an attribute-based access control model (ABAC) might be the first choice due to the lack of stable role structures. It is important to note that there is no authorization model that is suitable for all different kinds of scenarios—the best suitable authorization model must be chosen depending on the requirements.

The usual approach for implementing an access control system is to first decide which authorization model matches the requirements and then develop a software module to implement this authorization model. This approach has a major drawback: The software is bound to a single authorization model. This

E. Damiani and P. Liu (Eds.): Data and Applications Security 2006, LNCS 4127, pp. 267–281, 2006.
© IFIP International Federation for Information Processing 2006

means, that if the requirements change and if it is necessary to switch to a new authorization model, this would require substantial changes on the software.

This paper describes a generic approach that led to an authorization component that supports multiple authorization models and can easily be extended to support arbitrary authorization models. To accomplish this, a rule-based system is used to map authorization models to rule sets; an inference engine processes the authorization requests. Moving from one authorization model to another only requires minor changes on the software—different authorization models are represented as modules plus rule-base that can easily be replaced. To ensure that authorization models can be easily exchanged, the access control logic is kept in the separate authorization model and not interweaved with the business logic.

## 2    Fundamentals

### 2.1    Authorization Models

Authorization models are essential for access control. They represent all information that is needed to perform an authorization decision. This information consists of entities and their relation to each other. These entities and relations vary from model to model, but they have some commonality, like the subject (user) that requests the access, the object that is to be accessed and the operation that the subject requests to perform on the object. Operation and object together represent a permission. This paper focuses on two very popular and well elaborated authorization models, RBAC and ABAC.

The role based access control model (RBAC) is the de-facto standard for access control. The standardization process was initiated by the NIST [3]. It introduces an intermediation between user and permission, called role. Roles are assigned to users and permissions are assigned to roles. The NIST also defined two extensions of this basic Core RBAC model: Hierarchical RBAC and Constrained RBAC.

The attribute based access control model (ABAC) relies on attributes of the requesting subject as well as the object to perform the authorization decision. There is no common or standard model like for RBAC, but it can be found in many research works, e.g. DLAM [1,4] or UCON [8] as well as the XML access control language XACML [6]. An attempt to define a common ABAC reference model was made in [9][1],[10]. Permissions are assigned by defining which attributes a subject has to have in order to be able to access certain objects (with certain attributes). The ABAC model can be extended to take environment attributes into account or to directly compare the subject attributes with those of the object.

In general, an authorization decision is a simple yes/no query that can be described with a limited set of authorization rules. This characteristic allows representing authorization models in rule bases and performing authorization

---

[1] In this paper the authors refer to metadata-based access control (MBAC) instead of ABAC. However, the terminilogy has changed in more recent work.

decisions with inference engines. Such authorization module can therefore implement virtually any authorization model. In addition, the more complex an authorization model is structured, the more effectively rule based systems can perform their advantages over classical software architectures, that reflect the authorization model in their structure.

## 2.2   Rule-Based Systems

Rule-based systems are able to represent knowledge by storing structured information (called facts) and using rules to generate new facts from the already existing ones. Facts are represented by predicates, which—similar to tuples in relational databases—describe relations of some entities. A set of facts together with a set of corresponding rules is called a knowledge base. Queries can be run against this knowledge base by using an inference engine. When using a rule-based system for authorization decisions, the entities of the authorization model and their relations are represented by a set of facts. Additionally, rules are defined to state, under which circumstances access will be granted and when it will be denied. Authorization decisions are then performed by querying the knowledge base with a query like *granted(subject, object, operation)*.

Implementations of rule-based systems vary in their approach, flexibility and maturity. For the purpose of using a rule-based system as kernel for a Java-based authorization module, the Mandarax[2] distribution was chosen. Mandarax was found to fit best to our requirements. Mandarax is an open source Java library implementing a very flexible and extensible rule-based system. One of the main features of Mandarax is the possibility to load facts from any JDBC data source on demand (i.e. when they are needed to answer a query). This way, Mandarax can handle huge amounts of data as the data is not kept into main memory but rather read from the data source as needed. As an interface for communicating with the rule-based system, RuleML[3] was chosen, as this is a XML-based format capable of describing all important elements of a rule-based system.

# 3   Authrule Architecture and Design

## 3.1   Requirements

Authorization models represent the data and logic that are used to perform authorization decisions. As stated above, there is a vast variety of authorization models which differ quite significantly in the data and logic they use. The aim of this work is to design an authorization module that is able to execute any potential authorization model; this means that authorization models should be exchangeable and that new authorization models should be addable with only little effort. To make the implementation of a new authorization model as easy as possible, an easy format should be used for describing the elements of the

---

[2] http://www.mandarax.org
[3] http://www.ruleml.org

model. Furthermore, the system should be platform-independent and it should be able to support different data sources easily.

The choice of the authorization model of course in some way influences the functional requirements that can be divided into two groups: functionality necessary for performing authorization requests (called client functions) and functionality necessary to manage the authorization data (called administration functions). Additionally, the functional requirements can be devided into those that are specific to a certain authorization model (model-specific) and those that are not (model-unspecific). For the client functions for instance, the authorization request itself can be easily abstracted to a generic authorization request that has the same form regardless of the authorization model the software is currently applying. But there are also client functions that are model-specific and cannot easily be abstracted, e.g., for RBAC there must be a client function to create sessions and activate or deactivate roles. Some administration functions are model-unspecific, for instance creating or deleting users, objects or operations. Most of the administration functions however use specific characteristics of the authorization model and are therefore model-specific.

## 3.2    Realization of Authrule

As shown in Fig.1, the authorization module Authrule processes authorization requests from client business applications and additionally supplies a (separate) interface for administration. These services were implemented in an API consisting of Java interfaces. The interfaces are supplied by a class called *KnowledgeBaseManager*, which represents the software to the user.

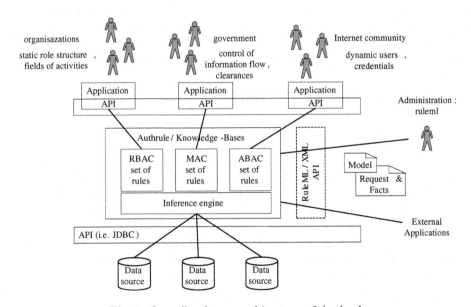

**Fig. 1.** Overall software architecture of Authrule

According to the requirements, these services are made available in a way that they are as generic as possible and at the same time offer all necessary functionality. Client functionality is provided by the Java interface *ClientI* (see Sec. 4) which forms the API for the applications in Fig.1. [4] For model-specific functionality, this interface was extended, e.g., the RBAC-specific functions (session management, etc.) are provided by the interface *RBACClientI*. Accordingly, the generic administration interface is *AdminI*, which is extended for model-specific functionality. For RBAC-specific administration (role management, etc.), the interface *RBACAdminI* was created. It is possible to use client functionality by using the generic *ClientI* interface—this allows a client business application to use Authrule for authorization requests without even knowing what authorization model is used. In contrast to the client side, administration of the Authrule can only be done properly, when using the model-specific administration interface, as the administration requires knowledge of the authorization model (e.g., for RBAC, the administrator must know that roles have to be used to assign permissions to users).

The API encapsulates the rule-based system, which actually processes the requests. A class derived from the abstract class *AuthorizationModel* transforms the method calls from the API to rule-based queries. This class also takes care of calls that require writing/modifying data, which cannot be done by simply querying the rule-based system. A helper class (called *PredicateDatasource*) was developed to provide an easy and abstracted way of writing and deleting data.

The representation of the authorization model as a set of facts and rules is described in a RuleML configuration file, which is loaded on startup. The RuleML format is human-readable an easy to understand and edit. This data format is mapped to the the internal, object-oriented and Mandarax-specific runtime representation of the rule-based system, which is not human-readable. The same format can also be used to directly query and/or as an intermediate step mapping calls from the Java API to query the the rule-based system. The core of Authrule is designed to be extensible in several aspects and therefore conforms to the above requirement. As mentioned above, the authorization model can be exchanged seamlessly. One class (derived from the class *AuthorizationModel*) includes all program code that is specific for this authorization model; by exchanging this class (and changing two configuration files), a new authorization model can be applied. Facts that have to be included in the knowledge base as they are necessary for the authorization decision (like user names, roles, etc.) can be added in two ways: If the amount of data for these facts is small, they can be manually added into the RuleML configuration file that is used to define a certain authorization model. This file should only comprise the set of rules (and some basic facts) that made up the model and are loaded into the knowledge base on startup. For larger amounts of data, it is more appropriate to map these predicates to a JDBC data source, this way the data does not reside in

---

[4] *Business applications* in Fig. 1 and the *SecurityProxy* in Fig. 3 are called *clients* from the perspective of Authrule. Not to be confused with *Client* in Fig. 3.

the knowledge base but is loaded into memory from the data source on demand. The mapping of predicates to data sources is configured in a different XML configuration file.

Administrative clients will use the administrative interfaces of Authrule. If they add new facts, this will internally result in adding a tuple to the database. If the access control model is modified, i.e. adding new authorization constraints, this will result in extending the authorization model with new rules.

## 4    Implementing Authorization Models

To implement an authorization model, only a Java class, two Java interfaces and two XML files have to be created, as described in Sec. 3.2. The elements of the authorization model are described as facts and rules in a RuleML file. Another XML file describes how the facts are mapped to data sources. Functionality for client use and administration is declared by extending the interfaces *ClientI* and *AdminI* (see Fig.2). An implementation of the abstract class *AuthorizationModel* is created to map the interfaces to requests to the rule-based system.

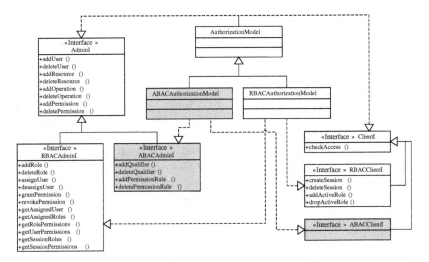

**Fig. 2.** Authrule application programming interface (with interfaces for RBAC and ABAC)

Each authorization model has to be assigned a unique ID, called *ModelId*. Each part of the authorization model implementation, i.e. the Java class derived from the class *AuthorizationModel* as well as the XML files for defining the rules and mappings, is tagged by this *ModelId*. Upon startup, Authrule loads the Java class and XML-files that are specified in the configuration file and checks if they all have the same *ModelId*. This ensures the integrity of the loaded authorization module.

## 4.1   Role-Based Access Control

The first step for implementing an authorization model is to describe the model itself, which is the static part of a RBAC policy, as a set of facts and rules. The following listing shows an excerpt of the RuleML file that forms the Core-RBAC model described in [3] translated to a rule-based representation.

```
...
<rulebase model_id="ifs.uni-regensburg.de/rbac-core/0.1">
<imp>
  <_head>
    <atom>
      <_opr><rel>granted</rel></_opr>
      <var>a User</var>
      <var>an Object</var>
      <var>an Operation</var>
    </atom>
  </_head>
  <_body>
    <and>
      <atom>
        <_opr><rel>hasRole</rel></_opr>
        <var>a User</var>
        <var>a Role</var>
      </atom>
      <atom>
        <_opr><rel>hasPermission</rel></_opr>
        <var>a Role</var>
        <var>a Permission</var>
      </atom>
      <atom>
        <_opr><rel>session</rel></_opr>
        <var>a Session</var>
        <var>a User</var>
      </atom>
      <atom>
        <_opr><rel>activeRole</rel></_opr>
        <var>a Session</var>
        <var>a Role</var>
      </atom>
... <!-- predicates to check existence of elements are omitted -->
    </and>
  </_body>
</imp>
</rulebase>
```

The RBAC model comprises just one rule for the predicate *granted* that represents the authorization decision. It is not necessary to declare the used predicates separately as they are declared implicitly when used in a rule definition. The use of predicates that represent the existence of elements (like user, role, object, etc.) are omitted in this excerpt:

Since the facts according to the predicates tend to be numerous and change frequently, they can be mapped to an arbitrary number of JDBC data source and therefore separated from the definition of the model.

The Java interfaces *RBACClientI* and *RBACAdminI* were created to extend the interfaces *ClientI* and *AdminI* with additional, RBAC-specific functionality like handling sessions and defining roles. Fig.2 shows theses interfaces and their methods as well as the class *RBACAuthorizationModel*, which implements them. Requests can be passed to the rule based system in several ways, see Sec. 3.2. The call *checkAccess()* of the interface *ClientI* results in a RuleML query similar to that in Sec. 4.2 that is sent to the rule-based system to find out if a user is allowed to perform an operation on an object. In other words, the implementation of interface methods like *checkAccess()* use the provided RuleML interface to implement their functionality.

### 4.2    Attribute-Based Access Control

Implementing the ABAC model requires—similarly to the implementation of RBAC-a Java class, two Java interfaces and two XML files. A major difference compared to RBAC is that an ABAC policy cannot be so clearly distiguished into a static model and its instances. The ABAC model itself is translated into some static set of rules that can be separated from the dynamic authorizations of some instance of the ABAC model, also translated into rules. These instances of the model are formulated into a separated set of rules and facts that are temporarily combined for an authorization decision. A second major difference is, that in this ABAC implementation the requesting user and the user's attributes (also called credentials) are external to the rule base and handed over when *checkAccess()* is called. The attributes can, for example, originate from a X.509 attribute client certificate [5].This is in contrast to most RBAC implementations, where server-side roles are derived from the identity without additional information from the client. Therefore, the parameter user that is used with the API is an object that has methods to get and set its attributes. Consequently, the RuleML query for handing the authorization request to the rule-based system is extended to take the attributes of the user into account when processing the query. This is shown in the following listing:

```
<rulebase>
<!-- facts added temporarly to knowledgebase for executing the query -->
  <atom>
  <_opr><rel>user</rel></_opr>
    <ind>Bob</ind>
  </atom>
  <atom>
```

---

[5] X.509: Public Key and Attribute Certificate Frameworks. ITU-T Recommendation, 2000.

```
<_opr><rel>hasAttribute</rel></_opr>
    <ind>Bob</ind>
    <ind>age</ind>
    <ind>23</ind>
  </atom>
<!-- the query, same for RBAC/ABAC -->
  <query>
    <_body>
      <atom>
        <_opr><rel>granted</rel></_opr>
        <ind>Bob</ind>
        <ind>DocumentA</ind>
        <ind>write</ind>
      </atom>
    </_body>
  </query>
</rulebase>
```

The rule base for the ABAC model is more complex. The following excerpt of the corresponding RuleML file show how ABAC can be formulated in rules:

```
<rulebase model_id="ifs.uni-regensburg.de/abac/0.1">
<!-- this rule maps the granted predicate to the hasPermission
  predicate and checks existence of the passed elements -->
<imp>
  <_head>
    <atom>
      <_opr><rel>granted</rel></_opr>
      <var>a User</var>
      <var>an Object</var>
      <var>an Operation</var>
    </atom>
  </_head>
  <_body>
    <and>
... <!-- predicates to check existence of elements are omitted -->
      <atom>
        <_opr><rel>hasPermission</rel></_opr>
        <var>a User</var>
        <var>an Object</var>
        <var>an Operation</var>
      </atom>
    </and>
  </_body>
</imp>
<!--  greater_equal (int) Operator -->
<imp>
  <_head>
    <atom>
      <_opr><rel>matchesQualifier</rel></_opr>
```

```
      <var>a User or Object</var>
      <var>a Qualifier</var>
   </atom>
 </_head>
 <_body>
   <and>
     <atom>
       <_opr><rel>qualifier</rel></_opr>
       <var>a Qualifier</var>
       <ind>greater_equal</ind>
       <var>an Attribute</var>
       <var type="Integer">IntValue 2</var>
     </atom>
     <atom>
       <_opr><rel>hasAttribute</rel></_opr>
       <var>a User or Object</var>
       <var>an Attribute</var>
       <var type="Integer">IntValue 1</var>
     </atom>
     <atom>
       <_opr><rel predefined="true">=&gt;</rel></_opr>
       <var type="Integer">IntValue 1</var>
       <var type="Integer">IntValue 2</var>
     </atom>
   </and>
 </_body>
</imp>
...
```

The *granted* predicate checks for the existence of the passed elements and then refers to the predicate *hasPermission*. The predicate *hasPermission* yields true, if one of the permission rules match the authorization query.

Permission rules use qualifiers [9,10] to describe what kind of attributes qualify users and objects for this rule. As qualifiers use operators (like *equal, greater than*, etc.), these operators must be first defined. The above excerpt shows the definition of the operator *greater_equal*[6] . Permissions are assigned by adding permission rules to the rule-based system. The following listing shows an example of a permission rule and the qualifier this permission rule uses:

```
<fact>
 <atom>
   <_opr><rel>qualifier</rel></_opr>
     <var>adult</var>
     <ind>greater_equal</ind>
```

---

[6] This is an example of a predefined predicate. It represents special functions that the Mandarax distribution supplies—in this example, it checks if the first term is greater than or equals the second term. To use predefined predicates with RuleML, the RuleML format was extended with a marker attribute predefined, as can be seen in the code example above.

```
      <var>age</var>
      <var type="Integer">18</var>
  </atom>
</fact>
<fact>
  <atom>
    <_opr><rel>qualifier</rel></_opr>
      <var>belongs_to_hemauer</var>
      <ind>equal</ind>
      <var>project_name</var>
      <var type=" String">Hemauer Project </var>
  </atom>
</fact>
<imp>
  <_head>
    <atom>
      <_opr><rel>hasPermission</rel></_opr>
        <var>a User</var>
        <var>an Object</var>
        <ind>read</ind>
    </atom>
  </_head>
  <_body>
    <and>
      <atom>
        <_opr><rel>matchesQualifier</rel></_opr>
        <var>a User</var>
        <ind>adult</ind>
      </atom>
      <atom>
        <_opr><rel>matchesQualifier</rel></_opr>
        <var>an Object</var>
        <ind>belongs_to_hemauer</ind>
      </atom>
    </and>
  </_body>
</imp>
```

Qualifiers are represented by a predicate called *qualifier* that defines the qualifier's name, an operation, an attribute type, and a value. In the above example, the qualifier *adult* is defined to match all users whose attribute age is grater or equals 18. The second qualifier *belongs_to_hemauer* matches all objects that have an attribute *project_name* indicating that they belong to the project "Hemauer Project". The permission rule that is listed afterwards uses these two qualifiers to specify that adult users are allowed to read objects that are associated to the project "Hemauer Project".

As shown in Fig.2 the Java interfaces for ABAC are quite straight forward. The API remains the same, however, the prerequisite must be met that the attributes are contained in the subject. Hence, only few additional functionality is required on the client side. This can be accomplished in transparent way using general APIs for authentication (like JAAS[7] , PAM,.etc.). On the client side, the interface remains the same, which means that this ABAC model can be used by means of the generic interface *ClientI*. This is made possible as the parameters for the generic interface *ClientI* are based on instances of the interfaces *UserI*, *OperationI* and *ObjectI*. These interfaces supply functions to get and set attributes. For this reason, these methods can be used regardless of the authorization model that is actually used. On the administration side, the generic *AdminI* is extended by the interface *ABACAdminI* with methods to create and delete qualifiers and permission rules.

## 5   Usage Scenario

In order to evaluate our approach and the Authrule module, we deployed it for access control in a component-based business application. Over the last years J2EE (Java 2 Enterprise Edition) evolved as a major framework for enterprise application development. This framework comprises the software component standard EJB (Enterprise Java Beans) [5]. EJBs are well suited for constructing business applications as they come with out-of-the-box solutions and mechanisms for a set of non-functional requirements like security. EJBs can also be made externally available as web services using JAX-RPC[8]. Unfortunately the EJB standard has been designed to be tightly bound to RBAC. This fact inhibits principals like application field neutrality, transparency and flexibility. EJB-based applications can be deployed in a variety of application domains that have different requirements for authorization see Sec. 1. A further substantial inconvenience of the EJB security approach is, that roles are derived from the users' identity on the server side see Sec. 4.2. Consequently, we consider the existent role based access control in EJB systems as a form of basic security, which needs to be supplemented by additional security measures. In Fig.3 an interceptor (called a "security proxy") is placed in the communication path between the client and a component transparently to the application logic. Each software component can be preceded with its own interceptor that can contain authorization logic in which we integrate Authrule to protect several EJBs. Consequently each piece of application logic in form of an EJB can be supplied with attribute-based access control with arbitrary authorization rules. The non-functional requirements transparency, flexibility, and interoperability have been taken into special consideration. Transparency in this sense means, that security should not be part of the application logic. In this way security unaware applications can be secured without requiring to change their code and security mechanisms are interchangeable.

Fig.3 depicts our approach in detail. A user/principal uses a client, which is linked to the authentication interfaces. On startup of the client application, the

---

[7] Java Authentication and Authorization Service (JAAS).
   http://java.sun.com/products/jaas/
[8] Java API for XML-Based RPC (JAX-RPC)
   http://java.sun.com/webservices/jaxrpc/index.jsp

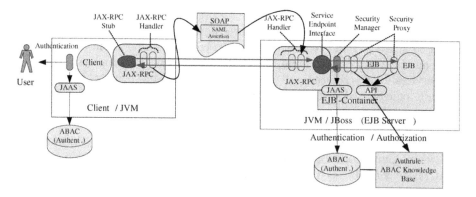

**Fig. 3.** Authrule for EJB access control

authentication process is being triggered. It calls the attribute-based authentication module, which is deployed in conformance to the server-side authorization module. The client is requested to provide the attributes, he wants to use and a *subject* instance containing these attributes is created. By invoking the web service methods the subject is transparently encapsulated. Server-side authentication is processed and a security context is established. Before invoking an EJB the interceptor forwards the attributes to Authrule in order to take the authorization decision. Depending on this decision the authorization enforcement within the interceptor/security proxy grants access to the bean or prevents the further invocation.

# 6   Related Work

Since it has been demonstrated that RBAC can be configured to also enforce DAC and MAC, RBAC has been considered to be a generic authorization model. The flexibility of RBAC and its ability to enforce MAC policies and a number of access constraints to realise the equivalent of Bell-LaPadula has been demonstrated in [13]. With the appearance of attribute-based access control models (XACML[6], UCON[8], DLAM[1]) authorization requirements have shown up, which eventually cannot be solved by RBAC. As a result, RBAC cannot longer be considered as "ultima ratio". A lot of RBAC implementations yet exist, one of it is described in [12]. It was implemented in a classical straightforward manner by mapping the static model to an equivalent software architecture. CSAP [12] afterwards has been extended with ABAC resulting in the above mentioned substantial changes on the software and runtime inefficiencies.

There have been other attempts to find a universal way of describing authorization models as set of rules and predicates. One of the broadest approaches is described by Bertino et al. [2]—however, the intention for describing authorization models in that work was to create a framework to compare them in respect to their expressiveness; it did not discuss how rule-based systems can be used to build a generic authorization module. Additionally, assumptions about the authorization models (e.g. that users are organized in groups) were made, constraining the generality of their framework. Other research works that use logics-based languages and reasoners for access control can be found in the area of the Semantic Web. For example, the KAoS framework [11] provides a collection of services for distributed policy management and enforcement. It uses the description-logics-based Web Ontology Language (OWL) to specify the policies. Likewise, the policy engine in Rei [6] can handle policies specified in RDFS (a subset of OWL).

In this work, we decided to use RuleML as basis for the input and output format when communicating with the application core. One might argue that the XACML[6] could be used as it is also able to formulate authorization requests and express the permission data for several different authorization models. In fact, XACML is a very versatile standard that is capable of mapping many different authorization models. However, XACML has drawbacks that make it unsuitable when a very generic, but simple approach is desired. One reason is that the versatility of XACML resulted in a very complex format, which is not easy to handle and involves a lot of overhead. Another reason is that XACML, though very versatile, is not generic enough to cover all possible authorization requirements. For example, even though core RBAC requirements can be easily implemented using XACML, a full-featured constrained RBAC [3] is hard to achieve as XACML rules are not as expressible as the logics used by a rule-based system. Using a descriptive format like RuleML ensures that the approach is so generic that it can capture all authorization models that can be formulated as set of predicates and rules—and, as we argued in this paper, every authorization model can be formulated as set of predicates and rules.

## 7   Conclusions

This paper presented an approach that led to a generic authorization module that supports arbitrary authorization models and can be easily extended. To accomplish this, a rule-based system was used to map authorization models to rule sets and an inference engine processes the authorization requests. There are different authorization models for different application fields with different requirements. Usually, authorization modules limit themselves to the use of a certain specific authorization model and a later change or modification of the model consequently results in a substantial effort for revising the software architecture. Rule-based systems are well suited to represent authorization models by mapping their elements and relations to facts and rules, which can be modified in a flexible manner. The implementation of the popular RBAC and ABAC (attribute-based access control) models with our approach was demonstrated, giving the deployment in a J2EE/web service scenario as a usage scenario. This scenario was chosen, because it also demonstrates how flexibility and transparency can be reached in conjunction with other state-of-the-art mechanisms.

Future work will elaborate on more integrative tasks. We will investigate different models, additional constraints, delegation, and trust, as well as the environment as an attribute source. We will also examine the semantics of exchanged attributes in web service scenarios.

# References

1. Adam, N.R., Atluri, V., Bertino, E., Ferrari, E.: A Content-based Authorization Model for Digital Libraries. IEEE Transactions on Knowledge and Data Engineering, Volume 14, Number 2, March/April 2002.
2. Bertino, E., Catania, B., Ferrari, E., Perlasca, P.: A Logical Framework for Reasoning about Access Control Models. In: ACM Transactions on Information and System Security, Volume 6, Number 1, pp. 71-127, Februar 2003.
3. Ferraiolo, D.F., Sandhu, R., Gavrila, S., Kuhn, D., and Chandramouli, R.: Proposed NIST Standard for Role-based Access Control. In: ACM Transactions on Information and Systems Security, Volume 4, Number 3, August 2001.
4. Ferrari, E., Adam, N.R., Atluri, V., Bertino, E., Capuozzo, U.: An Authorization System for Digital Libraries. In: VLDB Journal, Volume 11, Number 1, 2002.
5. Enterprise JavaBeans 3.0. Java Specification Request 220 Proposed Final Draft, http://jcp.org/aboutJava/communityprocess/pfd/jsr220/index.html
6. Kagal, L., Finin, T., Joshi, A.: A Policy Based Approach to Security for the Semantic Web. In: Proc. 2nd International Semantic Web Conference (ISWC 2003), Sanibel Island, FL, October 2003.
7. OASIS eXtensible Access Control Markup Language v2.0 (XACML). http://docs.oasis-open.org/xacml/2.0/access_control-xacml-2.0-core-spec-os.pdf
8. Park, J., Sandhu, R.: The UCONABC Usage Control Model. In: ACM Transactions on Information Systems Security, Volume 7, Number 1, pp. 128-174, February 2004.
9. Priebe, T., Fernandez, E.B., Mehlau, J.I., Pernul, G.: A Pattern System for Access Control. In: Proc. 18th Annual IFIP WG 11.3 Working Conference on Data and Application Security, Sitges, Spain, July 2004.
10. Priebe, T., Dobmeier, W., Muschall, B., Pernul, G.: ABAC - Ein Referenzmodell für attributbasierte Zugriffskontrolle. In: Proc. 2. Jahrestagung Fachbereich Sicherheit der Gesellschaft für Informatik (Sicherheit 2005), Regensburg, Germany, April 2005.
11. Uszok, A. et. al.: KAoS Policy and Domain Services: Toward a Description-Logic Approach to Policy Representation, Deconfliction and Enforcement. In: Proc. 4th IEEE International Workshop on Policies for Distributed Systems and Networks (POLICY 2003), Comersee, Italy, June 2003.
12. Dridi, F., Fischer, M., Pernul, G.: CSAP – An Adaptable Security Module for the E-government System Webocrat. In: Proc. of the 18th IFIP International Information Security Conference (SEC 2003), Athens, Greece, May 2003.
13. Osborn, S., Sandhu, R., Munawar, Q.: Configuring Role-based Access Control to enforce Mandatory and Discretionary Access Control Policies In: ACM Transactions on Information and System Security (TISSEC), volume 3, pages 85-106, 2000

# Aspect-Oriented Risk Driven Development
# of Secure Applications

Geri Georg[1], Siv Hilde Houmb[2], and Indrakshi Ray[1]

[1] Computer Science Department
Colorado State University
Fort Collins, Colorado, USA
{georg, iray}@cs.colostate.edu
[2] Computer Science Department
Norwegian University of Science and Technology
Trondheim, Norway
sivhoumb@idi.ntnu.no

**Abstract.** Security breaches seldom occur because of faulty security mechanisms. Often times, security mechanisms are incorrectly incorporated in an application which allows them to be bypassed resulting in a security breach. Methodologies are needed for incorporating security mechanisms in an application and assessing whether the resulting system is indeed secure. We propose one such methodology for designing secure applications. We begin by identifying the assets in the application that need protection. We then find the kinds of attacks that are typical for such applications. We show how to evaluate the application against such attacks. If the results are unacceptable, that is, they pose a high security risk, then some security mechanism must be incorporated into the application. We illustrate how this can be done and show how the resulting system can be evaluated to give assurance that it is resilient to the given attack.

## 1  Introduction

In the commercial world, designing secure applications is impacted by various parameters, such as time-to-market, cost and effort involved. The presence of these constraints often prevents the development of applications which are adequately secure. We propose a risk driven development approach for designing such applications. While designing an application one needs to understand the threats in the current design and the risks associated with those threats. If the risks are unacceptably high, the application must be redesigned. Redesigning the application means methodically incorporating security mechanisms into the application and evaluating whether the resulting application is adequately secure.

Security mechanisms are solutions to security problems in applications. For example, encrypting information is a solution to prevent malicious attackers from eavesdropping on sensitive information sent in clear-text. However, there might be several mechanisms to solve one problem. This implies that we need to evaluate to what extent the different mechanisms solve the problem for a given application and what is the cost associated with each. Security and risk management standards [1,2,6] were developed to aid secure systems development. Such standards often require extensive amount of work and

E. Damiani and P. Liu (Eds.): Data and Applications Security 2006, LNCS 4127, pp. 282–296, 2006.
© IFIP International Federation for Information Processing 2006

also include other activities that are necessary for evaluating security mechanisms. In this paper, our goal is to complement the above mentioned work on standards and show how to assess whether an application is indeed secure when a particular security mechanism has been incorporated. This is important because often the security mechanisms designed to thwart attacks are adequate; yet security breaches still occur because the security mechanisms are often bypassed in an application.

Our approach begins by specifying the *primary model* which represents the application functionality. The items that need protection are identified as *assets*. The attacks on the application are then identified and modeled. The *attack model* is then composed with the primary model to produce the *misuse model*. The misuse model illustrates the degree to which the application can be compromised and the risk posed by the attack. If the risk is unacceptable, some security mechanism must be incorporated into the application. The model of the security mechanism is then methodically composed with the application. The result, which we refer to as the *security treated model*, represents the application in which the security has been incorporated. Finally, we show how the security treated model can be analyzed to give assurance that the application is indeed resilient to the given attack.

Our approach is based on aspect-oriented modeling techniques. Complex software is not developed as a monolithic unit but is decomposed into modules on the basis of functionality. An attack is not confined to one module of the application but impacts several of the modules. Similarly, a security mechanism will impact multiple modules of the application. Modeling security mechanisms and attack models as aspects have several benefits - it allows the attacks and the mechanisms to be understood in isolation, which makes it easier to manage and change these models. Once security mechanisms or attack models are represented as aspects, then techniques for composing aspects with the primary model can be used to understand the effect of the attack or the effect of security mechanism on the application.

The rest of the paper is organized as follows. Section 2 describes the e-commerce system which we use to illustrate our methodology. Section 3 gives an example attack and shows how the attack can be represented as an aspect. This section also describes how to generate the misuse model from which we we can identify the impact of the attack on our example application. Section 4 shows how the security mechanism designed to thwart the given attack can be represented as an aspect and how this mechanism can be integrated with the application. It also shows how the resulting system can be analyzed to give assurance that it is indeed resilient to the attack. Section 5 discusses some related work. Section 6 concludes the paper with some pointers to future directions.

## 2   Example E-Commerce System

We illustrate the reasoning about security risk mitigation with the login service of an e-commerce platform. The ACTIVE e-commerce platform provides services for electronic purchasing of goods over the Internet. The platform was developed initially for the purchase of medical equipment, although it is generalized to provide services for any kind of goods. (For details, please see T. Dimitrakos et. al [2]). ACTIVE is a general purchase platform that can host a variety of electronic stores for vendors. The infrastructure consists of a web server running Microsoft Internet Information Server (IIS), a Java application server (Allaire JSP Engine) and a Microsoft SQL server running RDBMS. The communication between the application server and the database is handled using the JDBC protocol.

There are two types of consumer users in the ACTIVE system, *visitors* and *registered* users. Personalized shopping services are only available to registered users, but all users can browse and purchase items from ACTIVE. In addition, visitors cannot add any personal information to the system that will be retained for future shopping sessions.

The IST EU-project CORAS (for details see CORAS project report [7]) performed three risk assessments of ACTIVE in the period 2000-2003. The project looked into security risks of the user authentication mechanism, secure payment mechanism, and the agent negotiation mechanisms of ACTIVE. The example in this paper concentrates on the result from the risk assessment of the user authentication mechanism, and its impact on login services.

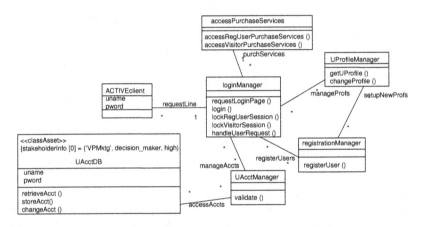

**Fig. 1.** Primary model (E-commerce login service) static diagram

We begin by creating a static diagram of the login service components. This diagram is shown in Figure 1. (We have simplified the diagram to only include model elements directly affected by the attack and its treatment.) There are several classes that play a part in the login process. A user wishing to login to the e-commerce system runs an *ACTIVEclient* in a web browser on their local machine. The browser communicates with a login manager (*loginManager*) which is located on a server across the Internet. The login manager has several related classes. An account manager (*UAcctManager*) and the associated database (*UAcctDB*) are used to authenticate users using a simple user name and password provided by the client web browser. A profile manager (*UProfile-Manager*) is used to keep track of personalized shopping information. A registration manager (*registrationManager*) is used to allow a visitor to become a registered user and a purchase service class (*accessPurchaseServices*) is used to access the different shopping services.

Risk-driven development (RDD) UML profile elements are also shown in Figure 1. These profile elements are used to annotate UML diagrams with additional information useful in risk treatment trade-off analysis. For example, the <<classAsset>> stereo-type is used to indicate that the *UAcctDB* class is an asset in the system. A RDD profile tag (stakeholder information) is associated with the asset. Stakeholder information is an array containing the name of the stakeholder ("VPMktg" in this case), the role of the stakeholder (decision maker), and the value the stakeholder places on the asset (in this case, extremely high value).

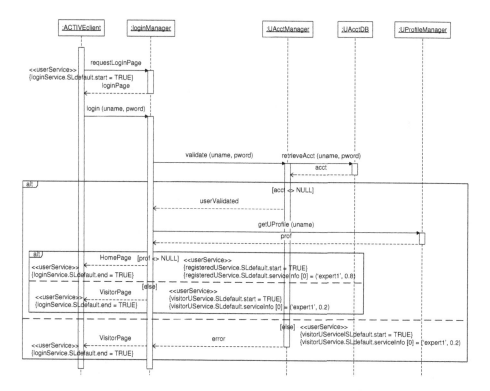

**Fig. 2.** Primary model (E-commerce login service) sequence diagram

The login sequence is shown in Figure 2. The *registrationManager* and *accessPurchaseServices* classes are not shown in this figure since they are classes whose services are used after a user has entered the system as a registered user or a visitor.

Figure 2 shows the sequence for a login operation. First, a user, through a web browser (*ACTIVEclient*), requests a login page from the e-commerce system by sending *requestLoginPage* to *loginManager*. *loginManager* responds with *loginPage*. The user enters his unique user name (*uname*) and password (*pword*), and this information is sent to *loginManager*. The server then sends *validate* message to *UAcctManager*. The *UAcctManager* sends an *error* message to the *loginManager* if the user account does not exist or cannot be validated. Otherwise *userValidated* message is returned to the server. If the user login information is valid, the *loginManager* sends *getUProfile* message to *UProfileManager*. The *UProfileManager* retrieves the user's *profile* and sends it to the *loginManager.* Using this information the *loginManager* creates an appropriate home page which is returned to the user's web browser. If the user's login information could not be validated, or the user's profile could not be obtained, a visitor page is returned to the browser. Although this is the end of the login sequence, the user can either continue as a visitor, or register as a new user in the e-commerce system.

In this example, our requirements are that users should have access to the e-commerce system and non-users should be allowed access as visitors. Consequently, we add several RDD profile elements in the login service sequence. The first defines the start of the login service with the stereotype <<userService>>, and the associated tag {*loginService.SLdefault.start = TRUE* }. This service begins when the *ACTIVEclient* sends a *requestLoginPage* message to the *loginManager*. Another set of user service beginning tags occurs when *loginManager* returns either a *HomePage* (*registeredUSer-vice*) or a *VisitorPage* (*visitorUService*) to the *ACTIVEclient*. These other user services have service information associated with them, namely the probability that they will be achieved, and the source of that information. In this example, "expert1" supplied the information, but there can be multiple sources of such information, including running system data from a honeypot. In this example, the probability of a user being registered is higher than that of a user being a visitor. Note that the visitor user service is achieved under two circumstances: 1) if the user name and password cannot be validated, and 2) if the user profile information cannot be obtained. Finally, RDD profile elements identify the points in the sequence when the login service has been completed, namely, at the end of the message when the login manager returns *HomePage* or *VisitorPage* to the *ACTIVEclient*. Note that the messages in the sequence diagram all have an explicit return message. This is required to be able to compose sequence diagrams according to our composition mechanism.

## 3    The Man-in-the-Middle Attack

The risk assessments performed as part of the CORAS project identified the login process as being vulnerable to man-in-the-middle attacks. During this kind of attack user names and passwords can be intercepted by an attacker, and used at later times to impersonate a valid user.

Each attack in our model is an aspect because an attack is not confined to one specific module of the application but impacts the entire application. We propose to represent those attacks that are not confined to one specific application as a generic aspect. Generic aspects are represented as patterns which are described using UML templates. These templates must be instantiated for each application to obtain a *context-specific attack model*.

In this section, we show how the man-in-the-middle attack can be represented as a *generic aspect*. Messages between a requestor and authenticator are intercepted by an attacker. This can only occur if all messages flow through the attacker and not through a direct association between the requestor and authenticator. The attacker either intercepts the message intended for the server, or the attacker eavesdrops on the communication medium between the browser and the server. In the first case, the attacker must pose as the server so that the message intended for the server really gets sent to the attacker.

The attacker then relays messages between the client browser and the server until the private information has been obtained by the attacker. In the second case the attacker does not impersonate the server, but rather just eavesdrops on the message flow. The attacker may not obtain all of the messages flowing between the client and server, but simply sample messages in the hopes of obtaining information. We use the first type of man-in-the-middle attack in this paper since the attacker can actually participate in complex protocols, and change messages if desired before passing them on to the client or server.

Due to space constraints, we not not show the attack model, but rather describe it. The attack model is shown as part of the misuse model described in the next section.

The generic attack model describes two service levels for the user service. The first is the default service level (indicated by *SL0*) which is the "best" level of service. This level of service is based on the physical connection. The second level of service described is level X (denoted by *SLX*), which means that either a non-user has gained access to the system, or that users have lost access to system services (that is, the system has gone down). In short, the service level X means that the system has been compromised. In addition, a requestor, authenticator, and an attacker must all be connected to the same network to enable a man-in-the-middle attack.

The annotations for the misuse service include service information such as that included for the user services in the primary login sequence, but they also contain other information. Misuse service information consists of the source of the information, the probability that the service level will be achieved, the average time it takes to achieve the service level (MTTM), the average effort it takes (METM), and the impact on asset value (IV). Probability information can either be supplied by an expert, based on experience with similar systems, or by a honeypot system that logs actual events. Different generic diagram with different probabilities, values of MTTM, METM, and IV can be created for cases where the connection is an Internet, LAN, or some other type of connection.

## 3.1  Generating the Misuse Model

In order to understand the impact the man-in-the-middle attack has on the e-commerce application, we need to generate the misuse model. The misuse model will indicate how much the primary model can be compromised by the attack. Two steps are needed to generate the misuse model:

1. Instantiate the generic attack aspect to obtain the context-specific attack aspect.
2. Compose the context-specific attack aspect with the primary model to obtain the misuse model.

**Instantiating the Generic Aspect:** The generic aspect is application-independent. It is specified using UML templates. These templates must be instantiated for a given application. This instantiation is done by binding names in the generic aspect to those in the primary model. Elements present in the generic aspect that do not have a counterpart in the primary model must also be instantiated. The instantiation of the generic aspect will be referred to as a *context-specific aspect*. For the e-commerce example, a context-spceific aspect is obtained by making the *ACTIVEclient* the requestor of an authentication, the *loginManager* the authenticator, and the login message the authentication request. The user service of interest is the login service.

**Obtaining the misuse model:** The context-specific aspect must be composed with the primary model to obtain the *misuse model*. The first step is to compose the class diagrams of the attack and primary models. For lack of space, we do not show the class diagram of the attack model or the composition process. The result from this composition is the class diagram of the misuse model shown in Figure 3. The misuse class diagram differs from the primary model class diagram in the following ways: (i) an *attacker* class is added, (ii) an association between *attacker* and *ACTIVEclient* is added, (iii) an association between *attacker* and *loginManager* is added, and (iv) direct association between the *ACTIVEclient* and *loginManager* is deleted because all communications now go through the attacker class.

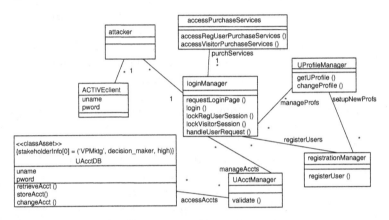

**Fig. 3.** Misuse model (primary model + man-in-the-middle attack) static diagram

The sequence diagrams describe the behavior of the primary model and the man-in-the-middle attack. The sequence diagrams must also be composed. The composition must be performed such that important properties of each model are preserved. Here again, we do not describe the mechanics of the composition process. The composed sequence diagram will serve to illustrate how much the primary model can be compromised.

The properties identified for the login service sequence that need to be preserved in this composition process are: (1) an application session is created, (2) users must be validated, (3) registered users receive a home page with profile information, and (4) unregistered users receive a visitor page. The properties that need to be preserved from the man-in-the-middle misuse are: (1) all messages from the client to the server through the duration of the session must pass through the attacker, (2) an authenticated session returned to the attacker indicates that the SLX service level has been achieved (3), no session returned to the attacker indicates that the SLX service level has not been achieved. The resulting composed sequence diagram is shown in Figure 4.

The main change in this sequence diagram from that given in Figure 2 is that an attacker lifeline has been inserted and all communication between the *ACTIVEclient* and

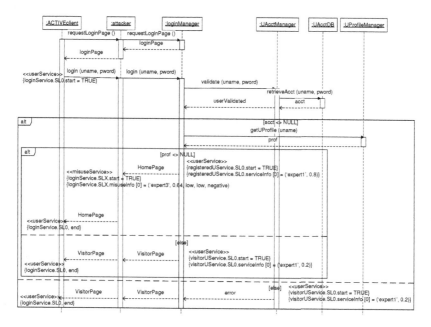

**Fig. 4.** Misuse model (primary + man-in-the-middle) sequence diagram

the *loginManager* go through *attacker*. The other change is in the probability associated with the SLX service level of the login service. This probability has been changed to reflect that the original probability is now included in an alternative sequence whose probability is 0.8 (the probability that the user profile exists). The value is calculated as part of the composition, by multiplying the outermost probability by the inner probability to obtain the new value of the inner probability.

**3.2  Evaluating the Impact of Attack on the Application**

The misuse model must be analyzed to determine the impact the attack can have on the primary model. The login service composed with the man-in-the-middle attack thus contains some properties that are undesirable. Paramount is the achievement of the SLX service level. The presence of the SLX service level means that some user service has been made available to persons not authorized to use it. Specifically in this example, an attacker gains knowledge of the user account login information, *uname* and *pword*. The class containing these items has been tagged as an asset in the primary static diagram, with a value that is "extremely_high". Once the *HomePage* message is returned to the attacker, the value of this asset has been decreased, as is indicated by the RDD tag stating that the impact on asset value is "negative". The ability of the attacker to extract these secrets can be formally analysed using tool support of the formal security analysis techniques developed by Jürjens [17]. To counter this attack, some security mechanisms must be incorporated with the application. The mechanism that we choose is TLS Authentication that is described next. We chose to use TLS since it is a follow-on to SSL (Secure Sockets Layer), which is a commonly available authentication mechanism used in web applications. Other mechanisms could also be used to provide a stronger authentication mechanim for the application.

## 4   Incorporating TLS Authentication in the Application

The security properties of integrity and confidentiality are compromised with the man-in-the-middle attack, so mechanisms that address integrity and confidentiality are potential risk treatments. We demonstrate the use of transport layer security (TLS) [10] to mitigate the man-in-the-middle attack risk. TLS is based on passing certificates between a client and server for authentication purposes, and to establish secret session keys for the encryption of all subsequent messages. In this paper, we use the version of TLS proposed by Jürjens [17]. The sequence of the TLS mechanism is shown as a generic aspect diagram in Figure 5.

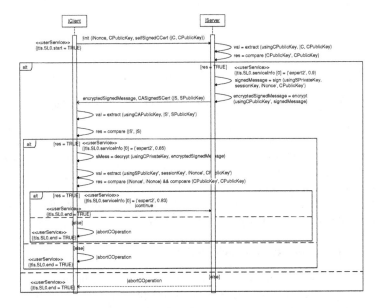

**Fig. 5.** Generic aspect of TLS mechanism sequence diagram

The TLS generic aspect contains two main classes: |*Client* and |*Server*. For this example, certificate creation and certificate authority public keys are assumed to be obtained in a secure manner. The client must have the certificate authority's public key, and the server must have a certificate, signed by the certificate authority (CA), of its name and public key. The notation in Figure 5 includes the concept of sent and received values, using a primed (') sent value name to indicate a value that has been received. Other assumptions include the fact that both nonces (unique identifier numbers) and session keys must change each time the protocol is initiated.

A TLS sequence begins with |*Client* sending an *init* message that contains a nonce (*iNonce*), its public key (*CPublicKey*), and a self-signed certificate containing its name and its public key (*selfSignedCCert(|C, CPublicKey)*). When |*Server* receives this message, it extracts the client name and public key using the client public key sent in the message (shown as *extract(usingCPublicKey, |C, CPublicKey)* in Figure 5). It checks to make sure that the public key in the signed portion of the message is the same as the public key sent in the unsigned portion of the message. If not, the entire operation is aborted.

If the client public keys match, the server creates a message containing the session key that needs to be used for encryption once the connection is complete, the nonce received in the original client message, and the client public key. This message is then signed using the server's private key. This signed message is then encrypted using the client's public key. The result, along with the server's certificate (signed by a trusted certificate authority) is sent to the client in a respond message. This is message labeled *encryptedSignedMessage, CASignedSCert(S,SPublicKey)* in Figure 5.

The client first extracts the server name and public key using the certificate authority's public key. If the name of the server in the message (|*S'*) matches the name of the server (|*S*) to which the original init message was sent, the protocol proceeds. Otherwise the client aborts the operation. The encrypted portion of the message is decrypted using the client private key (*CPrivateKey*), and the items in the resulting signed message are extracted using the server's public key. The received nonce value (*iNonce*) in the signed message is compared to the nonce originally sent by the client (*iNonce'*), and the client public key (*CPublicKey*) in the signed message is compared to the client's public key (*CPublicKey'*). If either of these items does not match, this indicates that an attack on the communication has occurred, and the client aborts the operation. If the items match, then the communication path is secure, and the client can encrypt its secrets using the session key and transmit them to the server.

### 4.1   Generating the Security Treated Primary Model

The sequence diagram in Figure 5 can be composed with the e-commerce sequence diagram in Figure 2 in order to add TLS capabilities to the e-commerce system. Similarly, the static portion of the aspect model can be composed with the static diagram of the login service, although the result of this composition is not discussed in this paper.

To compose the sequence diagrams, we use the same method as we used to compose the primary sequence with the man-in-the-middle attack sequence. The TLS aspect, specified in template form, must be instantiated for the e-commerce application. This instantiation is done with the following bindings: (i) |*Client* in TLS is bound to *AC-TIVEclient* in the e-commerce application, and (ii) |*Server* is bound to *loginManager*.

Properties in the login service sequence and in the TLS sequence are identified, and the properties that need to be preserved in the composed sequence are also identified. The resulting composed sequence diagram is shown in Figure 6.

The sequence shown in Figure 6 begins as the sequence did in Figure 2, with the *AC-TIVEclient* requesting a login page from the *loginManager*. The *loginManager* responds with *loginPage*. Now the TLS sequence is inserted; instead of *ACTIVEclient* sending a login message with a user name (*uname*) and password (*pword*), a different login message is sent. This new login message contains a nonce (*iNonce*), the user's public key (*CPublicKey*), and a self-signed certificate containing the user name and user's public key (*selfSignedCCert(uname, CPublicKey)*). The logic for the TLS handshake

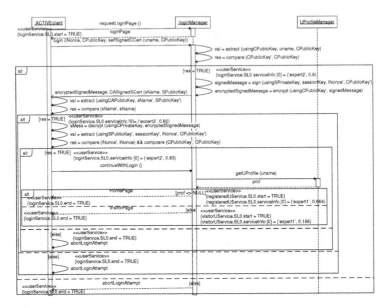

**Fig. 6.** Security treated model (primary model + TLS) sequence diagram

continues as in the TLS aspect model, with model element name changes per the bindings discussed above. Once the TLS handshake completes successfully, the *ACTIVEclient* sends a continue message to *loginManager*, which in turn causes the *loginManager* to get personal profile information (if it exists), and a *HomePage* is sent back to the user via *ACTIVEclient*. If the profile information does not exist, a *VisitorPage* is sent back to the user. Note that the probabilities of the *registeredUService* and *visitorUService* have been changed as was discussed in the previous composition section to reflect the probability that the third test is successful (0.83 multiplied by 0.8 and 0.2 respectively). We can informally argue that the properties identified for each model have been preserved in the composed model.

## 4.2   Analyzing the Security Treated Primary Model

Once the security mechanisms have been incorporated into the primary model, we need to verify whether the given attack is prevented in this new model. That is, we need to determine whether the TLS authentication adequately protects the application from the man-in-the-middle attack. We can reason about the effective security by composing the man-in-the-middle aspect with the security treated primary model.

The models are composed as before and the properties that need to be preserved in the security treated model are identified and used to create the composed sequence diagram.

Figure 7 shows the sequence when the man-in-the-middle attack is composed with the system protected by the TLS mechanism. We can reason informally about the composed sequence as follows. First, the properties identified as part of the composition are preserved in the composed sequence. Next, consider the *login* message parameters

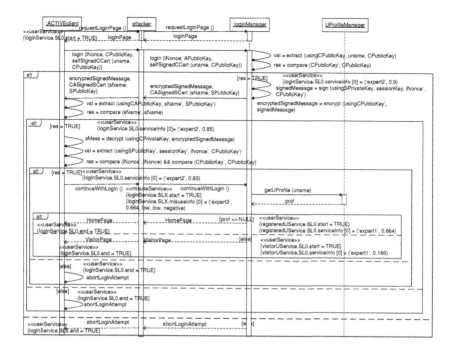

**Fig. 7.** Misuse model (security treated model + man-in-the-middle) sequence diagram

between the *ACTIVEclient* and *attacker* and between the *attacker* and *loginManager*. The *attacker* must replace the *ACTIVEclient* public key (*CPublicKey*) with the attacker's own public key. This must be done so that any messages from the *loginManager* that have been encrypted using the "client" public key are encrypted with the attacker's public key. This encryption means that the attacker can decrypt them. Since the attacker is posing as the *ACTIVEclient*, the client's certificate must be changed to include the client user name and the attacker public key. The result is that the login message parameters change to replace the client's public key with the attacker's public key, *APublicKey*. Once the *loginManager* receives this message, it uses the public key in the message to extract the name and public key in the certificate.

Since the public key in the message is the one used to encrypt the certificate, the first test comparison will work. Next the *loginManager* creates a signed message containing the attacker's public key, and encrypts it using that same public key. This message and the *loginManager's* CA-signed certificate is sent to the attacker, which decrypts the signed message with its private key. The signed message from the server is then encrypted with the *ACTIVEclient's* public key, and is sent to the *ACTIVEclient*, along with the server's official certificate from the CA.

The *ACTIVEclient* first extracts the server name and public key from the CA certificate using the CA public key. A comparison is made between the server name the *ACTIVEclient* has and the server name in the certificate. This test will work. Next, the *ACTIVEclient* decrypts the signed message from the *loginManager* using its private key. It then compares the message nonce included in that message with the one it originally sent, and the client public key included in that message with its own public key. This test will fail because the client key included in the signed message from the *loginManager* is that of the attacker. Therefore the sequence will always move to the third test failure alternative where the *abortLoginAttempt* message will be returned to the user of *ACTIVEclient* and the sequence ends. Thus, the treatment prevents the attack, and consequently the undesirable properties it allows, from occurring.

## 5   Related Work

Standards such as the ISO 15408 Common Criteria for Information Technology Security Evaluation [6] can help developers focus on processes and development activities that lead to more secure systems. However, these standards only address the development activities of the system, not its operational security. They are also based on assessment by certified assessors. Trade-off techniques such as Architecture Trade-off Analysis Method (ATAM) [19] and Cost Benefit Analysis Method (CBAM) [18] operate at an architectural level, and also require experienced assessors. Any of these assessments require a strong resource commitment on the part of the organization that uses them. Risk identification, assessment, and management are the targets of the CCTA Risk Analysis and Management Methodology (CRAMM) [3] and CORAS [7,21] frameworks. CORAS makes use of multiple standards, including the Australian/New Zealand Standard for Risk Management [1], ISO/IEC 17799-1: Code of Practice for Information Security Management [13] and ISO/IEC 13335: Information technology – guidelines for management of IT security [14]. CORAS adapts the asset-driven structured approach in CRAMM, and uses model-based risk assessment in integrated system development processes. Our Aspect-Oriented Risk Driven Development (AORDD) framework [12,11] makes use of the CORAS processes and the asset-driven approach of CRAMM. The analysis described in this paper is a part of the AORDD framework. It is lightweight in that there is no need for a certified assessor, and it also provides information that is directed to a single risk treatment, rather than to an overall system. Unlike the process-targeted frameworks and standards, it deals with system operation.

The aspect-oriented techniques we use are part of our on-going AOM research, where aspects are UML templates that are instantiated in the context of a system prior to composition (see France et al. [8,9] and Straw et al. [22] for details on the AOM notations and composition). Jacobson [15,16] and Kiczales [20] describe AOM techniques that require that an aspect contains information regarding where and how it will be composed with a system model. Our generic aspects are free of this information and thus can be reused in multiple systems by instantiating them in different contexts. Clarke et al. [4,5] describe AOM composition techniques that augment or replace model elements and behavior. Our composition also allows elements and behavior to be deleted from a composition, or to be interleaved with other behavior and elements. The latter capability has been particularly useful in our AORDD work with security risk treatments.

## 6   Conclusion

In this paper, we propose a methodology for designing secure applications. We identify the assets in the application that need protection. We then find the kinds of attacks that are typical for such applications, based on risk assessments that are beyond the scope of this paper. We show how to evaluate the application against such attacks. If the results of this evaluation indicate that the assets may be compromised, then some security mechanism must be incorporated into the application. Our focus is therefore on evaluating the ability of security mechanisms to protect against previously identified risks rather than on detecting new vulnerabilities. We illustrate how this can be done and show how the resulting system can be evaluated to give assurance that it is resilient to the given attack. A lot of work remains to be done. In this paper, all our analysis was done manually without any tool support. In future, we plan to investigate how this analysis can be automated to some extent. Specifically, we will look at how existing theorem-provers and model-checkers can aid this process.

## Acknowledgements

This work was partially supported by AFOSR under Award No. FA9550-04-1-0102.

## References

1. Australian/New Zealand Standards. AS/NZS 4360:2004 Risk Management, 2004.
2. Australian/New Zealand Standards. HB 436:2004 Risk Management Guidelines – Companion to AS/NZS 4360:2004, 2004.
3. B. Barber and J. Davey. The Use of the CCTA Risk Analysis and Management Methodology CRAMM in Health Information Systems. In K.C. Lun, P. Degoulet, T.E. Piemme, and O. Rienhoff, editors, *Proceedings of MEDINFO'92*, pages 1589–1593. North Holland Publishing Co, Amsterdam, 1992.
4. S. Clarke. Extending standard uml with model composition semantics. *Science of Computer Programming*, 44(1):71–100, 2002.
5. S. Clarke and E. Banaissad. *Aspect-oriented analysis and design.* Addison-Wesley Professional, Boston, 2005.
6. ISO 15408:1999 Common Criteria for Information Technology Security Evaluation. Version 2.1, CCIMB–99–031, CCIMB-99-032, CCIMB-99-033, August 1999.
7. CORAS (2000–2003). IST-2000-25031 CORAS: A Platform for risk analysis of security critical systems. http://sourceforge.net/projects/coras, Accessed 18 February 2006.
8. R. France, D.-K. Dim, S. Ghosh, and E. Song. A UML-based pattern specification technique. *IEEE Transactions on Software Engineering*, 3(30):193–206, 2004.
9. R. France, I. Ray, G. Georg, and S. Ghosh. Aspect–oriented approach to design modeling. *IEE Proceedings on Software*, 4(151):173–185, 2004.
10. TLS: Network Working Group. The TLS Protocol Version 1.0, RFC 2246, January 1999.
11. S. H. Houmb, G. Georg, R. France, J. Bieman, and J. Jürjens. Cost-benefit trade-off analysis using bbn for aspect-oriented risk-driven development. In *Proceedings of Tenth IEEE International Conference on Engineering of Complex Computer Systems (ICECCS 2005)*, pages 195–204, June 2005.
12. S.H. Houmb and G. Georg. The Aspect-Oriented Risk-Driven Development (AORDD) Framework. In O. Benediktsson et al., editor, *Proceedings of the International Conference on Software Development (SWDC–REX)*, volume SWDC–REX Conference Proceedings, pages 81–91, Reykjavik, Iceland, 2005. Gutenberg.
13. International Organization for Standardization (ISO/IEC). ISO/IEC 17799:2000 Information technology – Code of Practice for information security management, 2000.

14. International Organization for Standardization (ISO/IEC). ISO/IEC TR 13335:2001 Information technology – Guidelines for management of IT Security, 2001.
15. I. Jacobson. Case for aspects – Part I. *Software Development Magazine*, pages 32–37, October 2003.
16. I. Jacobson. Case for aspects – Part II. *Software Development Magazine*, pages 42–48, November 2003.
17. J. Jürjens. *Secure Systems Development with UML*. Springer, Berlin Heidelberg, New York, 2005.
18. R. Kasman, J. Asundi, and M. Klein. Making architecture design decisions: an economic approachn. Technical report CMU/SEI-2002-TR-035, CMU/SEI, http://www.sei.cmu.edu/pub/documents/02.reorts/pdf/02tr03.pdf, 2002.
19. R. Kazman, M. Klein, and P. Clements. Atam: method for architecture evaluation. Technical report CMU/SEI-2000-TR-004, CMU/SEI, http://www.sei.cmu.edu/pub/document/00.reports/pdf/00tr004.pdf, 2000.
20. G. Kiczales, E. Hilsdale, J. Hugunin, M. Kersten, J. Palm, and W. Griswold. Getting stared with aspectj. *Communications of the ACM*, 10(44):59–65, 2001.
21. K. Stølen, F. den Braber, T. Dimitrakos, R. Fredriksen, B. A. Gran, S. H. Houmb, Y. C. Stamatiou, and J. Ø. Aagedal. Model–based risk assessment in a component-based software engineering process: The CORAS approach to identify security risks. In Franck Barbier, editor, *Business Component-Based Software Engineering*, pages 189–207. Kluwer, 2002. ISBN: 1–4020–7207–4.
22. G. Straw, G. Georg, E. Song, S. Ghosh, R. France, and J. Bieman. Model composition directives. In T. Baar, A. Strohmeier, A. Moreira, and S Mellor, editors, *UML*, volume 3273 of *Lecture Notes in Computer Science*, pages 84–97. Springer, 2004.

# From Business Process Choreography to Authorization Policies

Philip Robinson[1], Florian Kerschbaum[1], and Andreas Schaad[2]

[1] SAP Research, Karlsruhe, Germany
philip.robinson@sap.com
florian.kerschbaum@sap.com
[2] SAP Research, Sophia Antipolis, France
andreas.schaad@sap.com

**Abstract.** A choreography specifies the interactions between the resources of multiple collaborating parties at design time. The runtime management of authorization policies in order to support such a specification is however tedious for administrators to manually handle. By compiling the choreography into enhanced authorization policies, we are able to automatically derive the minimal authorizations required for collaboration, as well as enable and disable the authorizations in a just-in-time manner that matches the control flow described in the choreography. We have evaluated the advantage of this utility in a collaborative engineering scenario.

## 1 Introduction

We present a system architecture and algorithm for automatically generating, installing and enforcing authorization policies that correspond to an agreed specification of inter-organizational collaboration. The planning and execution of inter-organization collaboration is known as *business process choreography* [1,7,16], with the specification document being referred to as a *choreography description*. From a choreography description we were able to automatically derive the corresponding authorization policies. Moreover, authorizations (which are determined based on authorization policies) are enabled only for the duration of their corresponding interactions in the running collaborative business process. We ensure that an organization is quickly prepared to fulfill its obligations in a collaborative business process, while obeying the least privileges principle. In collaborative business there is a need to reduce both the risk of losing market credibility, due to slow response, and the risk of exposing valuable information. This challenge is presented in collaborative engineering, where multiple organizations collaborate on a short term basis within a specific project, in order to exchange design objectives, detect and resolve conflicts, as well as generate new ideas and design options [2]. In order to support collaborative business processes such as collaborative engineering, new methodologies, specification languages and tools [1,7,10,16] are being produced, alongside which we position and evaluate our work.

E. Damiani and P. Liu (Eds.): Data and Applications Security 2006, LNCS 4127, pp. 297–309, 2006.

The paper continues with a preliminary introduction to business process choreography, authorization and collaborative engineering, outlining the problem domain. Secondly, we present the system architecture, elements and component interactions for deriving authorization policies from a choreography description. This is followed by the details of the authorization policy generation algorithm, and a discussion of its merits. We conclude with a discussion of the solution and related work.

## 2  Preliminaries

### 2.1  Business Process Choreography

Business process choreography is the description of how multiple organizations coordinate their activities in a collaborative business process. A choreography may have been agreed to, but it is then the job of individual organizations to provide authorized access to the systems and resources that will do the actual specified work. The basic building blocks of a choreography are interactions, such as web service invocations across organizations, and internal actions within one organization. [16] explains this as a three stage process:

1. create a common understanding of the inter-organizational workflow (or collaborative business process) by specifying a shared public workflow,
2. partition the public workflow over the organizations involved, and
3. for each organization, create a private workflow which is a subclass of the respective part of the public workflow.

The choreography description therefore defines the public workflow, which acts as a means of combining the private workflows of multiple organizations into one global control-flow.

The Web Services Choreography Description Language (WS-CDL) [7] is an emerging, XML-based standard for describing message-based interactions between web services. We however only discuss the elements that were important for generating authorization policies. For a more complete introduction to WS-CDL see [1,7]. WS-CDL offers an element for encoding a web service call, referred to as an <InterAction> element. This contains references to the source <roleType> and the receiver <roleType>. In addition the expected internal actions of participant organizations are denoted using the <SilentAction> and <NoAction> tags. As control-flow elements the WS-CDL specification offers sequential <Sequence>, parallel <Parallel>, branching <Choice> and looping <WorkUnit> composition, which we take into consideration when specifying dependencies between generated authorization policies.

### 2.2  Authorization and Access Control

Having described and agreed to a choreography, each collaborating organization still needs to provide the appropriate authorizations that allow the agreed interactions to be executed. Furthermore, authorizations should only be activated according to the control-flow of the choreography. An authorization is defined as a triple ⟨subject $s$, object $o$, action $a$⟩, stating that a subject $s$ can perform action $a$ on object $o$ [4,12]. Messages originating from a subject and targeted at an object are composed of a corresponding triple. Access control is then the process of intercepting every incoming message before it reaches its target, and determining whether or not the request can be granted [12]. The decision requires policies to be specified that consider the message plus the conditions under which it was received. A generic authorization policy is then specified as ⟨$s,o,a,q$⟩, where $q$ is a set of conditions that must evaluate to true in order for the ⟨$s,o,a$⟩ triple to be a valid authorization. A general architecture for access control therefore consists of a policy decision point (PDP), which makes the authorization decisions based on installed authorization policies, and a policy enforcement point (PEP), which intercepts all incoming messages and enforces the authorizations or denials resulting from policy decisions [12]. A message also consists of a triple ⟨$s,o,a$⟩, such that its authorization is evaluated according to a policy, whose ⟨$s,o,a$⟩ triple matches the corresponding elements of the message. In order for an authorization decision to be made, the PEP first authenticates the identity of $s$ in all intercepted messages, then forwards to the PDP. The PDP then makes decisions concerning if ⟨$s,o,a$⟩ is valid given $q$, a set of condition variables.

# 3    Collaborative Engineering

Having discussed the background of our work (choreography and authorization), we now consider this in the context of a specific application domain. We have selected collaborative engineering, as the issues of managing short-term, inter-organization control flow arise, along with the requirement to provide minimal access to sensitive documents and services. Collaborative engineering is a way in which multi-functional development teams coordinate their communication and work in order to improve the process of developing a new product. It involves different partners with different perspectives on the engineering tasks [2]. We draw an example from the aerospace engineering domain, as depicted in figure 1, where they use grid and web-service technology in order to share resources [3]. The engineering team partners, computational resources and data are not part of the same administrative domain. Therefore each organization maintains and administers its own PDP, PEP and services it provides, as well as the Policy Generation Component (PGC) introduced in section 4. Each partner has a right to protect access to the resources they own, yet must still maintain their obligations to complete the business process. The team partners involved are discussed with respect to their authorization and collaboration requirements:

- *Initiator*, in this case the Aircraft Company, specifies the overall requirements for the product to be designed during the project. The series of design documents need to be version controlled and accessed only for specific project tasks. Leaking the design documents could destroy the opportunity to gain a market or patent. The Initiator adds and removes partners in the

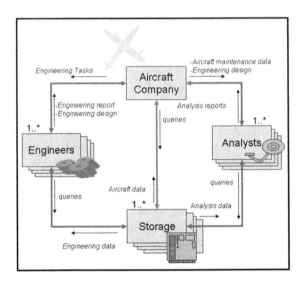

**Fig. 1.** Scenario for Collaborative Engineering in the Aerospace Domain

project based on their performance or changes in the environment (e.g. if a partner becomes a competitor).

– *Storage Providers* are contracted to store, version control and maintain access to large design documents, analysis reports and simulation data. A Storage Provider must ensure that access to shared resources does not violate the rules of the document owners nor the availability requirements of the contract.

– *Engineers* are contracted to provide models that meet the Initiator's requirements specification, using their own methods and tools. The Engineers may maintain models on their local machines or use the computational facilities of a Storage Provider.

– *Analysts* are contracted to provide models of the environment where the product is to be operational and therefore make predictions about how the final product will perform in a live environment. Their access is limited to very specific specification and design documents.

In order to coordinate the activities between the different specialist teams, a series of notifications and requests are interchanged, to which particular response actions occur. The notifications and requests are messages that state that an action is to be performed or an explicit attempt by a subject to perform an action on a resource such as read, write or delete. Coordination and authorization are critical throughout the lifetime of the project, with respect to confidentiality, availability and performance. For example, analysts should only be able to access design documents when a draft had been agreed in an earlier interaction, otherwise extra effort must be invested in organizational conflict analysis and resolution [2]. The partners may change during the lifetime of the project, such that the authorizations of old partners should be immediately removed. The required guarantees are that resources are available when they need to be available and only to whom they need be available.

# 4   System Architecture

The PDP and PEP components form the basic trusted computing base of our system architecture, but we introduce an additional component for authorization policy generation called the PGC. In addition to generating authorization policies, the PGC is also responsible for installing them on the PDP. Each of these components are assumed to be trusted, as there is no intermediate policy decision that intercepts their interactions and they are assumed to be in the same administrative domain. We do not cover the administration authorization model of these components in this paper.

- Policy Generation Component (PGC): interprets a choreography and generates authorization policies. In addition to the choreography (WS-CDL), the service description (WSDL) containing the end point references (EPRs) of the target objects, as well as the public key certificates (PKCs) of the selected parties in the choreography are received.
- Policy Enforcement Point (PEP): intercepts requests to the resources and extracts authorization queries of the form $\langle s, o, a \rangle$, authenticates the subject of the message $msg$ and queries a PDP for an authorization decision. Only authenticated and authorized messages $msg_{auth}$ are allowed to reach targeted resources. Typical examples of where PEP functionality is implemented are network routers, switches, firewalls, proxies, OS filesystem interfaces and database interfaces.
- Policy Decision Point (PDP): makes authorization decisions based on $\langle s, o, a, q \rangle$ policies that have been generated by a PGC. A PDP receives a triple $\langle s, o, a \rangle$ from the PEP and outputs either an authorization $msg_{grant}$ or denial message $msg_{deny}$.
- Resources: the objects to which access is requested, as agreed to in the choreography. We assume that there is a standard means of representing and exposing the interface to these resources as services, such as WSDL, but the issues of interoperability and interconnection are not discussed in the paper.

## 4.1   Component Interactions and Assumptions

Before describing the component interactions, there are some assumptions that we make with respect to a particular instance of the environment within which they interact. Firstly, we assume that the PEP, PDP and PGC are all in the same administrative domain as the resources being protected.

Each project partner's PEP is therefore situated in a logical DMZ (demilitarized zone), while the PDP, resources and PGC are in a protected domain. Secondly, we assume that there is a PKI (Public Key Infrastructure) in place that allows each project partner to validate the certificates of each other. The

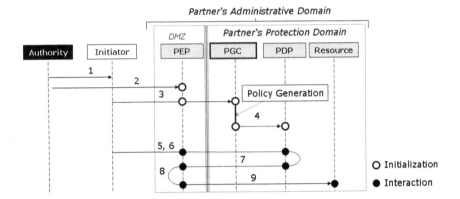

**Fig. 2.** Sequence diagram of component interactions

"Authority" in figure 2 represents a standard PKI Certificate Authority (CA). Finally we assume that each partner maintains a project management system that at least provides information concerning which projects are currently active. The component interactions are represented in figure 2 and discussed below:

1. The Initiator (i.e. Aircraft Company) must first be issued a public-key certificate (PKC) from an authority, asserting its identity and claim to be the initiator of a project with a unique universal identifier $PRJ_{id}$. The certificate has the format: $Cert(subject = Initiator, keyinfo = PK_{Initiator}, extension = Claim(isInitiator, PRJ_{id}), issuer = PK_{Authority})$

2. The identities of all partners must also be validated by an authority, as well as the claim that they have been selected to play a role $r_{name}$ in the project $PRJ_{id}$. $Cert(subject = Partner, keyinfo=PK_{Partner}, extension = Claim (r_{name}, PRJ_{id}), ..., issuer = PK_{Authority})$

3. The Initiator then sends the WS-CDL (choreography), WSDLs (service interfaces) and PKCs of all selected partners to the PGC of each partner, using the initiator certificate as its authentication token. Recall that the PGC is not directly accessible from outside the network, such that there must be an authorization in place that allows $s = Initiator, o = PGC, a = Add$, under the conditions $q : isActive(Initiator, Partner, PRJ_{id})$.

4. The PGC derives the authorization policies and installs them on the PDP, given that the above condition $q$ holds. This allows administration to simultaneously confirm participation in the collaborative business process and determine valid authorizations.

5. The Initiator issues an initiation message to all partners, indicating that the project is in the operation state. A PGC of partners implementing our proposed architecture must simply enable the first authorizations according to the choreography.

6. Incoming message requests are intercepted by each partner's PEP. We assume that there is mutual authentication between the communicating

parties. If the authentication is successful, the PEP extracts the authorization-relevant information ($\langle s, o, a \rangle$) and uses this to query the PDP.

7. The PDP evaluates the request by the PEP and returns its decision ($msg_{grant}$ or $msg_{deny}$). Every time a policy decision is made, the PDP updates its internal state with the next set of authorizations to be installed.

8. The PEP drops all $msg_{deny}$ and forwards all $msg_{grant}$ to the appropriate resource, e.g. analysis service.

9. The actual resource is then invoked using only authorized messages (requests and invocations) forwarded by the PEP.

We now proceed to describe the algorithm for implementing the policy derivation.

# 5    Control-Flow Aware Authorization Policy Derivation

Our policy derivation algorithm uses the control flow of the choreography in order to minimize the time a policy is enabled. In addition to extracting only the relevant <InterAction> elements and enabling them over the life-time of the choreography, we also use the control-flow of the choreography to trigger the enabling and disabling of the policies, given the following extensions to the basic specification.

## 5.1    Extended Authorization Policies

We extended the specification of authorization policies in order to develop a mechanism for supporting the control-flow of a choreography. Instead of representing the run-time control-flow (and monitoring it with a second component) we have chosen to represent the static control-flow and extend the policy enforcement and decision with two mechanisms to track the control-flow. Each authorization policy is annotated with two additional fields, one set of policies that are enabled and one with policies that are disabled after the policy has been successfully matched. Let $l_{enable} = \{policy - id_1, policy - id_2, \ldots, policy - id_n\}$ be the set of policies to enable and $l_{disable} = \{policy - id_1, policy - id_2, \ldots, policy - id_m\}$ be the set of policies to disable. Additionally we store the $policy - id$ of each policy as an unique identifying integer and the state of the policy. The state of a policy can be either *enabled* or *disabled*. Disabled policies are not considered when making a policy decision, but they have already been created and can be activated on-demand, i.e. $q : enabled(policy - id)$. This allows us to create all policies initially and then reference them by policy-id for enabling and disabling. The life-cycle of a policy is depicted in figure 3. Furthermore, a policy might be enabled and disabled multiple times during the execution of a choreography. Summarizing a policy is a 7-tuple of $\langle policy - id, s, o, a, l_{enable}, l_{disable}, state \rangle$ where $s$, $o$ and $a$ are the usual authorization policy elements mentioned above.

The sets $l_{enable}$ and $l_{disable}$ are evaluated by the PDP after a policy has been successfully matched. I.e. the PDP evaluates all enabled policies in order, comparing them to the request, and, on the first policy matching subject $s$, object $o$

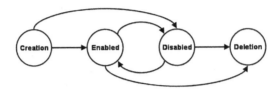

**Fig. 3.** Policy State Model

and action $a$ it allows access. All our policies are *grant* policies specifying an allowed access. The PDP has an implicit *deny* policy that is used for all unmatched requests. Since we only have *grant* policies there is no conflict specified by our policies. Furthermore, if all policies are generated by the policy generator they are non-overlapping. After a policy has been successfully matched to the request the PDP processes the set $l_{enable}$ of this policy and enables all policies in the set, followed by the set $l_{disable}$ of this policy disabling all policies in the set. This implies that a policy might disable itself after successful matching. Our algorithm ensures that no policy appears in both sets ($l_{enable}$ and $l_{disable}$), such that the order of evaluation causes no conflict.

### 5.2  Automatic Policy Generation

In this section we will describe the algorithm to populate the enable and disable sets of each policy. WS-CDL offers four activities for control-flow: `<Sequence>`, `<Choice>`, `<Parallel>` and `<WorkUnit>`. `<Sequence>`, `<Choice>` and `<Parallel>` are self-explaining and work like expected. It is important to note that `<Parallel>` introduces parallelism into the control-flow which complicates the analysis. `<WorkUnit>` encapsulates another activity and makes its execution conditional. The enclosed activity may be executed 0 to $n$ times depending on the guard and repetition conditions.

As we are interested in deriving authorization policies, the only activity that results in a (cross-domain) access to a resource is `<InterAction>`. Each `<InterAction>` represents an access from one party to another (i.e. no multi-party access).

We first present an overview of our algorithm and then detail its important steps. The algorithm steps are as follows:

1. Verify all partner certificates carry the role extension with the choreography role name. We place the canonical name of the subject of the certificate as the subject $s$ into the authorization policy. The PDP can then match the subject of the certificate presented for authentication to the subject $s$ in the authorization policy.
2. Derive control-flow with all intermediate nodes (i.e. XML elements, like `<Choice>` and `<Parallel>`) from the parsed choreography description.
3. Filter all `<InterAction>` elements that do not have oneself as a target, i.e. remove all `<InterAction>` elements that do not result in a local access (and therefore a local authorization policy).

4. Remove all XML nodes that do not contain `<InterAction>` elements by directly linking predecessors and successors. (Exception: Empty nodes in `<Parallel>` are simply removed.)
5. Create policies with empty $l_{enable}$ and $l_{disable}$ sets in disabled state.
6. Compute $l_{enable}$ and $l_{disable}$ set for each policy from the choreography.
7. Install policies on a partner's PDP and enable start policy (or policies) on request.

The derivation of the control-flow is straightforward from the syntactic constructs of WS-CDL. We store the predecessor and successor information in a two-dimensional array in the activity. Let $pred_i(N)$ denote the set of sequential predecessors of node $N$ for $i = 1, \ldots, p$ where $i$ is the $i$-th parallel activity, i.e. one of each $pred_0(N)$, $pred_1(N)$, $\ldots$, $pred_p(N)$ has occurred before $N$. Similarly let $succ_i(N)$ denote the set of sequential successors for the $i$-th parallel activity, i.e. one of each $succ_0(N)$, $succ_1(N)$, $\ldots$, $succ_q(N)$ will occur after $N$. Let $pred(N)$ and $succ(N)$ denote the union of all parallel activities, i.e. $pred(N) = \bigcup_{i=0}^{p} pred_i(N)$ and $succ(N) = \bigcup_{i=0}^{q} succ_i(N)$. Let $pred_N(M)$ and $succ_N(M)$ denote the set of predecessors and successors, respectively, of $M$ of that activity that contains $N$. Due to the syntax of `<Parallel>` and `<Choice>` in WS-CDL this set is unique. We use the same notation when applying predecessor and successor operators to sets, i.e. the operator is applied to each element in the set removing duplicate results. E.g. $succ(pred(N))$ denotes the set of all possible sequential and parallel siblings of $N$ (including $N$ itself).

The creation of policies in step 5 requires the subject, object and action information for each policy. We analyze each `<InterAction>` for this purpose. The subject is the canonical name as extracted from the certificate for the role (attribute `fromRole` in the `<participate>` element). The object is the web service EPR from the WSDL file referenced in the `<behavior>` element of the `<roleType>` with the name of the `operation` attribute of the `<InterAction>`. The action is the method of the web service that is called and, in our convention, is referred to as the `operation` attribute. With this information we construct a draft of each policy, such that all policies are disabled, but have a policy-id assigned. Each such policy is associated with a node in the control-flow and, after the removal of empty nodes, each node has one policy associated with it. I.e. we can use control-flow nodes and policies interchangeably.

The set $l_{disable}$ is the set of all alternative sequential choices, i.e. for each node $N$

$$l_{disable} = succ_N(pred(N))$$

Note that this includes $N$ itself, i.e. by default each policy is disabled after it has been activated unless the control-flow allows it to be reactivated.

The set $l_{enable}$ is the set of all successors of a node $N$

$$l_{enable} = succ(N)$$

Since a node may be contained in both $l_{disable}$ and $l_{enable}$, e.g. a loop to itself (in a `<WorkUnit>` activity with repetition), we postprocess both sets and remove all elements that are contained in both sets from the sets.

$$\phi = l_{disable} \cap l_{enable}$$

$$l_{disable} = l_{disable} \setminus \phi$$

$$l_{enable} = l_{enable} \setminus \phi$$

The policies are now ready for deployment and we only need to enable the start policies to allow the choreography to start.

# 6   Discussion and Related Work

An authorization is said to be passive with respect to a given condition, if for all possible values of the condition's variables the authorization remains unchanged. Conditions include tasks performed, time of day, resource availability and various other properties that can be used to describe a system's current operational state and behavior. The implications of "active", "just-in-time" or "need-to-know" authorizations have been discussed by various authors including [5,15,17]. We consider the authorizations generated from a choreography as active with respect to project membership, role, task and control flow. These therefore maintain the membership of a group and enforce access controls on resources and functions that are reserved for active and qualified partners of the group. When an organization needs to enforce an access control on a resource reserved for usage in a project, it is therefore important to have a means of validating the membership of the subject with the project, otherwise residual access could be granted to a requesting subject that is no longer an active partner.

## 6.1   Active, Task and Membership-Based Access Control

TBAC [15] has similar foundations as RBAC [11], with the goal of modelling authorizations at the enterprise and application level as opposed to restricting them to the system and resource level. TBAC authorizations are granted and revoked based on when tasks are scheduled and performed, such that permissions to objects should be granted to subjects only for the duration of a task that necessitates the subject performing some action on the object. TBAC's authorization policy extensions are two fields for activating or deactivating authorizations at runtime. A TBAC authorization has the form $\langle s, o, a,$ usage $u,$ authorization-step $as\rangle$. Each task in a workflow is associated with an authorization-step, representing the workflow's protection state when the task or activity is being performed. An authorization such as $\langle s, o, a \rangle$ is only valid when contained in the current authorization-step. Secondly, authorizations are conditioned by a usage or validity count $u$, specifying the number of times the authorization can be granted in the workflow. The authorization-steps are similar to our $l_{enable}$ and $l_{disable}$ sets, but seem to assume that parallel activities will conclude at the same time. Our approach therefore offers a finer granularity with the enabling and disabling of authorizations. Secondly, TBAC must be integrated with a workflow engine in order to function, creating a large trusted computing base beyond standard PEPs and PDPs.

TMAC (Team-based Access Control) [14] is a related framework to TBAC and RBAC, but adds the feature of authorization enabling based on team existence and membership. That is, a subject $s$ may be assigned a role $r_t$ containing a set of permissions $\langle o, a \rangle$, but these roles are only active when a relevant team $T$ exists and $s$ plays role $r_t$ in $T$. The authorizations are deactivated either by removing the role assignment or the team assignment. A project is a team of multiple participants, such that we achieve a similar membership-based access control activation and deactivation. We however support a finer-grained activation and deactivation mechanism, such that we achieve dynamic authorization based on role, task and membership.

## 6.2   Generation of Access Controls

[8] also addresses the idea of adding workflow states to the protection state variables of a system. They use Petri nets as the basis for modeling workflows, as the theoretical and practical understanding of Petri nets to modeling information and control flow are well established. The activities of a workflow correspond to the transitions in a Petri net, while the workflow state, data-stores and control flow are represented by the places and markings. Their extensions to the authorization policies are quite simple, as they express an authorization as $\langle s, o, a, task \rangle$, stating that a subject $s$ is allowed to perform action $a$ on object $o$ if $q : isScheduled(task)$. They also define a simple read/write $\{r, w\}$ policy that is associated with incoming and outgoing data of a task. That is, if a subject $s$ is assigned to a task $task_i$ with incoming data $o_i$ and outgoing data $o_j$, then $s$ should have read $'r'$ rights to the data-store of $o_i$ and write $'w'$ rights to the data-store of $o_j$. The claim of their work is that given the appropriate Petri net model of a workflow, by applying the $\langle s, o, a, task \rangle$ scheme and the $\{r, w\}$ policy the required authorizations can be derived and enforced at runtime of the workflow. They envisioned the enforcement being done by a workflow engine as tasks were scheduled. Again this is tight coupling of functionality and too large a trusted computing base. A workflow engine is already a complicated piece of software that must maintain state, manage concurrencies, handle exceptions and perform compensation actions. We believe that their simple derivation scheme could work, but suggest decoupling authorization and workflow management. [6] achieve this decoupling by using task-based capabilities, which are assigned to subjects that have specific roles in the workflow. A PDP maintains a matrix of tasks and objects, where the cells specify actions that holders of task-based capabilities are allowed to perform on these objects. Our architecture and algorithm manage to capture a combination of these concepts.

[9] have taken advantage of the existence of maturing standards for defining business processes and workflows, such as the Business Process Execution Language for web services (BPEL4WS). They have presented a conceptual integration of BPEL with RBAC in order to provide an authorization concept to accompany BPEL. They have defined a conceptual mapping between their interpretations of the meta-models of BPEL and RBAC. While what we achieve is also a transformation or mapping, this is still only a first step when considering

the requirements of collaborative engineering projects that need to meet tough
deadlines. The enabling, disabling and removal of these derived authorizations
must be supported with respect to the control flow of the process from which
they have been derived.

## 7   Conclusions

We have described an architecture and algorithm for deriving authorization policies from a business process choreography. This enables partners in e.g. a collaborative engineering project to focus on agreeing on the protocol for how they
collaborate and still have the assurance that their authorization requirements
will be addressed. Our approach has been implemented and is being applied in
the context of a larger research project – TrustCoM [13] – for security in collaborative business processes, which includes collaborative engineering as a main test
case, and also considers legal and business elements that influence the validity
and control flow of collaboration. Future work will therefore consider how these
can be included into our framework, as well as handling faults and exceptions.

## Acknowledgements

The developments presented in this paper were partly funded by the European
Commission through the IST programme under Framework 6 grant 001945 to
the Trustcom Integrated Project.

## References

1. A. Barros, M. Dumas, and P. Oaks. A Criticial Overview of the Web Services
   Choreography Description Language. BPTrends, 2005.
2. M.R. Danesh and Y. Jin. An Aggregated Value Model for Collaborative Engineering Decisions, Proceedings of the 5th ASME Design for Manufacturing Conference,
   2000.
3. A. Gould, S. Barker, E. Carver, D. Golby, M. Turner, BAEgrid: From e-Science to
   e-Engineering, in Proceedings of the UK e-Science All Hands Meeting, 2003.
4. M. Harrison, W. Ruzzo, and J. Ullman. Protection in Operating Systems. Communications of the ACM 19(8), 1976.
5. R. Holbein, S. Teufel, and K. Bauknecht. The use of business process models for
   security design in organisations. In Proceedings of SEC, 1996.
6. M. Kang, J. Park, and J. Froscher, 2001. Access control mechanisms for inter-
   organizational workflow. In Proceedings of the 6th ACM Symposium on Access
   Control Models and Technologies, 2001.
7. N. Kavantzas, D. Burdett, G. Ritzinger, T. Fletcher, Y. Lafon, and C. Bar-
   reto. Web Services Choreography Description Language Version 1.0. Available at
   http://www.w3.org/TR/ws-cdl-10/, 2005.
8. K. Knorr. Dynamic access control through Petri net workflows. In Proceedings of
   the 16th Annual Computer Security Applications Conference, 2000.

9. J. Mendling, M. Strembeck, G. Stermsek, and G. Neumann. An Approach to Extract RBAC Models from BPEL4WS Processes. In Proceedings of the 13th IEEE international Workshops on Enabling Technologies, 2004.

10. P. Robinson, Y. Karabulut, and J. Haller. Dynamic Virtual Organization Management for Service Oriented Enterprise Applications. In Proceedings of IEEE CollaborateCom, 2005.

11. R. Sandhu, E. Coyne, H. Feinstein, and C. Youman. Role-Based Access Control Models. IEEE Computer 29(2), 1996.

12. P. Samarati, S. de Capitani di Vimercati. Access Control: Policies, Models, and Mechanisms. Lecture Notes in Computer Science 2171, 2001.

13. T. Dimitrakos, S. Ristol, and M. Wilson. TrustCoM: A Trust and Contract Management Framework for Dymamic Virtual Organisations. ERCIM News Magazine, 2004.

14. R. Thomas. Team-Based Access Control (TMAC): A Primitive for Applying Role-Based Access Controls in Collaborative Environments. In Proceedings of the 2nd ACM workshop on Role-basedAccess Control, 1997

15. R. Thomas, and R. Sandhu. Task-Based Authorization Controls (TBAC): A Family of Models for Active and Enterprise-Oriented Autorization Management. In Proceedings of the IFIP 11th International Conference on Database Security, 1998.

16. Wil M.P. van der Aalst, Mathias Weske. The P2P Approach to Interorganizational Workflows, Lecture Notes in Computer Science, 2001

17. W. Yao, K. Moody, and J. Bacon. A Model of OASIS Role-Based Access Control and its Support for Active Security. Proceedings of 6th ACM Symposium on Access Control Models and Technologies, 2001.

# Information Theoretical Analysis of Two-Party Secret Computation

Da-Wei Wang*, Churn-Jung Liau**, Yi-Ting Chiang, and Tsan-sheng Hsu***

Institute of Information Science Academia Sinica, Taipei, 115, Taiwan
{wdw, liaucj, ytc, tshsu}@iis.sinica.edu.tw

**Abstract.** Privacy protection has become one of the most important issues in the information era. Consequently, many protocols have been developed to achieve the goal of accomplishing a computational task cooperatively without revealing the participants' private data. Practical protocols, however, do not guarantee perfect privacy protection, as some degree of privacy leakage is allowed so that resources can be used efficiently, e.g., the number of random bits required and the computation time. A metric for measuring the degree of information leakage based on an information theoretical framework was proposed in [2]. Based on that formal framework, we present a lower bound of the scalar product problem in this paper, and show that to solve the problem without the help of a third party, approximately half the private information must be revealed. To better capture our intuition about the secrecy of various protocols, we propose two more measurements: *evenness* and *spread*. The first measures how evenly the information leakage is distributed among the participants' private inputs. The second measures the size of the smallest set an adversary could use to obtain the same ratio of leaked information that could be derived in the worst case scenario.

**Keywords:** Privacy Analysis, Private Computation, Scalar Product.

## 1   Introduction

Privacy protection is one of the most pressing issues in the information era. The massive databases spread over the Internet are gold mines for some and, at the same time, one of the greatest threats to privacy for others. How to accomplish a computational task cooperatively without revealing the participants' private inputs has therefore gained a great deal of attention in recent years and the development of efficient solutions is now an active research area. In theory [11,7], it is possible to securely compute almost any function without revealing anything, except the output. Unfortunately, the theoretical results are not readily applicable to real applications due to their high computational complexity.

---

   * Corresponding Author. Joint appointment faculty member of National Yang Ming University Taiwan. Supported in part by NSC (Taiwan) grant 94-2213-E-001-030.
  ** Supported in part by NSC(Taiwan) grant 94-2213-E-001-007.
*** Supported in part by NSC (Taiwan) grant 94-2213-E-001-014.

E. Damiani and P. Liu (Eds.): Data and Applications Security 2006, LNCS 4127, pp. 310–317, 2006.

Most theoretical approaches adopt a computationally indistinguishable view of secrecy and try to find provable secure solutions, but such a definition leaves little room to quantify secrecy. Meanwhile, in application-oriented studies, researchers usually take an intuitive approach to the definition of secrecy and try to argue for the secrecy of protocols by refuting possible attacks. There is a gap between these two approaches in terms of provable secrecy. Although, privacy is a basic human right, it is not the only one. When multi-party private computation is applied in the public sector, sometimes privacy must be compromised in order to accommodate other important social values. The computation can also be applied in the private sector, such as in a business setting. For example, two (or more) companies might want to compute a function cooperatively; however, neither of them wants to share their private information. In both public and private sector applications, it would be beneficial to be able to quantify secrecy so that a tradeoff could be made, for example, between secrecy and computational efficiency. In [5], similar arguments are presented about ideal secrecy and acceptable secrecy. Meanwhile in [2], an information theoretical framework is proposed and two quantitative definitions of secrecy for multi-party private computation are defined, namely, *relative secrecy* and *absolute secrecy*. In this paper, we prove a lower bound for the relative secrecy of protocols that solve scalar product problems. We also propose two refined measurements, *evenness* and *spread*, for quantifying information leakage by multiparty private computation protocols.

The remainder of this paper is organized as follows. We give a short review of related works in Section 2. In Section 3, we present the formal framework proposed in [2]. In Section 4, we present our lower bound proof. In Section 5, we present our extension of the formal framework, and use three examples to explain our new measurements. Finally, in Section 6, we present our conclusions and a short discussion about possible extensions of our model. We also indicate the direction of future work.

## 2   Related Work

Secure two-party computation was first studied by Yao [11] and extended to the multi-party case by Goldreich et al [7]. Through a sequence of efforts, a satisfactory definitional treatment was found and precise proofs for the security of multi-party computation were devised . A full description of these developments is given in [6]. The general construction approach is as follows. To securely compute a function, it is first converted into a combinatorial circuit. Next, all the parties run a protocol to compute the result of each gate in the circuit. Both the input and the output of each gate are shared randomly and the final output is also shared randomly among all parties, who then exchange their share of information to compute the final result. Although, this general construction is impressive, it also implies that both the size of the circuit and the number of parties involved dominate the size, i.e., complexity, of the protocol. Note that the size of the circuit is related to the size of the input. Therefore, this general construction is not feasible for real world applications with a large input and/or a large number of parties [9].

The high cost of the general approach for large problems has motivated researchers to look for efficient solutions for specific functions, and many protocols have been developed to solve particular problems. There are specific protocols for general computation primitives, such as, scalar products [1,10], set union and set intersection cardinality [8], and private permutation [3]. In addition, there are protocols for specific application domains, for example, data mining, computational geometry, and statistical analysis. An excellent survey of secure multi-party computation problems can be found in [4].

Most of the above approaches are based on the notion of ideal secrecy, as observed in [5]. In that paper, the authors ask if it would be possible to lower the security requirement from an ideal level to an acceptable level so that an efficient protocol can be developed. A formal framework based on information theory is presented in [2] in which quantitative metrics of the security level of a protocol are proposed.

## 3   Framework

As our lower bound proof is based on the formal framework in [2], we include a brief introduction to the framework here. In multi-party private computation, $n$ players cooperate to compute a function. Each player holds some private input that is part of the parameters for computing the function. The goal is to compute the function and maintain the secrecy of each party's private input. Given a protocol, $P$, we use $X_i^P$ to denote the private input of party $i$, and $msg_i^P$ to denote the message received by party $i$. We use information theory to model the amount of information revealed after running $P$. Note that before running $P$, none of the parties has any information about the other parties' private inputs. However, after running $P$, each party may know something about some of the other parties' private inputs because of new information gathered during the execution of $P$. Let $H_i^P = H(X_i^P)$ denote the entropy of the random variable $X_i^P$, and $H_{ij}^P = H(X_i^P|msg_j^P)$ denote the entropy of the random variable $X_i^P$ given $msg_j^P$. The conditional entropy corresponds to the intuitive idea of the amount of information (uncertainty) of $X_i^P$ from party $j$'s perspective after receiving $msg_j^P$.

Two measurements, *relative secrecy* and *absolute secrecy*, of the secrecy of protocol $P$ are defined as $\min_{i,j}(H_{ij}^P/H_i^P)$ and $\min_{i,j}(H_{ij}^P)$ respectively.

## 4   Lower Bound

In this section we show that for any two party scalar product protocol, the relative secrecy can not be better than $\frac{1}{2}$. Without loss of generality, let us assume that the protocol proceeds in rounds, where Alice and Bob send messages to each other alternately, with Alice sending the first message. We can record the communication between Alice and Bob as a sequence of messages,

$msg = (msg_1^A, msg_2^B, \ldots)$. Given a message sequence $msg$, we say that an input sequence $X$ of Alice(Bob) is *compatible* with $msg$ if it is a possible record of the communication when the input sequence of Alice(Bob) is $X$. We use $I_A(msg)(I_B(msg))$ to denote the set of input sequences, that are compatible with $msg$, for Alice(Bob). Note that $msg$ is a possible record of the communication when Alice's input is in $I_A(msg)$ and Bob's in $I_B(msg)$. We use $I_{A,B}(msg)$ to denote $\{(X, Y)|X \in I_A(msg), Y \in I_B(msg)\}$. The set $I_A(msg)(I_B(msg))$ can be further partitioned into two subsets according to the output value $u(v)$. We use $I_{A,u}(msg)(I_{B,v}(msg))$ to denote the set of input sequences compatible with $msg$ and the final outcome. Note that, for all $X \in I_{A,u}(msg)$ and $Y \in I_{B,v}(msg)$, $XY = u + v$. Here, we consider the case where each number is from $GF(2)$ and the input vector is $n$ dimensional. A general lower bound can be derived by the same approach. Below, we present a high-level sketch of the lower bound proof. If after the execution of the protocol, the information content of the input sequence of Alice(Bob) is still high, it means that many input sequences should be compatible with the recorded conversation. However, a larger $I_A(msg)$ would imply a smaller $I_B(msg)$, since each sequence in $I_B(msg)$ paired with each sequence in $I_A(msg)$ has to satisfy the condition that their scalar product is equal to the sum of their outputs. We therefore derive a lower bound. To formalize the above sketch, we state some basic facts from information theory and linear algebra.

**Fact 1.** *Let $X$ be a random source with $n$ possible outcomes, $H(X) \leq \log n$. In other words, for a random source to have entropy $n$, we need at least $2^n$ possible outcomes.*

**Fact 2.** *Let $I_1$, $I_2$ be two sets of $n$-dimensional binary vectors. We use $dim(I_1)$ to denote the dimension of the subspace spanned by $I_1$.*

- *If $|I_1| \geq 2^k$, then $dim(I_1) \geq k$; and if $dim(I) \leq k$, then $|I| \leq 2^k$.*
- *If $I_1$ and $I_2$ are orthogonal, i.e., the scalar product between every vector in $I_1$ and $I_2$ is zero, then $dim(I_1) + dim(I_2) \leq n$.*

Given a message sequence $msg$, let $\mathbf{0_A} = I_{A,0}(msg)$, $\mathbf{0_B} = I_{B,0}(msg)$, $\mathbf{1_A} = I_{A,1}(msg)$, and $\mathbf{1_B} = I_{B,1}(msg)$. By Fact 2, we get $dim(\mathbf{0_A}) + dim(\mathbf{0_B}) \leq n$ and $dim(\mathbf{1_A}) + dim(\mathbf{1_B}) \leq n$. Now consider the relationship between $\mathbf{1_A}$ and $\mathbf{0_B}$. Assume that $dim(\mathbf{1_A}) = k$ and $(i_1, i_2, \ldots, i_k)$ form a basis of the subspace spanned by $\mathbf{1_A}$. Consider the set of vectors constructed by combining an even number of vectors in the basis, denoted by $I'$. There are exactly $2^{k-1} - 1$ vectors in the set, because the summations of the even terms and odd terms of a binomial sequence are the same. However, the zero vector is not included in our subset. Clearly $dim(I') \geq k - 1$ and the space spanned by $\mathbf{1_A}$ contains both vectors in $\mathbf{1_A}$ and $I'$. Using Fact 2 again, but this time for $I'$ and $\mathbf{0_B}$, we get $dim(I') + dim(\mathbf{0_B}) \leq n$, which implies $dim(\mathbf{1_A}) + dim(\mathbf{0_B}) \leq n + 1$. If $H(X_A|msg) \geq k_1$, then by Fact 1, $|I_A(msg)| \geq 2^{k_1}$. Without loss of generality, assume that $|\mathbf{1_A}| \geq 2^{k_1-1}$; therefore, $dim(\mathbf{1_A}) \geq k_1 - 1$. Since $|I'| \geq |\mathbf{1_A}| - 1$ and the the number of vectors in the space spanned by $\mathbf{1_A}$ contains every vector in

$I'$ and $\mathbf{1_A}$, we derive that there are at least $|I'| + |\mathbf{1_A}| \geq 2^{k_1} - 1$ vectors in this space. Therefore, $dim(\mathbf{1_A}) \geq k_1$. Hence, by $dim(\mathbf{1_A}) + dim(\mathbf{1_B}) \leq n$ and $dim(\mathbf{1_A}) + dim(\mathbf{0_B}) \leq n + 1$, we get $dim(\mathbf{1_B}) \leq n - k_1$ and $dim(\mathbf{0_B}) \leq n - k_1 + 1$. There are at most $2^{n-k_1+1}$ vectors in the vector space spanned by $\mathbf{0_B}$. However, half the vectors in this space are not in $\mathbf{0_B}$, so we get $|\mathbf{0_B}| \leq 2^{n-k_1}$; therefore, $|I_B(msg)| = |\mathbf{0_B}| + |\mathbf{1_B}|LIA \leq 2^{n-k_1+1}$. If $H(X_B|msg) \geq k_2$, then by Fact 1, $|I_B(msg)| \geq 2^{k_2}$. Now we have $2^{k_2} \leq |I_B(msg)| \leq 2^{n-k_1+1}$. Thus, we get $k_1 + k_2 \leq n + 1$ and the following lemma and theorem.

**Lemma 1.** *For any two-party scalar product protocol $P$, if $H(X_A|msg) \geq k_1$ and $H(X_B|msg) \geq k_2$, then $k_1 + k_2 \leq n + 1$.*

Since $H(X_A) = H(X_B) = n$, we get $H(X_A|msg)/H(H_A) + H(X_B|msg)/H(X_B) \leq 1 + 1/n$. The relative secrecy of the protocol is

$$min(\frac{H(X_A|msg)}{H(X_A)}, \frac{H(X_B|msg)}{H(X_B)}) \leq \frac{1}{2} + \frac{1}{n}.$$

**Theorem 1.** *For any two-party scalar product protocol, the relative secrecy is at most $\frac{1}{2} + \Omega(\frac{1}{n})$.*

## 5   Extension of the Formal Framework and Examples

Although the two metrics, relative secrecy and absolute secrecy, capture the amount of information revealed by a protocol, they fail to distinguish intuitively apparent differences between various protocols. For example, many two-party scalar product protocols have a relative secrecy of $\frac{1}{2}$, but, it is obvious that a protocol that allows Alice and Bob to send half of their respective inputs to each other is not acceptable. We try to capture the intuition by extending the definition of the secrecy metrics. First we introduce the concept of *evenness* to overcome the drawback of the above-mentioned measurements, which only capture a global view of information leakage. Now consider two protocols, each with relative secrecy $\frac{1}{2}$. In the first protocol, the amount of information leakage only reaches $\frac{1}{2}$ when all the input elements are considered. In the other protocol, however, the information leakage reaches $\frac{1}{2}$ when only a single input element is considered. Clearly, the first protocol is better than the second. We introduce the concept of *spread* to capture the intuition that the first protocol is better. Before we formally define evenness and spread, we introduce some notations. We present only the two-party case here, and defer the multi-party case to a full paper. Let us first generalize the definition of $H_i^P$ and $H_{ij}^P$ to any subset of input elements. Let $A$ and $B$ denote the two parties. For player $A$(the definition for party $B$ is similar), let $X_A^P = (x_1, x_2, \ldots, x_n)$, and $S = \{x_{k_1}, x_{k_2}, \ldots, x_{k_r}\} \subseteq \{x_1, x_2, \ldots, x_n\}$. We use $H(S)$ to denote $H(x_{k_1}, x_{k_2}, \ldots, x_{k_r})$ and $H(S|msg)$ to denote $H(x_{k_1}, x_{k_2}, \ldots, x_{k_r}|msg)$. Define $H_A^P(S) = H(S)$ and $H_{AB}^P(S) = H(S|msg_B^P)$. Let $r_A = r = min_S\{\frac{H(S|msg_B^P)}{H(S)}\}$, $rg_A = \frac{H(X_A^P|msg_B^P)}{H(X_A^P)}$, and $\eta_A =$

$rg_A - r_A$. In the above definitions, $r_A$ is the minimum ratio between the information of any subset of the secret input before and after the execution of the protocol, $rg_A$ is the ratio for the whole input. It is reasonable to replace $rg_A$ by $r_A$; however, we feel it is more informative to define evenness to be $\eta_A$, and interpret it as the measurement of the evenness of information leakage about player $A$. When $\eta_A$ equals zero, it means that player $A$'s input is leaked evenly. We define the spread for player $A$ as $min\{|S| : \{\frac{H(S|msg_B^P)}{H(S)}\} = r_A\}$; that is, the minimum number of input elements required to reach the maximum information leakage level. An ideal protocol should have relative secrecy as close to one as possible, evenness of every player as close to zero as possible, and spread of every player as large as possible. We use three two-party scalar product protocols to demonstrate the concept of evenness and spread. In the two-party scalar product problem, the two parties, Alice and Bob, have private input $X_A$ and $X_B$(two $n$ dimensional vectors), respectively. A solution to this problem is a protocol that, after running, enables Alice and Bob to correctly compute the numbers $u$ and $v$ respectively, such that $u + v$ is the inner product of $X_A$ and $X_B$, i.e., $X_A \cdot X_B$. Let $*$ be the matrix product operator, and $X_B^T$ be the transpose of $X_B$. Then, $u + v = X_A \cdot X_B = X_A * X_B^T$. Hereafter, we assume that $X_A, X_B \in GF(p)^n$, where $GF(p)$ is a Galois field of order $p$, and $p$ is a prime number. We also assume that $X_A$ and $X_B$ are uniformly distributed and that both parties are semi-honest, i.e., they both follow the protocol and do not deliberately deviate from it to get more information. Instead, they only deduce information from the messages they receive.

## Examples

Our first example is a naive protocol whereby Alice sends the first half of her vector to Bob, and Bob sends the second half of his vector to Alice. It is obvious that relative secrecy $r_g = \frac{1}{2}$, which matches the best protocol. However, it is also obvious that this is not a very appealing solution, because the evenness of this protocol is $\frac{1}{2}$. Thus one party has full information of half the private input elements. In addition, the fact that the spread is equal to one makes the situation even worse.

For the second protocol, we use the Chinese Remainder theorem to encode each element of the input vectors with the same base. Specifically, we pick two consecutive integers, $p_1, p_2$, such that $p_1 p_2 > p$ and encode each number $x$ as $(x \mod p_1, x \mod p_2)$. Thus, $X_A = ((x_{11}, x_{12}), \ldots, (x_{n1}, x_{n2}))$ and $X_B = ((y_{11}, y_{12}), \ldots, (y_{n1}, y_{n2}))$. Alice then sends the first coordinate of her private input, $(x_{11}, x_{21}, \ldots, x_{n1})$, to Bob and Bob sends the second coordinate of his private input, $(y_{12}, y_{22}, \ldots, y_{n2})$, to Alice. Alice computes $a = \sum_{i=1}^{n} x_{i2} y_{i2}$ $\mod p_2$, and set $u = p_1 p_1^{-1} a$; and Bob computes $b = \sum_{i=1}^{n} x_{i1} y_{i1} \mod p_1$, and set $v = p_1 p_1^{-1} b$, where $p_1 p_1^{-1} = 1 \mod p_2$ and $p_2 p_2^{-1} = 1 \mod p_1$. It is easy to see that the relative secrecy of the protocol is again $\frac{1}{2}$, but this time the evenness is 0, since half of the information of each private input element is revealed to the other party. However, the spread of the protocol is 1; for example, once Bob gets $x_{11}$ the information about $x_1$ is reduced to about $\frac{1}{2}$.

The third protocol [5] operates as follows. First Alice and Bob agree to an $n * n$ invertible matrix $M$ and a positive integer $k$ that is not larger than $n$. The rest of the protocol comprises the following steps:

| Alice | Bob |
|---|---|
| 1. Compute $X'_A = X_A * M$. | Compute $X'_B = (M^{-1} * X_B^T)^T$. |
| Let $X'_A = [x_{A_1}, \ldots, x_{A_n}]$, | Let $X'_B = [x_{B_1}, \ldots, x_{B_n}]$, |
| $\bar{X}_A = [x_{A_1}, \ldots, x_{A_k}]$, | $\bar{X}_B = [x_{B_1}, \ldots, x_{B_k}]$, |
| $\underline{X}_A = [x_{A_{k+1}}, \ldots, x_{A_n}]$ | $\underline{X}_B = [x_{B_{k+1}}, \ldots, x_{B_n}]$ |
| 2. | Alice $\xrightarrow{\bar{X}_A}$ Bob |
|  | Alice $\xleftarrow{\underline{X}_B}$ Bob |
| 3. $u = \underline{X}_A * \underline{X}_B^T$ | $v = \bar{X}_A * \bar{X}_B^T$ |

In this protocol, $M$ is an n by n invertible matrix. Without loss of generality, let $S = \{x_{A_1}, x_{A_2}, ..., x_{A_r}\}$ and $T = \{x_{A_{r+1}}, ..., x_{A_n}\}$. $H(S) = r * \log p$. Let $msg = \{msg_1, msg_2, ..., msg_n\}$. We have the following linear system of equations from Bob's perspective:

$$\begin{cases} a_{11} * x_{A_1} + a_{12} * x_{A_2} + \cdots + a_{1r} * x_{A_r} + \cdots + a_{1n} * x_{A_n} = msg_1 \\ a_{21} * x_{A_1} + a_{22} * x_{A_2} + \cdots + a_{2r} * x_{A_r} + \cdots + a_{2n} * x_{A_n} = msg_2 \\ \qquad\qquad \cdots\cdots\cdots\cdots \\ a_{k1} * x_{A_1} + a_{k2} * x_{A_2} + \cdots + a_{kr} * x_{A_r} + \cdots + a_{kn} * x_{A_n} = msg_k \end{cases}$$

$H(S,T|msg) = (n - k)\log p$. Moreover, $H(S,T|msg) = H(S|msg) + H(T|S, msg) = H(S|msg) + \max_S\{(n-r-k), 0\} * \log p$. If $r \le n-k$, $\frac{H(S|msg)}{H(S)} = \frac{r*\log p}{r*\log p} = 1$. Otherwise, $\frac{H(S|msg)}{H(S)} = \frac{(n-k)*\log p}{r*\log p} = \frac{n-k}{r} < 1$. Therefore, $\min_S\{\frac{H(S|msg)}{H(S)}\} = \frac{n-k}{n}$, where $|S| = r = n$. The relative secrecy for Alice's input is $\frac{n-k}{n}$. The evenness is thus $\frac{n-k}{n} - \frac{n-k}{n} = 0$, and the spread is $n$. For Bob's input, the relative secrecy is now $\frac{k}{n}$, however, the evenness and spread are the same as for Alice.

# 6   Conclusion and Future Works

In this paper, by proving a lower bound, we show that revealing half of the private information is unavoidable in two-party protocols that solve the scalar product problem by only allowing the two parties to communicate with each other. Although this seems intuitively straightforward, proving the claim without the help of an information theoretical formalism is non-trivial. Our lower bound proof not only confirms our intuition, but also demonstrates the advantage of the information theoretical framework. To better capture our intuition, we also propose refinements and extensions of the measurements of information leakage for two-party secure computation. We hope that analyzing protocols formally will not only provide solid certification of the secrecy of existing protocols, but also facilitate the design of better protocols. Using the Chinese Remainder theorem to design protocols is an interesting approach worthy of further investigation. In this paper, we assume that inputs are uniformly distributed. We feel it would be a very interesting and challenging task to develop a method that incorporates players' a priori information about others players' private inputs into the formalism. Finally, and obviously, extending the model to multi-party situations and analyzing some interesting problems is logically the next step.

## Acknowledgement

This work was supported in part by the National Science Council under the Grants NSC94-2213-E-001-004, NSC-94-2422-H-001-0001, and NSC-94-2752-E-002-005-PAE, and by the Taiwan Information Security Center (TWISC) under the Grants NSC 94-3114-P-011-001, NSC 94-3114-P-001-001-Y, NSC94-3114-P-001-002-Y and NSC94-3114-P-001-003-Y.

## References

1. M. J. Atallah and W. Du. Secure multi-party computational geometry. *Lecture Notes in Computer Science*, 2125:165–179, 2000.
2. Yi-Ting Chiang, Da-Wei Wang, Churn-Jung Liau, and Tsan-sheng Hsu. Secrecy of two-party secure computation. In *Proc. 19th Annual IFIP WG 11.3 Working Conference on Data and Applications Security,Lecture Notes in Computer Science, Vol. 3654, Jajodia, Sushil; Wijesekera, Duminda (Eds.)*, pages 114–123, 2005.
3. W. Du and M. J. Atallah. Privacy-preserving cooperative statistical analysis. In *Proceedings of the 17th Annual Computer Security Applications Conference*, pages 102–110, New Orleans, Louisiana, USA, December 2001.
4. W. Du and M. J. Atallah. Secure multi-party computation problems and their applications: A review and open problems. In *New Security Paradigms Workshop*, pages 11–20, Cloudcroft, New Mexico, USA, September 2001.
5. W. Du and Z. Zhan. A practical approach to solve secure multi-party computation problems. In *Proceedings of New Security Paradigms Workshop*, Virginia Beach, Virginia, USA, September 2002.
6. O. Goldreich. *Foundations of Cryptography Volume II Basic Aplications*. Cambridge, 2004.
7. O. Goldreich, S. Micali, and A. Wigderson. How to play any mental game, or: A completeness theorem for protocols with honest majority. In *Proc. 19th ACM Symposium on Theory of Computing*, pages 218–229, 1987.
8. M. Kantarcoglu and C. Clifton. Privacy-preserving distributed mining of association rules on horizontally partitioned data. *IEEE Transactions on Knowledge and Data Engineering*, 16(9):1026–1037, 2004.
9. Dahlia Malkhi, Noam Nisan, Benny Pinkas, and Yaron Sella. Fairplay – a secure two-party computation system. In *Proceedings of the 13th Symposium on Security, Usenix*, pages 287–302, 2004.
10. J. Vaidya and C. Clifton. Privacy preserving association rule mining in vertically partitioned data. In *The Eighth ACM SIGKDD International Conference on Knowledge Discovery and Data Mining*, pages 639–644, July 2002.
11. A. C. Yao. How to generate and exchange secrets. In *Proceedings of the 27rd Annual IEEE Symposium on Foundations of Computer Science*, pages 162–167, November 1986.

# Author Index

# Lecture Notes in Computer Science

For information about Vols. 1–3991

please contact your bookseller or Springer